WEYERHAEUSER ENVIRONMENTAL BOOKS
William Cronon, Editor

Weyerhaeuser Environmental Books explore human relationships with natural environments in all their variety and complexity. They seek to cast new light on the ways that natural systems affect human communities, the ways that people affect the environments of which they are a part, and the ways that different cultural conceptions of nature profoundly shape our sense of the world around us. A complete list of the books in the series appears at the end of this book.

PESTS

IN THE

CITY

Flies, Bedbugs,
Cockroaches,
and Rats

DAWN DAY BIEHLER

UNIVERSITY OF WASHINGTON PRESS
Seattle and London

Pests in the City is published with the assistance of a grant from the Weyerhaeuser Environmental Books Endowment, established by the Weyerhaeuser Company Foundation, members of the Weyerhaeuser family, and Janet and Jack Creighton.

© 2013 by the University of Washington Press
Printed and bound in the United States of America
Design by Thomas Eykemans
Composed in Sorts Mill Goudy, typeface designed by Barry Schwartz
16 15 14 13   5 4 3 2 1

UNIVERSITY OF WASHINGTON PRESS
PO Box 50096, Seattle, WA 98145, USA
www.washington.edu/uwpress

LIBRARY OF CONGRESS CATALOGING-IN-PUBLICATION DATA
Biehler, Dawn.
    Pests in the city : flies, bedbugs, cockroaches, and rats / Dawn Day Biehler.
        pages   cm — (Weyerhaeuser environmental books)
    Includes bibliographical references and index.
    ISBN 978-0-295-99301-0 (cloth : alk. paper)
1. Urban pests   I. Title.
    SB603.3.B54 2013
    632'.6—dc23   2013019967

Frontispiece: "Flies Are a Disgrace," *Bulletin of the North Carolina State Board of Health* 21 (May 1914).

For my parents, Jayne and Stephen Biehler

CONTENTS

FOREWORD

An Unruly Wildness Within
WILLIAM CRONON

ASK MANY PEOPLE WHAT FIRST OCCURS TO THEM WHEN THEY THINK
of wild nature, and their most likely answers will sound pretty familiar.
They conjure images of sublime landscapes, of Yosemite or the Everglades,
Everest or the Serengeti. If they favor humbler embodiments of the wild,
they may name a local park or woods or wetland where they watch birds or
hike or fish or hunt deer. If watery nature is their passion, their answer will
evoke the rapids of the Colorado, the lakes of the North Woods, the tide
pools of Maine or Puget Sound, the trackless expanse of the open ocean. If
they prefer their wildness animate, they speak of grizzlies in Alaska, wolves
in Yellowstone, lions and elephants and wildebeests in the Great Rift Val-
ley. In most cases, what counts as "wild nature" for them is relatively far
away and disconnected from their daily lives. Even if they live in Manhattan and regard the Ramble in Central Park as an icon of wildness—which
it most certainly is intended to be—it carries that value for them precisely
because its curving, rustic pathways feel so very far from the city's gridded
streets and avenues.

Such places and the organisms they shelter have long stood as symbols
of the world we humans did not make, the nature we cherish because it is
not us. But if by "wildness" we also mean the plants and animals and places
that resist human control, we need not look nearly so far afield to find it. A
vacant lot that stops being tended by its owner quickly fills with a tangle of
weeds that, however familiar (or exotic) they may seem to us, are certainly
not under our control. Quite the contrary: our difficulty in getting rid of
them is why we call them weeds. They may not be what we imagine when
we think of wild nature, but they are hardly tidy or tame. We may create
the habitats in which weeds thrive, but the exuberance they bring to their

invasion of those habitats is surely the expression of a wild life force whose vivid power is not of human making.

Nearer still are the creatures that live in our midst and sleep under our roofs. When these animals enter our dwellings unbidden—demonstrating like weeds their indifference to our illusions of control—we think of them not as wildlife but as vermin. Dawn Biehler catalogs some of the chief species among them in the title she has chosen for her fine new book, *Pests in the City: Flies, Bedbugs, Cockroaches, and Rats*. Such organisms rarely turn up in the work of nature photographers or grace the covers of magazines like *Audubon* or *National Geographic*. So it may seem perverse to suggest that they too are "wild" . . . but it would be even more perverse to call them "domesticated." Opportunistic in the extreme, seizing whatever openings we give them to set up housekeeping in the ecosystems we unknowingly create for them, these creatures are near perfect exemplars of what Baruch Spinoza called *natura naturans*: nature naturing.

In *Pests in the City*, Biehler sets out to explore the environmental history of the much-unloved wildlife that has so triumphantly colonized the domestic territories of human habitation. Comfortably straddling the disciplinary boundaries between history and geography, she pays careful attention to *space* as it has shaped the lives of people and animals in American cities since 1900. A core premise of her book is that one cannot understand urban environments without attending to the innumerable boundaries that divide urban spaces into outside and inside, public and private, open and closed, empowered and disempowered, along with the social distinctions among classes and occupations and races and ethnicities and genders and sexualities that cannot be expressed with such tidy dichotomies. Put them all together, and one discovers an intricate historical geography that Biehler explores and elucidates quite brilliantly in this book.

She begins, appropriately enough, with the animals themselves, focusing on a rogue's gallery of organisms that have played outsized roles in urban pest-control efforts since 1900. They find their way into our dwellings via different routes, occupy different spaces, interact with people in different ways, and pose different threats and annoyances as they pursue their own livelihoods. Houseflies concentrate in the kitchen and dining room (and outhouses, before the advent of indoor plumbing) but flit hither and yon in the most annoying ways as they seek out places to lay their eggs and breed the next generation. They land anywhere and everywhere, so their feet become vectors for transporting microorganisms from food to garbage and back again. Cockroaches make many of the same journeys between food and garbage but prefer tighter spaces as they go about their affairs, dropping egg sacks in dark protected places where their young can emerge by the dozens (and, if unchecked, by the hundreds and thousands). They scuttle everywhere, and the airborne dust from their feces may play an important role in promoting human asthma. Bedbugs choose the hidden spaces inside mattresses and upholstery as their preferred domestic ecosystems (though they can dwell in other household locations as well), for the obvious reason that warm sleeping bodies so reliably supply a nocturnal source of blood on which to feast. (A special horror of bedbugs is that their exhausted victims must somehow fall asleep knowing they'll be dined upon all night long.) And finally, rats—much larger in size and closer mammalian kin to humans—range farther afield and are just as capable of transporting disease. Major players among the things that scurry and go bump in the night, rats are scarier to encounter and have even been known to attack humans when cornered. All four of these species do what wild animals do everywhere—move about in search of food, eating and defecating and reproducing themselves—but because they do so in our walls and ceilings, in our kitchens and bedrooms, their companionship feels especially disturbing.

A big part of Dawn Biehler's story thus has to do with the long struggle to control such pests to improve the quality of life for city-dwellers across the United States. She opens with Progressive Era reformers who sought to institute public health protocols for identifying infested buildings and applying to them an ever-proliferating array of "pest-control" technologies. In so doing, they pursued the familiar modernist dream of using scientific knowledge in the hands of supposedly disinterested experts to promote the common good. Doctors, chemists, entomologists, engineers, health departments, settlement-house workers, and professional exterminators all became players in this drama, and Biehler analyzes their respective roles with subtlety and insight. The advent of seemingly miraculous pesticides like DDT during the 1940s led many to believe that technology would eventually triumph over at least the offending insects—and bedbugs in particular began to retreat quite significantly in the years that followed. Rachel Carson's *Silent Spring* in 1962 would provoke growing public doubts about such solutions to pest problems, yet for the middle decades of the twentieth century, technological approaches seemed to represent modern science at its best and most effective.

But *Pests in the City* is not just about human beings striving to control insects and rodents. It is equally about groups of human beings who have very different relationships not only with these creatures but also with one another. From the beginning of her story, Biehler is acutely aware that not everyone is equally exposed to the predations of rats, roaches, and other pests. Although they can in theory turn up anywhere, these pests have long tended to be most abundant in the poorest and most crowded neighborhoods, where the urban poor congregate. This makes their presence or absence a marker of class and racial status, which means that the environmental history of these organisms cannot help but be a history of environmental injustice as well. Early pest-control efforts tended to favor simple one-size-fits-all approaches in which a toxic chemical like DDT could be applied to "eradicate" an infestation whose causes were in fact far more complex, originating as they did from an intricate web of pest-people relationships. Far from being merely "environmental," these were powerfully linked to poverty, segregation, poor housing, bad sanitation, and urban infrastructures that were much less adequate in inner-city neighborhoods than elsewhere. Pests flourished most successfully in social spaces where neglect and crowding fostered the ecological conditions they preferred.

Although it was tempting for better-off Americans to blame the poor for the infested conditions in which they lived, those conditions had at least as much to do with insufficient capital investment and negligent maintenance by landlords as with any individual choices poor families made for themselves. People with little money more often than not found themselves living in run-down buildings, relying on secondhand furniture that sheltered bedbugs, and perennially struggling to clean up conditions that were not of their own making. Nothing demonstrated the systemic nature of these problems more compellingly than the speed with which public housing projects—constructed from the 1930s forward by reform-minded municipal governments, often with federal support—were invaded by the very pests they were supposed to keep away.

By the 1960s and 1970s, it had become obvious that the modernist dream of extirpating pests had been just that: a dream. Subtler, more systemic, longer-term efforts that went far beyond the broadcast deployment of poisons would be required if people and pests were ever to coexist on healthier terms. Furthermore, the heroic image of experts descending on infested neighborhoods with spray cans and traps was itself part of the problem. As the experts themselves began to realize, what was needed were day-to-day practices that the urban poor (and anyone else whose households were invaded by bugs and rodents) could themselves use to discourage infestation in the first place. Among the most intriguing and encouraging aspects of Biehler's narrative are the occasions when inner-city residents succeeded in working *with* experts to create a culture of caretaking in which their intimate knowledge of their own communities enabled them to make their residences less attractive to pests.

Pests in the City offers many lessons that speak as much to the present as they do to the past. Although people have long regarded flies, bedbugs, cockroaches, rats, and their kindred as creatures worthy only of fear and disgust, they are undeniably forms of wild nature that have been remarkably successful in colonizing *us*. The ecosystems we work to create for ourselves are often equally hospitable to them. It thus requires care, vigilance, and maybe even grudging respect for their tenacity if we are to design and maintain dwellings and neighborhoods that minimize their effects on our own lives. Because the urban poor have historically been forced to crowd into buildings whose owners have insufficiently cared for their upkeep, they have known and lived with these organisms more intimately than most. Although the literature of environmental justice has traditionally focused on pollution and toxic chemicals, Dawn Biehler makes a persuasive case that the buzzing of flies, the defecating of roaches, the scurrying of rats, and the bloodsucking of bedbugs also make potent contributions to the environmental costs of social inequality. Chemicals alone cannot solve such problems. No less important—as Biehler compellingly demonstrates in this pathbreaking book—is a wider and more generous understanding of the social geographies that separate people from one another to create the spaces of neglect and abandonment in which pests thrive.

ACKNOWLEDGMENTS

IT IS A HUMBLING TASK TO TRY TO UNDERSTAND HOW TINY CREATURES persist in our homes and cities. I am humbled anew as I think of the people whose wisdom, patience, generosity, and love have supported me through this task, and to whom I owe many debts of gratitude.

My first thanks go to Bill Cronon and Marianne Keddington-Lang, who have nurtured this project from its inchoate and sprawling beginnings to its current form. Bill always reminded me of my intellectual purpose when writing became difficult. I can never repay him for his faith in me, for his patience during hard times, and for his keen insight into the crafts of research and writing. Marianne has also shown extraordinary patience and good cheer through changes in the shape and timeline of the book. I am astounded at the hard work she has done to see this project to completion—a thousand mea culpas for the times I created more work.

I have benefited from the wisdom and kindness of several other mentors. Special thanks go to Gregg Mitman, who pointed me in the direction of this project in the first place and, more than almost anyone else, shaped my thinking about health, environment, and social justice. Lisa Naughton, Matthew Turner, Kris Olds, and Judy Leavitt gave creative ideas, incisive critiques, and much-needed doses of reality during the project's formative stages. Graeme Wynn, Paul Robbins, and Sylvia Hood Washington provided scholarly nudges at key moments. Thanks also to the anonymous reviewers who guided me toward important changes in the book's content, structure, and argument.

Several organizations provided generous funding that allowed me to visit archives, conduct interviews, and dedicate my time to working on this book. The National Science Foundation jump-started my research efforts, and the University of Maryland, Baltimore County, also provided funds for research travel and to hire research assistants. The American Association of University Women, the National Endowment for the Humanities, and the University of Maryland, Baltimore County, all provided generous support that allowed me to take time out from other responsibilities and focus my attention on writing. Thanks to Sandy Parker for being a constant advocate for me and my research. Thanks to the Wisconsin Alumni Research Foundation and the University of Wisconsin–Madison Department of Geography, which funded my graduate studies with scholarships and assistantships.

Many archivists and librarians have patiently guided me through their collections and pointed out sources that otherwise would have remained hidden to me. Thanks to Robert Battaly and Beth Jaffe of the Rockefeller Archive Center; Lyle Benedict of the Chicago Public Library; Tad Bennicoff at the Smithsonian Institution Archives; Philip Deloria and Thomas Hollowak of the Langsdale Library Special Collections; Allen Fischer of the LBJ Library; Derya Golpinar at the Lower East Side Tenement Museum; Tab Lewis of the National Archives in College Park; Eileen Lipinski of the Milwaukee Legislative Reference Bureau; and Micaela Sullivan-Fowler at UW-Madison's Ebling Library. Thanks to the Artists' Rights Society and Emory Douglas, the Chicago Public Library, the City of Milwaukee, the *Journal of Housing*, the *Journal of Mammalogy*, the University of Baltimore, and the National Pest Management Association for their kind permission to use images, and to the Rockefeller Archive Center for kind permission to cite and quote material. Thanks also to staff at the City of New York Municipal Reference Bureau, the Enoch Pratt Free Library, the Library of Congress, the Maryland State Historical Society, the National Library of Medicine, the New York Public Library, the Schomburg Center, Special Collections and University Archives at Rutgers University, and the Washington, D.C., Historical Society.

Material in chapters 1, 2, and 3 of this book was previously published in two journal articles: "Permeable Homes: A Historical Political Ecology of Insects and Pesticides in U.S. Public Housing," *Geoforum* 40 (2009): 1014–23; and "Flies, Manure, and Window Screens," *Journal of Historical Geography* 36 (2010): 68–78. Thanks to these journals for easing the process of using this material.

Several people have shared their stories about pests with me, taking time out from work and family, welcoming me into their homes and offices.

Helga and William Olkowski, William Jackson, Eugene Wood, and Wayne White were especially generous and welcoming, and Sarah Ruffin shared the most difficult story of all. For their time, insights, and suggestions, I thank Barbara Brenner, the Honorable Spencer Coggs, Stephen Frantz, Gregory Glass, Stuart Greenberg, Colin Ellis, Charlie Haug, Anthhu Hoang, Ruth Hopgood, Ray Lopez, Cindy Mannes, Kenneth Metzger, Gary Piper, Saint Prillerman, Silvia Salazar, Kathy Seikel, David Shangle, Doug Thiessen, Jill Viehweg, Emily Williams, and Mark Wyman. These individuals have helped make this story come alive.

Numerous friends have provided moral and intellectual support over the years. Kendra Smith-Howard, Eric Carter, Claudia Thiem, Gregory Simon, Brian and Stephanie Slattery, Chuck Wall, Tara Duffy, Lisa Uddin, Amy Muise, J.D. Ho, Laura Massie, Anna Kinsman, Adam Shapiro, Giselle Hicks, Bill Ross, Morgan Robertson, and Maureen McLachlan have been great cheerleaders, kind critics, and sources of humor and relief. Melanie McCalmont surprised me with unexpected primary documents that opened up new possibilities. My conversations with Yvette Williams helped push the book in new directions.

A long list of student assistants helped lighten the workload and seek out obscure information, starting with Maureen McLachlan. Julianna Kuhn, Molissa Udevitz, Matthew Haines, Matthew O'Connell, Eliza Ledwell, and Daniela Makembe also helped track down articles and images that have been crucial to the book.

My family—Cristine and T. J. Kirsch, Eric and Karen Biehler, Sharon and John Day, Caitlin Day and Tess Abellera, and Laura and Andrew Giarolo—have given hospitality, support, good meals, free and loving child care, and fun times that drew me out of the world of pests. This book is dedicated to my parents, Stephen and Jayne Biehler, who gave all of these things too and inspired me from a young age to think about animals and domesticity. This book would not have been possible without their support for my mind and my very being.

Alice Annie Day-Biehler came into the world in the midst of revisions on the book, and she grew up with the project during her first two years, sharing my fascination with "yuck bugs" when we moved into a condo infested with *Blatta orientalis*. She is a joy and an inspiration, showing me the world, including its most reviled creatures, through a fresh pair of eyes.

Finally, Nathan Day endured this project for the first several years of our married life, tolerated my ravings about pests, read every word of the second draft, and cheered me on when the writing got hard. Thank you for your compassionate criticism, your patience, and your love.

PESTS IN THE CITY

INTRODUCTION

History, Ecology, and the Politics of Pests

> Put cover on your garbage,
> Revamp the rusty screen,
> Drive out the rat and bedbug,
> The roach and fly obscene . . .
> Yes, clean the vacant places,
> Where rank disorder roam,
> Look wide beyond the fences,
> The city is your home.
> —Arthur Corwin, M.D.,
> "Clean Up," c. 1916

> Good night, sleep tight,
> Don't let the bedbugs bite.

DR. ARTHUR CORWIN'S POEM "CLEAN UP" AND THE TRADITIONAL BED-time rhyme about bedbugs evoke two very different facets of life with pests. Parents uttered the latter while tucking their children into bed, hoping to ward off a menace that attacked in people's most private moments. In contrast, Corwin's poem made ridding domestic space of pests a civic duty for individual urbanites whose material connections to the city stretched "wide beyond the fences." Together, these two poems suggest that living with pests is neither simply a private nor a public experience—it is both.

Indeed, the creatures in Corwin's poem—rats, bedbugs, roaches, and houseflies—have long scurried, hitchhiked, scuttled, and buzzed across the borders of public and private space.

Yet responses to pests in American cities often divided the public from the private—or at least attempted to do so. Health departments urged poor women to maintain window screens in their homes while municipal sanitation crews failed to clean up fly-breeding filth throughout their neighborhoods. Public housing managers longed for pesticide technologies that could kill bedbugs in individual apartments so they could avoid the complexities and cost of treating entire buildings. Apartment-dwellers tried to hide roach infestations in shame even as the insects ranged into their neighbors' units. Scientists and public officials envisioned grand housing rehabilitation schemes that would eliminate rat habitats but neglected to help residents keep rats out of their homes. Politicians dismissed rat problems in African-American neighborhoods as residents' private responsibility although racial segregation had consigned blacks to substandard homes that harbored long-established rodent populations. In all these cases, authorities—and sometimes residents themselves— assumed that pest problems could be contained to private or public spaces. Throughout the twentieth century, however, these animals have defied attempts at containment. Pests persisted to trouble people who already struggled against housing discrimination, neglectful governments, and social stigma.

For a time, one of these pests seemed to be contained, but it has since returned with a vengeance. Since colonial times, the bedbug had made an excellent living in the United States by hitchhiking from home to home, gaining passage to new abodes and hosts via secondhand belongings and human bodies in such public spaces as streetcars and movie theaters. In Arthur Corwin's day, families toiled for weeks or months to rid themselves of bedbugs, often dousing infested bed frames and other furniture with chemical remedies of dubious value.[1] The high labor and financial costs of effective treatments made it difficult for poor families to eradicate bedbugs. If they succeeded, a neighbor still might unwittingly reintroduce them during a visit or on borrowed belongings. Despite these troubles, elites who managed to escape bugs often faulted the poor for continuing to live with them. All the while, many families who lived with bedbugs tried to hide their infestations out of shame and fear of ostracism.

In the 1940s and 1950s, most bedbugs in the United States fell to DDT as exterminators and do-it-yourselfers applied this mythic modern chemical in homes and other structures. DDT made bedbug control affordable across the income spectrum, with the exception of an extremely unfortunate few. Bedbugs' downfall seemed so complete that by the late twentieth century two generations of Americans knew little of their existence except in the bedtime rhyme.[2] Beginning just before the dawn of the twenty-first century, however, bedbugs resurged, belying promises of modern pest control. The bedbugs' resurgence also reconnected Americans to the largely forgotten private history of bodily discomfort, stress, painstaking labor, and excruciating shame. In the early twenty-first century, again, families trying to rid their homes of bedbugs faced a series of arduous tasks: encasing mattresses, laundering entire wardrobes, eliminating clutter, and vacuuming repeatedly. Desperate families bought their dubious chemicals online. Some of the most isolated, vulnerable people became even more so as they tried to hide infestations from landlords, fearful of stigma and eviction. The old homily "bedbugs don't discriminate" has also returned, but the affluent can still escape an infestation much more easily than the poor. As in Corwin's time, bedbugs in the twenty-first century leave infested families itching, sleepless, stressed, and socially stigmatized.

Bedbugs also carry in their bodies the legacy of our past relationships with them. Many populations of *Cimex lectularius* in the early twenty-first century were harder to control than their ancestors because they had evolved resistance to common pesticides. Strains of bedbugs already resistant to one pesticide were also predisposed to evolve cross-resistance to other substances.[3] Also, with the bedbug resurgence, many communities relearned a lesson well known in early twentieth-century America: bedbugs tend to bite in their victims' most private moments, but they are creatures of community, and their ecology is inextricably connected to politics. Some infested communities found shared political strength in their efforts to manage these creatures. In Washington, D.C., in 2007, for example, residents of the Norwood—a mixed-income, ethnically diverse rental building just blocks from the White House—united to control the bedbugs, mice, and mold that spread from apartment to apartment there. Their common efforts to manage pests and improve their environment built solidarity as they faced possible eviction; their landlord hoped to sell the building as the neighborhood gentrified. Residents united by bedbugs succeeded in their struggle to keep their homes, in a city where affordable housing was all too rare.[4]

At the same time, bedbugs divided other communities and burdened people who tried to escape them. The university town of Madison, Wisconsin, enjoys a reputation for progressivism, but the bedbug resurgence exposed and heightened exclusions faced by some residents. In 2006, a resident unwittingly brought bedbugs home to her unit in a city-owned, low-income apartment complex on the ethnically diverse South Side—an area already marked by the stigma of crime and poverty in the minds of Madisonians from other neighborhoods. As bugs spread throughout the project, neighbors blamed one another for the infestation. The city paid for chemical treatments—along with heat and freeze treatments—but some residents worried about toxic exposure.[5] Troubled by both biting bugs and chemical odors, a few residents sought new housing. They discovered that would-be landlords could deny their applications on the basis of their past infestation. Bedbugs created ecological links among neighbors with their migrations but also alienated them from each other and from better housing options.[6]

Stories from the Norwood and South Madison echo pest control struggles across the twentieth century. Much as residents of the Norwood mobilized around bedbugs, past pest-control campaigns have often been tied to urban reform efforts, public health programs, and community activism. The spaces these campaigns targeted might seem remote from nature— from backyard privies to tenement bedrooms, from kitchens in public housing projects to the alleys running through blocks of row houses—but they nonetheless possess rich ecologies in which pests thrived and people struggled for healthy living conditions.

POLITICAL PESTS IN THE CITY

The opposition between reductionist techno-science and ecological thought has become a central conflict in narratives of twentieth-century American pest control. Stories about pest control in modern America often describe a war against nature waged with a series of chemical weapons, culminating in the rise of DDT and other synthetic pesticides after World War II. Narratives reach a turning point in 1962 with the publication of Rachel Carson's book *Silent Spring*. The historian Maril Hazlett has argued that Carson blurred lines between human bodies, animals, and the environment, between nature and culture—lines that reductionist pest controllers had drawn all too sharply in their attempts to eliminate pests from the ecosystems where they existed.[7]

Most histories that follow this trajectory have focused either on pest control in general or else on agricultural pests; several recent studies have also examined mosquitoes, which inhabit a range of domestic, urban, and rural landscapes.[8] These studies have largely been silent about animals that infest urban, domestic space, however. Like their counterparts in agriculture, landscaping, and mosquito control, urban reformers have struggled over pest-control methods and have drawn sharp lines between nature and culture. They have often disagreed about the necessity, effectiveness, and safety of chemical pesticides in residential neighborhoods on the one hand and, on the other hand, the potential for holistic environmental change to provide an effective method for managing flies, bedbugs, roaches, and rats.

Urban, domestic pest controllers have drawn other lines, however. In addition to lines between people and nature, many have also reinforced lines between the public and the private. Some reformers have targeted education campaigns at individual households, making pest control a private responsibility despite broader-scale factors that sustained infestation. Other reformers have launched top-down projects to modernize infrastructure and housing, taking public control of the environment while ignoring the small-scale dynamics of pest populations, human health, and human culture. These campaigns simplified urban ecology and society much as other pest controllers tried to simplify the webs that bound together insects, birds, fish, water, soil, and human bodies. The clearest problem with these private-public divisions was that pests—and sometimes pesticides—migrated across these spaces, connecting neighbors to one another and linking homes to the wider urban environment. Flies flew from manure-caked streets to germ-infested privies to kitchens where mothers prepared baby bottles. Bedbugs hitchhiked from home to home on secondhand belongings or neighbors' bodies. Roaches crept through the interstices of multifamily apartment buildings. Rats scurried across property lines and breached crumbling foundations. Pesticides seeped through shafts between flats or repelled pests into neighbors' apartments.

The public and the private were not only physical spaces, however. They were also political lenses through which urban reformers viewed pest problems. By narrowing their conception of infestation to either a public or private issue, reformers depoliticized urban ecology and sometimes even tried to isolate it from its community context. Thus, even pest-control campaigns that claimed to respect ecology might not offer a truly holistic solution. Sometimes chemical-based campaigns engaged communities in ways that "ecological" campaigns failed to do, crossing lines of public and private. Many other campaigns urged individuals to change their domestic ecologies without correcting the inequalities that made neighborhoods hospitable to flies, bedbugs, roaches, and rats.[9] To paraphrase a 1947 commentary on rodents in Chicago, pests were symptoms of other social problems that had long gone unsolved. The historian James McWilliams has described much American pest control as a "futile quest to remove ourselves from the inexorable realities of the insect world."[10] Similarly, depoliticized and individualized pest control attempted to remove pests from the realities of urban society.

Domestic pests' ecologies and changing pest control practices have long intertwined with social tensions and political struggles in American cities. Household pests persisted through and within these struggles; the ecologies of flies, bedbugs, roaches, and rats are entangled with urban history. Three enduring themes in urban history can help us understand the relationship between urban society and persistent infestation. One theme is the position of homes with respect to public life. Many histories of the home have examined notions of domestic space as a separate, feminine sphere, a haven from the city, and a site of family sovereignty. Household pest control required difficult, stressful, and often dangerous labor, and the problem often spilled past the bounds of the home.[11] A domestic advice columnist wrote in 1911, "the wandering tribes of insects" can "cause the housewife as much anxiety and hard work as comes to the man of the house in putting through a big business deal."[12] The notion that wives and mothers bear responsibility for the household and its health has informed contradictory public policies: on the one hand, aggressive attempts to teach women domestic skills; and on the other hand, public neglect of the home environment based on the assumption that a woman would take care of it. Many families targeted in pest-control campaigns sought to close off their homes to the prying eyes of the state. Others demanded public protection from landlords and authorities whom they saw as responsible for household infestation.[13] The story of pests shows that the home was not merely a private matter; rather, it was (and still is) an environment with important implications for politics, human health, and women's work.

A second theme is social injustice along lines of race and class. For much of the twentieth century, residential segregation gave landlords who rented to low-income blacks—and some immigrant groups—license to neglect their buildings. With few housing options, poor African-Americans in many cities were vulnerable to this exploitation, and their health suffered from exposure to pests, pesticides, and other home-based hazards. Meanwhile, affordable housing initiatives were underfunded and controversial, and municipal code enforcement systems were spread thin, leaving residents little recourse against neglectful property owners. Even in public housing, African-Americans faced the stigma of living in "the projects" within a culture that valorized private homes; government neglect of public housing projects sharpened this stigma.[14] Pests thrived in buildings long deprived of maintenance, new investment, and government inspections—conditions that the historian Gregg Mitman has called "the ecology of injustice." Yet many outsiders—and some insiders—blamed poor immigrants and communities of color for sanitary lapses that supported pests. Pests marked communities as "environmental lepers," to borrow from the historian Sylvia Hood Washington. Furthermore, activists in communities of color protested unhealthy housing, pests, and the stigma they carried. The story of urban pests thus broadens our understanding of environmentalism, human health, and environmental injustice.[15]

A third theme is the promise and failure of urban reform projects. From sanitary overhauls to housing rehabilitation to public housing, many government-funded projects promised modern, healthy living conditions for all. Projects have chronically fallen short of their goals, no matter how visionary the reformers who conceived them. Alleviating pest problems was often a secondary but very visible goal of these projects, and many affected communities enjoyed reduced pest populations, at least for a time. Communities targeted for these projects could only keep pest populations low under two conditions, however: first, if funding was sufficient to bring holistic change to environments that had supported pests; and second, if authorities cooperated with and empowered communities to sustain those environmental changes. Sometimes these conditions were present at the beginning of a project, but funding and community relationships often broke down later, reopening pests' niches in an unequal and unhealthy urban environment.[16] The story of urban pests thus challenges the sustainability and justice achievements of urban reform.

Indeed, as social and environmental problems persisted, so did the pests that were their fleshy manifestations. Houseflies, bedbugs, German cockroaches, and Norway rats may be less common in American cities now than they were a century ago, although statistics about their prevalence then and now are incomplete. Rat populations in some cities may have changed little since the 1950s.[17] Where pest populations have declined, the magnitude and sustainability of these declines have varied, as have the use of chemical pesticides, governments' engagement with communities, and the treatment of public and private spaces. Furthermore, changes in pest populations have been uneven across urban landscapes. We unfortunately lack the historical data that might allow us to compare infestation across urban neighborhoods in the past. We can, however, examine the history of communities targeted for pest control campaigns because of severe infestations or the perception thereof. In these places, social and environmental conditions supported thriving populations of flies, bedbugs, roaches, and rats. Residents had long tried to control most of these pests themselves, but beginning around 1900, the emerging field of medical entomology brought the attention of health authorities and housing reformers to urban infestation as well. Reformers along with residents attempted to control these creatures, often by modernizing urban infrastructure, living conditions, and citizens themselves.

Attempts to contain pests through modernization of cities and homes continued into the 1960s—the same moment when many other histories of American pest control reached their climax with the publication of Carson's *Silent Spring*. *Silent Spring* sparked protests against common pest-control methods for their potential to poison people, wildlife, and the environment. Meanwhile, in central cities, movements demanding civil rights and economic justice included protests against poor housing conditions and the failed promises of urban modernization and health projects. These protests criticized narrow, atomized, and depoliticized approaches to urban pest control. Communities demanded environmental justice amid persistent infestation and other dangerous and unhealthy living conditions.

PLACES AND PESTS

Cities across the United States have suffered infestations and launched campaigns to control flies, bedbugs, roaches, and rats. Those in the mid-Atlantic and Midwestern United States share similar climates, housing types, and urban histories that have shaped struggles over pests. In those regions, Washington, D.C., Chicago, New York, Baltimore, and Milwaukee have all been the sites of especially notable pest-control campaigns connected with housing reform activities. A range of human characters in these cities have shaped pest control—social reformers, public health officials, housing managers, scientists, pest-control professionals, politicians, and community activists and residents.

This book focuses on four animal characters who represent a range of pest types and associated public health problems. Houseflies are suspected of carrying germs on their feet as they fly from filth to homes and food supplies. Bedbugs crawl on human bodies, sucking blood, leaving itchy bites, and disturbing sleep. German cockroaches play a major role in allergies and asthma and, like flies, can foul food supplies. Norway rats foul food, too, and also cause stress, spread infectious diseases, and sometimes even attack humans. These four creatures are strongly associated with housing, and public health authorities have made them frequent targets of domestic pest control campaigns. From lice to mice, and from mites to mosquitoes, other pests also share Americans' domestic spaces and affect public health. They make brief appearances in this book as well, but fuller stories of their relationships with people would require another volume. All these pests—and the many pathogens that they carry—are tightly woven into the ecological fabric of cities and have long resisted our efforts to disentangle them.

PART ONE

THE PROMISES OF MODERN PEST CONTROL

MANY URBAN HOMES AND NEIGHBORHOODS IN THE FIRST HALF OF THE twentieth century teemed with pests. During surveys of Washington, D.C., in the summer of 1908, entomologists sometimes caught over two thousand houseflies with a single sheet of flypaper hung for two days in a residential area. At least half of residents entering Chicago Housing Authority projects in 1938 had lived with bedbugs in their old homes. One mortified New Yorker, writing in 1921, estimated that her exterminator removed thousands of German cockroaches from her kitchen—a not-unusual yield for her city just after the Great War. In the mid-1940s, ecologists in Baltimore found many central-city blocks that were home to two hundred rats each, with four hundred thousand rats residing in the city overall—and these estimates likely undercounted rats that lived inside houses.[1] Such infestations seemed primitive and backward in an era of modern architecture and housing, new domestic technologies, and advanced medical and ecological knowledge.

Urban reformers of many stripes responded to infestations like these by trying to rid city-dwellers' homes of pests, especially homes in low-income communities. Between the blossoming of medical entomology around 1900 through the 1960s, pests became one of many aspects of poor citizens' lives in which health and welfare crusaders intervened. Reformers promised modern living spaces, nearly free from pests, for the poor. Some reformers saw new urban infrastructure and housing as the solution to teeming pests. Rational, efficient sanitation could remove wastes that bred and fed pests from the city. Housing reform programs aimed to solve an array of social and environmental problems by either rehabilitating infested homes or else demolishing them and replacing them with modern, healthy structures that were less vulnerable to pests. Many reformers promoted modern pest control methods to be practiced by citizens or trained exterminators in residents' homes. Some tried to teach women how to make their homes healthy in the midst of the urban environment. Others promoted chemical technologies for controlling pests—sometimes as a magic bullet and sometimes in conjunction with other environmental changes. Pest-control reformers in the first half of the twentieth century placed their faith in the modernization of domestic and urban environments, whether they urged top-down infrastructure and housing projects on the one hand, or practices and technologies applied in the home on the other.

Many reformers failed to see the ways in which pests remained entangled in urban politics and communities amid these modernization and education projects. Only a few advocates for pest control combined sanitation, housing reform, domestic education, or pesticide use *and* the empowerment of people who struggled daily with pests. Even when campaigns were based on ecological knowledge, reformers often missed the ways in which pests' ecology was communal and political. Attempts to control pests without changing politics recall the words of preservationist John Muir: "When we try to pick out anything by itself, we find it hitched to everything else in the universe."[2] Muir's words were inspired by mountain meadows lush with sedges and lupines, but they apply equally to basements and back alleys swarming with rats. Pests were not only "hitched" to physical conditions such as the presence of garbage or house foundations in ill-repair. They also thrived on racial segregation, underfunded housing inspection programs, and cultural stigmas that led residents to try to hide infestations. Modern pest controllers promised to make homes healthy, but many tried to "pick out" pests from complex, enduring social struggles. Some campaigns succeeded despite their lack of social and environmental holism, but in other cases, the pests persisted alongside tenacious inequalities in American cities.

Each of the chapters in part one begins with a composite sketch of pests' life-worlds within one city where that species thrived in the first half of the twentieth century. These sketches are based as much as possible on descriptions of the cities themselves, as well as on contemporary and more recent science about the specific pest. The aim of these sketches is to illustrate the ways these pests encountered urban, domestic environments, and to show how pests sensed and moved through urban landscapes. The chapters end with a similar composite sketch, showing how the environment changed—and didn't change—from the perspective of the pest.[3]

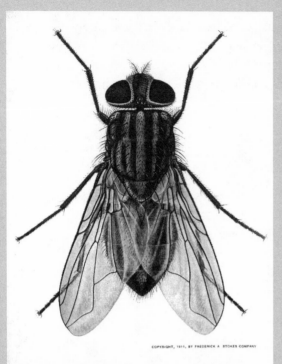

Housefly, *Musca domestica*. L. O. Howard, *The House Fly: Disease Carrier* (New York: Frederick Stokes, 1911).

TRAP THE FLY
THIS TRAP CAUGHT 500,000 FLIES IN ONE SEASON

THESE TRAPS CAN BE MADE AT HOME

HANG NEAR BACK DOOR

BAIT WITH
BANANA PEELING
SUGAR & VINEGAR
PIECE OF MEAT

A FLY TRAP FOR EVERY HOME
MAKE ONE OR BUY ONE

Biologist C. F. Hodge promoted domestic-scale, early-season fly trapping, using traps such as these, as the best means of controlling flies because he believed sanitation could never eliminate all fly-breeding. *Reference Book for the Lecture "Fight the Fly"* (Chicago: International Harvester Company Agricultural Extension Department, 1917).

In the 1910s, health departments promoted fixtures and tools with which house-holders could protect their homes from flies, emphasizing private responsibility for fly-borne diseases. Chicago Board of Health, *Clean Living* (May 1916). Courtesy of the Chicago Municipal Reference Collection.

The headline "Our Greatest Menace Is Domestic not Foreign" played on debates about the United States's entry into the Great War in Europe but also placed responsibility for fly control with individual families. Here, most of the flies come from trash in the man's own yard. Chicago Board of Health, *Clean Living* (July 1916). Courtesy of the Chicago Municipal Reference Collection.

Flies became part of the debate about infant-feeding practices in the early 1900s. This cartoon warned mothers that flies connected urban filth with domestic space and infants' food. Association for Improving the Condition of the Poor, *Flies and Diarrheal Disease* (New York: Department of Health, 1914).

Health department literature emphasized women's responsibility for fly control and the potential for flies to contaminate food and drink. "Flies Are a Disgrace," *Bulletin of the North Carolina State Board of Health* 21 (May 1914).

Tenement families in the Bronx in 1914 dumped garbage in their backyard in
the absence of better receptacles. The open windows, strung with clotheslines,
would permit flies from the backyard and nearby horse stables to enter domestic
spaces. Association for Improving the Condition of the Poor, *Flies and Diarrheal
Disease* (New York: Department of Health, 1914).

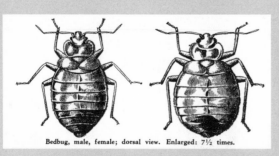

Bedbug, male, female; dorsal view. Enlarged: 7½ times.

Bedbug, *Cimex lectu-
larius.* Hugo Hartnack,
*202 Common Household
Pests of North America*
(Chicago: Hartnack
Publishing, 1939).

This cartoon illustrated a 1939 advertisement for DuPont's hydrocyanic acid gas (HCN) generator. Like bedbugs, HCN could penetrate into the narrowest crannies of homes and other structures, making it both highly effective and likely to spread to adjoining structures through unseen crevices. *Pests and Their Control*, July 1939. Courtesy of the National Pest Management Association.

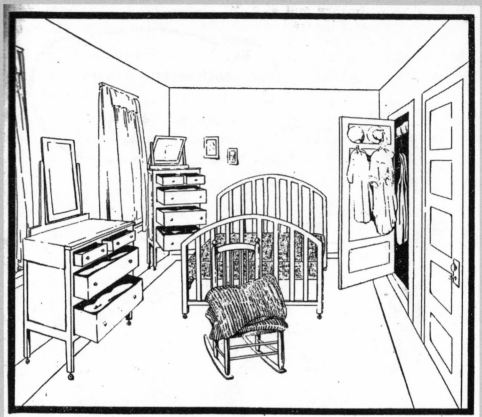

FIGURE 4.—Sketch of bedroom showing bureau and dresser drawers and closet door opened as they should be during a fumigation

A U.S. Department of Agriculture bulletin shows the proper way to prepare a bedroom for HCN fumigation, to facilitate airing out afterward. Failure to prepare a room thus could result in the retention of gas in porous items—a common cause of HCN poisoning. E. A. Back and R. T. Cotton, "Hydrocyanic Acid Gas as a Fumigant for Destroying Household Insects," *USDA Farmers' Bulletin* 1670 (1932).

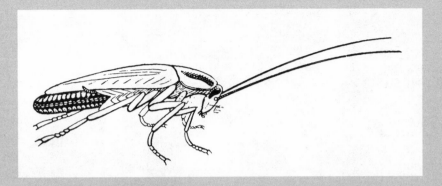

German cockroach, *Blattella germanica*, with ootheca, or egg case, which contains up to forty eggs, more than that for larger species of roach. Hugo Hartnack, *202 Common Household Pests of North America* (Chicago: Hartnack Publishing, 1939).

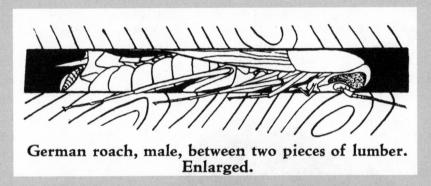

German roach, male, between two pieces of lumber. Enlarged.

A German cockroach squeezes into a tight space. The attraction to bodily contact with surfaces is called positive thigmotaxis; this behavior helps the species hide and move throughout buildings. Hugo Hartnack, *202 Common Household Pests of North America* (Chicago: Hartnack Publishing, 1939).

At this 1946 workshop in Springfield, Illinois, public housing maintenance staff learn to apply residual DDT. *Journal of Housing* (July 1946). Courtesy of the National Association of Housing and Redevelopment Officials.

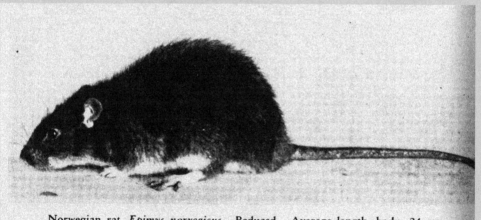

Norwegian rat, *Epimys norvegicus*. Reduced. Average length, body: 24 cm, tail: 20 cm.

Norway rat, *Rattus norvegicus*. Hugo Hartnack, *202 Common Household Pests of North America* (Chicago: Hartnack Publishing, 1939).

Baltimore schoolchildren participate in a clean-up day in 1953, part of a long tradition of neighborhood environmental stewardship in the city's black communities, which included rat and fly control. Citizens' Planning and Housing Association Collection, Series VIII, Box 1, folder 40-Clean-Up Day, 1953, University of Baltimore Archives. Courtesy of CPHA Collection—University of Baltimore.

Gaps in this house foundation in Baltimore allowed for rat ingress. This photograph was part of a 1941 survey of housing conditions that led up to the Baltimore Plan. Citizens' Planning and Housing Association Collection, Series VIII, Box 1, folder 85-Housing-Interior Shots, 1940s–1950s, University of Baltimore Archives. Courtesy of CPHA Collection—University of Baltimore.

Health officials in Baltimore believed that crumbling outhouses like this one harbored rats. This photograph was part of the 1941 survey that informed the Baltimore Plan. Citizens' Planning and Housing Association Collection, Series VIII, Box 1, folder 84a-Housing-Exterior Shots, University of Baltimore Archives. Courtesy of CPHA Collection—University of Baltimore.

1

FLIES

Agents of Interconnection in Progressive Era Cities

As temperatures climbed into the nineties in June 1900, a female Musca domestica *buzzed about a small stable in southeastern Washington, D.C. She alit upon a heap of horse manure inside an old wooden bin and deposited 120 eggs under a lump of dung. The young maggots emerged twenty-four hours later and then ate their way into the dung heap for four days. As they grew to their full larval length of about half an inch, they migrated back toward the edges of the pile along with thousands of well-fed cousins. They spun pupae around themselves; inside, they spent four or five more days transforming into adult houseflies. Still, the manure remained in the bin.*[1]

Some ten days after their mother laid them as eggs, the adult houseflies emerged from their pupae and climbed out of the pile. They joined a buzzing cloud of their kin in the tight space between the top of the manure heap and the lid. Some flew through a gap in the lid, but most remained until a man opened the bin to shovel in fresh dung. The hungry swarm burst out of the bin.

One fly flew through an unscreened stable window and a few yards toward a produce cart carrying, among other things, cherries that had begun to ferment during their transit from a farm on the city's outskirts. The fly alit upon a cherry, and the minuscule hairs on her feet, akin to taste buds, sensed a viable meal. She vomited digestive fluids onto the cherry's skin, extended her proboscis with its raspy, liplike lobe, and began to mouth and ingest the cherry as it softened.[2] *She flitted about the produce cart all day as it made deliveries to markets near the Capitol. Some grocers waved her and the other flies away, but others seemed unconcerned about their presence.*

She copulated with a male fly. Garbage pails and dairy trucks nourished her, and the eggs inside her, for five days. Then the fly detected a new scent: a heap of human waste excavated from a privy by a small-time scavenger and dumped illegally in a lot just across the alley.[3] *The heap's fragrance overpowered that of the horse dung in the street and even that of the block's half-dozen privies. The ammonia odor of urine fermenting on a steamy day not only attracted the fly, its chemical signal also induced oviposition, the deposition of eggs. She nestled into a sheltered area on the side of the mound and, over the course of the next day, laid ten dozen eggs.*[4] *The air above hummed with hundreds of other flies, residues of human feces and urine clinging to the hairs on their feet.*

Several flies alit and rested for a moment upon the outside wall of the nearest house. A mix of odors wafted from a window, and several flies found easy passage indoors. Some fed at a garbage pail and a sticky pot in the kitchen. Others circled the head of an infant drinking a bottle of milk, tickling the baby's ears.

IN 1900, THE EMERGING SCIENCE OF MEDICAL ENTOMOLOGY GAVE PRO-gressive reformers a troubling new perspective on urban houseflies. Could ubiquitous flies, bred in poorly managed horse manure, pick up germs from privies and human waste dumps? Leland O. Howard, chief of the U.S. Department of Agriculture (USDA) Bureau of Entomology, routinely found illegal dumps teeming with flies as he walked the streets of Washington, D.C. He described one dump, left under cover of a steamy night, that by the next day "swarm[ed] with flies in the bright sunlight." Indoor spaces provided no haven from flies bred outdoors or the germs they might pick up there. Howard observed that "within 30 feet [of the dump] were the open windows and doors of the kitchens of two houses kept by poor people."[5] Flies endangered infants and young children particularly; one educator estimated that over seventy thousand died each year in the United States from fly-borne disease.[6]

In the first two decades of the twentieth century, many urban reformers feared that houseflies would imperil city-dwellers at home so long as horse manure clogged streets and privies plagued poor neighborhoods. They saw flies as agents of interconnection, linking diseased bodies with healthy ones, delivering pathogens across neighborhoods, and weaving domestic spaces into the city's ecological fabric. Flies flitted from waste heaps to mothers in kitchens, babies in cradles, and families in crowded cottages. Reformers such as Howard pressed for better municipal waste management to protect families in their homes. Housing advocates also saw flies as markers of vice and social dissipation, and demanded sanitary homes for the poor. The first reformers to embrace medical entomology sought public and preventive solutions to the fly menace.

Modernizing manure disposal and replacing slums would require hefty public funding, however, and municipalities failed to make these matters budgetary priorities. Furthermore, some public health experts disputed flies' role in spreading disease; for some, flies in the home simply indicated personal slovenliness, not an immediate health threat. In the absence of support for broad-scale sanitation, welfare advocates and health departments who remained suspicious of flies increasingly called upon citizens to exclude flies from their homes. Health agencies urged families, especially women, to keep flies out of their homes by installing screens and maintaining vigilant watch over the borders of domestic space. Rather than limiting fly-breeding, this strategy required women to separate their homes from the ecology of the city. Urban nature and human culture resisted this separation. When urban fly populations did eventually subside, neither sanitation, housing reform, nor household fly control deserved the most credit. These efforts, though, used flies to justify the assertion of state power to contain citizens as well as insects.

FROM DOMESTIC COMPANION TO SUSPECTED VECTOR

By 1900, Americans had long regarded rats, roaches, and bedbugs as menaces, but popular opinion of houseflies varied. Material and popular culture shows that some nineteenth-century Americans considered flies pests, if not necessarily disease carriers. The song "Shoo Fly, Don't Bother Me," dating to the Civil War, attests to the nuisance role of flies—and to whites' appropriation of black culture. The white composer T. Brigham Bishop reputedly based the song on a comment overheard in the black company he led, and the song became popular as performed by both black singers and white minstrel groups.[7] Housewifery guides provided recipes for housefly poisons, such as cobalt in sugar water. As window and door screens became more available during the late nineteenth century, families who could afford these devices held both mosquitoes and flies at bay, though mosquitoes were more annoying than the nonbiting housefly.[8]

At the same time, many Americans believed houseflies to be harmless or even entertaining or useful. Some housewifery guides offered recipes for cockroach and bedbug control but none for fly control.[9] Children's books portrayed buzzing, flitting flies as benign domestic companions, ideal for piquing infants' curiosity. Flies' habit of washing their faces with their fore-legs gave an impression of cleanliness; they also seemed to act as the gar-bagemen of the insect world as they consumed organic matter.[10] For some, the ubiquity of flies in daily life bred amused resignation, as expressed in a popular quip about a customer in a dimly lit restaurant who mistook a custard pie crawling with flies for huckleberry. One entomologist deemed the nineteenth century "the Period of Friendly Tolerance" of houseflies. Another joked that "a few of them were nice things to have around, to make things homelike."[11]

Regular Americans varied in their views of houseflies, but a growing number of physicians and naturalists believed they could transmit germs.[12] In 1895, George Kober, a respected health officer and Georgetown Univer-sity dean, surmised that flies might have helped spread typhoid fever bacilli in the nation's capital. Over typhoid's course, patients develop high fevers, rashes, and delirium, and pass germs in infected diarrhea. Typhoid struck cities nearly every summer; Washington's 1895 epidemic sickened at least 800 people and killed 143. Kober blamed most cases on contaminated wells, but some cases appeared in clusters around city blocks with privies and ille-gal dumps, and at time intervals suggesting a source other than water. Kober attributed these to "the agency of flies," which "abound wherever surface pollution exists [and] may carry the germs into the houses and contaminate the food or drink."[13] Then, in 1898, during the Spanish-American War, U.S. Army surgeons also proposed that flies carried typhoid germs from primi-tive privies to mess halls at stateside military camps.[14] Camp conditions recalled those in urban neighborhoods lacking sanitary infrastructure.[15]

Naturalists and health experts subjected houseflies to new scrutiny at the same time as malaria and yellow fever studies focused in on vector spe-cies of mosquitoes. Flies lack the piercing mouthparts that let mosquitoes access human bloodstreams for withdrawal or injection of pathogens.[16] The housefly's accusers postulated instead that it served as a mechanical vec-tor, carrying microbes on its mouthparts or sticky, hairy feet. Given flies' attraction to fecal matter, gastrointestinal diseases caused the most worry: typhoid, cholera, dysentery, and the deadly annual outbreaks of infantile diarrhea known as "summer complaint."[17] These germs might cling to a fly until they brushed off during a visit to a milk truck, produce stand, or baby bottle.[18] Some speculated that flies might also deposit germs in regurgitated fluids or with bits of feces, euphemistically called "specks," that dotted window panes in infested homes by the thousands.[19] Experiments found germs on the feet and mouthparts of flies exposed to infected stools.

Cases of—and deaths from—these diseases peaked in summer, among both adults and young people, precisely when heat hastened flies' reproductive cycle. Growing fly numbers seemed to speed the circulation of germs. During Washington's steamiest months, new eggs matured into adults in as few as ten days. Even in cooler climes, maggots matured quickly in poorly drained privies as they slurped down accessible liquid nutrients. In D.C.'s climate, an overwintering female laying her first clutch of eggs in mid-April had the potential to leave 5.5 trillion descendants by mid-September, though many young flies died off.[20] In fall, most adults died off with the first frost, but some survived inside heated homes while juveniles went dormant in their pupal stage.[21]

Flight distances would determine flies' ability to connect diseased places with bodies elsewhere in the neighborhood or city. Howard asked, "Will the proper care of the stables and houses in a given city square relieve the houses in this square from the fly pest," even if adjacent blocks remained filthy? He conceded that "the house fly will seldom travel very much farther than it has to fly for food and a proper nidus"—disease ecologists' term for nest—"but as a matter of fact it is very hard to prove this." Experimenters who tracked flies found most within tens or hundreds of yards, but a few traveled for miles.[22] The scale at which flies could spread germs thus remained uncertain; a roving fly might connect polluted neighborhoods with clean homes across the city.

New findings about the vector roles of flies and mosquitoes—along with rats and their fleas—arrived amid other changes in public health agencies' activities and also their relationships with citizens. For much of the nineteenth century, urban health departments emphasized general sanitation to clean up rotting organic matter that generated disease-causing forces called miasmas. These sanitation activities served as preventive medicine for all residents. The rise of bacteriology in the late nineteenth century enabled health agencies to target sources of infection, such as contaminated food or human carriers, with increased precision—a development some historians say reduced attention to general sanitation. Medical entomology raised new questions about the most efficient, effective ways for health departments to control disease. Some reformers—such as Leland Howard in 1900—believed that medical entomology justified both a focus on general sanitation to clean up environments that supported vectors and also the use of state power to protect citizens from disease. Others insisted that screens, poisons, and traps—often deployed in people's homes—could kill insects and rodents even if conditions outside favored them.[23] These approaches expressed divergent visions of the role of the state, experts, citizens, and ecology in public health. Fly control would also occur in rather different urban spaces under these divergent visions. General sanitation promised to cleanse the entire fly-breeding landscape— manure-caked streets, alleys, and stables, along with any remaining privies. Meanwhile, approaches targeting flies themselves often focused on private homes and other spaces from which flies were to be excluded.

Medical entomology was one of many sciences that was applied and shaped by urban reformers in the late nineteenth and early twentieth century. Progressives pursued a variety of agendas, often with competing practical and philosophical priorities. Reformers who embraced medical entomology called for government interventions at a variety of scales, exerting a variety of different powers. The tensions among various reform agendas helped shape approaches to public health in general, and fly control specifically. Some Progressives sought increased power for experts to manage cities and apply science in pursuit of orderly, modern landscapes— for example, the draining of wetlands to eliminate mosquitoes.[24] Others sought to discipline citizens' conduct through education in sciences such as hygiene, home economics, natural history, and medical entomology—a top-down, paternalistic vision of relationships among the state, experts, and the people. Others, however, believed that government should first and foremost wield its power to protect and empower the least powerful citizens. These reformers, such as the activists at Chicago's Hull-House, used medical entomology to justify calls for democratic access, social justice, and environmental health for people living in fly-breeding landscapes.

SOCIAL JUSTICE, URBAN ECOLOGY, AND FLY-BREEDING LANDSCAPES

In the summer of 1902, typhoid fever killed some 450 Chicagoans, sickening many more. This was in spite of the new canal completed two years earlier—a feat that promised to ease the city's annual bouts with water-borne disease by diverting polluted river water away from Lake Michigan. The Board of Health responded to the outbreak with further measures to protect the entire city's water supply. Activists at Hull-House countered that the "peculiar localization of the epidemic" indicated a smaller-scale yet no less dangerous cause for many typhoid cases. Amid its engineering achievements, city government neglected landscapes where the most vulnerable Chicagoans lived. Hull-House stood amid one such landscape: the nineteenth ward. This district of working-class Greeks and Italians, along with Bohemians, Russian and Polish Jews, and Irish-Americans, suffered six times the city's average typhoid case rate.[25] Hull-House activists argued that humble houseflies wreaked death upon the community as they flitted from broken-down privy to unscreened cottage.

On the blocks at the center of the outbreak, investigators Maud Gernon and Gertrude Howe, along with the physician Alice Hamilton, found abundant opportunities for flies to breed in human excrement. Nearly half of residents enjoyed working flush toilets as required by an 1896 municipal law, but their homes were scattered among properties that relied upon privies lacking sewer and water connections or whose cesspits were seldom cleaned. If maintained properly, liquid would exit through a pipe or trickle through an older cesspit's permeable walls; hired scavengers were supposed to remove solids frequently enough to prevent clogs. Waste in basins several feet deep should emit little fly-attracting odor as it composted. In Chicago in 1902, however, a landlord who violated the law by keeping a privy instead of a flush toilet might also delay hiring a scavenger until long after the cesspit clogged. Trapped liquids mixed with solids, brimming up close to the unscreened toilet hatch and enticing flies with their fragrance. Wet sludge nourished fast-maturing maggots, who emerged as adults close to the surface.[26]

The area's two thousand human residents exceeded the capacity of sewer lines laid decades earlier when housing and population remained sparse. Landlords packed three or more families into units designed for just one.[27] "Only a moderate increase in rainfall" sent sewage spilling into yards and basements.[28] To Hamilton, Gernon, and Howe, these conditions recalled military camps where surgeons had blamed flies for spreading typhoid four years earlier. They watched flies emerge from exposed cesspits and flit to nearby homes. Many typhoid patients lived in homes with working plumbing adjacent to tenements with illegal privies. The women thought that only "the agency of flies" in carrying typhoid germs could explain this case distribution.[29]

Hamilton, Gernon, and Howe captured flies and tested them for the typhoid bacillus to determine whether germs survived the flight from a privy to a neighbor's open window. At one site, family members emptied typhoid patients' bedpans into a privy full to within three feet of the opening. Stool had splashed and stuck to the side of the pit just shy of the ground, within easy access for flies. Flies on a fence across the yard bore typhoid bacilli on their feet. The women also found bacilli on flies outside homes that had five typhoid cases; these homes had working toilets that would have flushed infected stools away from any flies, however. Nearby, a tenement housed sixteen families but no apparent typhoid cases. The tenement's cesspit had filled to the brim when the landlord finally hired a scavenger in August, but the scavenger left the night soil in the alley for a week at the height of the summer heat. "Naturally, the place swarmed with flies," observed Hamilton, Gernon, and Howe. They suspected that bacilli survived in the night soil from either a previous typhoid case in the tenement or a latent case there.[30] Flies that touched infected stools could deliver typhoid to the neighbors with good plumbing.

The women deflected blame from residents because many had complained to city inspectors only to see their cases overlooked or dismissed. Each inspector covered such a large territory that many complaints received cursory attention, and the ordinance that banned privies contained no provisions to ensure their removal. Inspectors responding to complaints were satisfied if landlords simply had privies cleaned—a process that could increase exposure if the scavenger dumped the night soil in an alley. Furthermore, property owners with connections to the ward's political machine often saw their cases dismissed. Cases that made it to court sometimes resulted in fines less than the cost of cleaning up the hazard. Almost 250 privies remained scattered across the nineteenth ward, breeding flies; other wards throughout Chicago harbored no fewer than a thousand additional privies.[31] Hull-House's report precipitated a scandal that swept several inspectors out of office.[32] To Hull-House activists, municipal officials negated the city's sanitary achievements when they failed to protect poor communities from flies.

Investigators from Hull-House drew upon medical entomology to explain the ecological unity of urban society, homes, and the city at large.

Hull-House centered its activism in homes and their surrounding neighborhoods as an expression of community support for domestic life and well-being. One Chicago activist called for municipal reforms to nurture "a city of homes, a place in which to rear children." The professional, Anglo women who lived in Hull-House taught courses for poor women, men, and children, many of them immigrants; their work set up a paternalistic dynamic based on education, class, and ethnicity.[33] It did so, however, in the context of activism that engaged community members, in hopes of creating a "sense of the economic unity" with "the large foreign colonies which so easily isolate themselves in large American cities."[34] For example, women in the community joined Hull-House residents to protest Chicago's privatized trash collection system, which left their district underserved—and a breeding ground for pests that thrived on garbage.[35] Hull-House called for the city to not only exercise its engineering prowess but also wield its power to protect families from those who profited from neglect of neighborhood environments. By contrast, other reformers used medical entomology to distance city government from regular people by shifting power to scientific experts or teaching citizens to regulate their own conduct.[36]

MANAGING WASTES, HOUSING, PEOPLE, AND FLIES

Like activists at Hull-House, reformers in Washington, D.C., called for municipal authorities to protect poor residents by eliminating fly-breeding landscapes. Health officer George Kober first drew attention to fly infestation in his report on the 1895 typhoid outbreak. The report called for the city to extend sewer services, eliminate privies, and replace poorly constructed homes that flies could easily infiltrate.[37]

Leland Howard of the USDA Bureau of Entomology backed calls to eliminate privies and also recommended speeding the flow of manure, the most prolific fly-breeding medium, out of the city. Howard studied Washington's flies to discern their nidus. Flies visited kitchen garbage pails for food, but few laid eggs there.[38] Instead, over 90 percent of flies in D.C. homes emerged from the horse manure that clogged city streets and stables. In late summer, as many as twelve hundred flies might grow up in a single pound of manure. Most other houseflies, though a small minority, had a more worrisome upbringing: they emerged from human excrement, where they could directly access intestinal pathogens.[39] Howard called for local government to charge unscrupulous scavengers with a misdemeanor for dumping night soil in residential areas—a common crime in alleys where police protection was lax.[40] For Howard, medical entomology informed efficient procedures for managing wastes and protecting public health.

Washington reformers' concerns about housing and flies centered upon African-Americans living in alley homes. Many established black families in D.C. made prosperous homes in black enclaves or a few racially integrated sites. Newcomers during and after the Civil War faced increasing racial discrimination, however, and in the days before further transit options became available, most housing remained concentrated in a limited land area close to the urban core. Developers packed tiny houses into back alleys on almost three hundred city blocks, from such fashionable spots as Dupont Circle to poorly drained areas in southeast D.C., exploiting high housing demand and the lack of options for black residents. As in Chicago's nineteenth ward, many D.C. alley homes remained unconnected to sewer lines; residents relied on privies, often in ill-repair. City authorities and the U.S. Congress—which oversaw the District—did little to intervene in the alley house boom, apart from condemning a few dwellings, until the 1890s. By then, some twenty thousand Washingtonians, most of them African-American, lived in alleys.[41] Unlike Chicago's "foreign colonies," which Hull-House described as isolated from the rest of the city, the alley-dwellers who were D.C. reformers' greatest anxiety lived on the same blocks as privileged residents. A labyrinth of fences and outbuildings obscured alleys from street-side neighbors, but flies easily spanned the distance between them.[42]

Concern for the poor motivated housing reform in Washington, but advocates lacked Hull-House's engagement with residents. Reports stigmatized alley denizens, asserting that alleys bred vice along with flies and disease. According to reformers' "breakdown hypothesis," the move from rural areas to the city degraded family life; squalid, fly-infested domestic landscapes both marked and perpetuated this breakdown.[43] Reformers hoped to uplift residents by destroying and replacing alley homes. A series of studies about Washington's alley homes began in 1895, led by George Kober as chair of the Committee on Housing the People, with help from the Women's Anthropological Society and the Associated Charities of Washington. Reports used flies as symbols of slovenliness encouraged by a disorderly environment. Surveyors portrayed residents breeding prolifically and wallowing in filth much like the flies that infested their communities. One noted: "To have swarms of children and let them die is characteristic of the alleys I have studied." Another described a mother with tuberculosis languishing under a "low ceiling . . . almost black with flies, which the sick woman drove away from her face occasionally with a weak motion of her skinny arm."[44] Some medical investigators suspected that flies picked up tuberculosis when visiting infected sputum in spittoons or on floors.[45] Images of flies evoked shame on both landlords and residents.

In 1902, President Roosevelt expressed shock over conditions "almost within the shadow of the Capitol Dome" and declared that all of Washington, not just its federal sections, must be made a model city. He called on Associated Charities president Frederick Weller to continue monitoring the alleys, while Congress supported demolition of more than five hundred alley houses and established two corporations to build affordable "sanitary housing." Mortality rates in the new homes were lower than in the alleys, but only a few dozen units were available to the lowest-income residents or blacks.[46]

Meanwhile, Leland Howard made Washington, D.C., a laboratory for the study of flies; research by USDA entomologists informed urban sanitation policy there and across the United States. Howard blamed copious horse manure for breeding flies that became prolific germ-carriers. Like other cities, Washington struggled to manage its manure. Automobiles had begun to compete with horsepower, but horse stables for household or business use persisted in areas across the income spectrum.[47] Many horse-keepers delayed manure disposal or kept manure in shoddy bins built over pervious ground and emptied at intervals longer than flies' breeding cycle. Even when haulers carted waste to farms in the hinterlands, manure spilled along the route could expose residents to flies.[48]

Based on the findings of his Bureau of Entomology, Howard prescribed new laws and processes for managing the manure that bred most of the city's houseflies. In 1905, summer typhoid deaths again alarmed the city, but the city health officer insisted that water pollution was the main cause. He stressed the need to improve filtration and disputed evidence that flies or privies were to blame.[49] Still, in 1906, the District adopted Howard's proposals to tighten government control over stables and manure haulers. The city ordered haulers to carry manure along routes that minimized exposure in dense neighborhoods.[50] Spilled or thinly spread waste helped juvenile flies evade control because maggots about to pupate instinctively migrate within their rearing media. If they reached the bottom of a pile of manure or human excrement, maggots might burrow into the substrate below, such as a dirt road or the soil of vacant lot, ready to escape upon removal of the waste.[51] Because of this and flies' rapid reproduction in Washington's summer heat, the city also mandated twice-weekly manure clearance. Such frequent sweeps interrupted flies' life cycle before they could mature or lodge themselves in the earth. The new law dictated that stables be surfaced with impervious materials and equipped with fly-proof manure pits. Violators convicted of keeping fly-ridden stables would be fined forty dollars. The Health Department collected a list of all stables in the city so it could monitor and control conditions there. Laws were especially strict in the most densely populated parts of the city, to protect families at home from flies.[52]

From Hull-House to George Kober to Leland Howard, reformers who called for government to clean up fly-breeding landscapes saw homes as part of an urban ecology. They differed in their engagement with communities, but all believed that city government could protect citizens by eliminating privies, illegal night-soil dumps, uncontrolled manure, and poorly constructed homes. So long as the urban environment teemed with houseflies, families at home would not be safe. Transformation of backyards, alleys, and stables would require hefty public investment, however—similar in magnitude to grand feats of engineering but expended at a more human scale. Advocates sought citizen support for expensive reforms by emphasizing the ways flies connected people and places throughout the city.

"DEMOCRATIC" HOUSEFLIES AND VISIONS OF A CLEAN CITY

In an article for civil engineers about vector-borne disease, the entomologist W. Dwight Pierce advised his audience to think ecologically: "Little by little it has sunk into the human consciousness that your health and my health depend upon the health of every other living creature in our community."[53] The editor of the text *Sanitary Entomology*, Pierce exemplified the rhetorical use of insects' natural history to enlist political support for broad sanitary reforms. Flitting with powerful wings and attracted to odors from manure to milk, the housefly "visits everything under the sun," explained entomologists who studied flies' role in the contamination of food.[54] Pierce contended that flies could wander for miles, broadcasting even isolated cases of disease. "If we allow a disease to fester in part of the social body," he warned, insects could deliver "poison thru the whole system."[55] Dr. Simon Flexner of the Rockefeller Foundation nominated flies as a possible vector for polio because they "possess the power to migrate over considerable territory" and "affect all classes of society."[56] According to this view of urban space, flies unified city-dwellers across social status and location. Middle- and upper-class citizens seldom saw or smelled fly-breeding landscapes. Still, reformers argued that by supporting fly control, the affluent would also protect themselves.

Washington's Associated Charities president, Frederick Weller, emphasized houseflies' tendency to cross social and spatial divides, unifying the body politic. "The democratic little house-fly carries disease germs from the disregarded plague spots and deposits them . . . upon the food alike of rich and poor, statesman and voteless citizen," Weller cautioned.[57] Associated Charities titled its 1908 study of alley-dwellers *Neglected Neighbors*, capturing reformers' frustration with Washington's privileged classes who gave little political backing for housing and sanitary reform. Government and charitable efforts failed to alleviate hazards that, Weller insisted, threatened the affluent along with alley-dwellers. Outmoded privies persisted in alleys, even after Congress passed a long-delayed act to eliminate such structures. Flies that visited these privies could sicken neighbors—rich and poor alike. Behind one alley home, for example:

> the toilet box was found, on several occasions, badly soiled outside with excreta. . . . The fact that flies carry typhoid fever germs from such privies to the food supplies of neighboring houses should have made the residents of better streets around "Snow Court" take interest in the death from typhoid fever of a young girl whose infected excrement was deposited in this open box. Flies have especially free access to this privy, for it not only has no lids (few privy boxes do, although the law requires them), but it is not even enclosed in a toilet house. . . . This case of typhoid might readily supply germs to infect the resourceful residents on Pennsylvania avenue, less than two blocks distant.[58]

Flies easily spanned the distances between the privies of alley dwellings and the homes of more privileged and powerful Washingtonians.

Economic relationships also connected germ-bearing flies to affluent homes. Nannies, laundresses, and grocers who hailed from Washington's alleys served elite and middle-class families. Weller noted that statesmen's "nurse girls take the babies for occasional visits to alley homes," feeding the infants bottled milk that both attracted flies and served as a prolific breeding medium for germs. Investigators from Hull-House also appealed to privileged Chicagoans by pointing to their connections with working people and horses that lived with houseflies in the nineteenth ward. "In this district are the stables of various large firms whose wagons are sent throughout the city and suburbs," reformers wrote, ". . . the peddler's carts which carry fruit and vegetables in every direction within a day's journey start in large numbers from this region and their supplies are stored here. With all these go the house-flies bearing, as we may believe, the typhoid germ."[59] Flies thus reduced the distance between the homes of working-class immigrants and the kitchens and bodies of comfortable citizens, connecting disparate social groups in cities.[60]

The "democratic" label for houseflies carried double meanings: flies both bridged class divisions and also, some reformers hoped, hailed citizens to demand sanitary reform. The residents most plagued by flies held little power to alter municipal priorities, but perhaps broad political support could place sanitary stables, streets, and homes at the top of city agendas. Many reformers believed that medical entomology could inspire citizens to demand fly management, an issue long ignored by politicians. The "municipal housekeeping" movement among middle- and upper-class women exemplified this push to mold an articulate and compassionate citizenry dedicated to healthy homes. Municipal housekeepers sought to expand an ethic of care from their own homes to the living spaces of all city-dwellers by demanding public investment in sanitation.[61] They interpreted medical entomology through this ethic and declared flies a public, political problem and not only one for housewives to deal with privately.

For example, Dr. Mary Waring, Health and Hygiene chair of the National Association of Colored Women's Clubs, framed environmental disease as a problem of racial injustice while also teaching blacks how to protect themselves against flies in the absence of government intervention. Many local chapters of the National Association promoted *both* hygiene education for households *and* political efforts to improve sanitation services in black communities. Waring disputed the common notion that "the

Negro has a predisposition" to environmental diseases, describing a litany of sanitary inequities to which blacks were subjected. Waring demanded: "Is it not a fact that in many localities the authorities allow certain sections in which poor people live to remain in an unsanitary condition? Have you ever noticed the irregularity of the passing of the garbage wagon in some localities? Have you ever known landlords to refuse to furnish tenants with the living needs for proper disposal of excreta and sufficient water supply?" All of these unjust conditions bred flies in black neighborhoods, but authorities left blacks to control flies themselves while also suffering with disease, infestation, and stigma. Waring called "conservation of health and national vitality" as important as that of "the forest and coal"—a duty for the state, not citizens alone, but one that authorities neglected in poor, black communities.[62]

Marion Talbot, University of Chicago Dean of Women and home economist, noted in her guide *Home Sanitation*: "A small proportion of the effort now expended in encouraging people to kill flies, if devoted to training them to demand effective scavenging, would be much more likely to accomplish the end sought."[63] Talbot urged readers, mostly educated women, to exercise their privileged citizenship position to advocate for the community's basic health needs. Talbot believed most other means of household infection were the duty of individual women to address, so her endorsement of a public solution to fly infestation is particularly telling.

Leland Howard similarly believed that a citizenry educated in the dangers of flies would demand "increased appropriations for public-health work."[64] In 1908, Howard launched a campaign to replace the benign name "house fly" with "typhoid fly" in hopes of prodding citizens to lobby for improved sanitation. The proposal earned him censure from some entomologists and health officials for the possible implication that *only* flies carried typhoid; most believed that far more cases resulted from contaminated water or filthy human hands.[65] The health director of Howard's home city of Washington doubted that flies caused many typhoid cases there, although he did support Howard's proposed stable regulations. Furthermore, in 1912, Charles V. Chapin, a respected public health leader, disputed Howard's charge that flies demanded municipal attention. Howard persisted, however, publicizing the fly's horrifying characteristics: its copious reproduction, its habit of vomiting digestive juices on food, its coat of tiny hairs that increased the surface area to which germs could cling, the "specks" that dotted walls, windows, and fixtures in infested homes. In 1908 he also had employees hang sticky flypaper at sites across Washington in hopes of proving an association between fly abundance and typhoid cases. The results were inconclusive, but a few sites yielded an impressive twenty-seven hundred flies in just two days.[66] Howard strived to motivate householders to not only destroy flies themselves but also to pressure officials for citywide sanitation.

Municipal governments never seemed to invest enough in sanitation to achieve satisfactory fly control, though, even as dwindling numbers of horses left dwindling amounts of manure in streets and stables. Manure management, privy removal, and housing reform progressed, but many reformers worried that homes remained vulnerable to flies. Early measures picked the low-hanging fruit, so to speak, but continuing sanitary problems and fly infestations proved more stubborn. By the 1910s, health departments and reformers expressed disappointment that flies persisted in their cities. In some cases, reformers stepped up holistic measures, proposing stricter sanitation laws and taking on new clean-up activities. In other cases, they experimented with more focused measures, many of which targeted domestic space.

SANITATION STRUGGLES AND GROWING RELIANCE ON TARGETED FLY CONTROL

Leland Howard hoped to use the horrors of "typhoid flies" to push for bigger sanitation budgets, but he and colleagues at the USDA were forced to admit that "very often it is lack of funds which prevents public health officers from taking initiative in anti-fly crusades."[67] Washington's experience shows how municipal efforts fell short of eliminating fly-breeding landscapes and fulfilling sanitary ideals in general. Like many city health departments, Washington's seemed trapped in a pattern of responding to emergencies, such as typhoid outbreaks, rather than budgeting in advance for comprehensive environmental and housing reform.[68] Howard complained of poor enforcement of the city's "excellent" stable ordinances, "the chief reason being the lack of a sufficient force of inspectors."[69] Also, "sanitary housing" built to replace alley dwellings represented but a "drop in the bucket" of all the District's substandard homes. Condemnation of alley homes had "intensified the housing problem" because landlords raised rents on the diminished supply of units. Residents invited more family members and boarders to share rents for their tiny dwellings, straining the capacity of toilets still unconnected to sewers.[70] Flies continued to thrive in Washington's privies and manure piles even as reformers strived to modernize the urban environment.

Washington, D.C., struggled not only to deploy inspectors to stables but also to dispose of manure, in part because of the city's expanding population and suburban footprint. U.S. cities had long exported organic wastes—horse and human manure alike—to farms on their outskirts to serve as fertilizer.[71] A year after the new regulations, Washington health officials lamented that "with the growth of the city, the volume of manure to be disposed of has increased, and the distances to which it must be hauled in order properly to dispose of it have lengthened." The connections between Washington's stables and their historic manure sinks (rural farms) were stretched to their limits, and many farmers declined to pay rising transport costs.[72] Health authorities called for a tax on horses to fund public manure collection services, but their proposal failed.[73]

Health inspectors soon stepped up enforcement of stable regulations, quadrupling inspections and entering some two thousand stables in the new city registry.[74] Horse owners searched for places to dispose of dung, and some of those who struggled to comply with city stable ordinances were alley-dwellers themselves. Many hewed to their rural origins by keeping an array of livestock in their new urban homes; affluent, established neighbors facing the street also kept horses, but had more resources to support them. Whether flies emerged from street-side or alley-side manure, however, they need travel but a few yards to find an open privy, potentially teeming with germs. Canvassers noted that the manure of a horse kept in "Snow Alley" bred clouds of flies that issued into an open shed where typhoid stools had been dumped.[75] Actions against horse-keeping in alleys recalled the crackdown on Italian and Chinese immigrants' chicken-raising practices, which, authorities charged, supported rats during San Francisco's 1907–8 plague outbreak.[76] In Washington, as in San Francisco, some regulations aimed at preventing infestation fell the hardest upon migrants—whether from abroad or the rural South—who brought their agricultural traditions with them to the city.

Leland Howard and other reformers strived to preserve ecological connections between cities and farms while also protecting city-dwellers from the flies reared in horse manure. Howard recommended applying pesticides to manure as the prospects for good manure management grew dimmer. One poison, borax, killed larvae when sprinkled over infested dung but seemed also to harm plants grown on the manure. Another, the plant-based hellebore, could actually improve crops but might be poisonous to livestock as well as fly larvae.[77] In his career, Howard grew disillusioned with other ecological control methods when efforts to deploy predatory insects against agricultural pests met with their own logistical failures.[78] Other entomologists recommended poisoning manure to prevent fly-borne disease; Illinois state entomologist John J. Davis boasted that iron sulfate would kill Chicago's flies and eliminate typhoid cheaply, and without damaging the value of manure.[79] These scientists began to resign themselves to pesticide-based methods of fly control in the face of continuing health threats from flies, while hoping to maintain the value of urban horse manure.

Cities' perpetual struggle to metabolize human and horse excrement led one reformer to declare the futility of efforts to eliminate fly-breeding landscapes: "In the city, the miles of gutters and sewers specially constructed to carry off filth, the public dumps and stray accumulations . . . and in the country the miles of roadsides and acres of barnyards and pastures, and the train-loads of manure from the cities, render attack upon the breeding-places of the fly utterly hopeless and impossible."[80] According to the biology professor and textbook author Clifton Hodge, organic wastes and the flies they bred would always evade state control and thereby endanger families, despite efforts to modernize urban infrastructure. Thus, Hodge called for citizen education in the sciences to inform and motivate home-based antifly campaigns.

Like other reformers, Hodge championed fly control as a means of citizen engagement with urban environment and community. Compared with Alice Hamilton or Leland Howard, however, Hodge saw the locus of pest control as much more decentralized. Asserting that municipal governments could never eliminate all fly-breeding, Hodge hoped to instruct citizens in scientific and hygienic principles so that they would alter their own conduct and take greater responsibility for fly control themselves. Individual environmental managers—women, children, and families—would learn about medical entomology from popular journals, public lectures, and school courses using Hodge's textbooks. Fly-control activities took place in the home but, Hodge argued, could eliminate flies across entire communities. Dr. Arthur Corwin's poem "Clean Up" conveyed a similar sentiment about the relationship between domestic sanitation, pest control, and civic spaces: "the city is your home." So did the American Civic Association (ACA), which promoted fly control as part of hygiene and city-beautification campaigns.[81] Hodge, Corwin, and the ACA insisted that homes were connected to urban society and nature but believed that environmental improvement must come from labor in the home, rather than reforms targeting the public sphere.

Hodge boasted that citizens of towns and small cities in Wisconsin, California, and Oregon had abolished flies through households' near-universal participation in early season trapping. He promoted a simple fly trap of his own invention that featured a screen dome a few inches in diameter to be affixed to a garbage can lid. An early model of the trap "merely set upon a pile of filth" caught over nine gallons of flies in a single week.[82] Hodge envisioned an urban landscape where fly traps stood vigil by every front porch and back door in early spring to catch flies emerging from hibernation before they could breed. Indoors, smaller traps and child-safe insecticides destroyed any flies that slipped past the borders.[83] Hodge supported municipal sanitation, but he remained pessimistic that environmental cleanups would ever protect families from fly-borne disease. Instead, citizens had to learn how to make their own homes safe, and with them, the entire urban environment.

Hodge aimed to mold children into citizens aware of their own ecological and social implications. He called for schools to instill in people from cities and suburbs alike an ethical and scientific concern for their environment.[84] For Hodge, this included not only beloved or useful organisms—flowers, pets, or wild fauna; crops, livestock, or honeybees—but also pests and microbes that did harm. For him, the civic space of the biology classroom could forge links to homes by helping young citizens to learn to protect their own bodies—and those of their families and communities—from household pests.[85] Hodge emphasized in his basic text, *Nature Study and Life*, that "one of the chief aims of this book is to unite home and school."[86] In other words, if school is a crucible of citizenship for young urbanites, then lessons must cultivate a sense of duty to the environment by teaching children to steward the ecology of their own homes.

Hodge's works for students as well as for adults stressed that responsibility for flies transcended public and private spheres. A good biological citizen would do her or his part in private space to help make the entire city clean, healthy, and free from pests. Hodge offered lesson plans that engaged children in making fly traps, observing maggots in glass jars, and tallying possible cases of fly-borne disease in their neighborhoods.[87] Hodge acknowledged that children might not want to discuss in class which insects infested their own homes, especially when bedbug problems might lead to ostracism; teachers must broach such topics with a "superhuman amount of tact" while making sure that the school did not become a point of dissemination for vermin.[88] Whatever creatures infested children's homes, Hodge believed that understanding the connections those pests made between nature, home, community, and health would produce responsible and healthy urban citizens.

Hodge's secondary-level text *Civic Biology*, like other school books with similar titles, aimed to provide older students with the scientific and moral foundations of urban and environmental citizenship. "Civic biology" advocates called for science courses in urban schools to teach young urban citizens to solve problems through cooperation and biological literacy. Students should learn to focus watchful attention on their homes, their bodies, and the bodies of their eventual children, particularly on the connections between bodies and the collective environment. For Hodge, houseflies exemplified those interconnections because "one careless or ignorant household can breed flies enough to infest all the houses within a quarter mile."[89]

Other educators aimed to make pest control a source of pride for schoolchildren. Some cities paid children bounties for catching flies, although Hodge warned that such incentives should be limited to early in the breeding season, when killing adults would have the greatest impact. In Chicago, a young girl proudly sent a fly she had swatted dead to the Board of Health, which ran a photo of the mangled corpse in its hygiene newsletter. School groups staged the play "Swat the Fly" in which domestic pets rally around a boy in his struggle to kill a diseased insect.[90] These activities aimed to instill in children a sense of their own effectiveness and duty in managing domestic environments.

Hygiene educators sent a stronger message to adults, especially housewives, to equip their homes with the means to exclude and kill insect invaders rather than rely on citywide sanitation. Messages to women and families ranged from disciplinary to scientific to outright fear-mongering.

Some insisted that women must attend to fly control with constant vigilance. Chicago's Board of Health advised that even in winter "every housewife should . . . go carefully over her house to see that there is not a fly now living in it."[91] Hodge explained that such vigilance was necessary because in colder climes, flies "hibernate as young adults in cracks about buildings. They come out of winter quarters ravenously hungry and feed for about a week . . . before beginning to lay."[92] Meanwhile, a North Carolina state health bulletin demanded: "Are you a careless housekeeper? Be sure the flies will find you out. . . . Flies are a householder's own fault. If you want to keep your own-self-respect and that of your friends and neighbors, don't let anyone find your house full of flies." The bulletin blamed one thousand to two thousand infant deaths on flies in that state alone.[93] As flies persisted despite sanitation efforts, hygiene educators called for citizens to manage flies at the bounds of their own homes.

Families could purchase a variety of implements to protect their homes against flies. Marketers seized upon suspicions about fly-borne disease to promote window screens in northern parts of the United States; yellow fever outbreaks and endemic malaria had already prompted public screening drives in the South.[94] Companies offered traps, swatters, flypapers like the brand Tanglefoot, as well as a variety of fly poisons. Many devices and chemicals had already been available for households who saw flies as nuisances; as suspicion of flies spread, companies could tout their products as lifesavers, with the endorsement of health authorities. Companies sent the implicit message that health was a consumer product women could choose for their families when they promoted gadgets, concoctions, and services to protect against germs in the home.[95] This contrasted with the message from other reformers that sanitation was a public good to be shared among all city-dwellers.

Bureau of Entomology chief Leland Howard lamented that the nation spent ten million dollars per year on window and door screens against flies when preventive measures would maintain cities in a healthier, more sanitary condition. "The whole expense of screening should be an unnecessary one," he argued, "just as the effort to destroy flies in houses should be unnecessary. The breeding should be stopped to such an extent that all these things should be useless."[96] Howard called for municipalities to remove the root causes of fly infestation by modernizing sanitation systems instead of leaving families to rely upon screens, traps, or swatters.

Howard's home city of Washington, D.C., however, rallied some twenty-five thousand households to "swat the fly" during a 1912 campaign.[97] Window screens, swatters, and household poisons reinforced the notion that private homes could be separated from the polluted city outdoors, contradicting notions of interconnection. By the 1910s, many reformers saw window screens as the answer to persistent houseflies.

Chicago's Board of Health conveyed mixed messages about screens. In a 1916 cartoon in its health education newsletter, a man installs a screen window while enormous flies swarm from his own curbside garbage can, carrying the demonic figure of disease. The caption read, "Our greatest enemy is not foreign, but domestic," punning on debates over the United States's entry into the Great War in Europe while also locating the source of the fly problem within the bounds of one resident's premises. Other Board of Health publications promoted screening, but this one seemed to suggest that citizens could better prevent fly-borne disease through better stewardship of their own garbage.[98] The cartoon portrayed a man doing the screening, but health departments aimed much fly-control education at women, making maintenance of screens and other household fly-control tasks part of mothers' duties to protect their infants and children. Flies became entangled with new ideas about scientific motherhood as well as anxieties about children's health and the cleanliness of the milk they were fed.

MOTHERS, CONTAMINATED MILK, AND FLY SCREENS

Reformers' responses to another public health trend paved the way for increasing focus on domestic-scale fly control by mothers. For much of American history, mothers' custom of breastfeeding babies through at least their second summer had protected infants from food- and water-borne illness. In U.S. cities at the turn of the twentieth century, mothers increasingly weaned their children onto cow milk and solids by three months of age. Babies this young could not yet fight off gastrointestinal germs for which cow milk provided a rich growth medium. As late as 1916, over thirty-four hundred Chicago infants died of diarrhea, 6 percent of babies born that year. At least 37 percent of all infant deaths were due to diarrheal disease.[99] Those who survived a bout of diarrhea suffered dehydration, poor growth, and susceptibility to other diseases. The shift toward early weaning brought flies into the ecology of infant feeding. Experts warned that cow milk—unlike milk suckled directly from mothers' breasts—suffered myriad microbial insults in its journey from udder to hungry belly, including those delivered by flies.[100]

Homes were not the only spaces where health advocates intervened to protect infants' food from flies; farms, milk trucks, grocers, and restaurants also became targets for regulation. The "scientific motherhood" movement had opened domestic space to scrutiny by the state and experts, making homes an important intervention site.[101] Household fly control became one element of domestic science taught in classrooms and by in-home educators. Visiting nurses promoted safe infant feeding when they checked new mothers' homes for flies along with other violations of cleanliness.[102] Educators implored mothers to prevent flies from touching milk and food. The association of fly infestation, infant mortality, and changing infant feeding practices made fly control a moral issue for educators and public health officials. For these advocates, mothers who fed their infants improperly had already failed in their maternal duties, and flies in a home marked women as poor mothers. For health educators, nurses, and social workers, the sight of flies crawling on babies' faces, milk bottles, and porridge bowls in districts with high infant mortality rates seemed to confirm maternal failure. Canvassers for Washington's Associated Charities considered it an indicator of alley-dwellers' moral degradation when they saw "nursing bottles ... lying on the floor or anywhere else, partly filled with souring milk and black with appreciative flies."[103] Associated Charities urged housing reform as a solution to such health hazards, but other reformers targeted mothers directly with fly-control education and surveillance.

In light of flies' persistence and continued deaths from infantile diarrhea in some sections, New York City's Health Department in the early 1910s considered adding a screening requirement to its health code.[104] New York hoped to intervene in poor families' homes to sever their connection with outdoor landscapes still marked by inadequate sanitation. In 1913, the Department of Health commissioned a study by the Association for Improving the Condition of the Poor to test the effectiveness of a variety of fly-control strategies, including screening, education, and sanitation, for reducing infantile diarrhea. Since its founding in 1843, the association had strived to aid poor families it deemed "worthy" by correcting conditions it believed contributed to residents' ill-health and moral failings. Its activities ranged from building and running model tenements, to teaching immigrant mothers about modern American child-rearing, to sending urban children to visit "fresh air" sites outside the city.[105] With the study of fly control and diarrhea, the association hoped to show correlations among outdoor and indoor environments, mothers' conduct, and babies' health. Screens would serve as a technology for sealing off the home from disease and also as a means for reformers to extend state power over citizens' hygiene in private space.[106]

In neighborhoods targeted for the study, both domestic spaces and outdoor and commercial landscapes favored flies. The association chose for the experiment an Italian tenement district in the Bronx that "boast[ed] all the equipment necessary for the lively perpetuation and joyful existence of the house fly." Poor conditions both indoors and out gave flies "a short circuit . . . between filth and food."[107] Nearby stables housed dozens of horses whose manure—and sometimes corpses—might remain long enough to nurture a generation of young flies. Four-story brick tenements on "congested" blocks were poorly served by both trash collection and sewers. Enclosed backyards functioned as illegal but convenient garbage dumps; many contained toilet sheds. Clotheslines ran between the open, unscreened windows of adjacent tenements.

In the first of two experimental years, investigators launched intensive fly-control efforts both indoors and out. The experimental design did not attempt to isolate the effects of outdoor sanitation from the effects of screening or education; the experimental blocks received all treatments, while control blocks received none of them. Visiting nurses taught some three hundred mothers on the experimental blocks about the dangers of domestic flies. Boy Scouts sealed seventeen hundred doors and windows with screens. Meanwhile, authorities performed intensive sanitation of stables, streets, alleys, and outdoor toilets.[108] Mothers' responses to the experiment left investigators unable to evaluate the effect of screening homes against flies, however. Most mothers found that screens stifled everyday interactions between domestic and public space. They removed the screens soon after installation so they could lean out of windows to communicate with family and neighbors outdoors. Investigators found that "during the warm weather"—the very moment when flies and disease pathogens reproduced most quickly—"it was practically impossible to keep the screens either in or closed. Not only were they taken out, but they were torn out, and in some cases destroyed."[109]

On the other hand, the association found that a combination of intensive outdoor sanitation and education protected children's health without the help of window screens. Even without window screens, fewer than half as many infants and young children contracted diarrhea on blocks cleansed of sewage, garbage, corpses, and manure than on adjacent, poorly served blocks. The association's 1913 study was one of the first to show the effectiveness of sanitation against fly-borne disease in a Northern city, albeit with a small sample size.[110] The experiment provided no evidence for the value of screens; it revealed only women's resistance to them. Still, the association and the Board of Health wished to sharpen their focus on household-scale interventions against flies. The association insisted that future studies must "be carried on in the home itself" and that "complicating outside general sanitary influences should be avoided" so researchers could "arrive at an accurate value" for home-based fly control.[111] A new experimental design tested whether homes could be isolated from filthy outdoor spaces.

The following year, mothers on the Lower East Side, most of them immigrants from eastern Europe, resisted the association's second screening experiment: "For the women of the lower East Side, a window possesses an importance of the first magnitude, and the suggestion of screening a window in such a way as to curtail ever so slightly its important social function will not readily be entertained. Even sliding screens, the installation of which amounts to a very considerable sum, were found to be quite impracticable."[112] The association imagined that unscreened windows exposed homes to the diseased public realm and that education about medical entomology would persuade women to exclude flies. For mothers, screenless windows and doors served as fluid conduits between domestic space and the public street, a function that reformers with the association and the Health Department failed to anticipate.

The Department of Health and the Association for Improving the Condition of the Poor continued to urge mothers to cooperate with household fly control. After women on the Lower East Side tore out window screens, nurses introduced nets for covering cribs and prams. After its second year of trials, the association claimed that if mothers were negligent housekeepers, practiced "artificial feeding"—as opposed to breastfeeding—and *also* refused both screens and netting, they placed their babies at risk for illness and possibly death.[113] The association and the Health Department sought greater control over domestic space to protect babies and their food from flies, even while evidence suggested that providing sanitation to under-served neighborhoods without screening improved babies' health.

One architectural historian has described screens as a "humane" inno-vation that allowed families to enjoy porches and cooling night breezes without annoyance or disease risk from mosquitoes and flies.[114] Women's resistance to New York City's screening experiments belies assumptions about the universal embrace of such domestic technologies. From the state's perspective, attempts to contain flies dovetailed with efforts to con-tain citizens. Screening, however, seemed to accomplish neither.

DWINDLING FLIES IN CITIES OF MODERN TRANSPORTATION

As the air warmed in mid-April 1920, in southeast Washington, D.C., a housefly broke free from the pupa in which she had spent the winter. She climbed toward the light that peeked through the loose slats of a two-hole privy soon due for a cleaning. The fly emerged into a world quite different from the one that had nurtured so many of her species on the same block just twenty years earlier.

She had spent her whole life in one of the poorest parts of the city, an area still neglected by city environmental services. But even the most neglected blocks in Washington had begun to change. Car garages now outnumbered horse stables. The remaining two stables had new, paved manure bins. Manure disposal still proceeded slowly, but with fewer horses there was less manure overall—and there-fore fewer places to rear maggots into full-grown flies. The privy from which the fly had emerged was one of just a few remaining on the block. As the fly searched for her first meal as an adult, she found fewer scents in the air than her forebears had twenty years ago. She finally flitted to a privy in which a family dumped its kitchen garbage. There she sucked bits of rotting meat from moldering bones.

The fly flew toward a small house that gave off cooking odors. Several flies were already crawling on a door screen, unable to enter the kitchen. The fly rested on the screen until she detected a strong movement of air around her. Sensing poten-tial danger, she beat her wings and then alit upon the house's outer wall. As she crawled toward the odor again, she found her way indoors through a gap between the door and its frame.

Early twentieth-century cities provided ideal ecological conditions for houseflies to thrive. Many commentators insisted that flies in any part of the city endangered all districts because of flies' ability to migrate across neighborhoods. Most accounts suggest that houseflies spent much of their lives in poor, immigrant, and black communities, however. It was also these groups who lived with the wastes that attracted and supported flies: horse manure left in place too long, privies by the hundreds or thousands that landlords failed to replace, illegal human waste dumps, and garbage poorly managed by either households or by public or private service agencies. The landscape of urban fly-breeding reflected these environmental and political inequalities.

Some of the early reformers who embraced medical entomology made infestation a political issue. Leland Howard called for citizens to demand a reordering of municipal priorities to put sanitation and its enforcement at the top of the agenda. Mary Waring and Colored Women's Club chapters addressed both the public and private sides of flies, condemning racial inequities in sanitation services while promoting household-scale fly control to communities for their own protection. Hull-House approached fly control holistically: it denounced code enforcers for leaving fly-breeding hazards in the nineteenth ward, while at the same time organizing protests and teaching hygiene there. Alice Hamilton, one of the leaders of Hull-House's study on typhoid, later retracted the fly-based explanation of Chicago's 1902 outbreak when the city Board of Health admitted to covering up a sewage leak that more likely caused the high case rate near Hull-House.[115] Even this revelation reinforced a larger point about infested communities. Immigrants, the poor, and blacks often lived with the city's worst filth, and authorities did too little to protect them from poor sanitation, regardless of flies' role.

Housing quality was also a factor in communities' exposure to flies and disease, and housing reformers in Washington, D.C., strived to make sanitary homes a political priority. Their attitudes toward flies, privies, horse-keeping, and other environmental conditions distanced them from communities rather than engaging them. Certainly, infested communities were in part responsible for the flies in their midst, particularly in the way they managed horse manure. Residents' sanitary failures were themselves abetted by public failures in code enforcement and waste collection and in the state's tolerance of racial segregation. Associated Charities portrayed flies as indicators of moral decline, justifying outside control over poor blacks' private spaces while failing to engage them in political efforts to improve conditions. Demolition of alley homes left residents more vulnerable to disease and their living situations more unstable, while offering them little help in controlling their own environment.

Halting fly reproduction through sanitation, health inspection, code enforcement, and housing reform proved a daunting, expensive task. Municipal governments balked at the cost of collectors, inspectors, and sanitary homes, leaving the job half-done. Flies persisted as sanitation and housing remained underfunded, leading reformers such as Clifton Hodge to urge devolution of fly-control activities to households. This shift in emphasis represented a distinct vision of urban ecology—more atomized and fragmented to the scale of the family, blind to structural inequalities. Visions of modern homes well kept by modern housewives eclipsed visions of efficient and equitable sanitation and code enforcement. Citizens whose homes still harbored flies became all the more backward in the eyes of reformers. For instance, in its own quest to show that control of the domestic scale was important for controlling flies and disease and to make mothers responsible for fly control, the Association for Improving the Condition of the Poor seemed uninterested that the results of its first study supported intensive sanitation. Meanwhile, another research team captured the difficulty of controlling flies once they already existed: "It is almost impossible to keep [flies] out of our kitchens, dining rooms, cow stables, and milk rooms."[116] Reformers who called on women and families to seal off their homes against swarming flies asked them to do the impossible given widespread pollution in neighborhood environments.

Modernization of citizens, homes, and sanitation were not ultimately the key to fly control; rather, it was modernization of urban transportation. Cars in garages replaced horses in stables; Washington's stables began to close by the hundreds in 1917.[117] Both Leland Howard in Washington and social workers at Chicago's Hull-House noted declining horses and flies coincident with the rise of automobiles and improved health.[118] The decline of urban horses brought more significant environmental changes than did public investment in sanitation, housing, or citizen education, severing ecological ties with one of the two urban species upon which flies relied the most. Public investment in the urban environment was seldom sufficient to bring about such dramatic changes in pest populations. Many other pests could still rely for their survival on the human species along with its homes, cities, and social inequalities.

2

BEDBUGS

Creatures of Community in Modernizing Cities

Hundreds of Cimex lectularius *rested throughout a long summer day in 1920 in a flat on Chicago's West Side. Most huddled together on the narrow wooden bed frame on the lodger's side of the flat's single bedroom. Some hid in grooves in a chest below the foot of the bed, others under peeling wallpaper or behind a framed picture, leaving a blotchy crust of feces and egg cases. A few squeezed between loose floorboards.*

As night fell, the lodger returned to his quarters, which smelled faintly of overripe raspberries. In the wee hours, the bugs finished digesting their previous meal. Roused by hunger, they sensed the lodger's breath and body heat and crept toward him.[1] The bugs crawled onto the lodger's limbs and trunk. Each one pierced his skin with two barbed mandibles, then inserted its other mouthparts, two tiny tubes. One tube delivered saliva that carried an anticlotting agent, and the other sucked up the host's blood—a process that might take five minutes for a nymph or ten minutes for an adult. The saliva provoked an allergic reaction, and itchy weals soon rose on the lodger's skin.[2] He stirred frequently, scratching bites old and new and smashing several bugs. As the bugs' engorged abdomens burst, the blood left red-brown spots on the sheet. Most escaped the lodger's thrashing, crawling off his body and back to their abodes.

The woman of the house and her daughters shared a bed on the other side of a partition. Two Sundays each month, dozens of bugs perished as the two girls spent the afternoon scrubbing kerosene into the bed frame and banging their mattress with a broom handle over a tub of used bathwater.[3] Thanks to this routine, their side of the partition had fewer bugs than the lodger's, but they never rid themselves of every one. Tough cases protected eggs from kerosene, and mother bugs' gluey secretions kept them stuck to the mattress.[4] Some impregnated adult females dispersed away from the main colony on the bed frame. These females laid a few eggs each day in hidden spots—cracks in the floor, between books on a shelf—while escaping both human control efforts and male bugs who attempted to reinseminate them by rupturing their abdomens.[5]

The nymphs emerged a week later, nearly colorless, and smaller than a millet seed, hungry for their first meal; incubation took longer in winter. Those bugs that evaded control turned a deep red hue from the blood they ingested. As their abdomens filled, adults bulged to the size of a sunflower seed meat. Between meals, their abdomens appeared to deflate; this, along with their color, earned them the nickname "mahogany flats."[6]

Bugs from the lodger's side of the partition replenished the population on the other side, migrating slowly on their own six legs or more rapidly as hitchhikers on the lodger's clothes that happened to drop off as he walked by. Bugs also rained upon the clothesline when the upstairs neighbor shook out her rugs. The lodger's mattress, bought from a neighbor, had been the original source of the infestation. Once, a bug rode the younger girl's coat home from school. Some bugs even traveled across town, joining the elder daughter in the handbag she carried to her housekeeping job. Her employer had recently hired an exterminator to eliminate bedbugs from the home.[7]

BEDBUGS HAD LONG PLAGUED AMERICANS OF ALL SOCIAL CLASSES, using the movement of human bodies and belongings to permeate communities large and small. In the early twentieth century, however, a confluence of trends altered bedbug ecologies and Americans' attitudes toward this widespread insect. First, Americans came to associate bedbugs with poverty as improved but costly control became available. Second, medical entomology raised suspicions that bugs might spread pathogens, in addition to causing stress and itchy welts. Third, the increasingly professionalized exterminator industry promoted bug control as a public health service while arguing that it should be provided by the private sector. With these trends, bedbugs became for some a more private problem, even a private shame, and for others a reason to intervene in infested homes.

Meanwhile, an effective but dangerous chemical became available that killed all bedbugs in homes where it was used: hydrocyanic acid gas, known as HCN. One exterminator called HCN "the ultimate weapon" against bedbugs, promising to free city-dwellers from troublesome and possibly disease-prone vermin.[8] Many public health officials and government entomologists supported HCN fumigation by private exterminators as a solution to continued bedbug infestations, which resurged even in affluent areas after the Great War. Bugs threatened public health, but health departments wanted exterminators to serve as private partners in controlling these vermin. HCN shared many characteristics with bedbugs, however: it was highly mobile and hard to control, crossing borders between households and hiding in unseen nooks in the domestic environment. Both bedbugs and HCN resisted efforts at containment within private space, especially in the most densely populated parts of cities, which were often the poorest as well. Some health officials condemned HCN use in homes because the gas was so hard to contain there. At the same time, reformers worried that bugs degraded norms of cleanliness and decency in poor districts where they persisted and where private exterminators did little business. Low-income residents, too, longed to rid themselves of these insects, not only to avoid stigma but to protect themselves and their children from bugs' unrelenting physical and mental insults. Prior to World War II, however, only a small segment of poor households enjoyed relief from bedbugs, thanks to families and reformers who acknowledged that bugs were creatures of community.

FROM UBIQUITOUS PEST TO MARKER OF POVERTY

Bedbugs arrived in the United States with European colonists and hitchhiked across the continent in their human hosts' belongings.[9] Wrote one entomologist: "Railroads and emigrant ships provided free transportation with meals. . . . By 1860 there was scarcely a hamlet . . . in which many homes had not been visited by this unwelcome guest." Traditional furnishings such as "old-fashioned wooden beds provided crack space for a teeming tribe."[10] The spread of central heating in the early twentieth century favored bedbugs in colder climes as indoor warmth sped their reproduction rates.[11] One physician blamed "the American house, with its fissures and passage-ways between the walls and its many coatings of wall-paper," for infestations worse than in European homes of masonry construction.[12] An exterminator industry leader, Hugo Hartnack, argued that better, more modern home construction should be the first step in preventing bedbugs.[13]

Bedbugs became so common throughout the United States that the entomologist Clarence Weed wrote in 1916, "those who do not recognize them are to be congratulated."[14] Public conversation about bugs was rare, however; some commentators charged that the silence and shame surrounding bedbugs hindered their control. In 1885, an unusually hot summer sped up bug reproduction from Manhattan's "lowly tenement houses" to "luxurious mansions of the upper-ten district," yet a *New York Times* reporter called it "the little insect whose name is not mentioned."[15] A physician quipped in 1908 that "its popular name is not pronounced in polite society." He continued: "It has become powerful through the silence of its victims," and the pretensions of those who claimed that the occasional bug sighted in their home "of course was brought in from the outside."[16]

For generations, rich and poor alike relied upon home remedies to control bugs. By the 1700s, expert exterminators counseled clients to prevent growth of bug populations with regular inspections, vigilance against bugs carried in by servants and on purchased goods, and avoidance of adorned beds and furniture.[17] Many families placed the legs of their bed frames in cans of oil to drown roving bugs on their way to a nighttime feast.[18] One former tenement resident from New York's Lower East Side, who shared his bed with a twin brother and two sisters, recalled that "once a month or so [family and neighbors] would take the beds apart, put a pot of water under the springs, and bang the bedbugs out of it."[19] The Beecher sisters, Catherine Beecher and Harriet Beecher Stowe, advised readers to fill cracks in walls and furniture with putty.[20] Women made searching out and killing bedbugs part of spring cleaning; bug populations were at their lowest then, before rising temperatures accelerated their reproductive cycle.[21] Occasionally, a property owner took drastic measures against persistent infestation, such as a Connecticut family who tore down their entire house after numerous remedies failed, including coating their walls with creosote.[22]

Traditional and commercial chemical remedies required hard work and exposure to toxic risks. The activist and author Lydia Maria Child recommended arsenic-based paint for filling cracks in bedbug-infested walls. For wooden furniture she suggested "an ounce of quicksilver [mercury], beat up with the white of two eggs, and put on with a feather" to reach into the fine grooves.[23] Many homemakers applied mercuric chloride, also known as corrosive sublimate, to infested furniture; this deadly poison flew off druggists' shelves during New York's 1885 bedbug outbreak.[24] Housewives also rubbed carbolic acid, kerosene, and gasoline into wooden furniture. The home economist and educator Mabel Hyde Kittredge advised that infested mattresses be soaked in naphtha and then kept in a closed room and away from flames "to allow the gas to pass off."[25] Naphtha was so commonly used for bugs and clothes moths that no explanation was warranted when the educator Marion Talbot recommended that bedding be "occasionally cleansed with naphtha."[26] Other commercial products sold as bedbug killers were of dubious value; most only worked upon contact with the bugs, and so would not reach lone females who hid away from the main colony like needles in a haystack.[27] Meanwhile, exterminators fumigated for bugs by burning sulfur candles, a procedure that was effective but could damage fabrics and metals.[28] None of these remedies ensured eradication, no matter how great the dangers undertaken by householders or exterminators and no matter how vigilantly the family toiled.

Only one female bug needed to survive to replenish a population, so long as she carried fertilized eggs inside her. She might hide under a strip of loose wallpaper or deep beneath a baseboard, evading treatments focused on the bed frame or mattress. One must be "a persistent and thorough housekeeper" even when using chemical remedies; the best professional exterminators disassembled bed frames and used lights to search out hidden bugs.[29] Bedbug eggs withstood substances that killed nymphs and adults, so infested families had to repeat the treatments as each new generation emerged. Given the near impossibility of eradication, many families "accept[ed] bed bugs as a necessary evil."[30]

Three factors limited bedbug control: the time a family could devote to applying chemicals and cleaning; the availability of bedbug hiding spots in the home; and the chances for introduction of bugs there. By the late nineteenth century, "people of means" overcame the time limitation when many "discovered that if enough domestic help was hired to clean thoroughly and if enough hot water and kerosene were applied in the right places, it really wasn't necessary to live with bed bugs."[31] New furnishings and appliances also changed the home environment for consumers who could afford them. Most important, metal bed frames deprived bedbugs of the harborages afforded by older wooden frames, and the growing fashion for modern furniture free from adornments cut down on hiding spots. Later, vacuum cleaners sucked up bugs, and washing machines enabled frequent laundering with hot water that scalded bugs.[32] Furthermore, economic segregation helped upper-income families avoid reintroduction. Those who could afford to hire staff to control bugs tended to live in neighborhoods with others who did the same. If the number of bedbugs in most households declined, so did the odds of reintroducing them during a neighborly visit. Affluent neighborhoods enjoyed many advantages over their poorer counterparts in controlling bedbugs, if not eradicating them.[33]

Some commentators suspected that a few stray bugs might remain even in homes of the upper classes, hanging on for dear life, unseen and unacknowledged by their hosts. A New York physician declared in 1908 that "there is probably not a house in this city which is free from the cimex, for where it once takes up its abode eternal vigilance may keep it down, but the most persistent campaign can hardly eradicate it." He instructed: "look behind the backs of pictures, examine the folds of the window and door draperies, pry up the edge of the wallpaper where it does not quite meet the molding," for in a "well-regulated" home the bed would be free from infestation. Any colony that grew large enough to attract notice by discreet household staff would be destroyed.[34]

An expert exterminator named Nathan Sameth noted in the early 1920s that the Great War had disrupted bug-control routines across the income spectrum. One problem was the housing shortage, during which "landlords stopped repainting . . . apartments were not repapered . . . [and] three families lived where one should live." He also blamed the tight wartime labor market and "high wages [which] tempted women out of the home into industry"; domestic staff took war-industry jobs, and "the woman accustomed to two and three servants came down to one." "Spring cleanings were passed over superficially" and women "made Red Cross bandages after working hours, instead of cleaning up closets . . . [m]eantime the bugs were multiplying." After the war, affluent households took a few years to regain control over infestations.[35] This bedbug resurgence showed the importance of housing conditions and women's labor. Even if a privileged household did eradicate its infestation, it remained vulnerable to resurgence or reintroductions, albeit less so than residents of poorer neighborhoods.

Many middle-class and poor families labored at the same bedbug control tasks as wealthier households' servants. With fewer or no hired staff, however, families might find themselves "sweating away for weeks, pursuing each unhappy little bug from crack to crevice," as one entomologist described the process.[36] Housing maintenance mattered; homes in need of repairs, often occupied by poor families, might be riven with crevices where bugs could hide. Each missed bug might leave new offspring before a family next had the chance "to haul the bedstead out into the backyard and treat it with some of that newfangled coal oil."[37]

Furthermore, the economic segregation that benefited well-off families trying to control bedbugs had the opposite effect on poorer families. In neighborhoods where families took weeks or months to control bedbugs, there were more chances for reintroduction via a visiting neighbor's clothing or a secondhand mattress picked up on the street. When a family moved out of an apartment, hungry bugs "crawl to the floor above." "Sometimes bedbugs also spread to flanking apartments, mostly where an intervening wall is weak," or they might "escap[e] through windows [and] pass along walls, water pipes, or gutters," possibly undoing weeks of bug-control work in a neighboring household.[38] Housekeeping practices in multistory tenements could help bugs spread; "cleaning of beds and shaking of bed-clothes out of windows from upper floors may be responsible for an occasional downward movement of an infestation."[39] Thus economic geography and poor housing quality compounded the difficulties of bug control for low-income city residents. A British public health officer explained that poor families often "wear themselves out and spend their entire savings in an attempt to rid their houses of the pest, and in the end have to give it up in despair."[40]

Many families in the United States shared their British counterparts' struggles and feelings of resignation. Many city-dwellers, no matter their class status, became hypervigilant about bugs, always checking their bodies and surroundings. Some avoided setting down purses or coats in streetcars, movie theaters, and neighbors' homes. Exterminators, home economists, and entomologists advised women to be on the lookout for bugs as part of their domestic duties. Domestic advice author Marion Harland noted in her newspaper column that, for women, "eternal vigilance is the price of immunity from these and other household pests."[41]

Although even wealthy households might suffer a brief relapse, the success of bedbug control in upper-income households and many middle-income ones left a stigma on families still unable to rid themselves of the insects. Families who had eliminated their infestations might instruct their children to "stop associating with those 'buggy' neighbors," whose homes could be identified by a "characteristic pungent odor" of the oil the bugs exuded.[42] Exterminators and entomologists warned upper- and middle-class homemakers that servants and laundresses from poorer districts were "a source of infestation that must be constantly watched."[43] Many cities had alleys or lanes called "Chinch Row" or "Chinch Street" after one of the bedbug's common names, including one of Washington, D.C.'s stigmatized alleys targeted for housing reform.[44] Thus, bugs marked both homes and neighborhoods as unclean.

Some exterminators deemed poor communities "tolerant" of bedbugs, their neighborhoods places where extermination "does not pay." A leading exterminator in Chicago, Hugo Hartnack, associated tolerance with the ethnic hodgepodge of his city's poor neighborhoods. He asserted in 1939 that "tenants of mixed races and nationalities crowded together are often too busy in acquiring the bare necessities of life to have vermin enter their sphere of interest."[45] Many residents did resign themselves to infestation, but not out of tolerance or lack of suffering. Unwillingness or inability to pay an exterminator might mask strenuous personal efforts to rid one's home of bugs.

SOCIAL REFORM, BEDBUGS, AND HEALTH

With their increasing confinement to low-income communities, bedbugs became a target for social reformers who hoped to bring poor families up to standards of cleanliness set by affluent households. Bedbug interventions brought both benefits and burdens to targeted households: reformers helped and supported poor families on the one hand, while stigmatizing and disciplining them on the other. Some feared that bedbugs accelerated falling property values in slums when they hitchhiked to uninfested dwellings via unwitting neighbors or when frustrated families abandoned control efforts.[46] Edith Abbott of Hull-House lamented in her decades-long study *The Tenements of Chicago*: "In addition to the wretched structural inadequacies of the tenements and the lack of modern sanitary conveniences is the never-ending struggle with house vermin."[47] The domestic science advocate Mabel Hyde Kittredge made bedbug control one of the first skills taught to poor girls and women at the home economics education centers she helped found in New York. Her courses and textbooks for girls and women urged vigilance in avoiding bedbugs; for example, homemakers must scrub bed frames weekly regardless of infestation.[48] Housing reformers believed that low-income residents needed more than self-discipline to achieve decent, healthy living standards, however. They advocated for publicly subsidized housing and increased enforcement codes to help residents escape the tenement conditions they lamented.

Housing reformers made bugs a moral issue, entangled with concerns over crowding in houses and tenements. Hull-House's Edith Abbott declared "overcrowding may, in fact, be looked upon as the crux of the whole tenement-house problem and at the same time the most difficult point to remedy."[49] Crowding did not just occur at the scale of the block or building, but at the scale of the room or bed itself. Families responded to unaffordable rents and close quarters by sharing beds and crowding multiple beds into tiny rooms. Sometimes families with a sufficient number of rooms and beds packed into a single room in winter to save on heating costs. Social workers who worked on Abbott's study marveled at the sight of "beds everywhere"—in closets, kitchens, and unfinished attics, rooms not large enough for sleeping quarters under the city housing code. Often every room in the flat was "occupied as a sleeping-room." About half of all households in poor and immigrant neighborhoods had fewer bedding units than residents, often far fewer.[50]

Siblings, parents, and extended family members shared beds. Nearly one-quarter of families took in unrelated lodgers to defray the cost of rent; sometimes night-shift workers slept during the day in beds used by others at night. For example, Abbott's study cited a case in which "a room containing only 841 cubic feet was occupied at night by a man and his wife, their one child, and three lodgers, while four other lodgers occupied the same room during the day."[51] Reformers worried that crowding of beds eroded standards of privacy and modesty and exposed young children to sexuality while also speeding the spread of tuberculosis.[52] Bugs thrived on the density of human hosts in every tenement room while heightening residents' discomforts and sharpening reformers' anxieties.

Like other threats to well-being, from tuberculosis to crowded beds, bedbugs symbolized the unsanitary and unhealthy conditions from which housing reform would deliver the poor. To poor communities, bedbugs were much more than symbols: they disturbed domestic life, draining residents' energies and threatening mental and physical health.

One health official noted: "Many individuals are so susceptible to its bites and to its offensive odor that it is impossible for them to sleep in a room in which bedbugs are present."[53] As many as 80 percent of people suffered allergies to bedbug saliva; bodies of those who lived with a severe infestation might be covered in raised, itchy weals. Bedbugs could pock a child's entire body with itchy bites and even withdraw enough blood to leave the littlest ones anemic. Scratched bites could open the skin to infections.[54] Bedbug colonies left bed frames, loose wallpaper, and other hiding spots encrusted with feces, egg cases, exoskeletons, and human blood.[55] Visual and olfactory bedbug signs served as stigma on poor households while bugs themselves led to severe fatigue, stress, and even paranoia. The author of a leading medical entomology text insisted that emotional responses were an extremely important kind of "disease" caused by insects and admitted that new knowledge of the infectious potential of insects worsened emotional responses among layfolk and entomologists alike.[56]

While reformers worried about crowded, infested housing, medical entomology raised concern about bedbugs' possible vector role. Like mosquitoes and fleas, bedbugs access human blood while feeding. This characteristic made them an obvious candidate for microbial testing. Typical laboratory studies allowed bedbugs to feed on a diseased patient; then, researchers ground up bugs or their excreta and injected a suspension of the powdered material into guinea pigs or other animals. One such test suggested that bedbugs might transmit yellow fever; another produced bubonic plague when bug excreta were rubbed on the skin. Other tests simply looked for pathogens in the bug or its excreta, or observed patterns of disease before and after bedbug control. Studies contributed to a long list of infections in which bedbugs might play a minor role: kala-azar, recurrent fever, anthrax, smallpox, and Chagas' disease, to name a few.[57] No experiment or documented case showed bugs to transmit pathogens from human to human in the course of normal behavior. Thus, health experts disagreed over bedbugs' potential to serve as a vector. Many agreed, however, that bedbugs' other health effects justified "extermination of bedbugs as a routine part of any program of sanitation" no matter how remote the risk of infection.[58]

The private exterminator industry showed growing interest in medical entomology, including findings about germs bedbugs might carry. Before

1900, exterminator businesses served cities and towns across the United States, but health experts thought of them as mere "rat-catchers." In 1905, Nathan Sameth was one of the first in the trade to use "exterminating" for a business name when he founded the Sameth Exterminating Company in New York.[59] Sameth seized upon emerging evidence about pests and disease as part of his endeavor to professionalize the industry and remake its public image. Sameth urged preventive pest control, advising architects and designers to make homes bedbug-proof from the start, while also embracing chemical technologies. He attained such respect from officials that the city bacteriologist tapped him to teach public health and medical students about pest-borne diseases.[60] Sameth also received praise for his charity work in providing free bedbug treatment to day-care centers. Housing code provisions soon formalized exterminators' role in public health: landlords found to harbor pests were often required to hire an exterminator.[61] Public agencies, unable to respond to all infestations themselves, seemed eager for the services of a professional exterminator industry. A building inspector gushed: "It is a far cry from the old-time bug exterminator to the professional status you have attained. . . . To you is allotted the task of making the world safe for mankind."[62] A sanitary engineer called exterminators "allies of the public health authorities."[63] Exterminator firms cited pests' threats to health and their role as a private partner with health authorities when they marketed their services as "preventive medicine" for families at home.[64]

By the 1920s, a new generation of exterminators staked out their place as providers of private health services for consumers. The entomologist Robert Snetsinger called this cohort of American-born, formally-educated strivers "the rat-catchers' children." They took over firms from immigrant parents who relied on traditional remedies and practices. Sameth, ahead of his time by a generation, often led the way for his younger colleagues as they adopted scientific findings, publicized their own expertise, and responded to new government regulations on their industry. "Progressive" exterminators claimed to possess scientific and technical mastery over domestic pests, the germs they carried, and the poisons their trade applied in homes. This expertise, they argued, qualified them as private health service providers.[65] The industry built its reputation for serving the public's health in part by ridding homes of bedbugs—one of the most common jobs performed in cities before 1945.[66] Exterminators sought to profit and to gain the trust of consumers and regulators as they deployed an extremely dangerous but highly effective bedbug poison: hydrocyanic acid gas.

THE DOMESTICATION OF AN UNRULY PESTICIDE

Hydrocyanic acid gas helped change home bedbug control and the exterminator industry's fortunes in the first three decades of the twentieth century, but it also sparked worries about domestic pesticide use. Soon after its first use in agriculture, health experts saw the potential for the gas, known as HCN or prussic acid, to free urban households of bedbugs. They also feared that its use in domestic and urban spaces would endanger neighbors of treated households. Residential environments differed from other spaces where HCN was applied. HCN was dangerous and difficult for technicians to control in all spaces, but homes and congested neighborhoods where bedbugs thrived posed special risks to residents. Private exterminators and health officials who supported use of HCN endeavored to domesticate the gas—that is, to develop methods and safety procedures for its application in homes and to bolster its reputation for household bedbug control. Other health officials argued that the gas could not be tamed for domestic use. The domestication of HCN allowed private businesses to offer consumers more effective household bedbug control, but many health officials feared the dangers of applying it in homes and demanded a more prominent public role in regulating its use in private space.

The story of HCN's changing uses reveals its unruly character along with shifting application procedures and safety concerns in various spaces.[67] Its career as a pesticide began not in homes but in citrus orchards infested with scale insects. In 1887, chemists from the U.S. Department of Agriculture (USDA) and the University of California "cover[ed] trees with oiled tents and liberat[ed] beneath the tents a . . . gas produced by treating cyanide of potassium with sulphuric acid."[68] HCN's properties made it powerful and effective against pests but also dangerous and tricky to control. Other gases left tiny pockets of fresh air in which insects could survive, but HCN penetrated spaces and diffused rapidly, killing pests in the smallest recesses. HCN could also seep through unknown crevices, condense into objects in the environment, or drift away—hence the need for oiled tents to trap it just long enough to kill orchard pests. HCN's tendency to penetrate and diffuse made it an effective pesticide but raised worries about technicians' ability to contain it.

Because HCN diffused well through large spaces, it soon became a popular fumigant in commerce and shipping. Sanitary companies treated ships and rail cars, grain and tobacco warehouses, and large factories. Government sanitarians gassed ships as a quarantine procedure against vector-borne disease.[69] Horticulturists applied it in nurseries and greenhouses. In 1899, USDA's head of entomology, Leland Howard, called HCN one of the top-three insecticide discoveries of the late nineteenth century.[70] As of Howard's writing, however, it was not yet a common procedure in homes.

As HCN fumigation became routine in several sectors, the procedure occasionally resulted in human deaths, often among technicians. Humans who inhaled the gas first lost higher nerve functions and then, unable to escape, died in as little as five minutes if no one came to the rescue.[71] HCN became notorious for intentional human deaths: prussic acid pills were a popular method for murders and suicides; American scientists promoted HCN as a chemical weapon; Nazi leaders employed the formulation Zyklon B as a tool for genocide.[72] During HCN's development as an insecticide, USDA, the Public Health Service, and chemical companies developed materials and procedures that made it safer, though not foolproof. These included gas masks, "airing-out" periods, sentinels to prevent premature reentry, indicator chemicals to test for HCN, and warning gases that mixed with HCN and caused eye irritation if they were still present.[73]

As of 1900, HCN remained a pesticide for agriculture as well as large commercial and naval spaces, but the need for bedbug control soon brought it into homes. The Public Health Service and the USDA hoped to bring the benefits of HCN to cities, where even ceaseless toil might not eradicate every bedbug in the home. "With the growth of our population and the ... crowding together of residences," explained a report on HCN, "the problem of the ... control of household insects is deserving of careful consideration from a sanitary standpoint." HCN stood apart from existing bedbug poisons because a single fumigation filled every nook and cranny in the home, killing every adult and nymph, and even extinguishing tough bug eggs. Between 1901 and the 1910s, USDA released instructions for HCN fumigation for a variety of room sizes and pests, calling it "undoubtedly the most efficient remedy for the bedbug."[74] Exterminators seized upon USDA bulletins and began obtaining the local licenses required by most cities to perform fumigation.[75] Home environments differed dramatically from the spaces in which HCN had been used previously, however.

Federal agencies made it possible for exterminators to provide HCN service to home consumers, but they conveyed an ambivalent message about its use in dense urban neighborhoods. Urban and domestic land-scapes increased HCN's hazards. Individual households in a block of apartments could hire a fumigator unbeknownst to their neighbors unless local laws required notification and evacuation.[76] By contrast, there were no residents to evacuate in a warehouse fumigation, and discipline on naval vessels helped prevent sailors from entering gassed spaces.[77] At sufficient concentrations, the gas could penetrate a solid brick wall, never mind a building riven with crevices.[78] Old tenements contained innumerable cracks through which HCN would seep if the fumigator failed to seal them up—the leading cause of HCN accidents. Also, although most gas dissipated rapidly, on cold days HCN could condense in porous items like upholstered furniture, clothing packed in dressers, and mattresses. When residents returned and retired to bed, their bodies heated the retained gas, releasing deadly fumes.[79] Federal bulletins showed the proper arrangement of a room to be fumigated, to expedite airing-out and minimize risk of retained gas: clients or fumigators must remove mattresses from beds and open dresser and closets and loosen tightly packed items. Furthermore, the USDA warned that "HCN should not be used in closely built apartments with single walls between" to avoid diffusion to adjacent units or buildings.[80] HCN was a risky pesticide for the many bug-infested homes that fit this description; its properties as well as the residential environment and its human occupants made HCN dangerous.

Federal agencies did little to regulate domestic HCN use even as they promoted it. No federal agency issued *legal* standards for HCN fumigation, in homes or elsewhere—only safety guidelines.[81] The Food and Drug Administration (FDA), charged with regulating residues on foods, offered no rules about HCN on food and food crops, though it did adopt an advisory position. The FDA offered no advisory position on household HCN.[82] In the absence of federal rules, local governments were left to grapple with the risks HCN posed to households, and to respond to accidents in homes as well as other spaces.

Municipal poison ordinances already governed HCN fumigation as well as other pesticides, but there was no uniform safety standard for the gas across jurisdictions to impose public authority on procedures performed in private space. As accidents occurred in cities across the United States, local health authorities began to study the issue and develop additional regulations. After one deadly accident in New York City in 1921—a shipboard accident in which naval discipline failed—the Health Department examined all of HCN's uses and tightened permitting procedures for urban and household HCN uses.[83] Local government claimed greater control over the procedure and thereby over both the exterminator industry and the home environment.

One of the most deadly HCN accidents ever occurred in a dense residential neighborhood—the kind of place where government bulletins cautioned against using HCN. On the evening of March 3, 1923, O. W. Hull of the National Hygiene Company fumigated a restaurant in South Chicago. He had been hired to control cockroaches, but the accident affected bedbug control too. Hull told the residents of the apartments above the restaurant to leave their windows open, though he did not specify how long. He fumigated the restaurant and then waited outside, watching the building overnight. In the wee hours, a storm blew through the city, waking at least one member of the prominent Kratzenberg family, who arose and closed the windows, assuming that the gas had dissipated. Hull failed to notice the closed window. The next morning neighbors discovered all six Kratzenbergs dead along with their pet birds and fish. The neighbors had returned home late, missing most of the gas and the storm. The accident gained national attention.[84] The coroner's inquest found "a shaft two feet by six inches leading to the flats above was not properly sealed and the gas . . . entered the first and second flats above." He warned: "The more extended use of this poison in the last year . . . is responsible for the increasing number of deaths. . . . The use of hydrocyanic acid as an agency for disinfestation of dwellings should be forbidden."[85] Health authorities in Chicago joined counterparts in other cities in turning a seemingly private activity—home pest control—into a matter for public intervention.

DOMESTIC HCN REGULATION AND THE HEALTH THREAT OF BEDBUGS

In the wake of deadly HCN accidents, the exterminator industry defended its expertise in protecting healthy homes and criticized new government restrictions on its use of the gas. Nathan Sameth upheld his industry's ability to control HCN in homes, maintaining that exterminators needed HCN because of the health threats posed by bedbugs. Sameth and other industry leaders insisted that new regulations on HCN were detrimental to public health because they raised the price of the service beyond the means of many householders and reduced the number of firms able to offer it. Progressive exterminators thus reasserted their role in private-sector health service by highlighting their protection of city-dwellers at home.

New York and other cities responded to accidents by making exterminators fulfill new requirements in order to apply HCN, to protect residents against the gas's tendency to evade control. Some cities required evacuation of several buildings adjacent to the fumigated home or business. Many required exterminators to obtain insurance policies for up to ten thousand dollars and to accept absolute liability for damages, injuries, and deaths that might result from a botched job.[86] The *New York Times* published an opinion piece by a client of Sameth's—anonymously, to hide the writer's bedbug and cockroach infestations—in which the client complained about New York's regulations on HCN. "Many householders who were perfectly willing and able to pay $5 are struggling along with the old-fashioned remedies instead of paying $25," the client lamented, referring to the price of HCN fumigation before and after the new regulations.

Sameth blamed a citywide resurgence of bedbugs in part on the new restrictions and higher cost of HCN service as well as on women working outside the home and the postwar housing shortage. According to his client, "all the exterminators in New York employed" HCN, and they "turned on the gas on suspicion," without confirming the nature of an infestation. This revelation may have backfired, because it suggested that exterminators exposed clients and their neighbors to unnecessary risks. In truth, industry leaders such as Nathan Sameth, Hugo Hartnack, and George Hockenyos emphasized preventive methods of bedbug control— sound housing design and maintenance, regular inspections, and vigilance against introductions—along with reactive ones when needed.[87] When residents began dying in HCN accidents, health authorities sought to seize some control over risks in the home back from exterminators.

Sameth responded to restrictions on HCN by alerting the public to diseases bedbugs might carry—another kind of health risk in the home. In 1924, one year after the accident that killed the Kratzenbergs, *Scientific American* magazine published an interview with Sameth in which he cited such eminent bacteriologists as Louis Pasteur and George Nuttall who blamed bedbugs for several serious illnesses. Sameth asserted that "there is evidence that the bug assisted in the spread of the influenza epidemic" of 1918. He called HCN "the ultimate weapon" against bedbugs and urged developers of apartment buildings and hotels to build gas chambers on their roofs for safer fumigation of belongings. Sameth argued that "when public opinion grows up to the [bedbug] problem," Americans would demand modern solutions including professional HCN fumigation in homes.[88] Exterminators hoped that consumers would also resist regulations that limited HCN use.

Industry leaders made one key exception in their opposition to regulation: they argued that fumigators should be required to undergo training and obtain city licensure. To exterminators, licensure by a city health department represented a stamp of legitimacy, like a physician's or pharmacist's diploma.[89] Such requirements would also exclude upstart firms from the fumigation market. According to industry groups, "fly-by-night" firms undercut established companies' prices and perpetuated the industry's bad reputation.[90] Exterminators hoped that regulators would recognize the industry's provision of expert health services, not control their work in the home environment.

Local authorities continued efforts to limit risks of HCN in the home, however, and for regulators, controlling risk meant controlling the exterminator industry. Other than licensure requirements found in most cities, regulations varied by locality and included provisions about insurance bonding, minimum airing-out times, evacuation of buildings, and use of sentinels and warning placards. Detroit kept careful records of HCN procedures, and even after it, like New York, enacted all of these provisions, one human still died for every two thousand HCN fumigations there. Boston and Detroit sought to require that all HCN be combined with a quick-acting tear gas to warn would-be victims to flee. HCN was lighter than tear gas, however, so it could separate from the mixture; technicians or residents expecting a warning gas could be caught unawares.[91] "So amazing . . . are the confusion and contradiction of directions concerning fumigation," remarked a health official, "that one . . . cannot read [them] without a constant smile, if not, indeed, without breaking into laughter."[92] Health agencies, like exterminators, seemed unable to grasp what would make HCN safe for use in urban and home environments.

Government agencies often seemed complicit in HCN deaths because they failed to understand and adequately control the gas, the exterminators who applied it, or the urban environment itself. A jury ruled the technician O. W. Hull not culpable for the Kratzenbergs' deaths in Chicago in 1923 because the city did not regulate HCN and because the USDA had recommended the procedure.[93] After that accident, Chicago mandated a two-hour airing-out period. In 1928–29, however, Chicago saw a record number of HCN deaths. The *Tribune* counted ten dead, many of them upstairs neighbors; it did not tally survivors who escaped. An industry leader, Hugo Hartnack, lost employees in an HCN job and was also the target of a lawsuit after nursing home residents died in an HCN job. After this deadly year, Chicago required exterminators to obtain a permit from a new Fumigation Board for every procedure, asserting tighter control over the industry.

Industry responded by accusing that "poorly trained" technicians and unethical firms caused HCN accidents. The industry journal lamented: "These fatalities are caused by fly-by-night exterminators, but the experienced exterminator receives the blame and the whole industry is looked at in suspicion."[94] Hartnack was no "fly-by-nighter," though. He knew gases well from working for the German military before immigrating to the United States and was one of very few PhDs among American exterminators. After his two HCN accidents, Chicago's Fumigation Board refused to grant Hartnack further permission to perform HCN jobs. Hartnack accused the board of reducing to two the number of firms in the city that could legitimately provide HCN fumigation to consumers. Hartnack admitted that he had performed illicit fumigations, without the board's approval. Despite government restrictions and his own transgressions, Hartnack argued that the state did too little to make HCN fumigation safe.[95]

Rather than blaming himself or the chemical for the deadly accidents, Hartnack blamed the City of Chicago's airing-out rules and federal pesticide researchers. His technicians perished despite waiting the required time before reentering the fumigated building. Hartnack suspected that not only upholstery but also wallboard could retain gas on cold days, and that prescribed airing-out times gave technicians a false sense of security when reentering a building after fumigation. He argued that HCN's behavior in homes remained poorly understood due to the failings of the very government agencies that promoted its use. "Nobody had worked out the special problems faced by the fumigator in the city" because of the agricultural skew of pesticide research. In other words, government pest researchers had neglected domestic and urban environments.[96]

Many health authorities disagreed with their colleagues' calls for regulations, insisting that exterminators could master HCN to protect families from pests. After a fatal HCN accident in a British housing estate, the medical journal *The Lancet* declared the gas too valuable in bedbug eradication to be banned.[97] Dr. Charles Williams, a U.S. Public Health Service quarantine officer experienced in ship fumigation, defended home use of HCN, calling it the ideal fumigant.[98] The physician and syndicated columnist W. A. Evans sought to calm the "waves of popular indignation" that followed accidents. He explained that when "done by trained, experienced men, the danger is not exceptionally great," calling it a "superior" method for eradicating bedbugs and other pests.[99] Other authorities maintained that HCN behaved too unpredictably in residential areas. At a forum on HCN at the 1935 American Public Health Association Conference, two city sanitarians warned, "There are so many things that may happen on a given fumigating job . . . that it is not possible to predict the ones most likely to occur."[100]

The debate over HCN pitted claims of mastery over the home environment against arguments that gas eluded control in domestic space. The exterminator industry's trade group, the National Pest Control Association, issued a set of recommended guidelines for HCN fumigation—another instance in which the private sector asserted its role in domestic environmental conditions.[101] As the debate among health authorities reached a stalemate, regulation remained local and piecemeal. Across the United States, exterminators who could comply with local laws continued to apply HCN for private households that could afford their services. For all the claims that HCN was necessary for healthy homes and bedbug eradication, however, the homes most afflicted with bugs had little chance of benefiting from it.

HCN helped further restrict bedbugs to the homes and neighborhoods of poor Americans, where few families could afford to hire a private exterminator, much less one that could comply with local HCN ordinances. Furthermore, blocks of poorly maintained homes found throughout many low-income neighborhoods made for the most dangerous and difficult environment in which to apply HCN. Debates over control of HCN in residential environments seemed urgent, but the segment of city-dwellers who suffered most with the insults of bedbugs had little support from government or private industry.

BEDBUGS, HCN, AND PUBLIC HOUSING

In the early twentieth century, several trends promised to contain prolific bedbugs: improved control in upper- and middle-income neighborhoods; the rise of medical entomology; the professionalization of the exterminator industry; and the expanded use of HCN in homes. Yet these trends mostly left behind infested low-income communities. Reformers continued to worry over tenements teeming with bugs. Residents still lost sleep, suffered itchy bites, and toiled away in vain as the insects hid in the creviced recesses of substandard apartments. By the late 1930s, however, a new trend in urban reform promised to free a limited segment of poor city-dwellers from bedbugs: the rise of publicly subsidized housing. The exterminator industry stressed the provision of private services to individual consumers with minimal government interference. Meanwhile, public housing reformers could only keep bedbugs out of the projects by treating the new developments as social and ecological communities.[102]

After years of advocacy by housing reformers, Congress passed the Housing Act of 1937, allocating funds to build public multifamily housing and creating local housing authorities to manage the projects. The act promised to eliminate "unsafe and insanitary housing conditions" and provide "decent, safe, and sanitary dwellings for families of low income."[103] At its founding in the United States, public housing inspired reformers and residents alike with its potential to free low-income people from exploitation by the housing market, to "decrease danger of epidemics," and to "raise general public health."[104] Modern, new homes offered improved ventilation and air circulation, more spacious units, and better-lit interiors than in the slums. One reformer wrote that the importance of "good housing . . . lies in its powerful aid to physical, mental, and moral health, which are themselves elements out of which a wholesome family life is built. . . . Family life at its best expands into neighborhood life."[105] Reformers believed that sound living environments, communal facilities such as nurseries and clinics, and social and educational clubs for people of all ages would improve and better connect citizens, families, and communities.

As the first projects opened in 1938, however, many local housing managers forgot the potential for bedbugs to infest communities. They soon regretted the oversight: "If the furnishings of but one family moving into the new building are verminous—the percentage is usually much higher—there is every possibility that the woodwork, cupboards, and fixtures of the apartments will have become infested before the management can bring the condition under control."[106] Public housing residents shared buildings, common spaces indoors and out, youth clubs, health clinics, parenting classes—and also bedbugs. Bedbugs' ability to colonize entire communities, linking neighbor with neighbor, called upon housing authorities to adopt collective pest-management practices in the projects.

Chicago's Sherman Aldrich was one of the first local housing authority managers to promote HCN for the improvement of home environments in American public housing projects. Aldrich exemplified the optimism, idealism, and paternalism of American housing reformers who planned to uplift poor city-dwellers by building modern homes and teaching residents how to live in them. Aldrich strived to build community pride and support residents' well-being. As the housing authority's first residents prepared to move in early in 1938, Aldrich "had our maintenance crews go through and see that everything was clean, the windows, the stairs, behind the doors . . . so that when the building was opened it was in first-class condition."[107]

As part of these preparations, Aldrich devised intricate plans for harnessing public resources to keep bedbugs out of public homes. He based his plans on the "disinfestation scheme" developed by housing managers in Leeds, Britain. Aldrich cited British officials' view of bedbugs: "The menace of vermin to human health and happiness is very great, and it leads to such deterioration of house property that the housing reformer will be wise to give most careful consideration to the best methods of prevention and cure."[108] In general, city agencies in Europe made bedbug control a more public matter than their American counterparts, and not only in subsidized housing.[109] In the United States, tenants often sued landlords over severe infestation; in successful cases, courts required the landlord to hire a private exterminator, but in Britain public bedbug service was available. Hugo Hartnack lamented that "some decisions [in the United States] do not permit the tenant to break his lease on account of bedbugs," contrary to standard rulings in many European housing courts. Based on his knowledge of European bedbug control, Hartnack complained that "there is no organized bedbug control in the United States."[110] Laura Thorne Hunter, author of a leading British pest-control text for women, declared serious bedbug problems "a matter to report to local health authorities" for treatment by public sanitarians—often with HCN.[111] Furthermore, public housing should offer a "clean start," and "the majority of tenants are not to be held responsible for the verminous state of their houses."[112] If the point of public housing was to improve the physical, social, and environmental well-being of low-income city-dwellers, bedbugs had no place there.

In their quest to give residents decent and healthy living environments, housing managers in both Leeds and Chicago relied upon a chemical that some health authorities feared was too dangerous in homes: HCN. Both British and American managers saw HCN as the best hope for the "clean start" they envisioned for poor families. HCN was just as mobile as the bugs it was used to kill, so ridding new residents' belongings of bedbugs at move-in time would require intricate safeguards. Both bugs and the gas that killed them were hazards with the potential to spread throughout entire communities. It was already housing reformers' main aim to harness public resources in building healthy communities of responsible citizens. Thus, housing managers called upon communities to cooperate in making the public projects safe from gas and free from bugs.

Managers in Leeds developed procedures to keep people away from places where fumigation was performed. In Leeds, small buildings meant that only a few neighbors had to evacuate their premises during fumigation.[113] American projects dwarfed the British estates, however, complicating safety procedures. In Chicago, for instance, early projects consisted of dozens of two- to four-story low-rises, along with some row homes. The Jane Addams Houses was the largest of the first three projects completed in 1938, all of them limited to white families; Addams included thirty-two buildings that housed a total of 1,027 families. A fourth project, Ida B. Wells Homes, was completed in 1941 and provided high-rise and mid-rise apartments and row houses for 1,662 African-American families. In each project, families clamored to move in as construction was completed, potentially carrying bedbugs with them. Additional families trickled in thereafter, also possible bedbug hosts. Aldrich did not want bedbugs to sneak in with any new residents, but he could not risk having families remain in their new homes during the fumigation of even one unit in the same building. Furthermore, they would have to stay away for twelve to twenty-four hours to leave a comfortable margin of safety for airing-out. Aldrich could only coordinate the logistics of fumigation and prevent infestation by enlisting support from families in the new public housing communities.

Aldrich developed a procedure that required as many families as possible in each new building to move their belongings in on the same day when the buildings first opened. Then they vacated the building, staying with relatives elsewhere for the night. Crews immediately fumigated the entire building and then aired it out before the new residents returned the next day. Fumigating each building all at once enabled Aldrich to secure a bulk rate from the exterminators he hired, bringing down the cost from eleven dollars to just over six dollars per family. As additional families joined the community, managers had their belongings fumigated in a vault off-site before move-in.

Aldrich initially worried that families would refuse to cooperate with the procedure. They certainly had grounds to do so because it brought unexpected costs, inconveniences, and intrusions. Every family went through the procedure regardless of their infestation status; Aldrich's deputy declared: "The singling out of individual families [for fumigation] carries with it a stigma which would not be socially acceptable."[114] Across the United States, it was common for more than 50 percent of families entering public housing to have lived with bugs. Neither federal housing officials nor the Chicago Housing Authority would pay for fumigation, so Aldrich had to charge families for the service, whether or not they had been afflicted with bugs in their old home. Aldrich was pleased to find that families not only cooperated with the fumigation procedure; they welcomed it. Some told Aldrich: "This is the best thing you have done with this project."[115]

From residents' perspectives, communal bedbug fumigation was one of many aspects of life in public housing that brought both environmental improvement and sacrifices of privacy—reconfiguring home as an ambiguous space, at once private *and* public.[116] Many residents seemed eager to open their homes to the eyes of the state if it helped them attain a healthy living environment for their families. The first generation of public housing residents knew the stress and stigma of vermin infestation, particularly the women who performed most tasks related to both children's health and domestic pest control.[117] Historian Rhonda Williams has explained that this cohort of residents cooperated with housing managers, know-ingly sacrificing privacy, in order to enjoy the state's protection from the insults—health and otherwise—of the private housing market.[118] As one mother, Lucille Rodriguez, explained, her old private apartment, crowded with extended human family members, was also "full of bugs of all kinds. I cleaned and sprayed and it did no good. The children were bitten all the time," but her new public unit was "wonderful."[119] American public hous-ing by the late twentieth century gained a reputation as a failed experi-ment, but in its early days residents saw it as a haven from an exploitative housing market and unhealthy, even dangerous homes.[120] To many, it was worth submitting to the fumigation procedure to free the community from bugs.

Public housing residents submitted to other instances of state surveil-lance in their homes as well as challenges to the very existence of public housing from business groups, politicians, and taxpayers. Aldrich's dis-infestation scheme and residents' responses to it are best understood in the context of this politics and discourse. The private housing industry, seeking to protect its market, appealed to a long-standing American bias against publicly owned homes as it lobbied to limit government housing provision.[121] Some Chicagoans predicted that low-income residents would waste tax dollars by despoiling their dwellings and wasting subsidized electricity. As residents settled into their homes, Aldrich defended public housing residents, insisting that they consumed energy conscientiously and that "there wasn't much bad housekeeping . . . the tenants took good care of interiors." At the same time, Aldrich and other managers weeded out housing applicants who they feared would taint the community, and kept mothers under the watch of nurses and social workers to uphold standards of modern housekeeping.[122] As in many such social programs, reformers hoped to reshape low-income families' conduct—to improve bodily and household hygiene, along with other aspects of daily life. Youth groups, parenting classes, and health clinics benefited families while also imposing reformers' values.[123] The history of public housing was marked by debates over public and private space and responsibility that shaped the ecology of pests and the practice of pest control there for decades to come.

New public housing managers across the country grappled with the question of how to deal with bedbugs that could spread rapidly through the projects, spoiling visions of healthy living for poor residents. Aldrich presented the details of his disinfestation scheme at a 1938 conference of the National Association of Housing Officials (NAHO), drawing support and interest from housing authority staff from several cities. Aldrich helped lead a symposium on bedbug control organized by NAHO, and the assembled managers and officials almost unanimously endorsed his communal fumigation scheme. Managers across the United States agreed that communal fumigation supported not only a healthy, decent living environment, but also "good tenant relations."

Managers bemoaned the costs and logistical challenges of communal disinfestation, however, and they hoped in the future to control pests in individual apartments.[124] An experienced manager named Abraham Goldfeld offered one solution at NAHO's bedbug symposium. Goldfeld directed a New York–based foundation that had managed low-income housing since 1928, and he had observed repeated reinfestations. He encouraged housewives to kill bugs with a spray device called a pistolator, which he had purchased for families in the project to share.[125] Families had to buy their own chemicals, which, Goldfeld conceded, were costly and only killed bug nymphs and adults, not the eggs. He justified use of the device by explaining that, with the pistolator, the woman of the house "feels that she can do something about the situation herself, and is really satisfied. I think it is worthwhile for management to invest in this kind of thing for the happiness of the tenants."[126] Perhaps women were also glad for one less intrusion into their units, since they did they spraying themselves. The pistolator gave women a sense of control over their home environments, even if relief from bugs was only temporary.

The pistolator appealed to NAHO members, but they agreed that the projects needed a technology that actually destroyed bedbug eggs. They examined other methods less hazardous than HCN fumigation, but none killed eggs, and most suffered from other drawbacks. As of 1939, the available technology, and the bugs that plagued incoming residents, meant that public housing projects were permeable environments and that pest control methods would have to engage the entire community. Managers pined for a method for treating each unit individually, however. They hoped science would deliver a chemical alternative "which is not dangerous to human life and which can be used for individual dwellings without endangering the neighbors."[127] Managers wanted to establish cohesive communities and healthy common environments, but the communal character of the projects made it difficult to keep them free from pests.

UNEVEN BURDENS OF BEDBUGS IN CITIES OF LIMITED HOUSING REFORM

The family packed their few belongings into the housing authority's moving van: a rocking chair; two beds with new metal frames; two chests of clothes and blankets; an old rug; a box of dishes; and a few sundries. They left the box and chests open, the bedding and garments loosely packed, the mattress and rolled rug propped against the inside of the van. The van doubled as a fumigation chamber, and the items' arrangement would facilitate the airing-out process later. Few bedbugs made it into the moving van; most remained in the family's old flat, holed up behind the loose baseboard molding and under strips of paper that had begun to peel away from the walls.

A housing authority staff member, licensed by the Fumigation Board, attached an HCN generator to the chamber. He turned the generator's handle, and gas wafted through the van, suffusing mattresses and clothes chests and penetrating cracks in the wooden chair. The last of the bugs perished as HCN crowded out the oxygen they needed to breathe. The next day, the family reunited with its belongings in their new apartment with its fresh paint and bare, unadorned interior, seemingly free from hiding spots for vermin.

Back at the old apartment, the remaining bugs easily survived the week without human hosts; their slow, meandering travels at mealtime led many into the walls of the building and some of them to the flat upstairs. Then a new family moved in. After a month in their new place, the family itched constantly and suffered fatigue from interrupted sleep. It was late 1945, and the mother had heard of a new bedbug remedy on the radio. She picked up a bottle of a pesticide called DDT on her next trip to the market.[128]

Bedbugs in the United States experienced a dramatic narrowing of their livelihood over the first half of the twentieth century, even before DDT became available for civilian use in 1945. Wealthy households reduced their burden of bedbugs through the assiduous labor of their housekeeping staff, setting a trend that middle-class and low-income families tried to meet with their own sweat, skill, and vigilance. Affluent families' urban geographies, social circles, and codes of silence about infestation blinded them to the privileges that freed them from bedbugs. Families who rid themselves of bedbugs through personal expenditures or their own labor advanced the illusion of individual, private control over domestic nature. Insects already considered shameful became an even more damning stigma, a supposed indicator of indifference toward bodily and household cleanliness, and possibly an infectious danger. Meanwhile, poor households suffered—and often toiled—in private against bugs whose mobility made them a community problem.

The rise of the exterminator industry, the domestication of hydrocyanic acid gas, and health officials' support of the two helped perpetuate the treatment of bedbugs as a private issue. Exterminators provided services that public health departments lacked the time and resources to offer, building their reputation in part by freeing householders from bugs and any germs they might carry. Exterminators and their allies in public health believed that HCN's benefits in bedbug control outweighed its risks; they promoted the gas and urged skeptical regulators to minimize interventions in exterminators' activities. Regulators themselves, while justified in their efforts to tighten control over HCN, shared with exterminators limited knowledge of its risks in residential environments. HCN was as mobile in communities as bedbugs themselves, and exterminators had to understand the surrounding environment to apply HCN safely, particularly in the most densely populated parts of cities.

Residents of the poorest such places often lacked the means to hire exterminators, however. Campaigns in new public housing projects brought HCN to some of the people who suffered most with bedbugs by emphasizing communal space and resources, while using the same acutely dangerous chemical technology as private exterminators. Reformers believed that poor families needed to be rescued from the bedbug scourge, not only for the sake of physical and mental health but also to uphold morality and decency. Bedbug eradication thus became another way in which public housing improved environmental health for poor families—a common good rather than a sign of individual mastery over one's home. The New York City Housing Authority boasted that it had saved residents from the "countless thousands of cockroaches, mice, rats, bedbugs and other vermin which thrive in the cracked walls and rotting floors of dilapidated tenements."[129] Reformers adopted HCN as a tool for giving residents a clean start, and residents cooperated eagerly to gain relief. The role of HCN in public housing casts the pesticide in an ambiguous light; regulators had good reason to tighten control over its use, but it also brought immediate relief to long-suffering families and unified new housing communities. As the historian Edmund Russell has written of the intermingling of pest control and warfare: "For some people, insecticides and chemical weapons were blessings; for others they were curses; and for some they were both."[130]

This communal use of HCN to create healthy living environments was limited both in scope and in longevity. For one thing, cities like Chicago offered public housing to only a small fraction of families who lived in substandard dwellings infested with bedbugs. In Chicago alone, hundreds of thousands of families remained in substandard or crowded private housing, many of them toiling against bedbug infestations. Furthermore, in public housing, managers dreaded the logistics of communal pest control and wished for a new technology that would break the projects into units where pests would be easier to manage. In 1945, their wish came true: a chemical became available that seemed to control bedbugs and other pests safely and effectively at the scale of the individual household.

3

GERMAN COCKROACHES

Permeable Homes in the Postwar Era

On the dry goods shelf at the market, a Blattella germanica left a sticky ootheca, one of eight she would lay in her lifetime, clinging to a sack of rice. The shopper did not see the purse-shaped egg case, smaller than a pea, as she lifted the sack from the shelf, nor did she see it later while packing her groceries. German cockroaches had already infested her New York apartment building so thoroughly that she would never notice the new brood she brought home. A female B. germanica, medium-brown and just over half an inch long, had the potential to leave four hundred thousand descendants in one year, many more than the larger American and Oriental roaches that had infested the basement and devoured rotted food that coated the garbage chute. German roaches thrived during the war years; pyrethrum and sodium fluoride were hard to come by, and the exterminator hardly ever visited.[1] By spring of 1946, roaches had diffused into every unit in the building.

The woman placed the rice sack in the cupboard. Within a few hours, thirty nymphs emerged from the ootheca, a structure that one exterminator called a "case of trouble." Some scaled the inside of the cupboard door with their sticky feet, reaching the next shelf. They feasted on spilled flour and sugar while sealed jars protected tomatoes and beets. Some crept into the adjacent compartment, crawling over plates and feeding on resident adults' molted skins. Foul-smelling oil from the adults' scent glands anointed the dishes.[2] That night, a few trekked down the wall to the thin gap between the range and the countertop, where shreds of food collected.

The baseboard molding had never been flush with the floor, and below the kitchen window it warped from water damage after a rainstorm, opening a gap that accommodated several roaches. The sensation of objects—including their fellow roaches—touching their bodies attracted them to tight spaces such as these, a behavioral characteristic called positive thigmotaxis. Even where the gap was as thin as a half millimeter, roaches squeezed underneath, single file, whenever a light turned on in the evening. Their antennae extended past the molding like a row of eyelashes. When the light turned off again, several roaches emerged from behind the baseboard and scrambled up the peeling wallpaper. A dish of cat kibble sat on the windowsill by the fire escape for a half-stray kitten. One roach was unlucky, however, for the kitten had climbed in the window. Attracted by the roach's movement, she pounced and pinned a large adult to the floor, breaking off its tiny legs and smashing its abdomen.

The space beneath the oven offered shelter as well as food—peas that rolled off the counter and teething biscuit crumbs that the baby threw from his high chair, both of which bounced out of reach. The broom was too thick to sweep out debris or roaches from the crevice. But along with the other groceries, the woman had brought home from the market a new spray that promised to kill these insects wherever they lurked.

Immediately following World War II, manufacturers, scientists, and government promoted DDT and related pesticides as miracle chemicals that would finally contain domestic pests. Household use of these chemicals demanded that DDT and its kin be contained as well. Developed as a pesticide for controlling malaria mosquitoes in tropical war zones, DDT was marketed as a domestic product appropriate to apply even for insects of trivial health or economic impact. The miracle chemicals also promised safe and easy application by untrained housewives in individual dwelling units. This represented a major advance over prewar pesticides, the most dangerous of which, HCN, permeated entire multifamily buildings and could only be used by licensed applicators.

DDT and related pesticides seemed the perfect remedy for the German cockroaches that teemed in cracks and crevices of kitchens, bathrooms, and, increasingly, living rooms and bedrooms. The roach was no *Anopheles* mosquito, but neither was its impact trivial. By the 1940s, health experts accused roaches of serving as mechanical vectors for myriad pathogens. Roaches also fouled household food supplies and inflicted stress and shame on families. Some residents reported that the war and its aftermath had been kind to German roaches. Bereft of funding, material, or labor for housing maintenance, private and public homes sheltered growing numbers of them. DDT promised to seal off individual homes against roaches, killing those that attempted to enter. The postwar years also brought new geographic inequities in housing investment, however; capital fled central-city areas for new suburbs. With limited funds for maintenance, many urban homes remained excellent cockroach habitats. DDT and related chemicals could do only so much to contain roaches when these insects fit so well in the niche provided by degraded domestic environments. In fact, modern pesticides interacted with homes in ways that made German cockroaches ever harder to control.

The miracle chemicals would not be contained either, regardless of the home's condition. Even if the new pesticides stayed in place, they could change roaches' behavior and genetics. The home environment allowed both roaches and chemicals to enter human bodies in unexpected ways. Homes and bodies remained permeable to pests and chemicals despite the promises of modernity and containment.

ROACHES AND ROACH CONTROL BEFORE 1945

By the early twentieth century, entomologists noted ominously that the cockroach family, Blattidae, was among the most "ancient and persistent" families of insects and that its members who share human households were "the most omnivorous as well as omnipresent." Of those, the German cockroach was "the most abundant and destructive" in the eastern United States by the early twentieth century.[3] The species did not actually originate in Germany; the entomologist James Rehn traced its origin to northeastern Africa. From there, it crept across what are now Greece and western Russia. It arrived in Western Europe via trade routes that passed from Russian through the Prussian states sometime after 1648's Peace of Westphalia stabilized commerce there. In the seventeenth century, partisans of the Russian and Prussian empires each called the small roach by the other's name. As Europeans introduced the species in the United States, the Prussian association stuck, and by the twentieth century, most Americans called it the German cockroach.[4]

New Yorkers also called it the Croton bug because they suspected that it had spread through the Croton water system that supplied the city.[5] *B. germanica* did not actually travel through water pipes, but modern domestic technologies and environments created the conditions for the species to thrive, particularly the consistent and abundant availability of water indoors. Most content in damp, dark, and warm conditions, German roaches took advantage of the spread of indoor plumbing in the second half of the nineteenth century and the early twentieth. Cornell entomologist Glenn Herrick recalled in 1921 that "dozens of inquiries have come to us regarding the little roach which had been never seen until the bathroom fixtures had been installed and the kitchen fitted with water pipes."[6] Indoor heating ensured warmth year-round, and heightened indoor temperatures raised reproduction rates. Multifamily apartment buildings allowed roach populations to expand their physical ranges year-round without migrating in the cold from home to home.[7] Building features that made for efficient construction and service provision—such as hollow wall voids, shared utility lines, and dumbwaiters—also sped the migration of roaches between units in multifamily buildings.[8]

While modernization of living environments helped the roach spread, medical entomology raised the possibility of more specific health threats than the stress and food spoilage with which it was already associated. Pest controllers and entomologists proposed that roaches served as mechanical germ vectors, much like flies, connecting germ-ridden parts of urban and domestic landscapes with household food supplies. The Chicago exterminator Hugo Hartnack remarked that upon seeing this insect, "one right away pictures a roach crawling around cuspidors [spittoons], toilets, garbage cans, sewers, and other filthy places and then transferring its interest to human food supplies and stored, clean linens."[9] The connections that roaches made between filth and food were especially troubling in light of their abundance in grocery stores, which became a source of infestation for homes.

Research on roaches' role in transmitting disease blossomed after 1940, revealing some forty bacterial pathogens that occurred in roaches, most of them involved with gastrointestinal infections.[10] Evidence of actual disease transmission remained circumstantial, but researchers cited an outbreak of salmonellosis in an infested Belgian nursery as reason not to tolerate German roaches, especially around children.[11] Many noted roaches' tendency to crawl onto sleeping humans' faces to obtain moisture from their orifices or, in the case of babies, to feed on dribbled milk that caked at the corners of mouths.[12] By the 1950s, a few physicians reported patients who suffered skin allergies to roaches, including a Brooklyn man so sensitive he had to discard a pair of shoes with which he had stomped on a horde of *B. germanica*.[13] One research team wrote: "Because of the lack of conclusive evidence that roaches can transmit disease, these insects have been regarded with tolerance by a large portion of the population, especially where roaches are difficult to control."[14] Many hoped that new evidence would motivate families and health officials to declare war on roaches, but these researchers likely overestimated householders' tolerance and underestimated these insects' tenaciousness.

Ridding a home of *B. germanica* required great persistence and resourcefulness—and entailed risks of its own. Glenn Herrick noted that "the croton-bug is the most difficult [roach] of all to get rid of" because "it seems to display more caution in avoiding traps and baits" and "increases faster" than others in its family, and because of its propensity to hide out of sight.[15] The Beecher sisters (Catharine and Harriet Beecher Stowe) recommended pouring boiling water down drains to kill roaches that hid there. For roaches elsewhere in the home, they suggested arsenic baited with cornmeal and molasses.[16] The home economist and educator Mabel Hyde Kittredge advised tenement dwellers to "every night sprinkle roach salt"— sodium fluoride—"in all cracks about sinks and tubs, brushing up in the morning before beginning to cook."[17] The activist and author Lydia Maria Child described a botanical preparation in which the root of the pokeweed was "boiled in water and mixed with a good quantity of molasses, set about the kitchen, the pantry, &c. in large deep plates."[18] One devious method involved offering roaches flour laced with dry plaster of Paris and a dish of water nearby; the mixture hardened in the insects' intestines. Many householders swore by boric acid—a powder that acted as a stomach poison but was less toxic to mammals than other roach remedies. They doused their kitchens with boric acid dust frequently and generously over the course of weeks.[19] Like bedbug remedies, many do-it-yourself cockroach cures posed risks to children or pets who might ingest a poison or to any household member who might inhale airborne dust. These control methods required women to labor persistently and patiently to rid the home of roaches as part of their regular cleaning tasks.

Commercial over-the-counter insecticide products required intensive efforts. Pyrethrum dust, made from a flower native to Persia, could be blown into crevices with a bellows.[20] Herrick warned, however, that "it is exceedingly difficult to inject anything into . . . cracks and crannies with sufficient force or in sufficient quantity to actually hit and kill the roaches." Herrick instead advised turning Buhach powder—a popular American pyrethrum brand—into a fumigant by wetting it, molding it into cones, drying the cones in an oven, and lighting them with a match. The smoke pervaded roach lairs, but only after time-consuming preparation.[21] Arnold Mallis, author of a leading pest-control guide, later recalled: "It was essential, when using [pyrethrum and sodium fluoride] powders to dust every crevice and hiding place in order to obtain control. The cockroaches were widespread, and if one hiding place was missed, this served as a breeding ground for the roaches."[22] Pyrethrum did seem to have one advantage over other poisons, however: lay and professional users believed that it posed no toxic risk to humans or pets.[23]

Home economists, exterminators, and entomologists saw an important role for preventive and nonchemical methods in German cockroach control. Chicago exterminator Hugo Hartnack, author of a leading pest-control guide, recommended simple homemade and commercial roach traps that required no poison. Popular trap designs involved ramps leading into a jar or coffee can baited with such favorite roach foods as stale beer.[24] More important, Hartnack advised caulking cracks and crevices to eliminate household harborages, and sanitation to deprive roaches of food. The parts of his guidebook dedicated to roaches suggest chemical remedies only as "very successful emergency measures," in contrast with his strenuous promotion of hydrocyanic acid gas (HCN) for bedbugs.[25] These roach prevention methods required careful attention to the domestic environment but had the benefit of limiting other pest species as well.

Other pest controllers and entomologists did recommend HCN for German roaches.[26] HCN's supporters considered bedbugs the best justification for use of this deadly gas because of its effectiveness against bug eggs. HCN also infiltrated German roaches' unseen lairs better than anything a householder could apply herself, wiping out both species when exterminators fumigated a home. Still, the drawbacks of HCN were the same regardless of the target species: the acute risks, the trouble of evacuating buildings, and the cost of hiring an expert exterminator. Managers who endorsed HCN for housing projects hoped for an alternative "which is not dangerous to human life and which can be used for individual dwellings without endangering the neighbors."[27]

Roaches strained housing reform efforts to improve urban living conditions and give families a sense of control over their home environments. Residents and reformers alike considered roaches dehumanizing and possibly pathogenic. Tenants of multifamily housing faced particular difficulties in ridding themselves of roaches because conditions in one apartment often affected those next door. Then, in 1945, a new family of chemicals brought fresh hope for controlling these insects in all kinds of homes, in all kinds of places, without cooperation among neighbors.

THE PROMISE OF DOMESTIC DDT AND THE DECLINE OF BEDBUGS

DDT and the family of pesticides to which it belonged, the organochlorides, went through a process of domestication similar to HCN's. DDT's career as a pesticide began in World War II, when it gained wide fame for protecting service members and civilians in war zones from mosquitoes that carried malaria and lice that spread typhus. DDT and its relatives adapted more easily to domestic use than HCN had, given HCN's acute dangers and mobility in residential environments on the one hand and DDT's reputation for safety and protecting human lives on the other. HCN required evacuation of entire buildings even if only one room was infested, but health officers had famously dusted refugees' bodies with DDT during a louse-borne typhus outbreak in Italy. In other words, few worried about contact with human bodies and living spaces in DDT's early days. Also, unlike in the case of HCN, manufacturers devised myriad do-it-yourself DDT products that offered effective, convenient, and safe application by householders. DDT came in multiple formulations: a housewife could apply surface sprays to walls and baseboards to form a long-lasting poison barrier, place dusts in hidden spaces like under-sink cabinets, or simply spray at an annoying insect. Federal agencies (including the Public Health Service and the USDA) promoted DDT to housewives, inviting them to wield the same power over their homes as the American military had over deadly insects abroad.[28]

A leading industry scientist, George Hockenyos, heralded "new standards for freedom" from pests and a dawning "era of pest prevention," in which chemicals, with or without building repairs, would prevent pests.[29] Hockenyos had long advocated thoroughness and care to pest-control technicians, urging a combination of chemicals, inspections, and sound building construction and maintenance. "For several years there has been increasing emphasis on the preventive phase of pest control work," he wrote in 1946. Hockenyos seemed to see no contradiction between older methods of prevention and the "preventive" methods offered by new organochlorides. He continued: "A principle obstacle in [preventive pest control] work is the fact that in many cases it requires a considerable outlay at one time for the necessary repairs to eliminate harborage and make reinfestation impossible. Many property owners will pay ten dollars a month for control service but will not spend two hundred dollars to permanently reduce or even eliminate the hazard. . . . With the advent of the residual type sprays, effective insect pest prevention in buildings really became possible."[30] The ease of killing pests with DDT seemed to reduce even further any incentive for property owners to invest in better maintenance. Promotions for DDT promised consumers that they could now avoid even minor infestations by maintaining a coat of pesticides all over the home.

The story of DDT and other organochloride pesticides dovetails with that of postwar suburbanization, consumerism, and notions of modern homes. Organochloride pesticides were one of many consumer products, from washing machines to polyester, that promised suburban consumers a convenient, modern lifestyle and a heightened sense of family sovereignty over the domestic environment. Popular media and government bulletins heralded the ease with which "Mrs. Postwar American" could put domestic nature in its place.[31] Advertisements and media reports often showed white models enjoying "pest-free" living in detached suburban homes.[32] The appeal and affordability of organochlorides also extended to low-income communities and central-city, multifamily housing. As of 1945, DDT symbolized the good life and control of domestic nature for residents of modern homes—be they public projects in the city or private homes in the suburbs. In its own way, the story of public housing in the postwar period was also entwined with the story of organochlorides and the changing fortunes of both bedbugs and German roaches there.

The organochlorides that Americans across the income spectrum and in cities, suburbs, and rural areas adopted in 1945 differed vastly from HCN. Both HCN and DDT could kill a broad range of rodents and insects, including bedbug eggs. HCN could also kill humans within seconds or minutes, but the new chemicals had a low acute toxicity, and chronic toxicity problems only slowly came to light.[33] DDT was far cheaper than

HCN, and few authorities questioned its availability as an over-the-counter chemical. Even low-income families could afford a bottle of DDT.[34]

DDT behaved quite differently from HCN in indoor environments in terms of both its safety and its function. DDT's properties seemed to render communal pest control unnecessary. The difficulty of controlling pests in multifamily housing came from the fact that "infested apartments and row houses . . . provide a constant source of infestation in adjoining premises."[35] Like bedbugs and roaches, HCN permeated entire structures; it reached insects in even the most hidden crevices but also made it necessary to evacuate entire apartment buildings before fumigation. By contrast, scientists in 1945 believed that organochlorides remained safely fixed where technicians or do-it-yourselfers applied them. A single application would not kill pests throughout a building, but neither did it require a full evacuation. On the other hand, housing managers had used HCN to keep bedbugs out of housing projects, but HCN left no residue to kill bugs introduced later. DDT surface sprays acted as residual pesticides: spraying them on a wall or other surface left a chemical barrier that would kill bedbugs for months.[36] Organochlorides seemed safe to use in a single unit, and they helped bound off each unit from adjacent units and the outdoors. The new chemicals possessed just the properties housing managers had hoped for in the 1930s; HCN use became rare with the introduction of residual pesticides.[37]

DDT reinforced the notion of the independent scale of the home and made it easier for individual families to perform their own pest control effectively. The narrowing scale of pest control had particular implications for women. Historians have noted that women in the twentieth century experienced growing isolation from other women performing domestic tasks. The historian Susan Strasser has explained that this "combined with the illusory individualism of consumerism . . . intensified the notion that individuals could control their private lives at home."[38] Promotions for do-it-yourself DDT products targeted housewives, assuring greater control over the home environment.[39] DDT helped make the home a space to be defended against unwanted nature, and women often assumed this job as one of many household tasks. A physician testified before Congress that in "the age of do-it-yourself . . . it is a rare . . . housewife who does not have a can of 'bug killer' handy for stalking flies, ants, clothes moths, or any other insect that moves across the threshold."[40] Advice about pest control had long emphasized housewives' individual agency, but DDT inspired new faith in the chemical technologies that women would wield, even in multifamily public housing with its founding ethos of collectivity.

Bedbugs' immediate responses to DDT reinforced the idea that women and families could control their homes individually. In 1940, exterminator industry scientist George Hockenyos said that "bedbug spraying [was] one of the most important pest control operations" in major urban areas.[41] By 1946, he noted "a reduction in the number of calls for bedbug control this season after only a year in which DDT has been available." Hockenyos predicted that residual sprays would bring bedbug control to the masses at little monetary or labor cost because "the poorest individual can buy a small bottle of DDT and a sprayer and thus assure himself a bed free of blood sucking bedbugs."[42] It seemed not to matter if a home was rife with bedbug hiding spots, because the bugs would eventually come in contact with a DDT residue. In 1952, one pest controller observed that "as [bedbugs] have become more and more uncommon, curiosity has tended to replace the abhorrence and disgust felt by older generations."[43]

DDT simplified bedbug control for householders and professional pest controllers alike. Most prewar chemicals did not control bedbugs completely, and the one that could kill all bugs in a home, hydrocyanic acid gas, was also acutely toxic and hard to contain. With DDT, a typical spraying routine called for a 5 percent solution in an oil base, sprayed "around the bedstead, mattress, spring and other furniture known to be infested as well as all cracks, mop boards, windows, door sills, mouldings and other hiding places"—a thorough coating over much of the home. Publications on DDT cautioned that one should not use furniture until the spray dried. Residual spray could kill each new bedbug that tread across it for six to ten months.[44] Bedbugs had already declined in the early twentieth century, and by the mid-1950s, infestations became rare across the United States.

DDT eased bedbug control at the scale of the household, but the effects of chemical applications extended beyond individual families in ways that few appreciated at the time. DDT helped reduce inequalities in the economic geography of bedbug infestation because, with fewer infested households even in poor neighborhoods, the chance of bedbug transmission there declined. Because bugs spread by migrating from home to home on human bodies and belongings, each time a family eradicated its bedbugs, the whole community benefited. Community-scale benefits of DDT for bedbug-infested families received little attention, however. Meanwhile, organochlorides along with changing policies toward public housing encouraged managers to move away from community-scale pest control.

DDT, GERMAN ROACHES, AND HOUSING DISINVESTMENT

As in millions of private homes in the United States, DDT became part of public housing residents' living environments after 1945. With the passage of the Housing Act of 1937, idealistic housing reformers strived to provide modern residences, complete with pest-control technologies to maintain high standards of health and decency. Much as they embraced hydrocyanic acid gas in 1938, local housing authorities now incorporated DDT into public housing's maintenance routines. Managers from across the United States shared tips with one another about new pesticide formulations and building materials such as wall paint and lumber manufactured with DDT.[45] Many housing authorities trained in-house staff to apply the new pesticides, while others chose to contract with a pest-control firm for regular service. In either case, a technician visited each project two to four times a year to reapply residual pesticides in tenants' units, utility rooms, and around the project grounds. Project managers believed that the regular appearance of a professional pest controller at residents' apartment doors assured them that the housing authority was diligently managing pests. Public housing residents, like other Americans, hoped to benefit from new technologies to keep their homes sanitary.

Housing managers as well as exterminators stopped using HCN for bedbugs, seeking the convenience and safety that DDT promised.[46] The Federal Public Housing Authority hired experts to train maintenance staff to use the new pesticides against a range of pests. At a 1946 workshop in Chicago, staff learned to stave off flies by applying DDT to screens once a month. They controlled the bedbugs that infiltrated projects by applying a 5 percent DDT solution to "all beds, cots, cribs, upholstered furniture, and a strip around the windows and corners of the room." Bedbug control seemed to be a straightforward matter of reaching likely hiding spots with DDT spray, but cockroaches, particularly German roaches, were another matter. Some German roach infestations were so severe that "a second spraying has been necessary after the first application has dried." DDT seemed more effective, convenient, and safe than HCN, but it still required what the instructor in Chicago called "intelligent applications"—that is, spraying the right solution of DDT in the right spaces at the proper time intervals.[47]

HCN fumigation had once required communitywide cooperation, but technicians could apply DDT on a unit-by-unit basis without any collective activity or spirit. The list of spaces where maintenance staff were instructed to spray is indicative of the new pest-control practices: "kitchen walls, shelves, under the sides of sinks, backs of refrigerators, plumbing, door casing, cabinets, and the shower stall." Technicians learned to focus on spaces within the unit interior but not to consider the ways roaches might move within the building or between units.[48] Residents who believed they had no pest problems could turn the technician away. Also, if a technician knocked on a unit door and no one answered, he would move on, and the unit might receive no treatment for months regardless of conditions there.[49]

By 1946, public housing residents in several cities across the United States reported tenacious German cockroach populations. In some cases, local housing managers maintained their dedication to "good tenant relations" by seeking new pest-control innovations. Local housing managers in New Orleans worked with the Federal Public Housing Authority to bring experimental formulations to roach-infested projects. Public housing in New Orleans became a testing ground for a powder called PCH, a synergist that, when mixed with DDT, expedited roaches' demise.[50] The manager reported that "the infested apartments were free of cockroaches," and residents applauded his efforts.[51] The Federal Authority advertised the chemical to local authorities across the United States. Furthermore, many housing authorities provided pest-control services at no additional cost to residents. This policy both supported "good tenant relations" and helped contain roach infestations promptly, because residents were less likely to hesitate in seeking extermination if it came at no extra cost. Many residents were accustomed to hiding infestations and attempting to control pests themselves to protect their pride or out of fear of reprisal from their landlords. Detroit housing manager James Oleniak justified the free service, explaining, "after an infestation has spread, it is difficult and often totally impossible to determine where the source of infestation had originally been"; if the original source remained untreated, the community would likely become reinfested.[52] DDT made household-scale extermination easier, but at least initially some housing officials still understood that community-based pest control served both social and ecological ends.

In other housing authorities, infestation sharpened tensions between residents and managers. Residents of Baltimore Housing Authority projects had from the beginning worried that they lived in an unhealthy home environment. Baltimore's mayor had appointed allies from the private real estate industry—which opposed public housing provision—to run the housing authority, and activists accused them of intentional mismanagement.[53] Extermination provided by the housing authority failed to control roaches, bedbugs, rats, and mice in several buildings, and residents had to pay for the service themselves. In 1946, an activist and public housing resident named Alverta Parnell sought help with cockroach control costs for a disabled resident. Activists like Parnell looked to state support for healthy living environments; as historian Rhonda Williams has noted, they made such issues as household infestation political rather than simply private.[54] Managers rebuffed Parnell's requests, though, telling her "they should not have vermin in their apartment and then spraying would not be necessary."[55] The Baltimore Housing Authority's response to resident concerns about pests presaged trends in housing authorities across the country. Recurring German cockroach infestations foreshadowed trouble for the projects as well as for the pesticides.

While public housing tenants in New Orleans enjoyed relief from German roaches, and those in Baltimore battled housing managers over pest control, residents of private apartments in the late 1940s struggled with roaches even while applying DDT "intelligently." In the years after World War II, deferred maintenance left many private homes and apartments vulnerable to roaches. Meanwhile, a nationwide housing shortage long in the making reached its peak, limiting the options of middle-class as well as low-income families. A writer named Louella Webster described for readers of *American Home* magazine the trials of housewives trying to rid degraded domestic environments of cockroaches in 1948, using her own struggle as an example: "It is an undisputed fact that the housing shortage has increased by millions the bug population in American dwelling units. With people forced to live in sheds, garages, caves, and other substitute abodes poorly equipped for the storage of food or the disposal of waste, the cockroach finds himself in heaven and the housewife finds herself on the brink of a nervous breakdown."[56] A chemical cure could do little to kill roaches when domestic environments provided such ideal conditions for them.

Even amid the hype about DDT, Webster knew that roaches would not die immediately upon traipsing across a residue on the baseboard or under the refrigerator; the poison needed hours or days to work. After that, "the residual spray would get the little beasties for weeks to come. . . . It would cling to their feet and, during their morning ablutions, reach their stomachs and shatter their nervous systems"—or so said the "suave voice" in radio advertisements. Roaches continued to pour through the cracks and crevices of Webster's apartment long after the poison should have kicked in, however.[57] DDT failed both because her crevice-ridden home provided so many retreats from the residue, and because population reservoirs in the community could replace roaches that did perish. Many residents in poorly maintained apartments faced this trouble with DDT.

Many entomologists, pest-control experts, and public health advocates stressed that DDT worked best in conjunction with sanitation, good building maintenance, and careful attention to cockroach movement between units. Health official and scholar M. Allen Pond did not as a rule oppose pesticide use but argued that vermin control should be addressed primarily through design and construction, especially in apartment buildings where units were interconnected with one another.[58] Pond warned: "The migration of domestic insect pests between dwelling units in multiple-family housing frequently assumes serious proportions. The main travel routes are along water, heating, power, and drain lines."[59] The USDA cautioned: "Dirt and filth help the roaches to develop in large numbers and make it more difficult for an insecticide to be effective. Sometimes a thorough cleaning would be more effective than an application of insecticide." Furthermore, regardless of whether a pesticide is used, "all cracks about pipes passing through floors or walls, as well as cracks leading to spaces behind baseboards and door frames, should be filled with putty or plastic wood, particularly if roaches are coming in from adjoining apartments, or from outside."[60] Professional pest-control operators who wished to get to the root cause of an infestation bemoaned their inability to overhaul poorly maintained homes.

The author of the preeminent American pest-control guide, Arnold Mallis, lamented: "Since the pest control operator cannot very well tear down and reconstruct the infested premises, he must concern himself with more practical aspects of the problem"—that is, how to eliminate the infestation without reconstructing the entire home.[61] Effective new pesticides made it possible in the short term to divorce pest-control activities from any effort to change the ecological habitat offered by crumbling buildings. Defects like the ones abhorred by Mallis riddled private and public apartments alike. Older private apartments like Louella Webster's became infested with roaches as part of a decades-long process of disinvestment and deferred maintenance. Many white, middle-class and working-class families soon escaped crumbling homes full of roaches as private developers and federal housing agencies invested in a massive expansion of suburban housing.[62] Meanwhile, the vast stock of private, urban housing crumbled amid disinvestment in the postwar years. Some public housing communities later became notorious for a variety of problems, including infestation, but in the 1940s and 1950s they still harbored fewer pests than adjacent low-income communities; many residents considered them havens from the brutal private housing market. Social welfare advocates attributed improved health, especially among children, to the environment that public housing provided: more sanitary than tenement neighborhoods in the same cities where "rats, mice, roaches and other kinds of vermin infest more than half the buildings."[63]

Yet roaches soon gained a foothold in public housing projects built upon ideals of health and modernity no more than ten years earlier. Despite housing reformers' idealism, opposition from the real estate industry kept federal budgets for public housing low; historians and critics have described early budgets as "miserly" and "inhumane."[64] Corner-cutting began with the very first projects. Local managers lodged many complaints—for example, that screen doors had warped in their frames, allowing "flies and other insects [to] come right into the houses."[65] In a 1948 report, maintenance staff in public housing reported many defects that could make building environments more vulnerable to vermin. Roaches and rodents could take advantage of poorly designed garbage receptacles, nonwaterproof floors, leaky walls, and rotting window and door sashes to find food, water, and hiding places. Unsealed gaps around pipes gave vermin routes into crawl spaces and thereby throughout buildings; pests could also gain passage via hollow wall voids and "cheap and flimsy" interior partitions between units.[66] Shared utility lines made for efficient water and power delivery but also provided avenues for roach movement.[67] At the same time that DDT promised to make homes less permeable to pests, the physical structures of public housing were becoming in many ways more permeable, allowing roaches to migrate from unit to unit.

DDT seemed to give managers license to neglect the interstices of buildings through which roaches moved. When housing authorities trained staff in DDT application, trainers called for spraying a wide variety of indoor surfaces but said little about the need to caulk utility insertion points or improve the process of garbage disposal.[68] An individual exterminator might visit eighty to ninety apartments in a single day, plus basements where many pests lurked, leaving little time to diagnose or treat problems like loose baseboards that harbored vermin.[69] These features of multifamily apartment buildings and their maintenance helped support the feeding, breeding, and movement of roaches. Construction and maintenance practices made public housing projects a highly permeable environment for roaches.

Despite these shortcomings, many in the first cohort of residents and managers saw public housing as a "paradise," or at least a place of possibility, and a vast improvement over infested, dangerous private tenements.[70] Political discourse on public housing soon demeaned the sense of social collectivity that the first residents and managers valued, while also contributing to the physical degradation of urban residential environments. Public housing advocates sought new federal support amid the nationwide housing shortage, which affected middle-class as well as working-class and poor families. The private real estate and construction industries renewed their own campaign against public housing, however, raising the specter of communism and accusing housing authorities of "squandering funds." Proposed legislation actually provided for "nine times as many private units as public units." The historian Lawrence Vale has explained: "Public housing was simply a small part of a more comprehensive housing program premised on massive but nonstigmatized government subsidies to support private housing ownership for the middle class."[71] Discourse and policy valorized private homes while diminishing public homes both rhetorically and materially. Pest-control practices—enabled by DDT and related residual pesticides—reflected this degradation in their increasing atomization of multifamily public housing.

Federal administrators had since the beginning tried to hold down public housing budgets to avoid drawing criticism from opposing politicians, leaving states and local authorities to do their best with limited funds.[72] The sections of the Housing Act of 1949 that addressed central-city public housing funded the acquisition and clearing of blocks considered "blighted" and also the construction of hundreds of thousands of new public housing units across the United States. Local authorities would now have to run more and larger projects. Authorities built projects on ground laid bare by the demolition of low-income tenements. Furthermore, Congress agreed to limit eligibility for public housing to the poorest of the poor to avoid competing with private developers. This meant that more of the tight budget for public housing would go into subsidies rather than other needs, such as community services and maintenance.[73] With the Housing Act of 1949, Congress supported the construction of many new projects while leaving housing authorities with limited funds to maintain them in sound condition.[74]

By cutting housing funds, Congress placed greater responsibility for environmental conditions in public housing with local administrators and residents themselves, leaving them to make do with tight budgets.[75] The New York City Housing Authority financed and managed its projects according to a set of policies different from other housing authorities across the country; New York's projects have not suffered the severe problems of projects in Chicago and other cities, but they still strained to maintain a healthy environment.[76] Even after setting aside inflation and the enormous increase in units that required servicing, maintenance costs soared in New York City as buildings aged and deteriorated; the authority was under strenuous pressure to contain costs.[77] Managers increasingly neglected the communal environment of housing projects—not just public hallways and common areas but also buildings' shared guts: the spaces between walls along with heating, plumbing, electrical, and trash-disposal systems. Vermin used these spaces to breed and move from unit to unit.

The trend toward central-city disinvestment after the war contrasts sharply with massive new federal subsidies on private, suburban housing.[78] While public mortgage support built new dwellings for white homeowners far from urban pest populations, central-city projects began to decay in the midst of established infestations of cockroaches as well as rats and mice. Cockroaches soon became living incarnations of dwindling public support for low-income, urban housing.

CHANGING PESTICIDE REGIMES AND CHANGING ROACHES

The reputation and effectiveness of DDT declined in tandem with funding for public housing maintenance. In 1947, public housing managers had been using DDT for only two years when inspectors performing local surveys in several housing authorities found "alarming . . . degrees of infestation" with German roaches. The Federal Public Housing Authority responded with a nationwide vermin-control campaign, using methods that, it boasted, had been "perfected during the war" and in Public Health Service experiments.[79]

DDT was the first of the organochlorides to achieve fame and wide use after World War II, but now the Velsicol Company unveiled the first pesticide that would succeed DDT as a tool for cockroach control: chlordane. Ads and consumer reviews promised easier control of a broad spectrum of pests with chlordane, "a brown, syrupy liquid with a wet-wood smell."[80] Consumers and professional pest controllers alike could purchase chlordane sprays and powders. It took up to six days to kill German roaches, but it paralyzed them more quickly and at a lower concentration than DDT.[81] Based on laboratory studies, *Readers' Digest* endorsed chlordane over DDT and other pesticides, and *Consumer Reports* called it "the answer to the housewife's prayer so far as cockroaches are concerned."[82] Promotions for chlordane emphasized its effectiveness and appropriateness for household use by untrained do-it-yourselfers.

Public housing managers seized upon chlordane as a quick fix that made it possible to serve the growing number of apartments built with federal dollars while adding only a limited number of new pest-control staff, if any. As late as 1952, the New York City Housing Authority praised chlordane for cutting labor and other costs of roach control. Trainers told workers that chlordane "made it possible to reduce the number of visits to each apartment each year, thereby decreasing the cost of service. This has been accomplished without any let-down in efficiency or control."[83] Chlordane initially reinforced the notion that modern chemicals could overcome domestic environmental problems and maintain healthy living spaces with little investment of staff or funds.

Problems with chlordane came to light within just a few years of its release for public use, however. By 1949, scientists and regulators raised concerns about its health effects. Chlordane's acute toxicity was only half that of DDT, but the FDA's director of pharmacology, Arnold Lehman, believed it to be five times as toxic over the longer term because the body stored chlordane in fat deposits and the liver. In 1950, Lehman explained to a congressional committee that "if it is used as a household spray, the potential hazard to living in these houses is quite great because of the ability of chlordane to penetrate the skin and because of the . . . possibility of poisoning by inhalation." Although "there are ways of using it safely in the household," Lehman believed it should not be available "in the open market for use in a spray gun by the householder"—in other words, chlordane might be safe only when applied by trained professionals.[84] Federal regulators called for limits on chlordane concentrations sold in over-the-counter treatments and approved the substance for spot treatments only.[85] That is, the user—whether a housewife, maintenance staff, or a hired pest-control operator—must be selective but thorough about where she or he applied the chemical.[86]

Instructions for spot treatment or other precautions were required by law to appear on pesticide labels, but that did not guarantee safe applications by household do-it-yourselfers or by hired pest controllers. Pesticide regulators stressed that federal pesticide laws have "no control over the actual user" of chemicals, particularly in the case of household pesticides—just as misuse was possible with other dangerous but legal products such as automobiles or guns.[87] Some regulators assumed that misuse was the responsibility of the user alone. As one stated of the 1947 law that governed pesticides: "The Federal Insecticide, Fungicide, and Rodenticide Act is a labeling law and not a prohibitory statute"—that is, it was up to the user to follow the label instructions; government would not ban substances that seemed safe to apply according to prescribed procedures.[88]

Systemic factors predisposed some pesticide applicators to misuse, however, affecting not only themselves but also people living in treated homes. Applying too much chemical endangered themselves and their clients, and missing an important harborage had dramatic consequences. Conscientious pest-control technicians knew they must search homes thoroughly, on hands and knees with a flashlight, to find the places where roaches actually hid.[89] The trainers who taught pest-control technicians in the New York City Housing Authority, for example, stressed the importance of targeting applications.[90] Housing authorities were looking for ways to cut costs and labor, however. Under such conditions, technicians might apply excesses of chlordane or other chemicals in places they assumed to harbor roaches, and they might miss hiding places beyond their immediate view—in the recesses of a kitchen appliance or behind a wall-mounted cupboard. Families in public housing and other rental homes often applied their own pesticides in addition to those sprayed by the housing authority staff or a pest-control contractor, especially if they distrusted the staff.[91] Double applications would expose residents to more of the chemical and possibly to multiple chemicals with unknown synergistic effects. Another problem arose as chlordane's reputation for quick, easy roach control spread. An extension entomologist later recalled: "New PCOs [pest-control operators] got into the business because chlordane allowed them to be successful with minimum effort and minimum training." Veterans accused neophytes of careless chemical use—a worrisome practice amid concerns about human health effects.[92] As regulators left domestic pesticide safety as a private responsibility, householders and pest-control operators had to address the consequences for human bodies.

Chlordane helped constitute the ecology of insecticide resistance in multifamily apartment buildings, including public housing. Four elements of resistance are important for understanding that ecology. First, the genetic and physiological mechanisms of resistance are not absolute but do evolve easily. One common and simple mutation results in a mechanism called knockdown resistance or "kdr"; the nervous systems of roaches who possess a kdr mutation are less sensitive than those of susceptible roaches to pyrethrum pesticides, organochlorides, and the organophosphates later adopted for roach control. In another mechanism called metabolic detoxification, an insect produces unusually large amounts of an enzyme that can disarm some of the toxin in the body. In both cases, however, a well-aimed initial dose of pesticides could kill even roaches possessing resistance genes if the population was never exposed to similar poisons.[93] Second, German cockroaches reproduce much more quickly and prolifically than other species in their family, and with each generation exposed to a pesticide, these physiological resistance traits could become more dominant in the population.[94] Third, many German cockroaches exhibited behavioral resistance to certain pesticides, whether or not they possessed the genetic bases for physiological resistance. Behavioral resistance means the ability to detect a pesticide and retreat from treated areas before picking up a lethal dose. Fourth, German cockroaches and many other insects tend to exhibit cross-resistance. This means that the mutations that allowed roaches to resist organochlorides such as chlordane predisposed them to evolve resistance to other pesticides that also worked on the nervous system.[95] These characteristics of roaches interacted with policies, environments, and pest-control practices in multifamily housing to support the evolution of resistance.

Residual pesticides once heralded for providing "preventive" pest control may have contributed to the evolution of chlordane resistance among German cockroaches in environments like multifamily housing. The entomologist Walter Ebeling pointed out that "an insecticide when originally deposited may result in the death of every insect coming in contact with it."[96] In the hours and days after a pest-control technician or housewife first sprayed the panels under the kitchen cabinets with chlordane, the roaches that frequented that part of the kitchen might all die regardless of their genetic endowments. Even roaches bearing genes for resistance might be unable to withstand the high toxic dosage of a fresh residue. As residues decomposed over the course of weeks or months, however, roaches emerged from lairs deep under the kitchen sink or within a wall void, untouched by the earlier spraying, and traipsed across the degraded chemical deposit. It was at this point that resistant roaches' mutations gave them the upper hand over susceptible roaches, securing their offspring dominance in future generations. Ebeling wrote: "When using insecticides with residues of gradually decreasing effectiveness, survival of exposed insects will occur, and some . . . selection of resistant individuals is inevitable." Once resistance became widespread in a population, "the dose required . . . [to overcome resistance] may be hundreds of times greater than that required in normal (susceptible) strains"—a dose too high to apply in human homes.[97] Like Americans in suburban homes, public housing staff relied on residual pesticides for roach control that seemed simple, effective, and safe at the scale of the individual dwelling unit. In practice, however, these chemicals behaved in complex ways in the social and physical environment of public housing.

Multifamily public housing possessed several characteristics that hastened evolution of insecticide resistance in roaches. Housing projects were subject to policies that degraded the physical environment and also strained the schedules of technicians who provided pest control. Amid these conditions, German cockroaches found ample opportunities and places to hide from the strongest doses of chlordane. As local housing authorities strained to limit maintenance costs, staff might do a poor job of inspecting individual units, spraying in obvious areas such as baseboards and beneath appliances, leaving other harborages that teemed with roaches untouched. When roaches later crept across degraded insecticide residues in their movements about a kitchen or bathroom, susceptible individuals died off, leaving those with the genes for resistance to thrive and reproduce. Lax construction and poor maintenance opened up more nooks and crannies in the home where roaches could hide from fresh pesticide deposits—both within individual units and between them in wall voids. Any clutter in the apartments made matters worse, offering additional untreated harborages. Resistance was not only a matter of pesticides selecting the most tenacious roaches; resistant roaches' ecology was deeply interwoven into the management of buildings, which depended upon the politics of public housing itself.

In 1951, pest controllers reported the first observed cases of German cockroach resistance to chlordane and another organochloride called lindane in a few Texas cities.[98] These were not the first instances of physiological resistance to the new pesticides; resistant fly and mosquito populations first appeared at least four years earlier, putting pest controllers and entomologists on notice that problems might arise with other insects.[99] These warning signals failed to change pest-control practices, especially among legions of undertrained exterminators and householders. By 1960 tests confirmed German cockroach resistance to chlordane in cities across the United States. Throughout the 1960s, the University of California entomologist Walter Ebeling conducted a series of experiments that revealed the connections among physiological resistance, behavioral resistance, pest-control practices, and domestic environments in a San Francisco public housing project. The identical units found throughout the Yerba Buena complex allowed for controlled experiments, and in 1965, Ebeling tested a different substance and method in each of the project's seven low-rises, constructed ten years earlier. Ebeling affirmed that when residents or managers sprayed repellent pesticides in individual units, roaches learned to flee into the open wall voids.

In the United States, houses and apartment buildings are commonly built with hollow walls. Cockroaches can move in and out of these hollow walls around utility pipes and conduits and imperfections in building construction. They can breed in the walls in enormous numbers and migrate via voids from one room to another and, in apartment houses, from one apartment to another. This type of distribution is accentuated by the application of insecticides with even a moderate degree of repellency.[100]

Roaches' ability to detect pesticides and retreat into cracks and crevices helped them thrive in public housing. Ebeling surmised that roaches "found new harborages free of insecticides in a wide variety of locations throughout the infested premises" due to the practices of technicians and the condition of the buildings.[101]

The pesticides that replaced chlordane for control of domestic German roaches could heighten evolutionary pressure on the species. In 1960, Arnold Mallis explained that pest-control technicians now turned to "organic phosphate sprays, pyrethrum-synergist sprays, sodium fluoride dusts, and silica aerogel dusts" instead of the organochlorides to which German roaches had evolved resistance.[102] Mallis warned that, except for the old roach salts (sodium fluoride) and the silica aerogels, the other new remedies "will have to be applied more frequently and more carefully if resistant German cockroaches are to be controlled."[103] Ebeling found similar problems in Yerba Buena.[104] Organophosphate pesticides such as malathion or diazinon were gaining popularity for outdoor uses when structural pest controllers began using them for cockroach control. Organophosphates decompose faster than the infamously persistent organochlorides, although many have higher acute toxicities.[105] Organophosphates ramped up selection of resistant roaches when used under conditions like those found in many public housing projects.

German roaches were so adept at learning to avoid residues of organochlorides and organophosphates that the urge to flee residues could override other instincts, such as their preference for dark spaces. In ill-maintained multifamily housing, however, roaches need not settle for a brightly lit space, because treatments seldom reached all their dark hideaways. Many housing projects offered myriad dark, warm, accessible retreats where the technician's sprayer and the resident's aerosol never reached. Ebeling explained: "Some cockroaches may leave treated apartments, and may invade untreated apartments via the wall voids or hallways."[106] A technician might flush roaches from an infested unit into the home of an uninfested neighbor, or the roaches might linger in hollow walls until the residue wore away. The management of the projects thus abetted roaches' changing behaviors and genetics in concert with increasingly repellent pesticides. Ebeling's findings revealed that pesticides applied in individual units actually rendered multifamily buildings more permeable rather than less permeable to cockroaches—at the very moment when community management of pests declined.

German roaches also expanded their range within any given apartment or home as human use of domestic space shifted. Since the days when they had first followed the spread of indoor water connections into homes, cockroaches had preferred to linger where plumbing fixtures made water constantly available, whether by a drip, a leak, or the film of water that remains after use of a sink or shower. Food also helped define their range— the availability of an errant crumb or unground scraps in an in-sink garbage disposal. In the mid-twentieth century, German cockroaches across the United States were adopting new "habits"—occupying an expanding range of spaces within homes, much as they had taken advantage of widespread plumbing in the early twentieth century. Pest controllers blamed this migration on changing patterns of human use of interior space and household appliances. People increasingly brought food into other rooms of the house, for example, eating in front of a living room television instead of in a kitchen or dining room, leaving crumbs. Air conditioners in other rooms also invited roaches when they dripped water.[107] German roaches crawled inside appliances from television sets to blenders to access warm, dark spaces close to food sources.[108] Such patterns characterized most American housing, but they became a more severe problem in apartment buildings, where roaches lurked in hiding spaces in and between units, ready to exploit any new source of food, drink, or shelter.

LINGERING BEDBUGS

Not only roaches but also bedbugs evolved resistance to the miracle chemicals. The first reports of bedbug resistance to DDT came in 1947 from a military barracks in Hawai'i.[109] Entomologists noted a few other resistant populations in the United States in the 1950s and 1960s, such as in a Pittsburgh public housing project in 1957 and, in 1958, in a Denver, Colorado, single-room occupancy hotel that provided housing of last resort to extremely poor residents.[110] Resistance evolved in myriad other locations in the United States and globally—not just to DDT but also to related pesticides, as bedbugs are prone to cross-resistance.[111]

Bedbugs' overall decline brought heightened stigma to the homes and communities where they remained or returned. Robert Usinger, the preeminent American expert on Cimicidae, the bedbug family, called C. *lectularius* "the bug that nobody knows" because so much of the American public denied its presence. Polite and abashed avoidance of the very topic makes it difficult to gauge how many Americans remained infested and how bedbugs were distributed among affluent and poor, rural and urban.[112] In 1954, Arnold Mallis observed: "Although this democratic creature draws no line between the impoverished and the wealthy, its presence is more evident in the poorer quarters since conditions for its survival are more favorable there."[113] Ebeling wrote in 1975: "Bed bugs may still be problems where there are primitive and unsanitary conditions."[114] Well controlled in most areas, bedbugs remained a stigma and a mental and physical menace for the very unfortunate few.

Reformers and pest-control professionals revealed the secrets of some poor communities and individuals that continued to live with bugs. The *New York Sun* reporter and housing advocate Woody Klein populated his 1959 narrative of Harlem tenement life with a variety of pests, including bedbugs. "That first night when I went to bed," Klein recalled of his own stay in the neighborhood, "I began to itch all over. I pulled the string to the light bulb in the ceiling, yanked the sheets off the bed and examined the mattress. It was crawling with bedbugs. . . . Sleep was impossible. . . . It was the worst night I had ever known."[115] Activists from the Nuyorican (New York Puerto Rican) collective the Young Lords published a photo of a toddler who lived in substandard housing covered in bedbug bites to expose conditions in their community amid demands for political change and empowerment.[116] Washington, D.C.–area pest controllers recalled the home of a low-income and seriously ill elderly woman crawling with bedbugs.[117] Anecdotes about bedbugs show that some survived the spread of modern pesticides under conditions where residents lacked community support, whether this manifested in poor access to pest control, unsanitary and poorly maintained homes, insecticide resistance, or a combination of these.

TENACIOUS ROACHES IN CHEMICAL CITIES

The exterminator visited the tenant less frequently than he used to a decade ago, but each of his visits brought a flurry of activity for the roaches. He knew he needed to spray under the kitchen sink. There, a pipe dripped intermittently and the floor beneath it had rotted, opening a moist, inviting harborage for dozens of roaches. What the maintenance staffer did not know, and what he never learned, was that dozens more huddled behind the back panel of the under-sink cabinet. When he sprayed his tank of pesticides under the sink—it was 1962, and he had recently switched to diazinon—most of the roaches there perished. The ones behind the cabinet, however, largely survived. A few emerged from their harborage and into the space under the sink, through the gap around the water pipe, which had never been caulked. They sensed the chemical residue and slipped back along the pipe.

The tenant's kitchen and that of her neighbor were mirror images of one another, sharing a common, hollow wall where each family's water, gas, and electric lines branched off from the main line. Several roaches continued to crawl along the pipe branch to find a similar gap leading into the neighbor's unit. The neighbor had been out at an appointment, and she missed the staffer's visit. He would not be back for months. The roaches passed undeterred into the space under the sink and then out through the loose cabinet door.

Weeks later, some of the roaches wandered back to their old harborage. Most could no longer detect the pesticide deposit under the sink. After walking through the deposit, several of the roaches died. Those that survived had been born to parents that resisted last year's malathion, and they would go on to spawn a new generation of survivors.

In the late 1930s, new public housing projects promised to put good health and modern living within reach for a select segment of poor city-dwellers. The first housing managers made freedom from bedbugs part of that promise. They fulfilled this goal by treating the projects as communities, involving all residents in the improvement of living environments there. The mobility of bedbugs and hydrocyanic acid gas reinforced the notion of home as a fluid space within the public housing community. For managers and residents alike, pest control became part of the collective ethos of public housing, even though communal methods were only chosen for lack of easier means.

When easier means became available, in the form of DDT, residents and managers had no way of knowing how their shared environment would change over the coming decades. For a time, managers and residents looked upon DDT and other new pesticides with optimism about improved health and convenience in their homes. "Good tenant relations" continued to motivate many managers, and residents returned the favor by cooperating with sanitation and spraying components of projects' pest-control programs. Pesticides were sprayed in individual units, but some managers maintained a spirit of community, in part because they knew roaches could spread quickly if tensions between managers and tenants led the latter to hide infestations or refuse to cooperate with control measures. But understanding of the shared environment of public housing soon dwindled as DDT and then chlordane offered seemingly easy fixes for roach problems. Furthermore, the political values that helped inspire the creation of public housing were eclipsed in both material and discursive ways. Housing policy favored not only private housing but also new suburban developments, sapping funding and interest in central-city landscapes and homes. Public housing would no longer be a "paradise," as many in the first cohort of residents saw it. Attitudes and budgets assured degraded living environments even under the best-managed housing authorities.

The new pesticides in many ways reinforced attitudes that favored private over public responsibility for home environments. DDT and chlordane seemed to offer inexpensive, easy, safe, and effective control over household pests. These pesticides changed not only the chemistry of pest control but also its social practice. Promotions for the pesticides promised individual sovereignty over the home environment. Like many technologies marketed to homeowners as well as apartment-dwellers, residual pesticides promised consumers the ability to control domestic environments as independent, private spaces. As Congress sent the lion's share of housing funding to the suburbs, DDT and its relatives looked like an inexpensive way to keep public housing pest-free in the midst of established and thriving pest populations. Optimism about the control of nature extended to control over the home, diminishing the sense that homes—even in multifamily housing—were interconnected ecologies.

German roaches, however, maintained those connections among neighbors, especially as the new pesticides changed their bodies and behaviors. Policy-makers and public housing managers set in motion a process of environmental change favorable to German cockroaches.[118] Despite growing roach problems, public housing remained a cherished resource for many residents who knew the difficulties of the private housing market for low-income people. German cockroaches brought confusion and anger to public housing projects in the postwar years, however. DDT, chlordane, and similar pesticides were hailed in advertisements, store displays, and public discourse as miracle cures. Yet residents saw that cockroaches returned again and again to their own homes. The promises of modern, healthy housing had failed.

4

NORWAY RATS

Back-Alley Ecology in the Chemical Age

A Norway rat emerged from his burrow as dusk fell over Baltimore's east side on an early spring evening in 1937. The air carried a faint scent of food, as well as scents of people, dogs, and cats. The high-board wooden fence surrounding the backyard provided reliable shelter from these minor threats despite its ramshackle condition—perhaps because of it. The rat's gray-brown fur brushed against the fence as he trotted along it, retracing the greasy line left a few inches above the ground by generations of his kin.[1]

He poked his nose under the fence, testing the space with his sensitive whiskers. His whiskers barely grazed the boards, signaling to him that he had more than enough room to pass through. On the other side, the rat found the neighbors' back stairs, atop which sat a bucket of kitchen scraps, its contents lean in these hard times, waiting to be dumped in a busted wooden barrel by the alley. The rat had seen this bucket there before. If he had not, he would have approached much more tentatively. His wariness served him well; new objects in the environment could be traps or poisons.[2]

One of the larger rats on the block, he easily reached the first step with his front paws and bounded up crooked wooden stairs until he reached the bucket and tipped it over. Another large male rat joined him, and the two licked juice from crab shells and nibbled at tiny scraps of meat left inside. Suddenly the light came on in the kitchen and a small dog barked from inside the back screen door. Startled, the rats reared up and squealed. The dog retreated, and the rats fled. They jumped down to the ground, scurried across the yard, and squeezed under the fence and into the alley.

Many of the block's two-hundred-some rats departed their burrows after sunset to eat, drink, and mate. Across the alley, a pregnant female lapped at a tub where rain had collected during a morning shower. She had given birth to five litters of six to nine young in the past year, but many of her pups died young from disease, starvation, or predation. A young rat peeked out from under the rotted and gnawed bottom of a privy-shed door and ducked back inside upon seeing a cat peering down from the back porch. Large adult rats had little to fear from dogs or cats, however.[3] Another young rat gnawed with her strong jaws and ever-growing teeth at the edges of a hole in the wooden platform of the back porch, enlarging the hole enough to squeeze inside.

Several rats made their homes in the house's cavity walls, rotting floors, and crumbling cellar. They enjoyed better access to stored food than their outdoor cousins, for the pantry consisted of open shelving without cabinet doors. They also transmitted fleas, mites, parasites, and bacteria to one another more easily than their backyard cousins. Indoor rats faced more frequent confrontations with human residents, which often proved fatal for rats, and sometimes injurious, infectious, or deadly to people.[4]

During the Great Depression, World War II, and the postwar years, city-dwellers across the United States struggled with rats and other pests supported by degraded housing and neighborhood environments. Authorities from both public and private sectors urged cities to support rat-proofing of ill-maintained homes. Still, many Americans attempted to control pests by applying pesticides in and around their homes, especially after 1945, when effective new chemicals became available for killing insects and rodents. Amid the pro-pesticide zeitgeist of the postwar years, some scientists and health advocates promoted an explicitly ecological and antichemical approach to pest control that was also funded by public resources. In the 1940s, Baltimore became the setting for two public health experiments that seemed to represent polar opposite views of rodent control. The first aimed to test a new chemical rodenticide and a community-based scheme to distribute the poison throughout the city. The other, called the Rodent Ecology Project, worked alongside a housing rehabilitation program called the Baltimore Plan and hypothesized that changes to the residential environment would reduce rat populations more sustainably without the use of chemicals. The experiments brought attention to Baltimore's rats from government, scientists, and private organizations—locally and nationally—and inflamed tensions between partisans of chemical and ecological rat control. Ecological pest controllers shared an important characteristic with pesticide supporters, however: both believed that science could overcome degraded environmental conditions.

With their emphases on science, rat controllers in Baltimore, regardless of their methods, were often blind to the political and community elements of rat infestation. Even "ecological" views of urban nature could rely on a kind of reductionism, and "reductionist" chemical approaches sometimes grappled with complexities ignored by ecological thinkers—though they also suffered their own blind spots. Ecologists and their public health allies found themselves particularly ill-equipped to understand three factors in the ecology of urban rats: the role of human communities in rat control; the relationships between public and private spaces in infested neighborhoods; and pests' ability to move between these spaces. Ecology's promises of healthy city environments proved nearly as elusive as the promises of postwar pesticides.

THE NATURAL HISTORY OF URBAN RAT CONTROL

Rodents' role in human disease and suffering has prompted collective interventions for centuries if not millennia. Mongolian nomads avoided marmots they suspected of serving as disease reservoirs, and some European cities killed off rats during bubonic plague outbreaks long before scientists discovered the bacillus they carried.[5] Folklore from across Europe and Asia mentions civic campaigns against rats, although the rats may be metaphorical additions to fact-based stories such as that of Hameln, Germany's Pied Piper.[6] Such campaigns remained sporadic in the United States until the early twentieth century, when microbiology affirmed rodents' role in human typhus and bubonic plague cases.[7]

In the absence of public rat control in homes, the job fell to private households and hired help. Popular methods included keeping a house cat, repairing holes in walls, laying out snaptraps and baits poisoned with arsenic or hemlock, or simply attacking rats with a makeshift weapon—though rats sometimes became aggressive toward those who wielded clubs or brooms against them.[8] Mom-and-pop "rat-catcher" businesses offered goods and services ranging from secret poison formulations to visits from a rodent-killing terrier.[9] New York's nineteenth-century rat-catcher Richard Toner dazzled rats with a lantern and grabbed the stunned animals with studded tongs he designed himself, charging fifteen dollars for every hundred rats caught. He profited a second time by selling the rats that survived to trainers of rat-catching dogs. Toner preferred live capture over rodenticides because poisoned rats could die, rot, and attract other vermin within a home's cavity walls.[10] Private control activities like these did little to address the systemic and ecological factors that supported rodents, though, even when rat-catchers carried away hundreds of them.

Public health agencies became active in rat control during the first outbreaks of plague and typhus after confirmation of rats' role in those diseases. Early campaigns welcomed the help of some citizens in controlling the environment, while imposing environmental control on others. When several San Franciscans died of bubonic plague in 1907, middle-class Anglo residents led efforts to trap rats and improve garbage collections.[11] Meanwhile, health enforcers paved yards, invaded homes, and banned activities such as chicken-raising in Chinese and Italian immigrant communities thought to harbor infected rats.[12] Like health officials in San Francisco, Baltimore's rat controllers engaged some residents in environmental reform while excluding others, but divisions in Baltimore were not based on race or ethnicity alone.

After emergency campaigns in San Francisco, officials at both federal and municipal levels took steps toward making rat control a regular government function. Aside from their role in epidemics, rats brought more day-to-day health, safety, and economic woes to the people whose homes and communities they shared. Rats fouled pantries, gnawed holes in buildings, and chewed electrical wiring—sometimes leading to fires—causing up to $240 million in damage each year within the United States by 1932.[13] In addition to disease hazards from rats' ectoparasites (such as fleas and lice), further research revealed that rats also spread lesser-known pathogens through bites, excreta, or direct or indirect contact. Symptoms long associated with rat bites—swollen limbs and faces, lockjaw, spasms, fever, and death—were caused by specific pathogens that came to be known as rat-bite fever.[14] Rat attacks on infants and small children were infrequent but horrifying and sometimes deadly. As these incidents attained the status of urban legend, parents in infested homes lost sleep worrying about their children's safety.[15] Health agencies increasingly intervened in rat hazards, poisoning and trapping rodents as well as changing the environments where they thrived.

Environment helped determine the degree to which rats endangered humans. Even before the wide acceptance of germ theory, Richard Toner sensed that the danger of a rat bite depended on the rat's location—those "that feed in the corn warehouse" posed little risk, but a bite from "one of them fellers what feed on hotel swill or slaughter-house garbage" could necessitate amputation of a bitten limb or even lead to a deadly fever.[16] Toner declared rat bites "poisonous" in 1876, long before knowledge of germ theory, much less rat-bite fever, became popularized. Studies in the 1930s suggested that indoor rats posed greater dangers to humans than those outdoors, and not only because of their proximity. Ectoparasites multiplied more rapidly on indoor rats than outdoor-dwellers. Thus researchers suspected that indoor rats exposed humans to greater risks for bubonic plague and typhus.[17] Baltimore's rat populations spanned alleys, backyards, and homes—along with such commercial areas as warehouses, ports, and railroads—and their use of territory in residential environments is key to the story of scientists and housing there.

The U.S. Public Health Service pursued a model rat-proofing program in Baltimore in the early 1930s to overhaul environments that harbored rodents. Staff installed galvanized iron sheathing over gnawed door bottoms and around pipe insertion points. They unearthed inadequate house foundations and shored them up with new concrete and fourteen-gauge wire mesh extending two feet below ground. They removed trellises under raised porches to eliminate hiding places. Meanwhile, other staff poisoned burrows with carbon monoxide and cyanide gases and placed traps around visible holes. Lab workers examined vast heaps of dead rats—and many live ones as well—for infectious disease.[18] Such labor-intensive efforts could not be sustained, however, or extended to the thousands of blocks in Baltimore where homes harbored rats.

Rats were only one of many hazards that menaced Baltimore residents in their homes and neighborhoods. Residents of substandard housing also suffered high rates of tuberculosis, burns from malfunctioning stoves, and exposure to water-borne disease in the twenty-six thousand privies that still stood in the city's backyards.[19] To understand rats' place in the history and the ecology of Baltimore's neighborhoods, we must trace the roots of housing reform there back to the 1930s.

ACTIVISM IN BALTIMORE: THE BALTIMORE PLAN'S ROOTS
AND DOMESTIC ENVIRONMENTALISM

By the mid-1930s, several studies had documented poor housing conditions in Baltimore, particularly in African-American areas. A 1933 report by the Maryland Joint Committee on Housing marked black neighborhoods as hazards, warning that infection could spread to white and affluent areas via the bodies of domestic workers, food handlers, laundresses—and rats. The committee seemed to draw parallels between blacks and rats: given "the well-known prevalence of rats and other vermin in Baltimore," the committee wrote, "the effects on the spread of contagion should be considered."[20] Meanwhile, Ira deA. Reid, an African-American sociologist who shared W. E. B. Du Bois's political spirit, blamed segregation practices for depriving Baltimore's blacks of healthy housing. Blacks only lived in homes "at the last stage of residential occupancy," after a long succession of white occupants had subjected dwellings to years of depreciation, leaving them obsolete and prone to infestation.[21]

These reports brought little action by authorities, but in 1936 a young, white social worker named Frances Morton conducted her master's thesis research in the city's fifth and tenth wards, home mostly to low-income African-Americans and some poor whites. Morton, who hailed from one of the city's more privileged districts, found landlord neglect, crime, crowding, and the highest tuberculosis death rate in the city. The *Baltimore Sun* picked up the story and published a series of reports on the city's "architectural gems."[22] Aided by this publicity, Morton rallied a network of professionals and middle-class reformers, and a few low-income Baltimoreans, to root out corruption in the city's new public housing authority and demand the Health Department's support for a new housing code in 1938. Among other provisions, the new code made Baltimore one of the first U.S. cities to mandate rat-proofing of all homes.[23] This code became the basis of a campaign called the Baltimore Plan, which, in turn, became the basis of one of the city's rat-control experiments after the war.

Morton and her network incorporated as the Citizens' Planning and Housing Association, hoping to become "the city's conscience" in matters of housing.[24] What Morton and the association conceived of in 1938 differed from later redevelopment programs that came to be known— and often despised by African-American communities and other local activists—as "urban renewal." Baltimore's health commissioner, Huntington Williams, helped lead a national committee of health officials that devised housing appraisal methods later used in urban renewal programs across the United States.[25] Morton, however, insisted on an approach to housing rehabilitation gentler than later urban renewal programs notorious for displacing African-American communities. Families were allowed to stay in their homes during and after rehabilitation, and code enforcers resorted to demolition only in rare cases. Morton observed: "Had the terms of the [housing code] been immediately and universally enforced in 1940, thousands of Baltimoreans would have been homeless."[26] The Baltimore Plan's advocates hoped that current residents would enjoy the health benefits of rehabilitation, unlike communities torn asunder by urban renewal.

The Baltimore Plan's approach to improving housing quality would—unbeknownst to its founders at the time—also suit emerging scientific thought on the ecology of urban rats. In most cities, housing inspectors responded to individual resident complaints about rats or other hazards, resulting in enforcement proceedings against individual property owners.[27] Yet rat populations spanned entire blocks. When housing courts required only one property owner to control rats, rats on the rest of the block continued to thrive and gradually reinvaded the improved lot. Instead of sending inspectors to individual properties, Frances Morton and Huntington Williams hoped to send inspectors and sanitary police to enforce the code on an entire block of housing at once.[28] Williams heralded the plan and the new code for its potential to "remove the last of the rat-harboring [privy] nuisances from the back yards of Baltimore."[29] The Baltimore Plan's founders thought little about rat *territories* at the time, but the block-based scale of the program later became important for the work of both communities and scientists endeavoring to control rats.

During the late years of the Depression and through World War II, the association and the Health Department struggled to apply the new housing code to Baltimore's two-thousand-some blocks of substandard housing. City judges had little time to devote to the multitude of cases that block-by-block code enforcement brought to court. Furthermore, materials and labor remained in short supply during the war; even sanitation services became erratic.[30] The Housing Act of 1937 had promised modern, healthy public housing, but the mayor's appointees—cronies from the real estate industry—ran the housing authority so poorly that many eligible families declined to apply. Rumors circulated that the public housing environment caused rheumatism, and resident activists clashed with managers over blame for a bedbug infestation. Limited numbers of public units were available for black families.[31] Public housing failed to deliver all Baltimoreans into healthy home environments. Block after block of substandard private housing remained, awaiting repair and teeming with rats.

Low-income African-American residents endured the worst conditions. Sixty thousand blacks arrived in Baltimore in the 1930s and 1940s, along with thirty thousand whites. New and established African-American residents made up one-fifth of the population, but only one-sixteenth of the city's residential space was open to them, according to Frances Morton. In 1944, she reported: "There are no vacancies for Negroes today—war workers or otherwise."[32] Landlords often carved up row houses built for one family into two or three units.[33] The Federal Housing Authority ramped up efforts to provide war-industry housing, but again, few units went to black workers.[34] With few housing choices, many blacks settled for ill-maintained dwellings that put them in close contact with rats. Still, blacks resisted poor housing and health conditions through political and civic activism and also their own physical labor. Some middle-class and low-income African-Americans joined the Citizens' Planning and Housing Association to demand investment in healthy housing and protection against exploitative landlords. Some also protested the new public housing agency's restrictive policies and systemic neglect.[35] Others engaged in community self-help projects, including neighborhood cleanups and gardening activities. Their work helped control rats, but black communities alone could not eliminate the ecological and political forces that supported infestation, including racial segregation.

By the 1930s, many African-Americans in Baltimore expressed a kind of domestic environmentalism through rat control and other civic activities, just as a small but growing number of scientists also began thinking about rats ecologically. Many neighborhoods celebrated National Negro Health Week, the culminating annual event in a movement for self-help and community betterment conceived by Booker T. Washington in 1914. The movement rallied blacks to promote health by, among other things, managing urban nature, including household pests. Washington had long encouraged African-Americans to plant gardens so that "more of nature's beauty shall pervade the home and its surroundings" and lift up the health and morals of the family.[36] Infestation degraded domestic beauty, morals, and health. By the 1930s, pest-control campaigns were among the chief activities of the week; thousands of communities across the United States, including Baltimore, organized rat- and fly-control campaigns.[37] Participants managed bodily health by exercising human agency over urban nature.[38] Like Washington himself, his movement opened itself to criticism about a weak and accommodating stance toward racial oppression. Health Week activities de-emphasized confrontation with landlords, government, and other authorities, despite the role these powerful groups played in perpetuating environmental degradation and injustice.

Baltimore's black newspaper, the *Afro-American*, also promoted rat control as an expression of good citizenship. Columnist Dwight Holmes noted in 1944 that rats "can be seen walking about our streets and alleys at almost any time of the day or night." Holmes lamented that Baltimoreans often went on crusades against rats, but "just as soon as the crusade ends they will be as thick as ever . . . if we clean up and stay clean, Baltimore will be a ratless town within six months." Holmes insisted that poverty was no excuse for infestation, writing that infestation "is a moral problem and in community life it becomes a social one. One dirty yard can spoil a neighborhood."[39] Many black activists strived to steward Baltimore's environment, making it healthier and more expressive of community and domestic values, despite constraints on their power to make dramatic changes.

Community efforts proved insufficient to control rats, however. Commitment not only from civic groups but also from the public and private sectors would be necessary to address overarching forces that supported rats: disinvestment, housing discrimination, and inadequate solid waste systems. Frances Morton had conceived the Baltimore Plan to apply public and citizen power to housing problems, but the plan languished for lack of funds, labor, and materials. While residents endured rats and substandard housing, advocates for healthy housing hoped to resume reform efforts after the war.

RATS IN PUBLIC AND PRIVATE SPACES: THE CASE OF CHICAGO

Other cities also grappled with rats during the Depression and World War II. In the 1930s and 1940s, for example, rat controllers in Chicago squabbled over public and private space and responsibility. The stakeholders there differed from those in Baltimore, but a digression into Chicago's story will help shed light on three key factors for Baltimore's story: the role of human communities; relationships between public and private spaces; and pests' ability to move between these spaces.

The Depression brought a decline in city services in Chicago—as in Baltimore—which in turn gave rats ample opportunities to invade homes. The city slashed up to 75 percent of health inspector positions in some distressed districts.[40] Basic code violations went unchecked, even as the Board of Health urged stricter rat-proofing provisions. In 1934, the affluent, white housewives of the Woman's City Club of Chicago noted that "a lean garbage pail makes a hungry and bold rat." In prosperous years, rats found plentiful scraps in alley trash bins, but when families wasted nary a morsel, desperate rats seemed to home in on homes.[41] Hull-House surveyors found a family huddled into two rooms of a tiny basement flat having abandoned the third room where rats climbed in through a broken window. A woman living near Hull-House told an activist that she feared bringing her baby outside because of the rats, but conditions indoors seemed little better: she hung food from the ceiling on strings to protect it from rodents.[42] Tenants reported seeking help from both landlords and the city but seldom hired exterminators on their own, perhaps because they saw housing codes as their ultimate recourse.[43] With the decline in enforcement, however, authorities did little to stop rats from entering human homes.

The city had cut its budget for trained inspectors, but federal work-relief money could fund the hiring of unemployed men to exterminate rats in both private and public spaces. In 1933, the Woman's City Club and the Board of Health secured a Civil Works Administration grant to do just that. The pilot project, centered near Hull-House, earned praise from residents. Building on the pilot's success, new funding from the Works Progress Administration (WPA) paid one thousand jobless men, most with no prior extermination experience, to serve additional neighborhoods.[44]

The program provided a unique opportunity to enlist community support and blanket entire rat territories with poison. Typical extermination activities targeted only individual private properties or public spaces, leaving a patchwork of spaces where rats could still thrive. Wary tenants often closed their doors to rat controllers, allowing rats to lurk indoors unscathed. Thanks to the program's early successes, however, residents "urged [workers] to place the poisoned bait throughout entire premises, including the interior of individual homes." "Such co-operative efforts on the part of private citizens produced very good results," because baiters could reach every rat hole, from backyards to basements.[45] Chicago's success inspired work-relief offices from New York to San Francisco to hire jobless men to poison rats.[46]

Where health officials saw the triumph of civic cooperation, industry leaders saw government infringement upon tradesmen's turf. William Buettner, president of the National Association of Exterminators and Fumigators, bristled at the insinuation that any "transient" could walk off the street and catch rats.[47] He insisted that consumers must take responsibility for infestation in their own homes: "There is no reason why the tax-payers . . . should pay for this work on the basis of rats being a 'public' nuisance."[48] Work-relief programs and the exterminator industry thus launched a turf war, much to rats' benefit. Chicago exterminators established a Committee on Pest Control Activities to assert their right to business on private property.[49] When the Chicago Chamber of Commerce backed the committee in 1938, the WPA cut off funding, against the pleadings of Chicago health officials. Meanwhile, the National Association of Exterminators and Fumigators successfully lobbied the federal government to cancel funding for all city rat-control programs.[50]

A few wily rats had survived five years of baiting in Chicago, and when the WPA halted the baiting program, their offspring "multiplied and swarmed over Chicago's districts without hindrance."[51] Meanwhile, the WPA campaign had done little to shore up crumbling homes. Residents feared for their health and safety as the rat population rebounded. Four children were bitten in May 1940 alone, and one of them, an African-American toddler named Carrie Bell, died of rat-bite fever. The *Defender*, Chicago's black newspaper, wrote that families like the Bells had been left vulnerable by the diversion of "billions [of dollars] . . . for war to kill men" rather than rats.[52] The city coroner called a blue-ribbon jury to investigate, recommending a new citywide rodent-control program, for which the City Council allocated five thousand dollars later in 1940.

The coroner called for a "preventive" program, but workers mostly gassed or dusted rat burrows with poison. The new program rekindled industry leaders' ire.[53] The National Association of Exterminators and Fumigators called on members to boycott travel to Chicago and any other city that offered free pest-control services, condemning "the use of public funds in competing with private enterprise."[54] In Chicago, other local businesses again backed the industry, leading to a new compromise with health officials. Publicly funded rat control was "limited to alleys and other public places."[55] Private homes would again be off-limits to public rat controllers.

The new spatial compromise and the city's failure to enforce the housing code created habitats where rats could breed undisturbed and left low-income households unprotected from rats. Rats exploited the fragmentation of public and private property. "When [the rat] realizes that other rats have been killed or threatened, it is quick to seek a safer locality," a health officer explained. Furthermore, "the rat may burrow into the ground or under a sidewalk or building only a few feet from the alley line and continue its existence unmolested."[56] Many families refused—or felt unable to pay for—private extermination, so domestic spaces became a "no man's land" for rat control.[57] Staff estimated that the proportion of all rats living in alleys declined from 90 percent to 40 percent; the missing rodents most likely migrated onto private premises.[58] As the state and businesses carved up urban space, rats resisted containment to either public or private territories. Families in poor housing suffered under the compromise as rat bites continued to increase. Chicagoans suffered 250 bites each year after the war, with several cases resulting in infections.[59]

In the first five months of 1943, more than twenty rat bites occurred in a four-block area near Hull-House, home to six hundred African-American and Mexican-American families. The community became a rare site of cooperation among the state, industry, and civic groups. The U.S. Department of the Interior hired private exterminators to gas rat burrows; women's clubs and Hull-House helped families acquire appropriate garbage cans and clean up lawns; and mothers planted vegetable and flower gardens in their place.[60] Elsewhere in Chicago, rats continued to enjoy free rein through the 1940s.

While industry leaders obstructed a valued program, government agencies fell down on their own duties to protect residents in their home environments, particularly in code enforcement and the maintenance of healthy housing. Buettner asked why the WPA didn't have work-reliefers haul away debris or repair homes to make their walls less permeable to rodents. He argued that a division of duties between private rat control and public refuse collection would have made each of the tasks more effective in permanently reducing rat populations.[61] One of Chicago's leading exterminators, Hugo Hartnack, agreed with Buettner, explaining that "rat campaigns with the purpose of killing rats are largely useless, because fecundity is the rat's main weapon. . . . The right kind of community effort is valuable. I mean by this, uninterrupted daily efforts, ratproofing, informing, keeping clean."[62] The *Tribune* agreed that as long as garbage went uncollected and homes unrepaired, rat-catcher salaries wasted public resources.[63]

The private exterminator industry also sought to make positive and preventive contributions to urban rat control in the 1940s; its stance toward government-supported rat control was not only oppositional or even primarily so.[64] The industry participated in a multiagency national urban rat campaign in the late 1940s and supported the adoption of model local programs. Local programs raised awareness of rats and their hazards among citizens and business owners, and often helped ramp up efforts to enforce housing codes against negligent landlords. Many private property owners chose to hire pest-control professionals rather than perform rat-control tasks themselves, benefiting local exterminator firms. Pest-control professionals lent their expertise to health officials conducting rat control on public property.[65] Private exterminator firms emphasized divisions of territory and responsibility in determining their support for public rat-control programs.

In 1940s Baltimore, conflicts did not pit exterminator firms against government-funded rat-baiters as they did in Chicago. Still, discord in Chicago echoed difficulties in Baltimore over community participation; divisions between different urban spaces; and rats' ability to transcend and take advantage of fragmented human territories. Furthermore, Chicago's public baiting programs failed to alter rat habitats and the larger problem of housing neglect and disinvestment that led housing to decay—the very problem the Baltimore Plan aimed to correct.

THE PROMISE AND PERILS OF COMMUNITY RAT POISONING

Baltimore's rats became the target of a poisoning campaign, one that brought federal, local, university, and community resources together in a search for an effective rat poison. The new poisoning campaign sought to simplify rat control in anticipation of wartime emergencies, but it engaged the community in complex and important ways. Like Chicago's program, it failed to rat-proof homes; meanwhile, the Baltimore Plan lay dormant. Military agencies worried that pests might hinder the war effort—or worse. Baltimore's teeming rat population seemed both a source of risk and the perfect test case for new poisons. The National Research Council (NRC) coordinated testing of new poisons for use against mosquitoes in the South Pacific, lice in Europe, and rats at home and abroad. The Rockefeller Foundation, which supported the research, explained that "there was fear that the enemy might resort to germ warfare, using rats to spread Bubonic plague." Furthermore, "rats were eating huge quantities of . . . grain at a time when food was so short as to be rationed." The NRC "sought the most efficient wholesale way of destroying this tough and wary animal," but from its perspective, rat-proofing would proceed too slowly to protect Americans from germ warfare.[66] Wartime shortages and trade obstructions had constricted the supply of time-tested poisons like arsenicals and red squill, so emergency rat control would require a new chemical.

In 1942, the NRC tapped physiologist Curt Richter of the Johns Hopkins Medical School, by all accounts a genius of animal studies, to find that chemical. The challenge in developing raticides lies in finding quick-acting toxins that wary rats cannot learn to avoid and that do not kill humans or pets who accidentally ingest them.[67] Richter's studies used rats to investigate the connection between nutrition and sense of taste. This research led him to test an industrial by-product called phenyl thiourea that had given the factory air a bitter taste for some DuPont employees. Richter found his lab rats unable to taste it, however.[68] Exposed DuPont workers appeared to suffer no ill effects, but Richter's lab rats died of pulmonary edema. Their deaths put an end to the civilian study but revealed a potential raticide.

Wild Norway rats possess more taste buds than laboratory-bred strains of the same species, allowing them to detect phenyl thiourea.[69] Richter tested related chemicals on wild rats caught near the medical school—in an area that happened to coincide with Frances Morton's study. A derivative named alpha-naphthyl thiourea (ANTU) killed wild rats quickly and escaped detection by their sensitive palates. Some pet dogs died in the field trials, but Richter insisted that in most nontarget animals, including humans, ANTU would induce vomiting before doing any damage. Rats are physiologically unable to vomit so cannot purge the toxin. ANTU's self-emetic property convinced Richter of its safety for use in human communities. DuPont was happy to gain a market for the by-product.[70]

Richter's ANTU studies seemed purely reductive at first, testing only the poison's effect on rats without considering their ecology. He also tested the human community's ability to steward its environment, however. The city Bureau of Street Cleaning initially provided the labor for trials, but residents stepped in when public resources could not cover the whole city. Volunteers led small community cleanups and monitored rats, querying householders about recurring infestations and distributing bait. Richter tried to understand rat territories, noting that "rats seemed to circulate freely between yards and alleys and often between houses and cellars, but rarely between blocks."[71] He had volunteers organize at the scale of the block, using rat territorial units to coordinate the poison trials and increasing engagement with low-income communities.

The participation of one African-American school gave Baltimore's black newspaper the chance to spotlight the problem rat poison could not solve: the racially segregated and unjust housing market. In 1943, students at the segregated Coleridge-Taylor School constructed traps that would help Richter collect fifty thousand wild test subjects. The *Afro-American* noted the link between living conditions and infestation—"Baltimore's housing problem and rat problem came up about the same time"—but observing the house-shaped traps, it joked, "the rat housing [problem] is solved." The newspaper noted with irony that "there will be no special houses for white or black rats."[72]

Volunteer involvement in the ANTU field trials became a double-edged sword for residents. On the one hand, community involvement diffused authority and made it easier for householders to take an active role in environmental management. When volunteers replaced municipal bureaucrats and laborers, they assumed greater power over their own blocks and homes and gained more immediate access to baiting materials. By late 1945, more than fifteen hundred citizens monitored some twenty-eight hundred blocks in the most densely populated areas of Baltimore.[73] On the other hand, the program gave volunteers license to coerce and blame their neighbors; Richter's secretary collected names of noncompliant families to report in the *Baltimore Sun*.[74] If Richter's assumptions about ANTU's safety had been wrong, he would have endangered hundreds of thousands of people and pets as community members were entrusted to handle and distribute a little-tested poison.

Richter saw communities as the responsible parties for rat infestation and assumed that infestation reflected residents' tolerance of pests. He made little comment about the disinvestment and segregation that created a generous niche for rats. Long sequestered in his lab and unfamiliar with the community surrounding Johns Hopkins, Richter blanched at the conditions he found during field trials. He even charged that "in these heavily rat infested districts most people apparently accepted rat bites as being inevitable."[75] He believed that the poor could and must do something about Baltimore's rats, ignoring forces beyond their control that supported infestation.[76]

Richter was quick to blame, but he also helped secure public aid for those who suffered most with rats. The NRC had charged him with averting the threat of germ warfare and food shortages, but he discovered far homelier health problems just beyond the university gates. Plague or typhus could ravage entire cities or regions, spreading beyond the homes or blocks where rat populations were concentrated. Baltimore doctors did report a handful of rat-borne typhus cases each year, signaling a potential threat; four cases had been fatal since 1935.[77] But Richter also found that hundreds of residents suffered rat bites and attacks, with effects ranging from small scrapes to serious infections to death. In just the neighborhood surrounding Johns Hopkins hospital—a primarily African-American area that Johns Hopkins often subjected to health studies—residents had suffered ninety-three rat bites in the previous four years. Furthermore, the environment in which these residents encountered rats mattered: many had rats living in the walls, floors, and basements of their homes, not just their backyards and alleys. Residents who came into contact with rats in their homes often contracted salmonellosis, leptospirosis, or rat-bite fever—germs unlikely to cause epidemics the way plague or typhus might.[78] Richter worried about these narrow, endemic effects of rats on the poor in their homes—not just rats' potential to cause widespread contagion.

The poison program at first glance appeared wholly reductionist, an effort to simplify a complex social and ecological problem with a chemical solution, but it brought a mix of burdens and benefits to target neighborhoods. It disciplined infested communities, much like crackdowns on immigrant communities in San Francisco in 1907. Richter placed residents at risk by distributing ANTU when he still had little knowledge of its effects on humans. ANTU also gave residents a sense of power and access to technology, however. Rather like Negro Health Week activists, Richter called for the exertion of human agency to manage urban nature and domestic space. Like Chicago's popular WPA program, ANTU allowed volunteers to "see the results of their efforts almost immediately," inspiring high morale.[79] Richter drew attention away from the distant risk of epidemics and toward immediate, endemic problems that menaced the poor. He failed to hold landlords or city policies culpable for harboring rats, much less the racism that consigned blacks to the city's worst housing. Yet he did give residents material resources and potent roles in managing their blocks and homes. Resident involvement ensured that the program encompassed dwelling interiors, spaces that were private, sensitive, and crucial for alleviating rat-borne health threats. Residents used their knowledge of domestic landscapes to distribute poisons to every nook and cranny, much like Chicago's WPA program. Richter believed poisoning campaigns would fail if they did not bait all indoor spaces, including cellars that harbored many rats.[80] Only with resident cooperation could Richter ensure that indoor as well as outdoor spaces received treatment.

Richter's use of rat poison brought him into conflict with Health Commissioner Huntington Williams, however. Richter refused to disclose the chemical formula of ANTU to Williams. In 1943, two children in the Eastern Health District ingested the poison. Unable identify the content of ANTU, doctors could not administer an antidote and had to pump the children's stomachs. Amid criticisms from Williams, the lame-duck mayor, Howard Jackson, withdrew the twenty-five-thousand dollars he had promised to Richter's campaign, and a City Council member demanded an investigation into Richter's rift with Williams. "The seriousness of the rat plague in Baltimore permits no dilly dallying," the member scolded. The new mayor, Theodore McKeldin, reinstated the twenty-five-thousand-dollar allocation and demanded Williams's cooperation, while Richter gave assurances that ANTU "was probably the least toxic of all" pesticides. Still, Williams was slow to cooperate; the health commissioner had pressed for the adoption of the Baltimore Plan before the war, and he hoped to resume the plan soon.[81] Williams believed that systematic enforcement of the new housing code would do more to control rats than any poison, while also alleviating other problems—from tuberculosis to criminality.

Johns Hopkins leaders soon initiated a new academic program linking pest control and health with ecological theory. Influenced by funding opportunities and the cachet of ecological science, administrators proposed a program to study mammals' and birds' roles as disease vectors, akin to medical entomology and game management.[82] The university shifted the institutional home of its rodent research. "Dr. Richter is a member of the School of Medicine," funders at the Rockefeller Foundation explained, "but rat control is a problem of public health, and the Johns Hopkins authorities decided that responsibility . . . should be transferred to the University's School of Hygiene and Public Health."[83] While medicine implied a focus on individual bodies, public health connoted interest in the whole environment.[84]

THE RODENT ECOLOGY PROJECT AND THE BALTIMORE PLAN

The School of Public Health began the Rodent Ecology Project in 1944, adding two young zoologists to the faculty: Dr. John Emlen, who had assisted with Richter's ANTU trials, and Dr. David Davis. Dr. John Calhoun came on in 1945. At first, it seemed that their work would complement Richter's experiments, and Richter served as an adviser for the project. Emlen, however, had worked with Aldo Leopold at the University of Wisconsin and embraced the eminent ecologist's teachings, which stressed that management of wildlife required genuine changes to animals' environments. Emlen remarked: "Although initially quite impressed with [Richter's] ambitious ANTU poison program . . . I was a solid convert to the ideas I had absorbed from Aldo Leopold back in Madison."[85] Davis's background in disease ecology made him even more skeptical about rodenticides than Emlen.[86] Ecology soon dominated rat-control discourse at Hopkins.

Early findings affirmed the ecologists' concerns about rodenticides. As Emlen and Davis tracked populations following a baiting campaign, they found that poisoning killed only 60 percent of rats on a block, and a block's population could recover within six to twelve months.[87] Resident complaints shot up 60 percent between 1943 and 1944, the largest single-year increase in at least ten years.[88] "Killing procedures," the Rockefeller Foundation reported, "merely make room for more rats to grow up and actually increase the yield of rat flesh per acre per year," and besides, "killing them proved an almost endless, tedious, highly repetitive, and expensive job."[89]

Emlen, Davis, and Calhoun found Baltimore's neighborhood environments ideally suited to rats. An initial census estimated that four hundred thousand rats lived in Baltimore, although the scientists admitted that their method counted mostly residents of outdoor burrows and probably missed many indoor rats.[90] Rats seemed to prosper in row houses, the dominant residential landscape found throughout Baltimore. Calhoun observed rats ranging freely from property to property across open backyards and alleys littered with construction debris.[91] "Wall fences of rotting wood" did more to shelter rats than to keep them out. Rats hid in other structures standing in backyards and alleys, including rickety "sheds attached to the rear of more substantial buildings." Thousands of privies, relics of landlord neglect, property-owner resistance, and the slow advance of sewers continued to harbor rats on many blocks. A Rockefeller Foundation report noted: "The broken floors, littered yards, sagging fences, and accumulated refuse provided ample harborage and places of escape from pursuers; the open garbage cans, kitchen shelves, and general insanitation provided plenty of food."[92] Funders and administrators boasted that these scientists "broadened [ideas of rat control] to include environmental factors." By implication, Richter's ideas had focused too narrowly on rat bodies rather than on the conditions that supported them.[93]

Initial data showed that infestation on any block correlated most closely not with human population or the rent that tenants paid, but the number of dwellings in need of major repairs. This study implied that rehabilitating dwellings could slash rat numbers.[94] As the war ended, Emlen, Davis, Calhoun (and their staff and graduate students) rethought the rat problem: once an emergency, rats now raised the question of how humans might use ecology to improve health over the long term.

Davis, who became project director in late 1945, applied ecological theory and research to support a nonchemical approach to rat control. His thinking dovetailed with that of health and housing reformers anticipating the Baltimore Plan's revival. He predicted that housing rehabilitation would not only improve human health generally, it would also "alter the balance [of population and environment] permanently." Rodenticides merely brought "temporary changes" to rat populations.[95] Davis did agree with Richter on one matter: the city block was the unit of rat territory. In a "homing" experiment, kibble dyed to turn rats' feces blue seemed to confirm that rats seldom ranged past their home block.[96] Furthermore, Davis observed that "when a market burned, hundreds of rats remained to die."[97] Ninety percent of rats released on unfamiliar blocks died or wandered away.[98] These findings gave ecological cachet to the Baltimore Plan's block-by-block rehabilitation scheme and seemed to affirm that rats would not simply flee to neighboring areas following code enforcement.

Richter's poisoning program continued for a time, but former supporters grew wary of it.[99] The National Research Council worried that volunteers might cause more accidental poisonings.[100] When authority for rat control shifted from Street Cleaning to the Health Department, officials denied Richter's requests to distribute more poison.[101] Richter complained about Davis's use of media to promote ecological rat control: he "has been sounding off in the press and on the radio . . . condemning the use of poisons and traps and advocating environmental sanitation as the only worthwhile method."[102] A convert to hands-on community work, Richter insinuated that Davis was "content to sit in his office simply dispensing advice about . . . eliminating sources of food and places of harborage." Furthermore, he called rat-proofing "purely defensive," insisting that rats required an offensive solution.[103] The head of Davis's department said:

> [Richter] seemed very critical [of the ecologists' work] and told me that he felt that it was not developing on [a] sound scientific basis. . . . His answer to the results that [show] the inadequacy of poison was that the work was not done correctly. All of us in the school who are in any way associated with the program disagree with Richter's point of view and we do not wish to have Dr. Davis and his group devote most of their energy to the studying of the effect of poisons.[104]

Administrators and funders shunned rat poison in favor of Davis's ecological approach as the Baltimore Plan emerged from years of dormancy imposed by the Depression and wartime shortages. The Health Department set in motion the block-by-block process of housing code enforcement that Frances Morton had first envisioned in 1938.

Even the city's largest typhus outbreak since the 1930s did little to shake health officials' confidence that environmental change would limit rat numbers. In late 1946 and early 1947, several residents contracted typhus from rats that occupied the rotting basement floor in a block of federally owned tenements.[105] One resident died, and at least 9 percent of residents on the block were exposed.[106] The city applied DDT and ANTU only sparingly, however, focusing instead on bringing the block up to code.[107] The response to the typhus outbreak affirmed the city's embrace of ecological rat control.

For Baltimore Health officials, supported by the Citizens' Planning and Housing Association, ecological rat control meant dramatic changes to the physical environment of home interiors, backyards, and alleyways. The city allocated two hundred thousand dollars to support immediate repairs and created a new housing court to recoup costs from landlords.[108] When the Health Department performed enforcement, rehabilitation procedures were exhaustive, spanning indoor and outdoor spaces. A typical block might host some two hundred rats before inspectors swooped in to appraise structures and lots and bring landlords to housing court: "Under [health officials'] orders the landlords and tenants tore down the wall fences, cleared the yards of refuse and resurfaced them with concrete, repaired the plumbing, replaced the defective kitchens with sound floors and other sanitary improvements, installed rat-proof bins and shelves for food supplies, covered the garbage cans, and sealed up all discoverable rat holes in walls and foundations."[109] A Rockefeller Foundation report boasted that "without . . . baiting a particle of poison," code enforcement brought about a gradual attrition of rat reproduction. The report continued: "Within three months the population had declined to fifty rats and at the end of two years it was down to twenty-five."[110] Block-based housing rehabilitation protected residents from rats far longer than did rodenticides—so long as it reached both indoor and outdoor spaces.

The city lacked the capacity to apply such exhaustive procedures to all two thousand blocks of substandard housing, however. The program plodded along, reaching only one hundred blocks by 1950, most of them in East Baltimore.[111] The work so strained Health Department resources that the department handed off enforcement tasks to the Sanitary Police on about two-thirds of all blocks.[112] These officers could force property owners to clear rubbish and debris from their lawns and alleys and repair broken fences without court action.[113] These were important environmental changes, but they left homes' structures and interiors unchanged. The Rockefeller Foundation noted that because "the regulatory powers of the Sanitary Police do not reach inside the houses . . . their changes of the environment are less drastic than those of the Health Department and usually effect less drastic reductions of the rat population."[114] A fully rehabilitated block starting with two hundred rats might have only twenty-five rats within two years, but a block attended by the Sanitary Police might still harbor three times as many rats.[115] Thus the Baltimore Plan fell short of the hopes of reformers and ecologists—and of the needs of residents.

Until 1950, the Baltimore Plan did little to involve and empower residents to sustain the changes it did bring. The community had clinched the success—however limited—of poisoning campaigns in Chicago and Baltimore, despite the shortcomings of chemical rat control. Meanwhile, Frances Morton lamented in 1951: "The most difficult phase of the law enforcement program is that of 'follow-up.' There are some landlords who . . . maintain their property in good condition [after rehabilitation]. Many more will not make even the minimum repairs unless forced to do so. Tenants in slum areas, moreover, are so fearful of reprisals and so ignorant of their rights under existing laws that they do not dare make protests to the proper agencies."[116] In other words, housing improvements could not be sustained without help from tenants, whom the Baltimore Plan had done little to help. The report concluded with disappointment that "even after being cleaned up, properties constantly tend to go downhill again" as officials left residents to fend for themselves.[117]

The lack of engagement in the Baltimore Plan contrasts sharply with participation in other civic environmental and health programs. National Negro Health Week and Richter's poisoning campaign inspired wide enthusiasm for environmental improvement and rat control. In the postwar years, residents also rallied to beautify the community. Children and block clubs competed for prizes offered by the *Afro-American* newspaper for planting the most attractive gardens and removing the most debris. Some ten thousand children participated each summer under the supervision of several hundred adults. A new prize recognized the block that showed "the greatest improvement in their backyards where old wooden fences have been torn down."[118] The Health Department and the Rodent Ecology Project failed to tap into this community spirit, much to the detriment of their goals of healthy housing and ecological rat management.

Noting chronic "up-keep" problems, Frances Morton helped create a new "pilot area" in 1950 in which resident engagement would be the top priority. On twenty-seven blocks bounded by Chase, Preston, Caroline, and Chester Streets in East Baltimore, three-thousand-some residents struggled to maintain both rental properties and an unusually high proportion of owner-occupied properties.[119] Rats huddled under slumping fences and porches and invaded open cabinets; mothers burned themselves on defective stoves; children suffered gashes and sprains playing in debris-strewn alleys; and families lacked modern bathing facilities. Since 1930, "the neighborhood had shifted from predominantly white to 80 per cent" African-American, including a range of income levels from "transients" to blue-collar workers (whose incomes were often suspended during labor strikes) to "prominent Negro professional men" excluded from suburbs by racial discrimination. African-Americans paid an average of ten dollars more for rentals, and their apartments were more likely to be substandard than those available to whites.[120] Other parts of Baltimore were poorer overall, but many working-class families hoped to purchase homes left by whites, meaning that they would be financially responsible for expensive repairs. Furthermore, many adults—both men and women—labored at backbreaking jobs with long hours, leaving little time or energy to remake the neighborhood with their own muscles and sweat.[121] If it had not provided additional support, the code enforcement program could have alienated and devastated these families while perpetuating the problem of poor upkeep.

The Health Department had rehabilitated the physical environment of its first one hundred blocks, attempting to alter their ecology, while doing little to overturn landlord neglect or racial and environmental injustice. Within the pilot area, however, social workers helped tenants do their part in holding landlords accountable. A suburban church purchased and renovated an old house as a demonstration project. An association of businesses calling itself Fight Blight, Inc., provided loans to homeowners unable to secure bank loans for repairs. The Baltimore Education Department won a national award for its role in addressing "community problems," including projects in pilot area schools that involved each grade in a different aspect of the Baltimore Plan, from rat control to housing law. With public and private support, residents paved backyards, replaced rotted wood fences with wire ones, cleared alleys, cemented old cellar floors, and reinforced foundations and interior walls. The Citizens' Planning and Housing Association called the process "building up a democracy" and argued that "neighborhoods in urban areas must be built up so that citizens will feel close enough to government to see strength in their own activities and thereby will develop in themselves the desire to participate."[122] Keeping homes in the pilot area healthy and ridding them of rats would require sustained resident engagement *and* robust public and private investment.

REBOUNDING RATS, ENVIRONMENTAL BLIND SPOTS, AND CHEMICAL RAT CONTROL

Four years after the Health Department and the Citizens' Planning and Housing Association poured their support into the pilot area, few rats resided on those twenty-seven blocks. Elsewhere, however, conditions had decayed since the housing inspectors had moved on. The *Sun* reported: "The new cement in the back yards began to crack. Some of the yards filled up with trash again. The rats, sensing perhaps that the humans' guard is down again, are finding easy pickings in the garbage-strewn alleys, burrowing under once-new concrete yards." David Davis continued to monitor rat populations, and his numbers confirmed what residents and the *Sun* suspected: "The rat total is climbing back to where it was at the beginning of 1948."[123] Davis had promised that "permanent changes" to the environment would permanently reduce rat populations. The Baltimore Plan brought lasting changes only on some blocks, however, and it mostly changed the physical environment, not the political disempowerment and long-term economic deprivation that marked segregated communities. Racial segregation still split Baltimore's housing market into two tiers, leaving blacks at a disadvantage when it came to demanding quality housing—and escaping daily life with rats. Rebounding rat populations embodied the failure to foster social justice, which is an environmental factor just as surely as are garbage and substandard housing.

If community engagement and genuine social justice were blind spots for the Baltimore Plan, the Rodent Ecology Project also suffered from two blind spots in its understanding of rats' movement among urban spaces. First, indoor rats went undercounted by the ecologists' census procedures—a major oversight, especially in instances where code enforcement did not extend inside homes. In Chicago, rats moved into private spaces during public baiting, and David Davis observed a similar process in Baltimore in 1949: "An obvious change in recent years is that, although the total rat population has declined, the proportion of the total that is in the houses has increased. Thus, in some areas with clean yards it is possible that the number of rats is underestimated because of their presence exclusively in the house."[124] Indoor rats could become a reservoir for repopulating a block if outdoor conditions declined again, and indoor rats could bring grave health consequences. Curt Richter observed that many of the rats who bit low-income Baltimoreans did so in the home, and indoor rats had high potential to spread diseases and ectoparasites. Officials suspected that indoor rats—namely those in a decayed tenement basement—had infected humans during the 1946–47 typhus outbreak.[125] Neither Davis nor the Health Department adequately accounted for the ways rats shared space with people and moved between indoors and out.[126]

Second, outdoor rat territories were more complex than the ecologists believed. Housing rehabilitation or demolition might disturb rat habitats so severely as to disrupt the seemingly fixed territorial unit of the block. Even if the Baltimore Plan did not create this kind of disruption, urban renewal brought more dramatic changes to wide swaths of Baltimore after the federal Housing Act of 1949, sending rats fleeing to adjacent areas. The *Sun* quipped in 1952: "Rats do not check in at the resettlement office to discuss desirable housing vacancies. When the razing crews start to work, the rats high tail it into nearby blocks, taking their fleas, lice, ticks, and disease potential right along with them."[127] By 1954, city authorities had discontinued the Baltimore Plan entirely in favor of federally funded urban renewal, disturbing rat populations wherever it went.[128]

Meanwhile, rats continued to thrive in parts of town never touched by the Baltimore Plan. City staff on Baltimore's west side performed chemical and physical control on individual properties rather than as part of a systematic treatment of an entire block. In June 1952, a reporter with the *Afro-American*, Ralph Matthews Jr., followed two such workers as they responded to complaints. The workers explained: "This block hasn't been surveyed, so we won't do the whole alley." Instead, they gassed burrows with cyanide, clubbed rats as they fled the gas, and set down poisoned baits of varying strengths depending on the severity of the infestation. Red squill, a time-tested botanical poison available again after a wartime shortage, "is the most frequently applied because it is mild and lessens the danger for humans who might get a swig." They used ANTU under somewhat worse conditions, and only "in extreme cases of rodent infestation" did they turn to another new poison: warfarin.[129] Workers outside the Baltimore Plan's target blocks knew that permanent rat-proofing would provide better control, but the city had not dedicated sufficient resources to transform the physical environments of all substandard areas.

While officials in East Baltimore relied almost exclusively on environmental change, and workers in West Baltimore preferred red squill over other rodenticides, rat controllers elsewhere flocked to warfarin after a brief surge in ANTU's popularity. Warfarin takes its name from the Wisconsin Alumni Research Foundation (WARF), which funded research by the biochemist Karl Paul Link at the University of Wisconsin in the 1930s and 1940s. Dairy farmers observed that their cows sometimes suffered internal hemorrhage after eating rotten clover, and Link isolated the anticoagulant substance for both rodenticidal and medical applications.[130] Humans take small doses of warfarin to treat clotting disorders, while rats die from internal bleeding after ingesting a series of larger doses. In cases of human overdose, Vitamin K restores normal clotting function. Along with warfarin's greater effectiveness, the sense of safety provided by this easy antidote gave warfarin an edge over ANTU in national and global rodenticide markets.[131]

Much like DDT for insects, warfarin made chemical rodent control in cities seem simple and safe for professionals and untrained householders alike—even more so than ANTU. Conscientious pest-control operators knew that warfarin worked best as part of a broader sanitation and rat-proofing campaign. Many unscrupulous or poorly trained exterminators applied warfarin without improving environmental conditions, however, because it seemed to kill rats with so little effort.[132] Both of Baltimore's rat-control experiments practiced a certain kind of reductionism—Curt Richter simplified the physical environment, while the Baltimore Plan and the Rodent Ecology Project reduced the complexity of urban society. Neither was as reductionist as the rat-control approach that gained dominance in the second half of the twentieth century, however.

REBOUNDING RATS IN CITIES OF INJUSTICE

A pipe running to the kitchen had begun to drip, and the rats that nested in the walls and the basement floor flocked to the collecting puddle for a drink. A young female arrived late and received a nip from her older, pregnant sister as she tried to squeeze into the crowd of rats.[133] Stealing a quick drink, she retreated to the corner of the floor void and the hole she had been gnawing in the masonry. A crack had formed, and water from a nearby downspout had eroded it over the years, giving the rat a head start in widening the hole. Probing with her whiskers, the rat now found the hole large enough to squeeze through. With her keen nose, she tested the air for odors both enticing and threatening.

She crept into a different world from the one in which her outdoor kin just a few generations earlier had thrived. Bare ground and pavement stretched out in all directions. Wooden fences once carved the alley into a blind labyrinth, providing ample cover for rats, but residents and code enforcers had replaced these with wire fences or no fences at all. The privy sheds had disappeared too, and the only brick piles were tightly packed with no crevices to squeeze into.[134]

The rat soon saw places to hide, eat, and drink. A large stray dog had knocked over a trash can, and what contents the dog did not consume remained strewn across a section of alley.[135] A landlord had laid wood scraps from a project across town in a haphazard heap in his tenant's backyard. One resident had set up a bench and a row of planters along her wire fence. The rat stepped tentatively toward the fence, then scurried toward the garbage cans. Two other young rats that had been born indoors soon emerged from the same hole, noses twitching in the air.

The story of Baltimore's rats in the 1940s and 1950s confounds easy conclusions about the reduction of ecological complexity at the line between private space and public responsibility. Curt Richer committed himself to chemical technologies and downplayed the importance of environmental and social change, but he also helped bring the private horrors of rats to public light. He made rat control a shared public-private responsibility and gave residents who lived with these horrors a meaningful role in control activities. Fifteen hundred residents helped control rats on some twenty-eight hundred blocks. At the same time, Richter shamed some residents, making their rat problems all too public, and he exposed citizens to risk in public and private spaces as he distributed a little-tested rat poison through community networks.

Meanwhile, ecologists who eschewed chemicals and favored grand public investment and holistic environmental change reduced the complexity of urban environments in more subtle ways, if we think about "environment" and "ecology" broadly. They neglected the habitats found in household interiors and did little to engage regular citizens. David Davis's methods, based on what he considered settled ecological principles, allowed little room for on-the-ground knowledge of rats in homes or rats running from block to block. Yet the people affected by the program had their own knowledge of rats—where they moved, where they lived, the waxing and waning of populations. In these ways, for all their beneficent intentions, the Rodent Ecology Project and the Baltimore Plan reinforced lines between public and private and discounted the ability of rats to cross these lines. For all their knowledge of rat movement, ecologists treated the walls of the home as impermeable barriers to science, when in fact rats posed great dangers to residents when they crossed that barrier and joined families inside.

Rebounding rat populations showed that private homes bereft of public support degraded quickly, but also that state-imposed environmental change was unsustainable without citizen involvement. Baltimore had no permanent system for ensuring that landlords would *maintain* healthy, rat-free conditions, and renters lacked the power to hold them accountable. Most of all, none of Baltimore's rat controllers attempted to overturn the system of racial segregation that had helped create crowded, degraded neighborhood environments. The people who had the most intimate and dangerous contact with rats could only do so much to maintain health while conditions remained unjust. An academic study of the Baltimore Plan's pilot area called the city's housing situation an example of "exploitation."[136] Meanwhile, in Chicago, where extermination turf wars and unmaintained housing also left residents vulnerable to rats, a *Daily Tribune* editorial aptly characterized the nature of rodent infestation:

> Rats . . . are a symptom, not a cause, of slum housing. The principal cause of slum conditions is the disposition of owners of property in blighted neighborhoods to operate it so as to liquidate their capital, instead of maintaining their property and earning a return upon the investment. The renting of slum homes is a process of exhausting a resource just as much as is the operation of a mine. The difference, of course, is that the so-called profits, which are really liquidation dividends on slum property, can only be collected at the expense of the health and safety of the tenants.[137]

As the mining analogy suggests, physical and economic exploitation of the landscape and its people were one and the same. Similarly, the biological ecology of rats could not be separated from the political ecology of cities.

PART TWO

PERSISTENCE AND RESISTANCE
IN THE AGE OF ECOLOGY

RACHEL CARSON'S 1962 BOOK *SILENT SPRING* DECRIED THE HUBRIS OF
modern pest control, which attempted to remove pests from environments
ideally suited to them. Instead of submitting to humans' will, nature both
suffered and struck back: wildlife perished, people became sick, and pests
evolved resistance to pesticides. Carson's followers raised their voices primarily against pesticides used in agriculture and landscaping—outdoor
uses that polluted water, killed birds and fish, and contaminated food.
Protesters in cities—whether or not they had read Carson—condemned
domestic and urban pest-control campaigns that attempted to isolate pests
from the conditions that sustained them. Advances in sanitation, housing,
housekeeping, and pesticides had promised to rid modern cities of pests,
yet many low-income city-dwellers still shared their homes with unbidden but persistent housemates. In the absence of effective pest control,
residents suffered exposure to disease, stress, and social stigma.

For pests and people residing in central cities in the age of ecology, two
trends emerged in the second half of the twentieth century. One trend was
the persistence of pests in urban homes despite advances that had promised healthy living environments and greater control over domestic space
for householders. By the 1960s, Norway rats and German cockroaches
remained steadfast inhabitants of many urban homes and neighborhoods. Some populations of pests became more tenacious as they evolved
resistance to pesticides. Pesticide resistance resulted not only from pests'

exposure to chemicals but also from the environmental conditions in which chemicals were applied.

City residents staged their own kind of resistance. A second trend was the rise of protests by householders and environmentalists against the conditions that allowed pests to persist in urban homes. Some protested common methods of controlling pests, including pesticides that they perceived as unhealthy for themselves and their children. Pest-control campaigns up to the 1960s mostly conceived of pest control as a technical problem and promised to control nature by modernizing cities—whether through sanitation, housing reform, citizen education, or chemical pesticide applications. Protests beginning in the 1950s and 1960s looked beyond the control of nature to the politics of pests. They often expressed a kind of ecological thinking that connected not only pests and their physical environment but also human bodies, and the political, economic, and social forces that degraded urban domestic environments.[1]

Social movements that protested unhealthy housing conditions combined the politics of tenant rights with environmental justice and, in the 1990s, an explicitly ecological approach to pest control called Integrated Pest Management. In the age of ecology, it became clear to urban protesters that infestations could not be contained in public or private spaces. Neighbors' common experiences with infestation helped unify social movements for healthy and just housing. Many found that they could not manage pests without cooperating to transform both the physical environments of their homes and the political structures that had degraded their homes in the first place. In this way, the very creatures that plagued communities also brought neighbors together to change the ecological conditions that sustained pests.

The four chapters in part one opened and closed with composite sketches of urban scenes envisioned from pests' perspectives. The two chapters in part two, along with the epilogue, open with contemporary cultural expressions about the relationships between pests and people, particularly pests and social inequities. This shift of perspective corresponds to the shift in perspective between chapters one through four and the rest of the book; the latter chapters emphasize activist movements among infested communities. Literary and other cultural references open another window on the meanings and experiences of people who lived with pests.

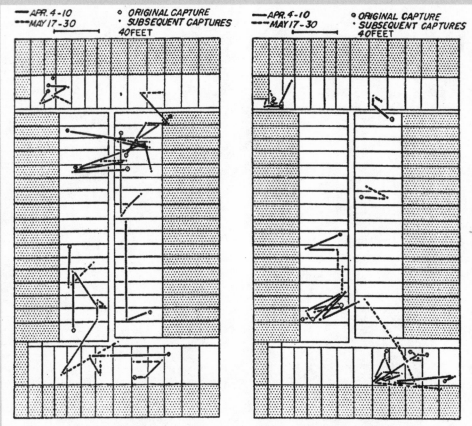

FIG. 1.—Movements of thirteen males (left) and twelve females (right), captured more than three times (see experiment 2).

Tracking experiments by the Rodent Ecology Project seemed to show that rats stayed within the confines of a single city block and that they moved freely among rowhouse backyards. David E. Davis, John T. Emlen, and Allen W. Stokes, "Studies on the Home Range of the Brown Rat," *Journal of Mammalogy* 29 (1948): 207–25.

Backyard scene from Baltimore Plan target block, 1947. The high-board wooden fences, construction debris, and other items provided ample harborage for rats. Citizens' Planning and Housing Association Collection, Series VIII, Box 1, folder 5-Alleys and Backyards, 1947, University of Baltimore Archives. Courtesy of CPHA Collection—University of Baltimore.

Wire fences in these Baltimore backyards provided no cover to rats, unlike labyrinths of wooden fences found in other backyards. Citizens' Planning and Housing Association Collection, Series VIII, Box 1, folder 5-Alleys and Back-yards, 1947, University of Baltimore Archives. Courtesy of CPHA Collection—University of Baltimore.

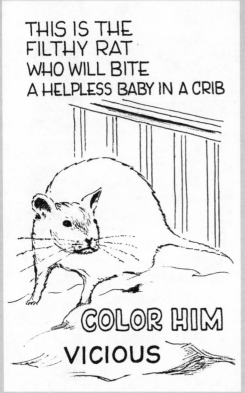

THIS IS THE
FILTHY RAT
WHO WILL BITE
A HELPLESS BABY IN A CRIB

COLOR HIM
VICIOUS

Many health departments used education of adults and children as their main approach to rat control, distributing materials such as this 1964 coloring book created by the Cleveland Health Department. The book suggested, among other things, that landlords and tenants could cooperate to control rats. Meanwhile, tenants striking in Harlem withheld rent from landlords and displayed rats caught in their homes as tactics for demanding improved living conditions. Rileigh Coleman, *The Dirty Rat Coloring Book* (Cleveland: Division of Health, Community Action for Youth, 1964). Courtesy of the City of Milwaukee.

THESE ARE
LANDLORDS, CUSTODIANS,
TENANTS, SANITARIANS
COLOR THEM
COOPERATIVE

THIS IS AN
EXTERMINATOR

COLOR HIM
EXPERT

ANNOUNCING A
CLEAN-UP
IN YOUR ALLEY
Tomorrow Morning
STARTS AT 9 A.M.

- HELP MAKE YOUR BLOCK CLEAN AND GET RID OF RATS.

- EARN A FREE METAL GARBAGE CAN BY PARTICIPATING IN THE CLEAN UP.

RAKES, BROOMS, AND SHOVELS WILL BE FURNISHED.
CITY TRUCKS WILL HAUL THE RUBBISH AWAY.

THE HEALTH DEPARTMENT WILL PUT OUT RAT
POISON IF SIGNS OF RATS ARE FOUND.

FREE MOVIES TONIGHT!
AT THE ENVIRONMENTAL VAN

SPONSORED BY THE INTENSIVE RAT CONTROL PROJECT
CITY OF MILWAUKEE HEALTH DEPARTMENT

The Milwaukee Intensive Rodent Control Program attempted to "educate and motivate" residents to steward garbage. This poster uses the figure of a fashionable man in an attempt to lend an air of cool to environmental citizenship. *Intensive Rodent Control Progress Report, 1969–1973* (Milwaukee: Municipal Reference Bureau, 1973). Courtesy of the City of Milwaukee.

"Black Misery! Ain't We Got a Right to the Tree of Life?" by Black Panther Party
Minister of Culture Emory Douglas. Douglas's portrait contrasts with images
of women afraid of rodents; the woman's grip on the rat suggests determination,
courage, and fury. ©2013 Emory Douglas/Artists Rights Society (ARS), NY.

A roach adorns this 1972 Emory Douglas poster supporting Shirley Chisholm's campaign for the Democratic nomination for president. Douglas used roaches as a motif in his posters to illustrate unjust living conditions in homes and prisons. ©2013 Emory Douglas/Artists Rights Society (ARS), NY.

A rat-control survey in Baltimore in the late 1970s found dented cans and lids, indicating the difficulty of maintaining rat-proof sanitation infrastructure. Trash cans must be closed tightly to keep rats from eating their contents. Citizens' Planning and Housing Association Collection, Series VIII, Box 1, folder 121-Rats, University of Baltimore Archives. Courtesy of CPHA Collection—University of Baltimore.

Loose trash in a Baltimore alley provides food and harborage for rats. Scenes such as this result from both community members' failure to store their waste in appropriate receptacles and the strains placed on sanitation systems and households by increasing reliance on disposable packaging. Citizens' Planning and Housing Association Collection, Series VIII, Box 1, folder 121-Rats, University of Baltimore Archives. Courtesy of CPHA Collection—University of Baltimore.

5

THE ECOLOGY OF INJUSTICE

Rats in the Civil Rights Era

IN THE MELODRAMATIC FIRST SCENE OF RICHARD WRIGHT'S 1940 NOVEL *Native Son*, Bigger Thomas's day begins with a fight against a "huge black rat" in his family's "tiny, one-room apartment."[1] His mother and sister huddle on a bed, screaming and "gaz[ing] open-mouthed at the trunk in the corner," where the rat last appeared. Bigger orders his brother to block a "gaping hole in the molding" so the rat cannot escape. Meanwhile, Bigger corners it, wielding an iron skillet. The rodent "squealed and leaped at Bigger's trouser-leg and snagged it in his teeth," ripping a long gash before Bigger can shake it free. After a chase about the room, Bigger finally hurls the skillet, hitting his mark. He then "took a shoe and pounded the rat's head, crushing it, cursing hysterically." He dangles the body in front of his sister, who faints into her sobbing mother's arms. Wright shows that mundane violence occupies the very walls of Bigger's home and all of Bigger's waking hours. Bigger himself lives in fear while his family—including two weak female characters—relies on him for protection. Wright drew parallels between rats and people in Chicago's Black Belt. One literary scholar has noted that the "buildings of the ghetto produce an endless stream of hungry and fearful rats," and Bigger stands for an "endless stream" of young black men shaped by racism in the slum environment. By the novel's end, Bigger faces execution for rape and murder, viewed by authorities and society as a threat to be crushed.[2]

Over a decade later, rats still plagued low-income African-Americans in their homes, but in real life the story often played out differently from that

149

in the Thomases' fictional home. In late September 1957, Mrs. Eva Ray had had enough with the rats that shared her Harlem apartment. They sometimes chased her children about their flat on West 142nd Street. Finally, one of the children killed the most menacing rat. Harlem's *Amsterdam News* ran a photo of Ray dangling the rat by its tail and staring defiantly at the camera. Unlike Bigger Thomas's mother and sister, she declared: "I'm not afraid of any rat."[3] *News* editors knew that rats represented more than an individual problem; women and men struggled not only against rats but also against the political and ecological forces that supported rodents. In an era when new suburban homes, urban renewal, and miracle chemicals promised to usher in an era of modern living, rat-infested neighborhoods seemed to have been left behind. Low-income, central-city African-American communities in the late twentieth century became associated with rats in popular discourse and research about infestation, along with urban protest movements by communities themselves. Residents and activists in these communities, along with reformers from the outside, constructed ecological theories about the causes and cures for persistent rat infestation there.

Black activists, journalists, and artists seldom, if ever, used the word "ecology." Yet they, along with many residents of low-income neighborhoods of color, understood rats as part of a web that entangled the physical environment with racial injustice, urban politics, and even federal housing policy. Residents suffered material, immediate effects of living with rats, but they and community activists saw rats as symptoms and symbols of larger problems. Racial discrimination in the housing market still limited African-American families' options as landlords of dilapidated buildings exploited their lack of choices. Substandard dwellings were so abundant in cities like New York that housing courts and city revolving funds could barely keep up with the need for rat-proofing. Federal funds for housing and community development largely flowed to new suburban communities, bypassing central cities where homes had languished for years without physical improvements. Insiders in infested communities saw rats as fleshy manifestations of the ecology of injustice and demanded that the benefits of American postwar prosperity be extended to their homes. In the face of persistent rats, communities resisted racism, stigma, and disinvestment. Many demanded support from government agencies to create healthy neighborhood environments.[4]

Meanwhile, outsiders also hoped to modernize infested neighborhoods through rat control, but plans for doing so often divorced rats from the ecology of injustice. Some believed they could reduce the complexity of urban ecosystems by simply poisoning rats, making few changes to the physical environment or the social factors that caused housing to decay. Other outside reformers hoped to reform residents into modern environmental citizens. Finally, some critics opposed any government support for rat control in cities, blaming infestation on civic disorder and residents themselves rather than any systematic oppression or injustice.

While black communities struggled against both rats and the stigma they brought, and outside reformers denied or downplayed the role of systemic environmental injustice there, rats themselves persisted and in many places thrived. The rodenticide warfarin had promised to make rat control simple and safe, much as DDT had promised for insects. But warfarin did not work as its promoters intended under the ecological conditions found in many disinvested urban neighborhoods. Warfarin's failures sparked fears of "super rats" resistant to the chemical and also brought new blame, stigma, and surveillance to low-income communities of color. Persistent and resistant rats belied the promises of modern chemistry, citizens, and cities.

RAT BITES AND THE "ULTIMATE RAT POISON"

Mrs. Ray's children suffered little physical harm from the rats in their apartment, but other Harlem families were not so fortunate. Henry and Willa Mae Collins had complained for years to their landlord's agent about rats and other code violations in the unit they rented for thirty-seven dollars a month. A hospital in New Jersey owned their building on 128th Street. On August 14, 1957, the couple awoke to find that a rat had gnawed through muscles and connective tissue in their newborn's arm and leg. Baby Keith spent the next two months at Harlem Hospital, and doctors doubted he would ever walk. The Collins family's ordeal inspired activists to publicize Harlem's housing conditions. Talk of "four-legged rats" led to criticism of another key species in the urban ecosystem: "two-legged rats"—landlords, officials, and politicians who perpetuated housing discrimination and neglect. The *Amsterdam News* became a national gadfly that demanded justice for low-income black families living in dehumanizing environmental conditions. Editors used the Collins case as a rallying cry for the Sharkey-Brown-Isaacs Bill in City Council, calling the bill the "ultimate rat poison."[5] Signed by Mayor Wagner in late 1957, Sharkey-Brown-Isaacs made New York the first U.S. city to ban housing discrimination on the basis of race.[6] The *News* interviewed parents of rat-bite victims, tracked housing court cases, and ran photos of mothers showing off rats killed in their apartments.[7] The *News* exposed the physical and emotional violence of rat infestation while placing it in the broader context of social and environmental injustice.

Some readers accused the newspaper of drawing too much attention to a shameful stigma on their community. They charged that the *News* fomented unrest—including local riots in 1959 and 1964—and sullied the image of black neighborhoods. Instead of blaming a racist housing market, critics of the *News*—many of them African-American Harlem residents—faulted families for allowing the environment to degrade. A social worker questioned the paper's accounts of the Collins case, blaming Mr. and Mrs. Collins. "The Sharkey-Brown-Isaacs bill can bar discrimination in housing," she wrote, "but it cannot protect little children against negligent parents." Another reader charged that coverage of rats "did nothing to bolster race or community pride. It gave a false impression of those of us who live in Harlem and have self-respect enough to keep clean homes free of rats."[8] Editors gave mock apologies "for devoting so much of its front page and its Society Page to rats," and said it had used "ghastly pictures of rats in Harlem homes [to] shock the moral conscience of this city."[9] Some readers agreed, such as a city court clerk who had witnessed foot-dragging at work. He wrote: "Without a doubt, the four-legged rats probably showed more courage and fight than many of our two-legged rats—leaders who are nothing more than parasites."[10] Even Harlem residents disagreed about the causes, solutions, and meanings of infestation and the stigma it carried.

City officials at first tried to respond to the Collins case with holistic solutions that protected residents from rats as well as other domestic hazards. Health and housing authorities ramped up code enforcement in Harlem over the next three years; between late 1959 and early 1960, courts tried more than a thousand owners of properties in Harlem. Like the owners of the Collins' building, many were absentee landlords, and some had taken over buildings in receivership—meaning that the previous owner had little money to invest in the property. The Health Department claimed that 90 percent of the hundreds of convicted landlords made the needed repairs. Reported rat bites across Manhattan dropped from their peak in 1959 until 1962.[11] The Collins family won a ninety-thousand-dollar judgment against their landlord, New York's largest award ever in a rat-bite case.[12] With political prodding from the *Amsterdam News* and community members, and an ecological intervention in Harlem's housing conditions, residents for a time felt more protected from rats.

UNJUST URBAN ECOLOGIES

By the 1950s, urban ecosystems like Harlem's were caught up in political, social, and economic currents far bigger than rats themselves. In the 1960s United States, 62 percent of poor black families lived in substandard rental housing, compared with 35 percent of poor white families.[13] Buildings in densely populated neighborhoods where substandard units were concentrated suffered more wear and tear on infrastructure and higher concentrations of waste, both of which supported rats. Petty criminals stole garbage cans frequently, leaving residents to dispose of trash in bags unprotected from rats.[14] Meanwhile, suburbanization sapped central-city tax revenues and public and private investments that central-city governments might have used to maintain homes and neighborhood environments.[15] The wealthiest 20 percent of American households, well-heeled enough to maintain their own homes, received twice the amount of government housing subsidies per family as did the poorest 20 percent.[16] Such policies helped make up the ecology that supported rats.

Rats filled the niche created by the forces of racism and disinvestment. Where disrepair was widespread throughout a building, block, or neighborhood, rats became entrenched residents, with many alternative harborages should any one family patch up holes with steel wool or cement. As one "resourceful housewife" lamented to the *Amsterdam News*, such measures "[keep] the rats out for a while, then they're back again."[17] Rats worsened decay by gnawing new holes or widening old ones. Tenants reported that rats entered through cracks around stove pipes, heating ducts, or water lines.[18] Some affluent homeowners might experience infestation due to disrepair, and crumbling sewage systems under communities of any income level often crawled with rats, but systematic injustices worsened infestation in poor, black communities.[19]

Baltimore achieved mixed success with its comprehensive code enforcement program in the 1940s, but within a decade housing courts and health officials again strained to keep up with negligent landlords, decaying buildings, and teeming rats.[20] Black leaders accused officials of shielding landlords from prosecution.[21] Full housing code enforcement would have ejected thousands of New York families onto the streets in the name of protecting them from poor living conditions. Many landlords "mortgaged [their properties] close to the full extent of value"—meaning that violators facing a lien on their property might choose foreclosure rather than make repairs.[22] Without repayment from landlords, cities' revolving funds for repairs dwindled. Furthermore, "maintenance enforcement is never-ending": repairs provided no guarantee against future decay and infestation.[23] Landlords might be jailed or fined for violations only to return to court months or years later when another tenant suffered a rat bite.[24]

In the 1960s, U.S. residents suffered at least fourteen thousand rat bites per year; underreporting meant the actual incidence was likely much higher.[25] More than half of victims were under age two, and most others were small children, the elderly, and the infirm. Following a bite report, some health departments relocated families permanently and prosecuted the landlord, while others sent families back after a quick rat-poisoning campaign. As many as one-third of bites occurred at addresses with multiple bite incidents, an indication of both the need for evacuation and the spatial concentration of rat problems. In some incidents the victim or his or her caretaker fought off the rat before it could nibble through flesh, but even small wounds could become infected. Among those unable to resist, gnawing rats could cause permanent deformities or even death by blood loss. Rats' habit of chewing on corpses could leave families and medical examiners uncertain whether a rat bite or some other cause had killed a deceased baby.[26] Survivors required antibiotics and sometimes reconstructive surgery or rabies shots.[27]

Contact with rats spread diseases that received little attention from the medical community. Physicians' knowledge of the two bacterial agents of rat-bite fever, *Spirilla* and *Streptobacilli*, remained scanty in the 1960s. In addition to fever, the infection caused rash, vomiting, diarrhea, and painful swelling of the joints; if untreated with antibiotics, it could prove fatal.[28] In the 1960s, U.S. health professionals recognized at least six thousand cases of rat-borne disease each year, including rat-bite fever as well as leptospirosis and salmonellosis, which could spread through contact with rats or their wastes.[29] Many physicians remained ignorant of this microbial scale of rat ecology.[30]

People who lived with rats also felt dire strains on mental health. For many parents a glimpse of a rat at home by day meant mounting feelings of dread and worry for young children's safety by night. Some parents kept vigil over their babies all night, their fears stoked by local reports of bites.[31] White psychologists, however, suspected that constant contact with rats led to feelings of hopelessness, defeat, and abandonment of efforts to improve homes and neighborhoods. Where activists hoped that rats could inspire protest, health experts saw a self-perpetuating cycle of rats and resignation.[32] Education programs often followed the latter line of reasoning, blaming residents' lack of motivation and poor environmental stewardship for rat infestation. Many who lived with rats also responded to them politically and creatively, however; rats may have numbed some into complacency, but they inspired others to action.

RATS AS POLITICAL SYMBOLS

Despite coverage in the New York Amsterdam News, the passage of Sharkey-Brown-Isaacs, and the 1959–60 rat drive, by 1963 more than twenty-two thousand New York City landlords were again in violation of housing codes. Rat bites in Manhattan rebounded.[33] Amid backsliding housing conditions, the housing activist Jesse Gray harnessed rats' power as symbols of racism and neglect. Critics called Gray a "rabble-rouser"; supporters praised his use of dead rats as props in activist spectacles. Gray understood Harlem's rats in terms of a broad and political ecology. He insisted that rat control would do nothing for homes in which toilets leaked, walls and ceilings crumbled, and heating systems failed.[34]

As the head of Harlem's Community Council on Housing, Gray convinced one thousand families from sixty buildings to withhold rent from their landlords—a bold move in late fall, when eviction could mean getting thrown out in the cold. In a rent strike, tenants can charge landlords with constructive eviction, meaning that the landlord has allowed conditions to degrade so severely as to force the resident from the dwelling, breaking the lease.[35] To prove a constructive eviction and gain a court order forcing landlords to make repairs and perhaps reduce or waive rents, residents must present evidence of those poor conditions. After first stringing together rubber-rat necklaces for protesters to wear in court, Gray convinced strikers to save corpses of real rats caught in their buildings to display at eviction hearings.[36] In addition to gaining judges' sympathy, the rats drew attention from the popular media and won public sympathy for the strikers' cause. Legal scholars praised Jesse Gray's use of visceral imagery in housing court. One pointed out that "in most jurisdictions the success of a rent strike will depend primarily upon its 'nuisance value,' and its ability to create public interest in the needs of the slum areas."[37] By January 1964, the city arranged for residents to pay their rent into escrow accounts until the landlords made necessary repairs.[38] Gray and the strikers had successfully turned rats into icons of social and environmental neglect.

As news of the victory spread, renters on Chicago's West Side copied Gray's rent strike tactic with support from the chapter of the Congress of Racial Equality. Local leader Roy Patrick explained the ecology of West Side housing in terms of not just rats but also mice and "roaches, bugs, and other crawling insects that get into [residents'] food, their beds, their dishes—their lives, period."[39] Also amid the strike, the CBS drama *Eastside/Westside*, set in Manhattan, won an Emmy for an episode starring James Earl Jones and Diana Sands as parents of a baby who dies from a rat bite. The episode further rallied Harlem residents, especially after southern CBS affiliates got the series canceled, objecting to its racially integrated cast and progressive subject matter.[40]

Jesse Gray and the Community Council on Housing saw the escrow arrangement as only a first step. They called for the establishment of a permanent housing arbitration board for New York State, more thorough inspections, and "a massive drive by the federal government to eliminate slums."[41] The council further urged state government to allocate funds that would build sturdy homes to protect people from rodents and the elements. Supporters enclosed rubber rats in missives to legislators and the governor. Gray hinted that Harlem wildlife might join a planned march on the state capitol in Albany "if the governor has not made efforts to assure more low income public housing or grant emergency repairs in our present buildings."[42] Some lawmakers attempted, with limited success, to legally fortify the constructive eviction defense to protect future rent strikers against eviction. Albany and City Hall, however, prioritized emergency repairs and a new rat extermination program aimed at "recalcitrant property owners."[43]

The rat extermination drive funded by the city and the state helped chip away at rat populations but failed to answer residents' larger demands. Protesters' rat displays had not been mere requests for pest control but demands for healthy, sound living environments for people largely excluded from the suburbs. Officials interpreted rats in too limited and literal a way. The program took steps toward alleviating the horror of life with rats, and it held government and property owners responsible. The city jailed and fined landlords who allowed rats to thrive and slashed rents if landlords did not comply swiftly.[44] But the major effort went into poisoning rats. When new surveys by the city reported decreased infestation, politicians representing Harlem contested the results, accusing the city of underestimating the problem.[45] Most important, killing rats did not go far enough for Harlem residents. One asked: "What good is getting rid of rats when you haven't got any heat or lights? We can beat off the rats with a stick, but how are we going to keep warm?"[46] The rat-poisoning program fell far short in a city where black residents paid steep rents to live in some of the worst environments.[47]

The social agenda supported by Jesse Gray and other activists went far beyond the issue of rats in Harlem; their proposals echoed the economic justice concerns of national civil rights organizations. Harlem activists called for rent supplements, legal protection for tenants, and massive public investment in housing.[48] Civil rights leaders from Dr. Martin Luther King Jr. to Whitney Young of the Urban League called for a grand program of reinvestment, a "domestic Marshall Plan" to rebuild American cities and overcome the uneven economic geography of metropolitan regions. Young proposed a $145 billion allocation to create jobs and overhaul distressed housing and other social and physical infrastructure.[49] Young and others believed that such an investment, if allocated as part of a program that genuinely engaged the community, could remake neighborhood environments where families lived in undersized units with broken plumbing, faulty heating, infrequent garbage pickup, and rats.

A "CIVIL RATS" BILL

Lyndon Johnson's administration, eager to garner black votes, strived to show that it understood the ecology of injustice. While New York officials failed to grasp the greater meaning of rats, Johnson made rodents a matter of racial justice with his 1967 proposal for the Rat Extermination Act. Johnson and ally Senator Abraham Ribicoff of Connecticut noted the bias in federal spending on pest control toward agricultural and aesthetic pests rather than urban pests.[50] Congress had recently funded removal of hyacinths that tangled in boat propellers in Southern waterways.[51] Johnson himself had funded a vast program to control the screwworm, a parasite attacking calves on ranches along the Mexican border. As of the 1960s, federal funding supported modern pest control for white, rural, and suburban citizens more than for black and urban citizens.

The proposed Rat Extermination Act was more closely tied to the War on Poverty and Great Society initiatives than to prior federal pest-control projects. It also diverged from rat-control education programs operated by many local health departments, which often stressed personal responsibility while providing little support for environmental change.[52] Instead, Johnson framed rat control as an issue of housing, civil rights, and health, not reducible to individual actions or public education alone. He intended to place the program within the two-year-old Department of Housing and Urban Development (HUD), where rat-control activities could be coordinated with urban reinvestment and community empowerment programs. Johnson's Office of Equal Opportunity had already piloted rat-control programs, known as Operation Rat. The Rat Extermination Act of 1967 expanded upon the "Model Cities" programs within HUD and the Office of Equal Opportunity. Model Cities involved communities in decisions about how to use federal funds for revitalizing the urban environment. The bill before Congress linked rat-control target areas with Model Cities sites, so neighborhoods would receive rat-control support as part of a larger, well-funded housing rehabilitation program.

The administrative location of the proposed rat-control program revealed that the president connected environmental health, housing, and racism in ways that few national politicians had before. Johnson's Commission on Urban Problems spoke to the inseparability of environmental and social issues. The founding mission of HUD called for "a decent home and suitable living environment for every American family," echoing the idealism expressed at the founding of public housing in the United States.[53] Furthermore, the placement of rat control in HUD rather than in the Department of Health, Education, and Welfare reflected the belief of Johnson and his staff that health agencies had failed to offer systemic solutions to urban environmental problems. A staffer explained: "[Rat-control] measures are far more closely related to the code enforcement, rehabilitation, and other 'urban environment' responsibilities of HUD than to the health and medically oriented responsibilities of the Department of Health, Education, and Welfare."[54] Johnson saw existing health programs as too narrow to overcome systemic neglect of the urban environment. By placing the rat-control program within HUD, he gave the federal government a major role in supporting holistic solutions to infestation.

Johnson hoped that HUD would improve quality of life for communities of color, but urban renewal, supported by the Housing Act of 1949, often sharpened inequality—and heightened exposure to rats. Vector-control experts with the Public Health Service noted that "rat-bite incidence increases when the ecology of an infested area is disrupted by expressway construction, building destruction, land clearance or similar activities."[55] Such acts of creative destruction pushed rats from demolished buildings to nearby apartment blocks all over New York as the planner Robert Moses strived to modernize city parks, housing, and transportation. The Public Health Service urged health departments to eradicate rats—and their fleas, lice, ticks, and mites—prior to "disruptive activities such as construction or demolition" lest these creatures simply spread disease to new locations.[56] The same activities that displaced communities of color also increased their chances of coming into contact with rats. Johnson's program promised instead to meaningfully involve communities in redevelopment *and* rat control.

The scale of Johnson's housing programs and the rat-control proposal fell far short of what civil rights leaders demanded, however. The War on Poverty agenda scaled back Whitney Young's urban Marshall Plan proposal; it dedicated hundreds of millions of dollars to the Model Cities program, rather than hundreds of billions. Johnson sought tens of millions in rent supplements, but Congress frequently fell short of his requests, struggling to control budget deficits as the war in Vietnam sapped funding and attention from domestic concerns.[57] The rat bill itself asked for only forty million dollars over its first two years. As Johnson and Congress scaled back black leaders' visions, the rat-control proposal served as a modest gesture toward alleviating the horror of rats in poor African-American communities.

When the rat-control bill came up for debate on July 20, 1967, rural members of Congress not only opposed but openly mocked it. Virginia representative James Broyhill joked, exaggerating his own drawl: "The rat smart thing to do is to vote down this civil rats bill, rat now."[58] Ohio representative Delbert Latta, who in 1966 had sought funding to poison blackbirds and starlings in his home state, sniped: "The matter of putting out a little bit of rat poison should not be requested of the Federal government."[59] Congress supported control of aesthetic and agricultural pests, but many legislators could not fathom that cities, like farms, might overwhelm the people who were part of their ecologies.

While Johnson and black leaders saw urban rats as ecological manifestations of injustice, opponents believed that rats thrived upon civic disorder—a concept infused with racial assumptions and imagery. Congressional critics of public rat control argued that residents themselves were to blame for failing to manage their own environment. They imagined low-income African-American communities as places where human sloth and carelessness allowed nature to run amok. The quip about "civil rats" mocked a movement that aimed to deliver the *rights* of citizenship to communities underserved by the state. Meanwhile, rat bill opponents sought to enforce the *duties* of citizenship upon underserved communities. They also sought retribution for civil unrest in Newark just days earlier; the same House members who rejected rat-control funding attempted to enact tough new federal punishments against rioters.[60] For partisans of the ecology of civic disorder, rats and riots were symptomatic of undisciplined, racialized urban nature.

The administration reacted swiftly to the bill's rejection. Many argued that rats and riots were entwined in a vicious cycle. Johnson attributed riots to deplorable conditions such as rat infestation and interpreted his detractors' response to the bill as revenge for the riots. In a televised address on the evening of July 20, Johnson observed: "We are spending federal funds to protect our livestock from rodents and predatory animals. The least we can do is give our children the same protection we give our livestock."[61] That night a baby died in a suspected rat attack in Washington, D.C., and newscasts juxtaposed his death with the laughter in Congress.[62] An administration official obtained medical examiners' photographs of infants and children who had been disfigured or killed by rats and sent prints to opponents in Congress.[63] The Fish and Wildlife Service sent rodent-control experts to assess the threat of infestation in Detroit after a riot there just days later. Liberals across the United States expressed shock at the dismissal of the Rat Extermination Act, and some reasoned that that summer's riots should have assured the bill's passage. A Los Angeles educator named James Jones retold the story of the Pied Piper of Hameln, with Congress as the stingy town fathers who refused to pay the piper. "But the summers grew hot," Jones wrote in a letter sent to the Johnson administration, "and the rat nest teemed with new life that came out of the alleys and the basements and began to march the streets like men looking for sustenance of survival." Jones saw that summer's riots as the price exacted by the piper: two hundred million dollars in property damage, thousands of injuries, and dozens of lives lost.[64] From Johnson's inner circle to the Department of the Interior to regular Americans, rat bill supporters believed that feelings of neglect and frustration that came from living with rats had helped spark the uprisings.[65]

Civil rights leaders equated rejection of the rat bill with racism. Congress had dismissed poor, black communities' struggles and denied them the means to alleviate a daily danger. Mamie Reese of the National Association of Colored Women's Clubs said: "I cannot remain silent while one of the primary objectives for which NACWC was founded is being shattered. We were organized in 1896 for the purpose of raising the standard of living for the Negro family. Controlling the rat menace is in line with this goal."[66] Jesse Jackson led journalists on a tour of a Chicago tenement to illustrate the daily trials of living with rats.[67] Whitney Young renewed calls for an urban Marshall Plan.[68] Jesse Gray organized a group of protesters to storm the floor of the House, where they shouted "rats cause riots!" until Capitol police arrested them.[69] While speaking to reporters about the riots, Martin Luther King Jr. contrasted Congress's daily expenditure for the Vietnam War—eighty million dollars—against the denial of half that amount to control "rats in the ghettoes" for two years.[70] Although the rat-control bill had been a modest gesture, its failure amid mocking in Congress was a dire insult to people for whom living with rodents was one of many impacts of the state's neglect.

Public disgust at legislators' callous humor ensured that rat control would become a federal budget item—the Urban Rat Control Program, adopted in December 1967. Congressional conservatives, however, hoped to discipline black communities, emphasizing individual responsibility over investment and racial justice. In this context, Johnson allowed Congress to move the program into a health-spending bill, weakening its ties to HUD's housing and community programs. Local health departments would receive federal grants to deliver rat poison while educating communities to be good stewards of wastes in the neighborhood environment; improvement of housing conditions fell to no better than third among program priorities. The revised program was a mixed bag for communities: they received modest funding to address the immediate problem of rats, but local grants came attached with strings of discipline, blame, and demands for physical work matched by limited new investment. Links between housing rehabilitation activities and health department activities varied. The people who took on the important and daunting task of cleaning up garbage might not see a federal investment in neighborhood infrastructure commensurate with their efforts. Congress narrowed the scope of thinking about rat control, isolating the issue from the problems of racism and disinvestment in which both Johnson and black leaders had situated it.[71]

Those leaders understood rats as fleshy, biting incarnations of racism, but some officials who administered local rat-control programs interpreted rats as indicators that black communities were out of control. Local health officials and politicians often asserted that rat problems resulted primarily from blacks' failure to take personal responsibility for proper garbage disposal. Certainly, it is important for communities to exercise agency in the stewardship of their neighborhoods. Rat-free environments are not created only by government intervention; rather, partnership and support between residents and the state are necessary to sustain environmental changes, as Baltimore's rat-control and housing intervention in the 1940s and 1950s showed. Yet even well-planned attempts to educate African-American renters failed to sever links between rats and poor housing conditions. Milwaukee's federally funded rat-control program earned praise from public health experts and rodent controllers across the United States, but it also shows that the ecology of civic disorder was at best an incomplete way of understanding urban rats.

ECOLOGIES OF GARBAGE AND HOUSING IN MILWAUKEE

Much as in Harlem, Milwaukee experienced sporadic antirat campaigns in the mid-twentieth century. A local housing judge declared, "we are not going to permit American citizens to live in rat-infested premises in 1960" and fined several absentee owners "who [take] money out of Milwaukee and [put] nothing back."[72] In 1966, middle-class activists living near a new expressway demanded that the Health Department provide new garbage cans, decorating City Hall with a garland of dead rats in protest. When the Health Department refused, a resident used his own funds to purchase hundreds of galvanized steel cans for his neighbors.[73] Such progressive judges and privileged residents blamed landlords and city government rather than fellow residents. Their rat-control efforts were not part of any organized, sustained program, however.

Meanwhile, much like Congress, the Wisconsin State Assembly treated publicly funded rat control as a joke. In December 1967, a Milwaukee delegate tried to amend a bill funding a bounty on coyotes and foxes—persistent problems for farmers—by adding money to reward citizen rat-catchers as well. Rural lawmakers mocked his proposal, offering to send barn cats from their districts. The Milwaukee delegate retorted: "The rats in [Milwaukee] are big enough to eat those cats of yours."[74] In Washington and Madison, rural lawmakers belittled urban problems through the proxy of a seemingly trifling animal. The journalist Ernest Boynton explained: "The House is a white man's world, and in such there are no rats."[75] To white, rural lawmakers, foxes, screwworms, and starlings were more worthy targets for modern pest control.

The Health Department faulted residents when "in 1966, the city experienced a dramatic increase in rat infestations in the inner core area," along with rising reports of rat bites.[76] Officials repeated the "breakdown" hypothesis developed by reformers in the first decade of the twentieth century who had studied problems in Washington, D.C.'s alley communities. They explained that new residents arriving from rural areas "furnish[ed] a food supply of improperly stored garbage and additional shelter in the accumulations of rubbish." They believed that new African-American residents settling in on the North Side and Puerto Ricans on the South Side were unaccustomed to the garbage disposal practices necessary to avoid rat problems in cities, as evidenced by their neighborhoods' heaping trash cans.[77] The U.S. Public Health Service also saw race and rural-to-urban migration as factors in rodent ecology: "The average annual rate of emigration of nonwhite citizens from rural areas [into cities] has been 2 $\frac{1}{2}$ times greater than that of white citizens. The bulk of this influx gravitates into the central slums and carries rural habits of environmental sanitation into an already poorly controlled urban milieu, from whence nearly all rat-bite complaints already emanate."[78] Mayor Henry Maier called for a program to "acculturate" residents to the urban environment—that is, "to educate newcomers that they cannot—as they might in rural Puerto Rico or rural Mississippi—simply throw garbage out the window."[79] Like many cities, Milwaukee aimed to overcome ecological decay and rat population growth by teaching new residents how to steward their garbage in urban space.

Milwaukee's Health Department won one of the first grants under the federal Urban Rat Control Program. It hired educators to teach residents of target neighborhoods about stewarding the urban environment. On twelve hundred blocks on the North and South Sides, women learned to keep kitchens spotless and wrap food garbage in heavy paper; men were instructed to close garbage can lids and clean up dog droppings promptly.[80] Residents of infested blocks would have to be more vigilant about house-keeping than residents in communities with better-maintained homes and lower rodent populations. Middle-class African-Americans from neighborhoods on the edge of the target zone staffed the program, and they established positive relationships with the community.[81] Public health experts and ecologists considered Milwaukee's program one of the best-designed among the fifty-two funded by federal rat-control grants. William Jackson, a graduate of the Johns Hopkins rodent ecology program and a global rat expert, believed that resident engagement made Milwaukee's program more successful than those in other cities where poisoning was emphasized over education. Health educators stressed the shared respon-sibility of citizens and government for rat control.[82]

Residents could adopt better garbage disposal practices, but many aspects of the environment proved difficult for them to control. Educa-tion staff soon found that treating garbage as a personal responsibility still left room for rats to thrive; residents took better care of their garbage, but their exercises of stewardship met with further obstacles. On many blocks each property still had a built-in ash pit, remains of a time when fuel or trash was burned in the home. It was common practice to use these as garbage receptacles—especially if landlords did not provide regular trash cans—but collectors often failed to clean pits out completely.[83] Regardless of whether residents disposed of trash there, rats found safe, comfortable homes in ash pits. Furthermore, the city only collected garbage every three weeks. Between pickups, householders had to store refuse, including food waste that attracted rats with its fragrant odors.[84] The infrastructure of target neighborhoods supported rats while residents strived to change their own practices.[85]

Neglectful or financially strapped owners also invited rats. More than half the dwellings in the target neighborhoods were not rat-proof, with rats gnawing holes in foundations or squeezing through gaps around pipes. Housing inspectors and judges strained to enforce rat-proofing mandates on thousands of homes. The city received HUD funding to coordinate housing rehabilitation with community rat-control activities, but the grant only covered six blocks.[86] Meanwhile, volunteers and staff tore down hundreds of ash pits. Staff installed hardware cloth over exposed foundations and metal flashing on the bottom of gnawed doors; thousands of housing units needed such repairs.[87] As in 1940s Baltimore, years of disinvestment left a backlog of costly repairs that city government and landlords would or could not completely pay for. Health officials eked out funds and staff for building repair, but public funding could not keep up with the improvements needed to support and sustain citizens' rat-control labor.[88] Staff in Milwaukee strived to broaden the program with its limited resources when it became clear that stewardship of garbage was important but insufficient for rodent control.

Staff who lived in Milwaukee's target area praised the program for helping reduce rat populations, making residents feel safer in their homes and community.[89] In 1980, however, the U.S. General Accounting Office (GAO) found that projects across the United States had faltered, issuing a report titled "The Urban Rat Control Program Is In Trouble." The program defined a local project as successful when fewer than 2 percent of homes "exhibit[ed] exterior signs of active rat infestations" and met one of two measures of proper garbage disposal. Not only were local programs unable to maintain this level of success, they also failed to monitor indoor rats. Especially in colder northern cities, large numbers of rats moved indoors where they exposed residents directly to disease, stress, and injury. Indeed, the GAO estimated the number of rat bites each year in the United States at forty-five thousand.[90] As urban rats persisted and public rat controllers repeated the errors of 1940s Baltimore, local activists engaged in more overt forms of resistance.

"COMMUNITY CONTROL OF MODERN TECHNOLOGY": RAT CONTROL AS ACTIVISM

The sort of rat control performed by the State of New York and the Milwaukee Health Department did not go far enough to satisfy the demands of groups like Jesse Gray's Community Council on Housing, which viewed rats as symbols and symptoms of much larger problems. For some activists, however, the ability to control rats for themselves signified an important victory. For these often self-taught rat controllers, grassroots extermination campaigns were means of seizing the scientific knowledge, economic self-determination, and environmental mastery that had been denied to communities of color by neglectful, exploitive, and discriminatory power structures. In the years after Jesse Gray turned rats into potent symbols in struggles for decent housing, other African-American leaders established programs that attacked infestations directly. Grassroots organizations made rat control a matter of, as the Black Panther Party put it, "people's community control of modern technology."[91] Beyond the need to revitalize housing and improve garbage collection services, these groups also believed that communities of color had been denied the benefits of pest-control science.

Some leaders envisioned that pest control would provide not just better services for black neighborhoods, but also community economic development and a career path for local youth. Washington, D.C.'s Pride, Inc., trained local "street dudes," many of whom carried a criminal record, in a variety of trades while also involving them in political protest.[92] Pride's leaders saw extermination as a profitable skill and a means for locals to gain skills while providing much-needed environmental services in their own neighborhoods.[93] When Washington received a federal rat-control grant, Pride helped provide the services and community organizing while also working with the Model Cities program to better link the "War on Rats" with housing rehabilitation.[94] One Pride leader, Rufus "Catfish" Mayfield, dreamed of founding "the International School for Rat and Pest Extermination," which would "bring hundreds of low-income-area residents to Washington from all over the country and train them in scientific methods of pest control."[95] Mayfield never succeeded in establishing this school, but his thought revealed links some black leaders made among environmental conditions, self-determination, and extension of science and technology to struggling communities.

Also in Washington, D.C., the Anacostia Neighborhood Museum presented an exhibit on rats to engage the community with programs like the War on Rats. Museum education specialist Zora Martin Felton conceived the exhibit in 1969 as community residents told her about troubling encounters with rats. Youth spoke of rats climbing over the walls from the nearby mental health hospital; parents were afraid to let their children outside even as far as the garbage can at night; and one woman recalled with horror feeding what she thought was a kitten in a dark lot, only to discover it was a large rat. The exhibit centered upon a simulated backyard environment populated with several live rats. Like Harlem residents who resented the *Amsterdam News* for publishing rat stories, some residents criticized the exhibit for airing the rat issue in the museum that was the neighborhood's public face. Others welcomed frank exposure of a serious environmental problem and public discussion of the ecology and politics of rat infestation.[96]

Philadelphia's Students and Neighbors Action Program (SNAP) likewise aimed to bring the benefits of science to communities that lacked access to elite knowledge about pests. African-American college students formed SNAP to reverse environmental decline in their neighborhood, deeming rat control the most urgent problem. SNAP leaders described a neighborhood abandoned by both residents and public services: "Vacant houses contain dirt which harbors rats and other pests. . . . Rubbish is dumped in backyards because there are not enough trash containers for people to use. . . . Almost all the buildings on one block are vacant." A chemistry professor helped them choose an effective rat poison, and they enlisted residents to help clear debris that harbored rats. Members learned from a rat-control expert to bait the blocks systematically before clean-up activities. This sequence of activities helped ensure that few rats would survive to invade uninfested homes and adjoining blocks.[97] In the absence of state resources, groups like SNAP sought to develop skills and expertise to help communities become self-sufficient, safe, and healthy. The project's geographic reach remained limited, however, because it depended upon volunteer labor and community resources.

The Black Panther Party (BPP) developed pest-control expertise and delivery systems to serve low-income African-American communities. Representations of the BPP often focused on its "self-defense" agenda, but they also called for self-determination, "decent housing, fit for the shelter of human beings," and "people's community control of modern technology." The BPP acted as a shadow state that fulfilled unmet needs for everything from ambulance services to affordable meals for children. In Detroit, Houston, and other cities, the BPP volunteers provided free pest control as part of its "Serve the People—Body and Soul" program. Members of the Houston branch blamed housing conditions as well as exterminators for persistent infestations: "As is natural to this capitalist economy, which feeds on poor people's every misfortune, exterminators who are equipped with the skills and tools to control or eliminate pests charge excessive prices for their work. Thus, the exterminator makes a house free of roaches and rodents a luxury and not a human right."[98] While SNAP couched its rhetoric about pest control in terms of democratic science, and the BPP in terms of socialism, both groups sought to develop expertise and resources that they found less accessible to low-income African-Americans.

Radical black artists used images of life with pests to argue that poor African-Americans had been left behind while white Americans enjoyed the benefits of modern technology and clean environments. Posters by Emory Douglas, minister of culture for the BPP, portrayed African-Americans confronting oppression and squalor. In one, a woman clutches an oversized rat, a look of defiance and determination on her face. The poster's title—"Black Misery! Ain't we got a right to the tree of life?"—along with the subject's compelling posture and tight grip on the rat, suggested that regular people could turn pain into action. Douglas portrayed women fighting off rats in defense of babies and thinking of killing "greedy slumlords" for "forc[ing them] to live in these inhuman conditions." Many of his posters used cockroaches as motifs, dotting the background in images of families in crumbling hovels. In 1976, Douglas collected stories from residents about health threats and indignities in public housing. Residents explained: "I have rats and roaches in my apartment. It needs effective extermination," and "we need more garbage pick-up."[99] These testimonies became the basis of an illustrated storyboard about an archetypal project run by a black man named "Mr. Sellout." Portraits of injustice and resistance rallied community members and offered expressive outlets for anger.

In a 1967 speech, Lyndon Johnson said: "The knowledge that many children in the world's most affluent nation are attacked, maimed, and even killed by rats should fill every American with shame." In his 1970 poem "Whitey's on the Moon," the performance poet Gil Scott-Heron elaborated on this sentiment and highlighted racial divides that Johnson left unstated. The poem begins: "A rat done bit my sister Nell / And Whitey's on the moon." Scott-Heron juxtaposed the mundane hazards of dilapidated housing and the lingering impacts of the rat bite—Nell's swollen face, unpaid doctor bills—against the high-tech wonder of a lunar landing. On the surface, the poem clearly criticized the allocation of technology and taxpayer dollars to outer space instead of urban space. At a deeper level, Scott-Heron's piece also condemned Americans for looking to the sky for inspiration and national pride at a moment when they might have found these by providing basic health and decency for earth-bound communities.[100]

Low-income black communities desired the health, safety, and modernity promised by postwar pesticides and housing—desires much like those other Americans projected onto these chemicals. Infestation carried cultural meanings for poor black communities that it did not for affluent whites, however—meanings that transferred to pesticide technologies. Black activists and artists believed their own communities had been denied the privileges of pest-free living enjoyed by affluent whites. Rat-control programs run by public health departments, and general public discourse about rats, often blamed infestation on blacks. Infestation not only threatened mental and physical health; it also brought racialized social stigma and a sense of exclusion from modern American life. Thus, pesticides symbolized dignity and equality for some low-income African-Americans in ways they did not for affluent whites. Although grassroots extermination programs sought to bring modern living standards to poor communities of color, they inadvertently brought heightened pesticide exposure to both applicators and residents. By the late 1960s, public health researchers began to find that poor blacks carried higher body burdens of pesticides than affluent whites, for whom lower quantities of chemicals provided better results.[101] Ecologists focused new scrutiny on low-income black neighborhoods as they believed rodenticides were changing the very bodies and ecologies of rats there.

"SUPER RATS": COMPLEX BODIES IN URBAN ECOLOGIES

Government-funded rodent management programs along with grassroots and do-it-yourself rat controllers made abundant use of the rodenticide warfarin in urban neighborhoods. By the 1950s, warfarin's popularity exceeded that of Curt Richter's ANTU, both in the United States and worldwide; it gained a reputation as a magic bullet much as DDT had for insects.[102] Also like the postwar insecticides, warfarin's effectiveness depended upon environmental context. In neighborhoods where rats enjoyed ample supplies of food waste, many rats survived doses of warfarin that were diluted by a rich diet of garbage. Individuals resistant to warfarin came to dominate local rat populations. The very chemical that had promised to subdue urban nature changed the bodies of the rodent denizens in neighborhoods neglected by social institutions, making it harder to control these creatures.

Before the late 1950s, ecologists and health experts expressed no worries about resistance to rodenticides, even after mosquitoes, flies, and cockroaches had evolved resistance to organochlorides in the 1940s and 1950s. Resistance traits required generations to gain dominance in a pest population, and rat generation times exceeded those of most insects, although they reproduced faster than most mammals. As of the 1950s, no mammalian pest population had ever resisted any pesticide. Some humans, however, failed to respond to coumarin, the blood-thinning drug that provides low doses of warfarin to patients at risk for strokes and blood clots. Discovery of this human trait foreshadowed news from rural Scotland in 1958, and the Netherlands a few years later, that some local rat populations no longer responded to warfarin.[103] Human technological and environmental practices revealed hidden complexities in rat bodies.

Warfarin-resistant rat populations appeared in more locales abroad, and in 1968 the U.S. National Pest Control Association and the North Atlantic Treaty Organization sent the American ecologist Dr. William Jackson, a Rodent Ecology Project graduate and global rat expert, to investigate. At resistance sites in Europe, Jackson found farms that offered abundant food alternatives to the warfarin-laced baits absentee owners had strewn about their properties. Rats thrived in ramshackle outbuildings and storage bins, feasting on spilled grain and feed between doses of warfarin. Farmers and government pest controllers laid out baits at will rather than on a regimented dosing schedule that would expedite buildup of the poison in the rats' blood. Alternate food sources and lax baiting practices often rendered warfarin ineffective, and in this case they did even worse: rats that resisted warfarin came to dominate local populations.[104]

Jackson predicted that old farm estates in the U.S. South would foster resistance to warfarin because they resembled European farms where resistance had emerged: absentee owners, careless warfarin use, and structures that had gone years without repairs. Indeed, North Carolina tobacco growers saw some of the earliest U.S. cases.[105] Yet Jackson wrote: "In the large urban rat control programs [in American cities], I would not expect resistance to develop" because he saw few similarities between U.S. cities and neglected European farms.[106] He had worked with U.S. health departments and trusted that they used warfarin properly under the Urban Rat Control Program. Soon after Jackson's return from Europe, though, Chicago pest-control operators reported that the rats on their turf no longer responded to warfarin.[107]

For a rat to succumb to warfarin, it had to consume multiple, regular doses of poison, which could be purchased in pellet or brick form, premixed with such flavors as coconut or chicken. Other poisons targeted the nervous system or lungs, but warfarin disabled the body's Vitamin K cycle that produced blood-clotting factors. Rats poisoned with warfarin died of internal bleeding from an accumulation of everyday injuries that would normally heal in the absence of the poison. Warfarin posed a lower risk than acute rodenticides to nontarget species—humans, pets, and wildlife—that accidentally ingested it. This feature also made it easier for rats to survive, however. A rat might nibble a butter-flavored warfarin brick occasionally, but frequent feasts on food wastes in garbage cans diluted the warfarin, allowing the Vitamin K cycle to reset itself. Many neighborhoods targeted by the Urban Rodent Control Program lacked adequate trash collection, or even trash receptacles, and thus supplied enough alternative meals to dilute rats' dosages of warfarin. A restaurant Dumpster or family trash bin might even provide leftover spinach pie, collards, or other foods rich in Vitamin K, warfarin's antidote. Other poisons could kill a rat with its first meal, but warfarin had to become the main course every day for several days.[108]

Competent pest controllers and public health workers knew that warfarin alone would not control rats and that rodent management required holistic environmental reform. The very environments that supported the most rats were also those that most reduced warfarin's effectiveness, however. Professionals and residents there faced a double struggle against both rats and garbage.[109] Meanwhile, warfarin's reputation as a miracle rodenticide tempted unscrupulous or untrained people to misuse it. In 1967, David Davis called warfarin "the worst thing that [has] happened to rodent control." A Rockefeller Foundation officer recalled Davis's explanation: "With the immediate success obtained with this material, the remaining requirements (of stoppage, sanitation, education, etc.) were prematurely omitted from rodent control operations."[110]

By 1973, toxicologists reported that lab tests found that up to 70 percent of rats in Chicago's Austin, Englewood, and Lawndale neighborhoods were not susceptible to warfarin.[111] These three sites had the highest rates of resistance among urban test sites in the United States, most of which belonged to the Urban Rat Control Program. In the Lawndale neighborhood on the West Side, an extremely poor and almost entirely African-American area, investigators reported resistance rates as high as 89 percent by 1979. According to Jackson and colleague Daniel Ashton, Lawndale was "characterized by a highly transient human population, absentee landlords, low-income housing, and poor sanitation." The health department and other authorities had been saturating the area with warfarin since the 1950s. Jackson and Ashton surmised that "this combination of long and regular use of anticoagulants and poor environmental conditions associated with a transient human population has selected for a high incidence of resistance in the rat populations."[112] Disinvested city neighborhoods shared more with neglected farms than Jackson had realized.

Discovery of resistance brought new state and scientific scrutiny, along with social stigma, to low-income, racially segregated neighborhoods. Media dubbed the resistant rodents "super rats," representing nature in these communities as malignant and mutated.[113] In Chicago, residents and health authorities disputed responsibility for persistent rats much as they had in 1967 over the failed extermination bill. In 1977, Austin's community association demanded more frequent street-cleaning and garbage pickups, and more appropriate pickup locations. Meanwhile, the city's rodent-control director called Austin "putrid" and charged that residents "don't give a damn." Residents demanded that the director lose his job over the insults.[114]

Heavy snows in the winter of 1979 shut down garbage collections in Chicago, leading, later in the year, to a rat population spike and a rise in bite reports in the city.[115] Blame again fell upon black neighborhoods. The city's African-American newspaper, the *Defender*, printed a commentary by a white writer who accused his black neighbors of leaving trash to pile up in the weeks when pickups were suspended.[116] The *Sun-Times* quoted Jackson calling the West Side "a prime example of a very serious [resistance] problem in an inner-city area." The reporter raised the specter "of rat attacks on people and of intracity migrations" by super rats. New York rats made national headlines when they attacked a woman on the street in 1979, and the *Sun-Times* made the sensational suggestion that the pack in question might have been super rats. Anticoagulant resistance does not predispose rats to viciousness, however.[117] The phrase "inner-city area" conveyed an innuendo of the racial identity of infested areas; the menace of intracity migration and attacks by resistant rats echoed white fears about poor blacks invading their neighborhoods. Meanwhile, the mainstream press seldom mentioned inequities in housing quality and trash collection that made black neighborhoods susceptible to infestation and warfarin resistance, nor did they provide positive reports of residents and officials cooperating to clean up infested areas.[118] Rats were already a stigma on black neighborhoods, and reports of super rats added to stereotypes about failed environmental stewardship there.

Jackson dismissed the media hype over "super rats"; still, he believed that areas with high resistance rates required state and scientific scrutiny.[119] The U.S. Public Health Service, which administered the Urban Rodent Control Program, monitored rats from all program sites.[120] This research made new demands of residents while also bringing new resources. Researchers used neighborhoods such as Lawndale to test new control methods, including "second-generation" anticoagulants that were more potent than warfarin and thus required fewer doses to kill their target. Jackson insisted on better sanitation in testing areas. He selected experimental blocks where he found householders at home during the day to let researchers onto the property and help with intensifying clean-up efforts. Most of these residents were women, and Jackson attributed much of the experiments' success to their hard work; presence of organized women's clubs or women at home during the day was a strong predictor of program success. Ashton and Jackson boasted over 70 percent control in the blocks where they worked closely with residents.[121] Lawndale did not receive increased funding for code enforcement or assistance from sanitation officials as Baltimore had during its efforts at ecological control. Instead, scientists and health officials contained resistant rats by enlisting the labor and cooperation of residents.

At least one scientist, however, raised doubts about rats' resistance to warfarin and therefore the need for second-generation anticoagulants. Dr. Stephen Frantz had, like William Jackson, studied under David Davis, but Frantz adhered more closely than Jackson to his mentor's antirodenticide stance. Frantz charged that stronger poisons exposed people, pets, and nontarget wildlife—including those that eat rats—to needless risks.[122] He also feared that careless rodenticide application practices would leave cities bereft of effective poisons should an infectious disease emergency arise. Upon retesting "resistant" rats, Frantz reported that at least half became susceptible to warfarin again after a period of nonexposure. The gene for resistance may switch on through exposure to warfarin. Frantz's research located the problem of resistance not in rats, but in the human follies of unsanitary environments and misuse of anticoagulants.[123]

STIGMA AND PROTEST IN INFESTED NEIGHBORHOODS

Black Panthers, exterminators, and some health officials placed their faith in chemical rodenticides and insecticides. Other health officials and many politicians placed their faith in resident education. Editors of the *Amsterdam News* placed their faith in the Sharkey-Brown-Isaacs bill. Neither technology nor environmental citizens nor antisegregation laws fulfilled the promise of modern, rat-free cities, however. Lyndon Johnson, Jesse Gray, and the General Accounting Office all urged holistic reforms that had been recommended decades earlier but remained perpetually delayed and incomplete for lack of funds. Rats persisted in poor neighborhoods not for lack of modern fixes—be they technical, disciplinary, or legal. What Baltimore lacked in 1950, many cities still lacked in 1970: the funds, capacity, and political will necessary to rebuild and support long-neglected communities.

Compared with the need for urban reinvestment, the Urban Rat Control Program represented a modest gesture to urban African-Americans who were eager for relief from a small but menacing creature. The program spread a mere twenty million dollars each year among fifty-two projects in central cities across the United States. The Urban Rat Control

Program deserves credit for shifting more federal pest-control dollars toward cities amid entrenched funding patterns that favored pest control on farms and in suburbs in spite of urban growth. As passed by Congress and implemented by local health departments, however, the program did too little to place rat problems in their ecological and social context. Urban funding grew under Lyndon Johnson's Great Society, but it only slowly rebuilt millions of homes that harbored rats and other health hazards.

Like other social welfare, public health, and environmental issues, rat-control programs cast public and private actors into roles loaded with political values and meanings. It held central city-dwellers responsible for rats without correcting the entrenched imbalance in housing support that favored suburbs over cities. Rats were already a stigma on black neighborhoods, and the program did little to shift that stigma to negligent landlords or urban policy in general—where Jesse Gray had tried to place stigma with his protest tactics. Residents who stewarded garbage and tidied their homes and yards remained confined to their segregated neighborhoods; Milwaukee was one of the most segregated cities in the country.[124] Deteriorating dwellings proved far more difficult to police than individual residents and their environmental practices, however.

Lawmakers and officials who blamed infestation on the ecology of civic disorder framed the issue in narrow terms. Rat bodies meshed with broad social and economic forces in the interstices of urban homes and neighborhoods. Many neighborhoods faced a constant threat of rat invasion, which residents could only counter with constant vigilance. By the early 1970s, programs in cities across the United States scrambled to repair crumbling homes as resident education and rat poisons proved insufficient to control rats. Not only rat populations, but changes to their very bodies showed the complex ways in which creatures were entangled with urban social conditions.

In 1972, the Milwaukee Health Department held a rat-control parade led by a band of Pied Pipers waving a banner bearing a single word: "ecology."[125] The image evokes questions about the breadth of the term, and the breadth of thinking about rats by the state, activists, and citizens. Had Jesse Gray, Emory Douglas, or Gil Scott-Heron been involved in organizing this parade—a job that would have suited Gray's showmanship, Douglas's art, or Scott-Heron's poetry—the ecology banners might have been joined by banners demanding sound, affordable housing and an end to racial dis-crimination. The ecology of injustice expands the frame of the rat-control problem, showing that racist housing markets, central-city disinvestment, and state neglect account for infestation at least as much as do household garbage disposal practices.

6

INTEGRATING URBAN HOMES

Cockroaches and Survival

IN THE ESSAY "EYE TO EYE: BLACK WOMEN, HATRED, AND ANGER,"
Audre Lorde recalled sitting down next to a white woman on a crowded
subway train as a small child in the late 1930s. The woman "jerk[ed] her
coat closer to her" with a look of horror on her face, and the young Audre
assumed that there was something disgusting on the seat, "probably a
roach," and so pulled her own coat toward herself as well. "Suddenly I
realize[d] there [was] nothing on the seat between us," Lorde remembered.
"It [was] me she [didn't] want her coat to touch."[1]

Lorde's 1974 poem "Brown Menace, or Poem to the Survival of Roaches"
elaborates upon this sense that many whites in her time perceived and
treated blacks as pests. Yet African-Americans had survived and would
survive hatred and disgust, attempts to contain them, and even threats
of extermination.[2] "Call me/your deepest urge/toward survival," the
cockroach narrator says. "Call me/your own determination/in the most
detestable shape." Lorde makes roaches' stubbornness an inspiring trait,
even amid the trials of living with them. Roaches also embody the sense
of shame that Lorde believed blacks internalize through the experience of
racism—just as the young Audre sensed that there was something dirty,
roachlike, about her own body because of incidents like the one on the subway. Furthermore, roaches themselves "alter— / through your greedy pre-
occupations / through your kitchen wars / and your poisonous refusal—/
to survive." Attempts to put roaches in their place remade roaches as an
ever more tenacious part of the environment.

Across the United States, German cockroaches had survived and changed long past the introduction of DDT and a succession of other pesticides. For decades, residents of the Chicago Housing Authority's Henry Horner Homes, a segregated project on the Near West Side, felt shame and visceral disgust about the roaches that became ever more tenacious members of their households. Families declined to host Thanksgiving dinners for fear that a roach would sneak into the turkey only to reveal itself as the guests sat down to eat. Mothers worried about both the chemicals that the exterminator sprayed, with their lingering, putrid smell, and also the effects of roaches crawling on their food or into their children's ears, polluting the entire home environment—sometimes just days after a pesticide application. One woman was mortified when a roach crept out of her purse during a job interview.[3] Roaches made the other insults of living in segregated public housing all the more tangible, corporeal, and humiliating.

Each encounter with roaches signified the disregard and dehumanization to which the housing authority subjected them. A resident leader named Sarah Ruffin recalled that infestation "was just an everyday thing, and [there was] nothing we could do about it"—although many applied their own pesticides when they saw the exterminators' did not work. While residents tried to put roaches in their place, they themselves had been consigned to a poor, crime-ridden neighborhood by the housing authority's Jim Crow policies. The housing authority had long neglected Horner's physical environment, and the effects of that neglect extended into the residents' very bodies. Roaches became part of Horner residents' struggle against racial injustice by the state—a struggle to survive in their own homes. The Chicago Housing Authority completed construction on the final annex of the Henry Horner Homes complex in 1961, just a year before the publication of Rachel Carson's book *Silent Spring*, which condemned the reductionist thinking behind contemporary pest-control practices. Carson popularized ecological thought and, as the historian Maril Hazlett has put it, blurred the lines among human bodies, animals, and the environment, helping to galvanize the modern American environmental movement.[4]

Carson showed that attempts to put pests in their place had sent pesticides coursing through the veins of entire ecosystems; under contemporary pest-control regimes, neither pests nor pesticides were contained. Entomology and ecology researchers called for a more "integrated" approach to controlling pests, which accounted for the complexity of natural ecosystems rather than trying to simplify ecological connections with quick chemical fixes. Carson and the mainstream environmentalists and scientists who took up her rallying cry did not, however, integrate the problems of environmental pollution and those of social injustice. Environmentalists demanded information about and regulation of the pesticides used on their food, on suburban streets, and in parks, but few seemed to think about landscapes like Henry Horner in the years after *Silent Spring*'s publication.

Residents of Horner developed their own ideas about the interconnections among health, animals, environments, and justice. Mothers grappled daily with the effects of roaches on their children, and some came to think of injustice as part of the ecology of their homes. They understood, much as Audre Lorde did, that roaches were not only pests but also incarnations of racist public policies—and visceral, contradictory symbols of both racism and survival.[5] This broad conception of ecology merged with the legacy of *Silent Spring* in the 1990s, opening new paths to integrate both housing and long-divided fields of political struggle.

SEGREGATED HOMES, DISINTEGRATING HOMES

The history of racial segregation in Chicago Housing Authority (CHA) projects helped shape both the ecology of the projects and later struggles against cockroaches and pesticides there. The CHA's first federally subsidized projects in the late 1930s and early 1940s were segregated by design, and the projects' tenants reflected the racial makeup of the neighborhoods in which they were constructed. Projects such as Julia Lathrop Homes were sited in white neighborhoods and admitted only white tenants, while Ida B. Wells Homes was located on the black South Side and admitted only blacks.

After World War II, planners estimated that it would take more than 270,000 new or refurbished units to properly house the Chicagoans who lived in substandard or overcrowded homes.[6] The Housing Act of 1949 funded acquisition of "slum" tracts for demolition and building of new public housing; most of the areas that qualified for demolition were in African-American neighborhoods. The federal government would also support a maximum of forty thousand units for Chicago—far fewer than the number required. Demolition of existing homes—however decrepit, crowded, and infested—would only subtract from the meager gain in housing units and would displace mostly African-American citizens. The CHA therefore proposed to build new public housing projects on vacant land, most of which was found in or near white neighborhoods, both to preserve housing units and to support racial integration of the projects. Chicago's mayor Edward Kennelly, the city alders, and many white Chicagoans opposed this siting plan. After a protracted public battle, the CHA extended prewar Jim Crow policies: each new project would be either all-black or all-white and located in a neighborhood of the same color.[7]

Under this segregated siting plan, CHA built Henry Horner Homes in a largely African-American and low-income neighborhood to house African-American tenants. The CHA erected the vast project's eighteen buildings, containing some three thousand units, in two phases, completed in 1956 and 1961, on the near West Side.[8] Horner occupied a long strip of blocks, with a long, narrow layout that included playgrounds in the central courtyards. The first residents to move in, in 1956, found the new buildings "dazzling," a vast improvement over homes they had rented for too much money on the private housing market. Horner offered events for children and adults in the midst of a community that bustled with commerce and political activity despite its poverty. And, in spite of its miserly budgets, managers and residents seemed determined to make a better life than residents had known elsewhere.[9]

Just five years after Horner's completion, residents from other projects sued CHA, charging that it had violated the Fourteenth Amendment and other federal civil rights laws by deliberately selecting public housing sites to "avoid the placement of Negro families in white neighborhoods." The suit soon charged the new Department of Housing and Urban Development with supporting the CHA's civil rights violations.[10] The case came to be called *Gautreaux*, for Dorothy Gautreaux, the lead complainant and a resident of Altgeld Gardens, a project on the South Side. Horner clearly belonged to the pattern of segregation that was the subject of *Gautreaux*.

Gautreaux originated amid the Chicago Freedom Movement, called "the most ambitious civil rights campaign in the North" and led by Reverend Martin Luther King Jr. and Al Raby. Chicago's 1963 Fair Housing Ordinance already promised an end to racial discrimination in both public and private housing, but residents and activists remained dissatisfied with enforcement.[11] The Freedom Movement's Open City Project called for the CHA to integrate public housing projects, build low-density projects in suburbs, discontinue construction of high-rises, and rehabilitate existing structures. Freedom Movement members called attention to unjust housing conditions with nonviolent marches through public spaces and white communities. Some of these were met with angry counterdemonstrations.[12] While Freedom Movement activists held demonstrations and negotiated with city officials, the *Gautreaux* plaintiffs and their American Civil Liberties Union lawyers pursued legal recourse.

Public housing residents protested not only segregation by the CHA but also physical conditions in public housing. Many considered the environments within the projects inhumane, with their cheap fixtures, shoddy maintenance, and high-rise architecture.[13] Public projects showed their age long before their time, as researchers John Atlas and Peter Dreier explain: "A cycle of government neglect and underfunding" set in, leading "to poor construction design, inadequate maintenance, racial segregation, stigmatization, and further concentration of the very poor."[14] For their part, Horner residents grew more frustrated with the housing authority each time the elevator broke down, the stairwells leaked, or the heaters stopped working during the frigid Chicago winter—or when cockroaches pervaded their apartments. These environmental concerns seemed a far cry from the American environmental movement that gained momentum in the 1960s after the publication of *Silent Spring*. Yet both activist movements addressed environmental hazards that threatened human well-being, and the concept of integration was important to both, though in very different ways.

INTEGRATED PEST MANAGEMENT AND THE URBAN ENVIRONMENT

While Horner residents settled into their apartments, and other Chicago Housing Authority tenants pursued justice in court, entomologists and ecologists in Berkeley, California, were rethinking pest-control practices in the wake of Rachel Carson's *Silent Spring*. Some scientists had worried about DDT and related chemicals since the first signs of pesticide resistance appeared in houseflies and mosquitoes in the late 1940s; later, the death of nontarget wildlife including fish and birds also raised alarm among conservationists. Many had for decades advocated "biological control" of agricultural pests—that is, supporting predatory insect populations to hold down the numbers of insects that destroy crops. Beginning in 1962, the growing environmental movement gave new momentum to the development of pest-control methods that nurtured the complexity of ecological systems. Informed also by theoretical trends in the discipline of ecosystem ecology, researchers conceived the concept of Integrated Pest Management (IPM).[15]

The entomologists and ecologists who first formalized the idea of IPM based their thinking on agricultural settings rather than public health campaigns or structural pest control, although some of their ideas recall David Davis's rat studies in 1940s Baltimore. They argued that the chemical-based pest-control methods long practiced in the United States did not only contaminate the environment; they also severed feedback loops between farm environments and farmers' practices. The appearance of pests, they believed, should signal to a producer that the ecosystem of his farm was somehow unhealthy. For example, a monoculture of one crop might invite pests to thrive; poor soil or underlying disease might leave plants vulnerable to pests. Early IPM scholars called for farmers to become effective "ecosystem managers" by promoting soil health and designing cropping systems that supported resistance to pests. Farmers should also integrate themselves into the ecosystem's feedback loops, learning to interpret signs of crop health and infestation. Rising pest populations on a crop indicated a need to change practices or perhaps to introduce a natural predator. Spraying scale insects, beetles, or nematodes merely killed the messenger.[16] The same could be said of pests in an apartment building, but as of the mid-1960s, few IPM researchers gave their attention to such environments.

One of the key elements of agricultural IPM was the economic injury level. According to IPM theory, an infestation reached this action threshold when there were enough pests to cause damage costing more than the labor, materials, and equipment required to control them. Only if the pest population on a field or crop reached this threshold should ecosystem managers—in agricultural situations, the farmer—take action to manage the pests. Even then, the farmer should begin with the delicate tool of biological control before resorting to the blunt instrument of pesticides.[17] It was not immediately apparent how to apply these principles of IPM to domestic environments and pests that did not destroy crops but rather disturbed health and well-being.

The University of California at Berkeley became a hotbed of research and thought about IPM, focused largely on agriculture. There, Dr. Robert van den Bosch attracted several graduate students to his lab while also sparking controversy with scathing critiques of the chemical industry.[18] One of van den Bosch's PhD students, William Olkowski, was also an activist at Berkeley's Consumer Cooperative, where Olkowski and his wife, Helga, promoted household waste recycling—a kind of ecological feedback loop that engaged domestic environments. The Olkowskis embraced the logic of the ecosystem theory that informed Integrated Pest Management. They soon combined William's entomological expertise with Helga's practical vision of domestic ecologies to bring IPM to urban households. Helga hoped to translate IPM into practice for regular people through civic activism and scientific education. Much as agricultural IPM advocates urged farmers to become ecosystem managers, so she promoted domestic IPM as a kind of citizen-science, a way for housewives and other householders to better understand and nurture the ecology of their homes. In 1971, she published her first guide to domestic IPM, *Common Sense Pest Control*, just as surveys revealed that at least 72 percent—and perhaps as many as 93 percent—of all American households used chemical pesticides either indoors or outdoors, and perhaps both.[19] Helga Olkowski also led workshops to help community members give up the sprays, aerosols, and other products based on organochlorides and organophosphates that had become fixtures in almost every home. She offered readers choices for how to deal with unwanted creatures in their homes and gardens—choices other than chemicals.[20]

Rachel Carson had sought to make scientific information accessible to the public in *Silent Spring*. Following that example, Helga Olkowski encouraged householders to seize knowledge about pesticides, ecology, and health for themselves, rather than rely on chemical manufacturers for information: "Will you risk the health of your family and pets because insects are frightening or distasteful to you? Pesticide companies and their distributors thrive on your fears and lack of information about the toxicity of their products. Protect your home environment, and don't let persuasive advertising for such products tempt you to bring these poisons into your house."[21] She insisted that reliance on pesticides represented a vain attempt to separate the home from nature. Such actions merely muted information feedbacks while exposing families and nature to danger. Translated for the home environment, IPM meant that householders should not try to beat back insects and other creatures in the home; rather, they should try to understand the information pests bore about environmental conditions. Cockroaches or mice, for example, might indicate a need to repair a home's foundation, caulk baseboards, or store food in pest-proof containers. Like pest management advice to farmers, Helga Olkowski's IPM stressed the agency, knowledge, and choices of ecosystem managers, but in this case those managers were housewives and other household members rather than farmers.[22] Instead of monitoring citrus groves, fields of soybeans, or herds of cattle, they monitored basements, kitchens, and bathrooms.

In 1973, William Olkowski helped translate IPM for urban practice by introducing the concept of aesthetic injury level—analogous to the economic threshold in agricultural IPM—the size of an infestation beyond which residents could tolerate no more pests. A small but growing cohort of urban IPM advocates embraced the concept and applied it to decisions about pest-management activities in spaces from city parks to homes. Under typical regimes for synthetic pesticides, both household do-it-yourselfers and pest-control contractors applied pesticides regularly to maintain a residue that was supposed to prevent infestation. Olkowski proposed that householders could avoid "unnecessary treatments" by refraining from applying pesticides until pest populations reached the aesthetic injury level. He reasoned that since aesthetic thresholds are subjective and individual, they could be altered through education and other cultural influences. Thus William Olkowski saw a critical role for scientists and environmentalists in raising Americans' tolerance for household pests.[23]

According to the Olkowskis and other urban IPM advocates, cultural conceptions of nature and sanitation influenced aesthetic injury levels. They believed that Americans' alienation from nature amounted to an irrational fear: entomophobia. The Olkowskis blamed the pesticide and pest-control industries and their supporters for promoting compulsive pest-control behaviors based on "fear of contamination, penetration, and/or filth."[24] In Common Sense Pest Control, Helga Olkowski broached the topic gently, beginning: "I think anyone has the right to exclude other creatures from one's own living quarters if one finds them undesirable." She asked readers to consider, however, "to what lengths are you willing to go to keep your home devoid of other forms of life?" The Olkowskis observed that modern taboos guarded the borders between food and waste, indoors and out, pets and pests. Helga Olkowski challenged these borders, pointing out that they contradicted humans' ecological history: "We live in the midst of the rest of nature and many of people's house companions have been associated with them since their days in caves."[25]

The Olkowskis sought to lead by example, launching a demonstration project called the Integral Urban Home to model the integration of urban nature and its signals into a working household. With support from the Fallarones Institute, a green architecture and appropriate technology foundation, they purchased a fixer-upper in an old Berkeley neighborhood, fitted it with solar panels and a composting toilet, and turned the grounds over to food production with a vegetable garden and chicken and rabbit coops. The Olkowskis and staff at the Integral Urban House taught visitors to become ecosystem managers in urban, domestic space by involving them in pest control, food production, and household waste management.[26] The composting toilet, small livestock, food composting bin, and busy kitchen all had the potential to attract insects and rodents, especially given the worn condition of both the house and its surrounding neighborhood. Indeed, when the Olkowskis first began the project, the compost bin, composting toilet, gardens, and animal manure fed a plague of houseflies. The flies irritated the Olkowskis so badly that they designed household routines such as regular kitchen scrap disposal to stop fly-breeding. Meanwhile, vigilant home maintenance prevented the infiltration of other pests while also conserving heating and cooling energy. The Integral Urban House, and the Olkowskis' guide of the same name based on their experiences there, became one of their best-known legacies—a living, urban laboratory of IPM and ecosystem ecology.[27]

By the mid-1970s, other entomologists joined the Olkowskis in promoting urban IPM, and many of them hoped to overcome entomophobia through education. William Olkowski's fellow Berkeley graduates Gordon Frankie and Gary Piper joined with psychologist Hanna Levenson to study householder attitudes toward pest control in several U.S. cities. Nearly half of respondents from a range of income levels reported changing their overall thinking about pesticides in recent years, since *Silent Spring*'s publication. Many had come to oppose pesticide applications in agricultural and park settings. Few altered their own domestic pest-management practices, however. Moreover, most respondents could name neither the insecticides that pest-control operators sprayed in their homes nor their potential side effects. Many could name nonchemical means of control, but they expressed dissatisfaction with those methods—and release of parasitoid wasps to kill roaches in homes was never a serious proposal.[28] Both the pest-control industry and IPM advocates blamed consumers for the unpopularity of a traditional remedy, boric acid, that was low in human toxicity.[29] Experiments by the University of California entomologist Walter Ebeling showed that boric acid could kill more German roaches than organophosphates like diazinon—albeit more slowly—because boric acid did not repel roaches.[30] One researcher wrote that methods like boric acid, "while much safer, are far too slow for the average urbanite. . . . We are, as a society, addicted to the use of chemical shortcuts to cure biological problems."[31] Pest-control technicians wanted to satisfy householders with a quick fix and believed that householders preferred nearly invisible residues of organophosphates over white, powdery deposits of boric acid. IPM researchers strived to alter cultural attitudes toward pests and pesticides, to persuade Americans to tolerate some insects in their homes.

Urban IPM research in the 1970s targeted Americans who lived with just a few bugs, in homes where low tolerance for pests led to heavy pesticide applications. The Olkowskis inspired many householders to become ecosystem managers, helping to raise tolerance of minor infestations. Educational efforts such as *Common Sense Pest Control* and the Integral Urban House assumed that householders exercised a high degree of control over their home environments, however. The desire to live free from pests meant something quite different for residents of affluent neighborhoods who seldom saw pests—and even more seldom pests that affect health— than for residents of poor neighborhoods plagued by cockroaches or rats. Early IPM advocates' focus on the fear of nature, the corrupting influence of pesticide companies, and householders' agency neglected other dimensions of urban life that influenced pesticide use and the potential for IPM adoption.[32] Housing tenure—that is, one's status as a renter or homeowner—and income, housing age, and neighborhood composition shaped residents' ability to manage their home ecosystems. So did the institutions and procedures that managed low-income housing, and, more broadly, urban politics and power relationships. In the 1980s and 1990s, some housing activists, IPM researchers, and health advocates began to focus on a different aspect of "integration": bringing politics into their conception of urban ecosystems.

GERMAN COCKROACHES, PESTICIDES, AND PERMEABLE HUMAN BODIES

Helga Olkowski's pitch for higher tolerance levels made sense when she was speaking to, as the stereotype went, the "average suburban home-owner" who "is a victim of the chemical salesmen," including those "fanatical housewives who pick up the aerosol can at the buzz of a mosquito."[33] It was an entirely different matter, however, to suggest that residents of highly infested homes should become more tolerant of hordes of German cockroaches and endure the injuries these insects wrought. The Olkowskis hoped to measure and thus defuse emotional responses to pests with the concept of aesthetic injury level. Infestation was about more than aesthetics in places like Henry Horner Homes: roaches were health hazards, a social stigma, and a sign of government neglect.

In many urban households, insects and rodents caused injuries that exceeded the aesthetic. By the 1970s, roach control in multifamily buildings like Henry Horner was not just a matter of residents cleaning up their own apartments. Certainly, many families made it easier for roaches to prosper in their units by allowing clutter to accumulate, creating an environment rich in roach hideouts, or by leaving dirty dishes in a sink or throwing food scraps in a trash can without wrapping them in plastic or paper. Others might keep a cat—perhaps in violation of their leases—and fail to clean up its litter box or leftover kibble, leaving food for roaches. Sometimes roaches congregated in some part of the apartment that seldom received cleaning, like under the bathroom sink. Residents of buildings with few roaches often get away with similar housekeeping habits, however, without attracting infestation.[34] In a building with few roaches, residents may enjoy the privilege of letting dirty dishes pile up without worrying about vermin. In a building where many units were already infested, roaches could almost literally emerge from the woodwork, ready to exploit even a minor lapse in sanitation. The condition of buildings and the spread of pesticide-resistant strains made it easier for roaches to move between units and escape extermination. Furthermore, for an infestation to develop, roaches must somehow be introduced into a building via a connection with another infested place, such as a tenant's previous home or a grocery store where a tenant shops. Thus, location, housing management practices, residents, and the roaches themselves all shaped the ecology of apartment buildings.

Sarah Ruffin, her husband, and their four young boys had little experience with German cockroaches when they moved to Chicago from rural Mississippi in the late 1960s. Ruffin remembered an occasional large bug inside her childhood home, but she knew nothing like the multitudes of tiny insects that greeted her family when they secured a unit in Henry Horner Homes in 1970. Ruffin found the physical and social environment of the city a dramatic change from her rural upbringing, a difficult setting in which to raise her children, including a fifth boy born after the family's arrival in Chicago. The Ruffins treasured the opportunity to move into Henry Horner Homes, however—it was secure, affordable housing, and it seemed safer than the other places in Chicago where they had been able to afford the rent.[35]

Residents valued their homes but also endured myriad environmental problems. Ruffin remembered: "We had an issue with the building starting to go down . . . so [the residents' council] was fighting to try to force [management] to keep it fixed up." In particular, "we had a lot of problems with our water running . . . [management was] saying they were going to allocate some money for it. We just kept waiting and waiting for years, without them doing anything about it." A journalist observed that "thirty-year-old kitchen cabinets, constructed of thin metal, had rusted through. They were pockmarked with holes."[36] Once a pipe burst near a drafty stairwell in the dead of winter, leaving slick ice on the steps.[37]

Cabinets full of holes gave roaches easy passage into dark hiding places; dripping fixtures gave them a steady water supply. Ruffin explained: "We know that [water leaks] can cause roach problems." Mouse infestations were severe, and "the roaches were just like an ongoing thing. It was like the more we tried to bait them down, the more they'd come. Even when [management] came to exterminate, it was like they'd get drunk and stagger all over the place, but then they would come back double." Ruffin insisted: "Each apartment that I ever been in they had a big problem," regardless of residents' sanitary habits. "No matter how clean the kitchen was at night, you'd come in and turn the light on and you'd see them all over the sink." Roaches took up residence in kitchen cabinets; inside, they slipped under flaps of breakfast cereal boxes and burrowed into sacks of potatoes and bags of snacks. They not only pervaded the kitchen but also "get all in the bed, in the drawers with your clean clothes. It was just absolutely a mess." Once a roach crawled into Ruffin's ear while she slept, necessitating a trip to the emergency room to have it removed. If roaches crawled across her face while she slept, they most likely did the same with her boys—a horrifying prospect for a parent trying to protect her family.[38]

While residents of projects like Horner endured the grinding stress of life with roaches, physicians and researchers also found evidence that German cockroaches inflicted injuries at a more micro scale. In 1964, allergists suggested that continuous exposure to high levels of German cockroach proteins heightened children's risk of developing asthma, a burgeoning problem in many central cities that was only worsened by other indoor and outdoor pollutants such as cigarette smoke, diesel fumes, or ground-level ozone.[39] Further studies accumulated evidence that German cockroaches could be a major cause of asthma in apartments that were highly infested.[40]

Living roaches circulated prolifically through infested buildings, and so did all their leavings. In the kitchen, bedrooms, and bathroom, wherever they crept, each of the hundreds of roaches living in a severely infested apartment occasionally molted its outgrown exoskeleton. The molting process revealed a fresh, soft, new skin that soon hardened in place. A roach that reaches a ripe old age of six months might molt as many as six times as it grew to its adult size.[41] Roaches recycled many of the exoskeletons themselves by eating them, but some skins disintegrated. These exoskeletons became part of the house dust that circulated in the air and that a household member might occasionally sweep or wipe up. The roaches' saliva and feces also turned to dust, as did the bodies of whole, dead roaches. A roach here and there did not produce enough dust to provoke a reaction in most human bodies, but a major infestation could sensitize human immune systems, particularly in young children.[42]

At Horner, "a lot of people had developed asthma. Some already had asthma when they moved in." These sensitive individuals came to believe that the housing authority's sprays made their asthma worse. The Ruffins' second youngest boy was one of many who grew up sickly and asthmatic. Sarah Ruffin wondered whether the environment of the Chicago Housing Authority project, so different from the one in which she had grown up, had anything to do with her son's condition. Indeed, the boy's pediatrician suspected that roaches contributed to his asthma. Ruffin recalled that "even with the medication he would have to go to the hospital, we'd be at the doctor's office at least three or four times a year."[43] Another boy with severe asthma sometimes relied on a mechanical respirator to help him breathe. His family and neighbors were horrified when a roach crawled into one of the oxygen tubes and became lodged there.[44]

Dissatisfied with services offered by management, frustrated and disgusted residents were tempted by pesticide products that promised easy and safe relief from cockroaches and other insect pests. Residents spent their own money on over-the-counter pesticides, attempting to control the problem themselves. One resident purchased at least twenty cans of roach spray each year and sometimes sprayed the aerosol directly at the roaches.[45] Such responses seem to run contrary to the mainstream environmental movement that bloomed during the very same years. Residents' heavy use of pesticides might seem to affirm the notion that environmentalism is a middle-class cause, not a concern for low-income Americans. Those who chose to pursue a chemical solution to cockroaches in their units expressed environmental concern in a way that made sense in the context of their lives, however. Horner residents who applied their own pesticides sought control over the ecology of their homes at a time when they held little political control over the state of the projects. They hoped to provide a healthy living environment for themselves and their children based on the belief that roaches violated their very bodies, their sense of dignity, and their sense of home. Some of the earliest public housing residents in Chicago had likewise participated in communal fumigation programs to protect themselves and their children and to feel that they could exercise a measure of sovereignty over their home environments.[46]

Sarah Ruffin and other residents were suspicious both of domestic intrusions brought by the exterminators' visits and also of the pesticides themselves. Many believed that the lingering smell of the pesticides indicated they were unhealthy.[47] They reasoned that the pesticides must have little effect anyway, since the roaches always returned so soon after a spraying. Ruffin's physician suggested that the chemicals might contribute to her own respiratory difficulties; she and other residents obtained physicians' notes stating that for health reasons their apartments should not be sprayed.[48] Such actions reveal a kind of environmental thought among residents, a concern that chemicals in their homes could move into their bodies and contribute to ill health, and that even modern chemicals could fail. Residents tried to balance worries about pesticides against the constant trials of living with these roaches.[49]

At the same time as allergy researchers revealed the links between cockroach infestation and asthma, other researchers affirmed the suspicions that led some Horner residents to refuse pesticide applications in their homes. A report coauthored by the Olkowskis warned:

> Of all the sites where pesticides are applied, the home reveals at the same time the greatest variety of pesticides, the most diversified kinds of exposure, the most susceptible members of the population (children), the least skill in application, the greatest and most sublime ignorance of the hazards, and the poorest system of protective controls. Home and garden pesticide use results in more hospital-admitted poisonings and more deaths than occupational use does.[50]

These were only the acute pesticide emergencies; chronic problems remained the subject of uncertainty and debate. The organophosphate pesticides that increasingly dominated the market for many different uses quickly decompose when exposed to the elements outdoors, but "toxic materials used indoors are protected from degradation by ultraviolet light and microbial action."[51]

In 1980, the National Academy of Science found that householders and contractors now relied on chemicals more dangerous than DDT, which had been banned in the United States, and chlordane, which no longer worked for German roaches. The report found that two of the organophosphates, chlorpyrifos and diazinon, "are of marginal safety for use in households, but they are used as cockroaches become resistant to materials less hazardous to human beings."[52] Housing authorities such as New York City's applied chlorpyrifos heavily for cockroach infestations as late as the 1990s.[53] Furthermore, urban and domestic pesticides remained in a kind of regulatory limbo; unlike pesticides in agriculture, "no one federal agency had specific overall responsibility for urban pest management."[54] Thus, the private space of the home remained outside any organized framework of government protection. Pesticide applications in homes were not merely a private matter but contributed to growing public health worries.[55]

Low-income residents appeared to face the worst exposures among urban residents. A 1964 study compared pesticides stored in human fat tissue across income brackets, becoming the first to suggest that low-income people carried high body burdens of pesticides.[56] A handful of studies that followed surmised that residents of low-income housing confronted particularly severe infestations and therefore exposed themselves to more pesticides than affluent people.[57] New revelations about the connections among human bodies, pests, and pesticides in the domestic environment heightened confusion residents faced about toxic risks and cockroach troubles.

The competing health threats of roaches and pesticides left residents of infested homes in a quandary that received little attention from mainstream environmentalists. Urban pest control in general remained a neglected research and regulatory area. Health advocates and scientists had done little so far to curtail—or even to examine—pesticide applications in cities. Public funding for pest-control research—involving both chemical methods and IPM—was heavily skewed toward agriculture. This skew reflected in part the size of the agricultural sector, but still, in 1973, of $134 million in public dollars spent on pest-control research, just over $5 million was spent on "control of insects affecting man" or public health. Most of the latter funds were spent on mosquito-control research—perhaps the most important vector in the world because of its role in malaria, but far from the only pest affecting human health in the United States.[58] In 1978, the National Academy of Sciences found that the Environmental Protection Agency had "largely limited itself to regulating the use of pesticides in agriculture," resulting in unequal protection for central-city and even suburban residents. The National Academy followed up by convening a committee on urban pest management, which itself was frustrated by the fact that "the data assembled to date are inadequate to allow quantitative analysis of pesticide use in urban areas."[59] Furthermore, for all the systemic *environmental* thinking of IPM scholars and advocates, they had thought little about the systemic *social* problems that also made up the ecology of infested homes.

THE PERSISTENCE OF COCKROACHES AND THE DECLINE OF COMMUNITY

Residents of public housing projects and private multifamily buildings across the United States shared similar experiences with those at Henry Horner Homes, with some variations. Early guides to household IPM were directed at individual householders and their own management practices.[60] In public housing projects across the United States, however, institutional arrangements such as the competitive bidding process also shaped household pest control.[61] Under competitive bidding procedures, the lowest bidders might be what conscientious pest management professionals dismiss as "spray jockeys" or "baseboard jockeys"—technicians who apply pesticides indiscriminately, missing some pests' hiding spots and overapplying in others, aiding the process by which insects evolved resistance to a series of insecticides. Poorly trained or careless technicians might also lack knowledge about cockroach resistance to some pesticides and the availability more effective and less toxic formulations such as silica aerogels.

As housing authorities built new buildings in the 1950s and 1960s, some added few or no new staff to manage pests in thousands of new units. Staff were left to cover more units in the same amount of time. Housing authorities might fire their old contractors if another firm offered a lower bid, making it impossible for pest controllers to accumulate valuable knowledge about the ecology of buildings, places that harbored pests, and other ongoing problems—knowledge that would be essential for effective ecosystem management. By the 1970s, many such pest-control contractors kept housing projects on a pesticide treadmill, dousing units with new and often more toxic chemicals as roaches evolved resistance to each one.[62] Practices were varied and were not always predictable based on whether the housing authority used outside contractors versus staff on payroll; for example, in four North Carolina cities, an entomologist found that contractors in low-income buildings did more preventive pest control, while maintenance staff responded only to complaints.[63] In the 1980s, the Olkowskis began offering guidance to housing authorities and other institutions about hiring and working with pest-control contractors to shift toward IPM methods in housing projects and other large buildings.[64]

Early research on urban IPM said little about multifamily buildings, the environmental connections among apartments, or the responsibilities of landlords or housing authorities. Pest ecologies transcended individual dwelling units, however, as did the effects of management practices and pesticides applied to any unit or building. Even if a resident kept her own apartment relatively clean, members of the building's roach population could range into her unit and find a minor housekeeping lapse upon which to thrive. The Extension entomologist Eugene Wood endeavored to overhaul the Baltimore Housing Authority's roach control program in 1976. Wood reported that in otherwise clean apartments, roaches might make their home atop refrigerators, a place where many residents—and indeed, this writer, and perhaps many readers of this sentence—seldom clean or even see.[65] Based upon his work in Baltimore and on other roach experts' research, Wood believed that "most roaches are provided to the whole building by one (or two) apartments which are called focus apartments."[66] Under such circumstances, using pesticides might seem to the resident more effective and less labor-intensive than improving household sanitation that already seemed fairly thorough. Individual residents might also possess limited resources for performing tasks like caulking that could keep insects and rodents at bay; besides, residents expected the housing authority to perform this type of maintenance. For public housing residents, simply cleaning their apartments did not make them "ecosystem managers"—it would take a grander scale of intervention.

In the 1930s and 1940s, the ideals of collectivity and "good tenant relations" had motivated the first public housing managers in many cities to involve residents in maintaining healthy home environments. Residents gladly joined in the program to live in a healthy, pest-free community, despite its logistical hassles and monetary cost. Even when housing authorities clashed with residents over pest control, as in 1940s Baltimore, activists like Alverta Parnell tried to protect their neighbors from accusations and monetary costs levied by managers.[67] By the 1970s, the contractors who controlled pests in many projects actually worsened tenant relations. Disunity among residents could turn into angry suspicion. Residents sometimes accused one another of feeding the project's roach population, showing how divided their communities had become despite a contiguous living environment.[68] In such rancorous and isolating—and sometimes dangerous—communities, many residents shut their doors to officials of any kind, including staff or contractors performing pest control.

German cockroaches themselves embodied poor practices of building and pest management and the decline of community. The chlordane resistance trait became particularly common in some cities' public housing projects, leading managers and residents to search for other chemicals that might still kill roaches.[69] For example, between the 1950s and the 1980s, Baltimore's housing authorities climbed aboard a pesticide treadmill, trying and discarding several chemicals as roaches evolved resistance to each in turn: chlordane, malathion, diazinon, propoxur, and the branded products Baygon and Ficam. Eugene Wood predicted: "The German cockroach can probably become resistant to any synthetic, organic insecticide we can develop."[70] In Baltimore, many of these treatments still worked on German cockroaches outside public housing, in neighborhoods where resistance had not become prevalent. Those populations lacked exposure to the selective pressures and opportunities for evasion found in public housing.[71] Housing reformers had once promised state protection of housing quality, but the state's neglect and clumsy, careless pesticide use produced stronger strains of insects than in other home environments.

While cockroaches displayed behavioral and genetic resistance to chlordane and other pesticides, residents of public housing began to stage their own kind of resistance to official pest-control practices. The persistence of roaches fueled residents' distrust of managers amid other chronic problems in public housing; fears of crime are among the more famous problems, but residents also suffered with routine elevator breakdowns and burned-out hallway light fixtures that managers never replaced. Eugene Wood believed that chemicals like chlordane had planted the idea in many pest controllers' minds that roach control was quick and easy. "We still assume that new residual sprays should control roaches with just a squirt," he lamented, yet by the late 1970s and early 1980s, "roach control in multiple family dwellings is currently the toughest problem in urban pest control." Wood explained of the situation in Baltimore public housing: "Because the crews had less time to treat each unit, application became less thorough. Tenants disliked the fogging process and refused to allow the crew to treat for roaches. . . . The crew's rapid roach control treatment fostered distrust by tenants and helped to develop an overall negative attitude toward an obviously ineffective control program."[72] Wood's program strived to overcome the animosity that contractors had provoked; it opened up discussion about roach control in community meetings to establish cooperation and mutual understanding.

Wood helped the projects where he worked to reestablish the kinds of relationships that the first public housing managers had cultivated. Like Sherman Aldrich, the manager who had introduced communal bedbug control in U.S. public housing in the 1930s, Wood reduced the cost of pest control for residents while dramatically increasing satisfaction—over 90 percent of residents were happy with the results.[73] In many projects, though, the Progressive ideals upon which reformers had founded public housing crumbled along with the physical infrastructure and daily upkeep of the projects themselves. The dream of modern living environments and communal services decayed into a nightmare of government neglect and danger.[74] In contrast with the first generation of tenants who traded privacy for public protection of well-being, subsequent generations found it necessary to fight with public officials for even a semblance of healthy and decent living environments.[75]

THE *GAUTREAUX* DECISION, PUBLIC HOUSING REFORM, AND HENRY HORNER HOMES

While public housing communities across the United States struggled with environmental conditions, *Gautreaux* worked its way through the courts. In 1976, ten years after the original filing and several months after the death of Dorothy Gautreaux herself, the U.S. Supreme Court ruled in favor of the Chicago Housing Authority residents. This ruling required the CHA to provide some forty thousand families new "mobility" within the greater Chicago region.[76]

Chicago's decades-long segregation practices surely contributed to the decline of public housing in the city. Public housing was conceived to provide poor families with a chance at a better life, but the CHA and the city of Chicago instead limited the life-chances of very low-income African-American tenants by limiting the places where they could live, treating them almost like pests to be contained. Housing authorities had tried to solve the problems of housing poor families with quick, cheap solutions, much as many Americans believed that postwar pesticides would be a quick, cheap solution to infestation.[77] If public housing was a failed experiment, it was because federal government, housing authorities, and the city of Chicago set it up that way; the Supreme Court's ruling affirmed the state's complicity.

Yet popular and political discourse about public housing ascribed the failure to other factors: their design, the residents, the very idea of subsidized housing itself. Amid talk of the failure of public housing, roaches became one of many symbols of its decline. In 1981, Chicago's mayor, Jane Byrne, moved into the notorious Cabrini-Green project as a way of spurring management to address the project's chronic problems with crime, drugs, and environmental degradation. Upon arrival, she and her spouse were greeted in their unit by hundreds of cockroaches that a "last-minute barrage of insecticides" had failed to disperse. During Byrne's stay, managers applied an "Armageddon of pesticides" in addition to stepping up police patrols against endemic crime and evicting many human residents. Critics of public housing used the roach-control incident as an allegory of the hopelessness of attempts to clean up the projects, inviting parallels between teeming, persistent pests and residents who lived there for decades without moving on to "permanent" housing.[78]

While Byrne's publicity stunt brought bad press to Cabrini-Green, and the *Gautreaux* case made Chicago public housing infamous for its segregation policies, Henry Horner Homes gained its own national fame and notoriety as writers made it, too, a touchstone for troubled public housing. In 1987, the journalist Alex Kotlowitz followed two boys growing up in the project for his book *There Are No Children Here*. Kotlowitz reported that the boys' mother compulsively cleaned the apartment whenever gang battles broke out in the neighborhood—a frequent occurrence—but she struggled to keep up with the dirty dishes produced by her seven children. Kotlowitz mostly blamed the housing authority, however, for the fact that "roaches were everywhere." He explained: "In keeping with the developers' tight-fisted policies in building these high-rises, the housing authority continued its miserly regard for their upkeep. Maintenance was a bare minimum."[79] Other media outlets issued their own commentaries on Horner Homes and, by extension, the state of American public housing. A writer in the *New York Times* called Horner "Hell" and a manifestation of "the pathology of the black lower class," suggesting, "surely we can impose some minimal discipline within which a reconstruction of decent life can begin."[80] For many Horner residents, however, the project remained a haven from even more dangerous neighborhoods elsewhere in the city, despite the project's troubles and the residents' many complaints to the housing authority. To them, public housing was still "the best housing in the community," even as Americans elsewhere came to see the projects as the housing of last resort.[81]

COMMUNITY-BASED IPM COMES TO SEGREGATED HOMES

For scientists steeped in ecology scholarship, the "I" in Integrated Pest Management stood for the need to reweave parts of nature that had been torn apart by reductionist pest control. Modern pest-control practices attempted to purify farm fields and homes by eliminating pests, rather than attempting to understand and respond to these animals' ecologies.

Improved knowledge and flow of information would knit the two back together. "Integration" implied the reunification of fragmented pieces of an ecosystem.[82]

As holistic as urban IPM advocates strived to be, however, a fully "integrated" pest management would also have to address the politics and social inequalities that left some communities to endure severe infestations. "Integration" carried its own meanings for low-income city-dwellers and people of color who faced a limited range of housing options—and who, in part because of those limited options, often endured greater degrees of infestation than more affluent and white residents of cities and suburbs. The story of infestation and the introduction of IPM in Henry Horner Homes illustrates just how *disintegrated* an urban home could be—at the same time as it was racially and economically *segregated*. IPM came to Chicago's projects in large part through the activism of mothers in Horner, such as Sarah Ruffin, who were also galvanized by the *Gautreaux* case. These women's struggles for healthier homes for their families echo the ecological thought of Rachel Carson and Helga Olkowski while also extending traditions of civil rights and environmental justice activism into the home environment.[83]

The *Gautreaux* ruling against the Chicago Housing Authority guaranteed certain concessions to residents of Horner and other projects. By the early 1990s, however, both the federal and city government were looking for ways to withdraw from the business of housing low-income people. The Chicago Freedom Movement activists of the 1960s, the *Gautreaux* plaintiffs, and many civil rights and housing activists across the United States had called for increased provision of housing for very low-income people in more affluent neighborhoods, even suburbs, to "deconcentrate" poor families.[84] Popular discourse and policy shifts in the 1990s echoed calls for deconcentration, but as part of an overall plan to reduce the number of units available to families at the lowest income levels. Many policy-makers aimed to shrink the role of government in housing very low-income families. A new federal program called HOPE VI provided housing authorities with funds to demolish projects that were deemed troubled and gave residents vouchers to subsidize private housing elsewhere in the city. The *Gautreaux* decision similarly required CHA to provide forty thousand Chicago families with vouchers for private-market housing. Some HOPE VI grants funded rehabilitation of projects; in most such cases, overhauls resulted in a reduced number of units overall, with some of that number offered to middle-income families at market rates. While many embraced the aim of economic integration, housing advocates and many tenant groups criticized the net loss of units for low-income families at a time when cities like Chicago had thousands of families on public housing waiting lists.[85] Furthermore, the first families to receive vouchers discovered that private landlords in other Chicago neighborhoods often refused vouchers, viewing them as a stigma on would-be tenants.[86]

Horner residents learned that CHA intended to apply for a HOPE VI grant to rehabilitate their project. Despite the environmental and other problems at Horner, residents worried even more about crime and danger in adjacent neighborhoods with affordable market housing. "We had told them that we weren't going to move out," Sarah Ruffin remembered, "because we saw what they did to the people at Lake Park." Lake Park was one of the first projects to receive a new rehabilitation grant from the federal government. The CHA had told Lake Park residents "that they were going to move them out to another place, and then when they finished with the apartment then they were going to move them back. But then they didn't do that. The people lost their apartments" because of the number made available to people at higher income levels.[87] The idea of economic integration had many supporters, but at the same time, many residents objected to the net decrease in units for people at their income level and the CHA's inability to guarantee a right of return.

Ruffin and her neighbors formed the Horner Mothers' Guild and launched their own lawsuit against the housing authority, in which they alleged that the poor conditions constituted a de facto demolition. They demanded renovations.[88] The suit galvanized Horner residents as a community and helped them see a healthy home environment as a right of citizenship. Mothers' Guild members commiserated with one another over the terrible pest problem and the health dilemmas it presented, lamenting the impossible choice they faced between competing risks of pesticide exposure and asthma caused by cockroaches. They called the housing authority to task for failing in its duties to provide healthy living spaces to residents.[89] In addition to saving their community from demolition, the Mothers' Guild named the cockroach problem their top priority.[90]

By positioning themselves as mothers, Sarah Ruffin and her neighbors claimed special knowledge of domestic environments and children's health as well as a special moral position.[91] Their children's illnesses, as well as the stigma that fell to them as the presumed homemakers, helped inform these women's demands that the housing authority do its part to make their homes healthy. The Horner Mothers' Guild moved beyond maternal pleas for a clean environment, demanding state protection of their families' well-being in publicly financed dwellings although the state and public housing critics might see the home as a private space and its management a private responsibility. For these women, homes carried meanings of security and sovereignty; as trying as life there could be, Horner was the community where they and their families had made a haven.[92] Ruffin and her neighbors staked their claims to Horner on the basis of rights to housing, health, and a decent living environment.

In 1991, the housing authority agreed to renovations and to the right-of-return for very low-income Horner families if 51 percent of resident families voted in favor of the plan; in fact, 85 percent supported it.[93] The Mothers' Guild's pro bono lawyer, Tom Finnerty, had contacts within a new IPM advocacy organization, the Safer Pest Control Project (SPCP), whose mission was to reduce chemical pesticide use in homes, schools, and other buildings in the Chicago region. The SPCP brought new meaning to the "I" in IPM: based in the city, it possessed expertise in the science of IPM, the complex politics of citizens and institutions, and community organizing. In 1995, Finnerty, the Mothers' Guild, SPCP staffer Jill Viehweg, and a local IPM practitioner and contractor, David Shangle, together developed a plan for rebuilding Horner as a pest-free complex in which only low-toxicity IPM methods would be used in perpetuity.[94]

Mothers' Guild members became ecosystem managers according to IPM principles. Donning a hardhat, work boots, and a construction mask, Ruffin and several other women residents caulked utilities and fixtures in hundreds of units throughout the campus, denying roaches and mice their old passageways and hideouts. Meanwhile, Shangle's workers applied nonvolatile baits, a newly patented pesticide product with little risk of becoming airborne and inhaled by children and other residents with respiratory troubles. They dusted wall voids with low-toxicity boric acid, that old home remedy found effective by Walter Ebeling but largely forgotten during the heyday of DDT. Finally, they vacuumed roach corpses out of old crevices, leaving no bodies to become pulverized into allergenic dust.[95]

After the residents moved back in, Ruffin helped her neighbors learn how to monitor for roaches and maintain their homes in a pest-free state, much as Helga Olkowski had encouraged citizen engagement with urban ecosystems. Caulking, vacuuming, and boric acid kept roaches out of wall voids, and baits killed remaining roaches. Meanwhile, families exercised greater vigilance over food and water within their own units, a task eased and encouraged by new and improved fixtures—well-made kitchen cabinets and sound plumbing. "We gave out little packages of clothespins" to close up food packaging, Ruffin explained, and taught neighbors "how to sanitize your kitchen [with] bleaches, to wipe it down. Tying up everything. Make sure there's no water left in the sink overnight." Within a few weeks, families who had lived with hundreds and sometimes thousands of cockroaches watched roach numbers dwindle to near zero.[96] The Horner IPM program rewove the ecological fabric of public housing communities. Residents' very bodies as well as their political positions had been part of a sick and unjust environment, but work by the residents and investment by the housing authority brought health, pride, and a sense of power.

By the time Henry Horner's environment was remade, Sarah Ruffin's family had lived with roaches for more than two decades. Her own children were grown, and her husband had passed away long ago. As much as Ruffin celebrated the Mothers' Guild's political and environmental victory, "at the same time I was devastated that [the housing authority] had us living all this time, with them [the roaches], when something could have been done."[97] The changes made to the project were dramatic and expensive, but they raised the question of why Horner residents had had to live with such poor conditions for so long.

The IPM program at Henry Horner Homes was one of the first in the United States spearheaded by the activism of low-income residents, and some subsequent efforts have used it as a model for how to empower residents to control their environment and demand help from housing authorities.[98] The Horner project is not a representative case of IPM in low-income housing, however. Changes in public housing funding and policy since the 1990s have reduced opportunities to stay in the projects after renovations, and even at Horner, the rehabilitation came at the cost of hundreds of units designated for very-low-income residents.[99] Compared with some 3,000 units, the rehabilitated project offered 764 homes, "271 for public housing, 132 for affordable housing, and 361 market-rate units."[100] After several of the high-rises were demolished, the remaining ones were rehabilitated, and a mix of townhouses and two-flat buildings were added to the neighborhood.[101]

The *Gautreaux* ruling also afforded Horner residents unique legal leverage with the housing authority, requiring that they be allowed a voice and a vote in matters relating to the renovation plan. The project cost eighty million dollars, supported in part by the federal HOPE VI program that awarded rehabilitation grants to only a small number of competing proposals.[102] The case shows ecological change cannot be separated from communities' power to improve their living conditions. Cockroach control could only proceed in these buildings on the basis of solidarity and empowerment—as public housing managers knew in the case of bedbugs in the 1930s. While residents retained private spaces and responsibilities, the cockroach-control project succeeded because it treated environment as a matter of community.

Ironically, during the same years when Sarah Ruffin and her neighbors moved toward a holistic and community-based solution to long-standing cockroach problems, families across the United States exposed themselves to grave danger in desperate attempts to free their homes of pests. Beginning in the mid-1980s, pest-control businesses in several states sprayed buildings—most of them homes—with methyl parathion, an organophosphate approved only for outdoor and agricultural use. Like other organophosphates, it decomposes quickly under outdoor conditions but persists for years indoors; enclosed environments concentrate fumes to which occupants are exposed.[103] When investigators discovered the illegal practices in 1994, several pest-control operators were jailed, and twenty-four hundred people from rural Mississippi to Chicago were displaced from their poisoned homes in dozens of cities. Many of the clients who purchased these illegal services were low-income apartment-dwellers who, like the Horner families, had lived for years with cockroaches.[104]

The Environmental Protection Agency designated these homes a Superfund site under the federal program that funds emergency cleanup of toxic contamination. The name Superfund often conjures images of bulldozers or dredging equipment removing poisoned soil or sludge from the site of an old toxic waste dump. By contrast, decontamination of structures sprayed with methyl parathion required staff to discard furniture, gut houses to remove and replace surfaces that had been touched by pesticide residues or vapors, and sometimes demolish entire buildings. The incident now known as the methyl parathion disaster became one of the most diffuse Superfund sites ever, and one of the most expensive to address thus far in the program's history. It also left residents to bear high body burdens of methyl parathion even years later because of the time they had spent exposed to the chemical indoors.[105]

SURVIVAL IN CITIES OF HUMAN-ANIMAL RELATIONSHIPS

One scholar who studied householders involved in the methyl parathion disaster marveled at residents' choice to have this pesticide applied in their homes. He observed that residents perceived great "personal benefits from home-use" of this dangerous chemical.[106] One might be tempted to read into these residents' behaviors a pathological fear of nature like that critiqued by the Olkowskis. These families lived with not just a few roaches, however, but with intense and persistent infestations. Life with pests presents confusing and contradictory health risks, and pests like roaches strain householders' sense of dignity, safety, and sovereignty that our culture teaches us to associate with our homes. The philosopher bell hooks has argued that the private home provides the ultimate haven and source of pride for many people who face hardship and discrimination in public, especially African-American women. This insight suggests that those who find themselves sharing that space with teeming, allergenic, stigmatized insects have all the more reason to pursue a greater sense of sovereignty over their homes. Audre Lorde might say that it was a matter of survival.

This is not to say that the choice to use dangerous pesticides is only a matter of individual agency; rather, people choose pest-control services or practices in the context of the meanings and politics of home as well as householders' social position. Political, social, and cultural complexities of home help explain householders' pest-control practices, but they do not fully account for the ecological implications of pest control. The development of domestic Integrated Pest Management since the 1960s required weaving the home's meanings and politics into ecological thought. Helga and William Olkowski took the first steps by showing the home's ecological significance, arguing to both scientists and householders that the home was rightly a part of nature. IPM could not reach a broader, more diverse range of households, however, until its advocates recognized the political, cultural, and social complexities that drove pest control for people who have limited control over their homes. The partnership between the Horner Mothers' Group and the Safer Pest Control Project, informed by the knowledge and conviction of people like Sarah Ruffin, made IPM sensitive to the privileges and injustices that bequeath to different families very different experiences of infestation.

Then there are the pests themselves. Ecology teaches that complex systems have emergent properties—properties that humans often fail to anticipate or even notice. We are part of nature, but many individuals and institutions have missed or ignored signals from the rest of nature. The persistence of pests is one emergent property, a signal that we might use to better understand our environments. The entomologist Walter Ebeling observed many processes that helped explain persistent German roaches, including one that might inspire new respect for these creatures: "The continual selection of those individuals that are best able to modify their behavior to meet the day-to-day exigencies of a man-made environment would result in the development of a population with a sufficiently increased plasticity in behavior to result in a corresponding increase in the difficulty of control."[107]

To distill Ebeling's wordy prose: the roaches were learning. Behaviorally and genetically, flies, bedbugs, roaches, and rats have evolved over the millennia as humans have made and remade our domestic and urban environments. Ecosystem theory tells us that information moves in feedback loops among members of an ecological web—including information that shapes organisms' genomes and behavior. In essence, humans' habits and movements, our building designs, the chemicals we apply, and even our politics and social inequalities have helped remake the creatures we call pests, again and again. These animals have learned much from humans, our cities, and our homes. The persistence of unjust urban environments raises the question of whether *we* have learned enough from *them*.[108]

EPILOGUE

The Persistence and Resurgence of Bedbugs

BEGINNING IN THE LATE 1990S, A GROWING NUMBER OF HOUSEHOLDS
and businesses—all along the income spectrum—suffered with infestations of bedbugs.[1] Only the oldest pest-management professionals could
recall the days when, as George Hockenyos described in 1940, bedbug jobs
were one of the most common services their firms performed in urban
homes.[2] As of 1952, Reece Sailer observed that few enough Americans had
encountered bedbugs that some began to regard the bug with curiosity
rather than disgust.[3] When bedbugs made headlines again in the 1990s
and the 2000s, that curiosity had combined into a strange mixture with
humor, paranoia, and hype—and, for those who lived with them, the old
sense of stress, sleeplessness, disgust, and shame.

In the first decade of the twenty-first century, the "bug that nobody
knows" became the bug that Americans couldn't stop talking about—
except perhaps those residents who tried to conceal an infestation out of
shame or fear of ostracism or eviction.[4] The bedbug resurgence spurred,
among other things, a burst of new cultural narratives, both tragic and
comic, dedicated to bugs. A common theme among bedbug poetry, parodies, and media coverage is the bugs' reputation for crossing class lines.[5]
News of bedbugs in luxury hotels, high-end retail stores, and the homes
of celebrities has inspired fascination and, it would seem, more than a
little satisfaction that the wealthy have been brought down to the level of
the common folk by this tiny bloodsucker. The blues group Matt Skoller
Band sings in "Bad Bed Bugs": "Bad bed bugs don't care who you are / A

nobody or a movie star." In an episode of the television sitcom *30 Rock*, the powerful media executive played by Alec Baldwin becomes infested with bedbugs. Shunned and unable to get his usual limo ride home, he deigns to ride the subway. At the end of the episode, Baldwin's character joins a group of African-American men in working-class dress singing on the train, suggesting that he has found a kind of humility and authenticity among regular folks.[6] In the early twentieth century, affluent people who rid themselves of bedbugs interpreted the insect as a marker of shame and poverty. With the bug's resurgence in the early twenty-first century, many people reinterpreted it as a social equalizer, an insect that cut the wealthy down to size.

Similarly, one of dozens of YouTube video parodies was set to the tune of the theme song of *The Jeffersons*, a 1980s television sitcom in which an African-American couple "mov[es] on up" from a working-class section of Queens to a luxury high-rise in Manhattan. The parody's creator wrote that "bed bugs are no longer a problem of the slums and low-income housing. They are now found in the posh areas of New York."[7] The parodist invited parallels between the Jeffersons—although their Queens neighborhood was not a slum—and bedbugs. By remarking upon the bedbugs' ascent into the homes and shops of the wealthy, he seemed to assume that bedbug infestation in low-income communities was expected and normal. There are at least two problems with these representations of bedbugs and social class. First, why do many people seem to accept infestation when it appears in a poor community, implying that pests are an inevitable part of life there? Second, the bedbug savors the blood of rich and poor alike, but the rich can escape more easily than the poor—just as was the case in the early twentieth century. Like representations of pests from throughout the twentieth century, these new bedbug narratives remove infestation from its community, social, and political contexts.

Municipal officials, landlords, hoteliers, retailers, pest-management professionals, members of Congress, and the growing number of householders who have hosted bedbugs joined the news media in their agitation over bedbugs. City health and housing agencies whose pest-control divisions had atrophied over the years responded to resident outcries by creating "stop bedbugs" task forces.[8] Property owners became wary about tenants' infestation histories. Landlords felt the strain of hiring pest-management professionals for bedbug eradication; pest-control costs increased by 300 to

400 percent for many, exceeding the capital reserves for even well-heeled property owners. The owner of one eighteen-floor complex, for example, paid five hundred thousand dollars to eradicate bedbugs from the building, only for bugs to be reintroduced within thirty days.[9] Luxury hotels and high-end retailers braced for the public-relations nightmare of bedbug infestation. Two members of Congress in 2009 introduced the Don't Let the Bed Bugs Bite Act, which called for federal aid to help state and local officials control bugs, especially in hotels and low-income areas.[10]

The bugs certainly deserved attention, as many a host family will attest. Health researchers remained unable to prove that bedbugs can transmit any infectious diseases; efforts to pin a disease on bedbugs, encouraged by progressive exterminator Nathan Sameth in the early twentieth century, picked up again, with hepatitis as leading candidate. Researchers failed to find evidence of bedbugs' vector role, but the stress that infested households suffered rose to the level of a serious mental health problem.[11] Bedbug hosts lost sleep, suffered itchy bites, felt anxiety about whether treatments were working, and worried about the financial and time costs of eradication as long as bugs remained in their homes. Then, even if a family managed to eliminate its infestation, many continued to suffer for months from a type of paranoia called delusory parasitosis. Unable to turn off the sense of paranoia and vigilance that bedbugs had stimulated, they still imagined seeing, feeling, and smelling bugs. Furthermore, scratched bedbug bites are vulnerable to infection of all types, and health experts in the 2000s worried especially that *Staphylococcus*—including dangerous drug-resistant strains known as MRSA—could spread more rapidly in infested communities.[12]

C. lectularius undoubtedly received more news coverage than any other U.S. pest-control issue in the first decade of the twenty-first century. Amid the bedbug hype, however, other stories about domestic vermin—some of them decades old—went largely unnoticed by the media. While bedbugs constituted a worthy target of attention and public health efforts as their numbers surged in the United States, other vermin that have long plagued communities have attracted much less notice—despite established health effects of both the pests themselves and the chemicals used to control them.

BEDBUG HYPE AND THE PERSISTENCE OF INFESTATION

The novelty of bedbugs—at least for most Americans—helps account for the attention they received. So does the broad demographic affected by them; middle- and upper-class "hosts" are accustomed to demanding political and media attention when they suffer upsets to their quality of life. Both in the early twentieth century and the early twenty-first, bedbugs gained a reputation as "democratic" vermin that can infest households of any income level. Stories of infestations among wealthy families and at high-end businesses both titillate and suggest visceral commonalities across classes. For example, one of the earliest such stories, in 2004, revealed that a show-business power couple, comedian Maya Rudolph and director Paul Anderson, along with their infant daughter, fled their luxury apartment upon discovering an infestation and sued the property owner for failing to disclose conditions there.[13]

Affluent families much more than those with working-class or lower incomes enjoyed the means to effectively escape an infestation, however. They could move into temporary housing, pay for treatment by a skilled professional—and perhaps even confirm that treatments worked by hiring a firm that employs a bedbug-sniffing dog. The best-off host households could afford low- or no-chemical treatment such as steam, which, because of high labor costs, can run into hundreds or thousands of dollars.[14] As the entomologist Michael Potter put it: "The poor suffer most"; talk of the "democratic" insect ignores different experiences of living with bedbugs across income levels.[15] Indeed, those unable to afford professional treatment might have to labor for days to achieve even minor relief from bugs—and low-income families often have little time to spare.

Meanwhile, pests that menaced less privileged and less empowered communities have received little attention. German cockroaches remain pervasive in private and public low-income housing, and many children's immune systems became sensitized to allergens from this persistent pest, often leading to asthma.[16] Yet struggles against these insects received little media attention, and no specific congressional legislation to support improved control. Even flies became a problem for communities living with poorly managed garbage dumps.[17] Rats, too, persisted as a source of stress and possibly infectious diseases, such as *Leptospirosis* and *Salmonella*, that spread through rat excreta and contact with foods. Baltimore once was home to a rat-control program that made great claims to holism, but its rats still troubled residents into the late twentieth and early twenty-first century, when residents lodged between fifty and one hundred complaints about rats to pest-control staff each day, and when municipal buildings such as the city courthouse stank of decomposing rats whenever temperatures spiked.[18] It is notable that no ridicule accompanied the introduction of the Don't Let the Bed Bugs Bite Act in Congress in 2009, although one of the sponsors, G. K. Butterfield of North Carolina, felt it necessary to warn against perceiving the bedbug resurgence as a "humorous" topic.[19] By contrast, members of Congress in 1967 considered rats that afflict poor neighborhoods worthy only of their jokes but not serious attention.

PESTICIDES, INTEGRATED PEST MANAGEMENT, AND ENVIRONMENTAL JUSTICE

Research on the bedbug had waned for several decades preceding the insect's resurgence, but investigations on control methods and genetics rebounded with it. By rapidly shifting their research foci away from other domestic insects, entomologists Dini Miller of Virginia Polytechnic Institute and Michael Potter of the National Pest Management Association and the University of Kentucky emerged as two of the leading bedbug experts of the early twenty-first century United States. As the first decade of the century ended, Miller and Potter both predicted that bedbugs would continue to spread among and infest American homes for the foreseeable future.[20] Infestation is unlikely to reach the levels found in the 1930s, when public housing officials noted that more than half of households in some low-income communities had bedbugs.[21] Miller and Potter both predicted that infestation of households at all income levels would remain common, however, for at least the first few decades of the twenty-first century.[22]

Part of the reason for Miller's and Potter's predictions was that, like German cockroaches and Norway rats, wild bedbug populations had evolved resistance to the pesticides that brought about their decline in the 1950s. Like roaches and rats, bedbugs are unruly creatures entangled in ecological webs that encompass human habitats and technologies. Chemicals that might still prove effective, such as the synthetic carbamate propoxur, have been banned for household use, deemed too dangerous for small spaces in which they might recirculate.[23]

Bedbug researchers urged policy-makers to consider reviving "known chemistries" for their control—that is, pesticides like propoxur that have already undergone the extensive toxicity studies required for approval by the U.S. Environmental Protection Agency. The process of obtaining sufficient toxicity data to satisfy EPA's requirements would likely have taken $170 million and more than ten years. For this reason, Miller insisted that infested families and anxious business owners should not place their faith in new technologies. Bedbugs had evolved resistance to many old chemicals such as DDT, and most resistant strains show cross-resistance—that is, resistance to one pesticide increases the likelihood of evolving resistance to others.[24]

In 2010, the radio shock-jock Howard Stern joined critics of pesticide regulation when his limousine became infested with bedbugs. Stern declared: "They gotta bring back DDT. Stop being a bunch of pussies." Stern not only ignored the history of pesticide resistance among bedbugs, he also echoed decades of gendered language about pesticides. Pesticide supporters once labeled Rachel Carson as "emotional" because of her calls for caution and limits in the use of these chemicals. Stern found bugs in his limousine—the very emblem of wealth—and studio and was able to clear them within a few weeks of discovering them; this experience reflects a privileged side of the bedbug resurgence.[25]

In the absence of effective over-the-counter chemicals or affordable, quick treatments, some desperate families and business owners turned to dangerous—and illegal—treatments, as those suffering with German cockroaches did during the methyl parathion disaster of the 1990s. In the first decade of their resurgence, bedbugs had already driven their human hosts to desperate and dangerous methods. The landlord of the Norwood, a mixed-income building in Washington, D.C., told the tenant who first reported a bedbug infestation to spray her apartment with diesel fuel. As bedbugs spread throughout the building, the community's nascent tenants' association recognized diesel treatment as not only ineffective but also unhealthy and dangerous, but they did turn to chemicals advertised online along with topical insecticides. Adults with sensitivities as well as children reported acute illnesses after applying the Internet remedies as well as large quantities of DEET.[26] Other individuals across North America and the world have sustained acute poisoning and burns—both chemical burns and burns when flammable substances ignited—when they applied over-the-counter remedies improperly or tried to devise their own concoctions.[27]

Bedbugs received attention that might have been more evenly shared with persistent but more familiar pests like German cockroaches and Norway rats. Similarly, news of poisonings from botched bedbug-control jobs overshadowed more mundane, chronic exposures in media coverage. While the methyl parathion disaster of the 1990s received some attention as a widespread case of contamination inflicted by rogue exterminators, commonplace exposures inflicted by do-it-yourselfers upon themselves and their families do not make such a compelling story. A thriving black market supplies many urban communities with illicit products such as "Chinese chalk" and "tres pasitos"; the latter means "three little steps," which is how far a cockroach is said to walk between coming in contact with the poison and falling down dead.[28]

Amendments to the Federal Insecticide, Fungicide, and Rodenticide Act in 1996 required the Environmental Protection Agency to reevaluate pesticide toxicities, but the organophosphates diazinon and chlorpyrifos remained on retailers' shelves for some years after the review cancelled their registration for home use, while pest-management professionals protested that chlorpyrifos was effective and posed no risk when properly used. Research by the environmental justice organization West Harlem Environmental Action revealed that pesticide consumers in poor neighborhoods were more likely to find these products at their corner store than those in affluent communities.[29] Meanwhile, the libertarian commentator Deroy Murdock accused environmentalists of racism for banning effective roach killers that could protect inner-city children from asthma. Murdock posed a stark choice between pesticide use and cockroach exposure despite the building evidence that chlorpyrifos threatened children's health too, and in spite of the promise of IPM to eliminate both health risks.[30]

Indeed, many epidemiologists came to consider the cumulative effects of many legal pesticides hazardous, particularly for developing fetuses, infants, and small children. Because many suffer from higher levels of infestation at home, lower-income families often find themselves pressed into circumstances where pesticides seem a viable option for protecting children's health and overcoming the stigma and stress of infestation. Findings about low but constant levels of pesticide exposure and the disproportionate exposure of poor communities helped motivate the growing healthy housing movement to promote ecological *and* political thinking about the home.[31] Environmental justice organizations such as Chicago's Safer Pest Control Project, Cleveland's Environmental Health Watch, and New York's West Harlem Environmental Action all launched Integrated Pest Management programs in low-income communities that empowered residents with knowledge of pest ecology, the health effects of pests and pesticides, and the political and legal resources to demand support from government agencies and private landlords. Environmental justice organizations joined state attorneys general who filed suit against the Department of Housing and Urban Development for doing too little to promote IPM as a means of protecting residents from pests and pesticides.[32] Perceptions that labor and financial costs of IPM exceeded those of conventional pest control inhibit private as well as public landlords from replacing their current exterminator contracts, however.[33]

Furthermore, IPM programs in multifamily housing have been marked by tensions over who should bear the most responsibility for those labor and financial costs—tenants, landlords, or the state.[34] For low-income families, IPM represents an opportunity to overcome two health problems at once—exposure to pests and pesticides—but also a potential strain on their time that residents of better-maintained housing seldom appreciate. IPM requires intricate knowledge of the home environment, to inform meticulous housekeeping of the sort urged upon women by health and housing officials throughout the twentieth century. Insofar as women have remained the primary caretakers of domestic space into the 2000s, IPM programs would make demands on their household labor to achieve healthy home environments—and, as in the case of Chicago's Sarah Ruffin, women's political labor as well.[35] When residents "chose" to use pesticides, their actions did not necessarily reflect mere ignorance or carelessness about toxicity, but instead a trade-off adopted under constraints on time, resources, and options.

PRIVATE VIGILANCE AND PUBLIC SUPPORT FOR INFESTED COMMUNITIES

Bedbug hosts who try to address infestation by themselves—whether out of financial necessity, shame, or distrust of pest-management professionals—find not just their time strained but also their awareness of domestic ecologies. Americans at all income levels in the early twenty-first century lacked the day-to-day knowledge and skills passed down from their great-grandparents to their grandparents' generation about avoiding and managing bedbugs. Few Americans knew how to detect or recognize an infestation within the home. Thrift shoppers might not check secondhand furniture for signs of infestation. What were once regular chores like banging the bugs out of the mattresses or scrubbing furniture with kerosene had long ago disappeared from weekly or monthly to-do lists.[36]

In the early 1920s, the exterminator Nathan Sameth had already noticed the decline of some of these practices. He especially blamed the growth of defense industry jobs and civil defense volunteerism during the Great War, which "tempted women out of the home" and reduced standards of housekeeping. As they fortified the home front in the international war, Sameth charged that women had forgotten the literal home front in the "war on vermin." As "slack housekeeping prevailed on every cross-town street in New York . . . meantime the bugs were multiplying."[37] Furthermore, affluent families had grown complacent as bedbug infestations became rare in their neighborhoods. The "eternal vigilance" prescribed by domestic advisers in the previous decade had waned as attention turned away from the home.[38]

In addition to reevaluating pesticides that regulators have banned for use in homes—or from all use—entomologists today insist that individuals and families must relearn the skills that waned among the past two generations. At the 2010 Congressional Bed Bug Forum, entomologist Michael Potter evoked the forgotten sense of "vigilance" that past Americans exercised to keep bedbugs at bay. As Nathan Sameth had almost ninety years earlier, Potter questioned whether Americans had lost their ability to focus on the mundane and literally homely concerns involved in bedbug management. Potter did not cite women's neglect of domestic space as Sameth had, but instead pointed to all Americans' relentless focus upon work, long commutes, and pursuits outside the home. Potter pointed especially to the way "distractions" intruded upon domestic time and space through the portals of Americans' personal electronic devices. Bedbug management, he predicted, would require that Americans turn their attention back to the home.[39] Potter thus shares much with the ecological thinkers in the history of American pest control who have called upon individuals to heighten their awareness of the intricacies and importance of domestic environments—from the Progressive Era home economist Marion Talbot, to African-American reformer Booker T. Washington, to the Integrated Pest Management pioneer Helga Olkowsi.[40]

The entomologists and health experts who tracked the bedbug's resurgence at the start of the twenty-first century also knew, however, that private space was not only private, especially given the bedbugs' ability to spread in communities via humans' own movements. Like Sherman Aldrich, the Chicago Housing Authority's first manager and the initiator of communal bedbug treatments in 1938, pest management professionals, health experts, and housing advocates came to recognize within a decade of the bedbug's resurgence that pest management requires attention to the home not only by private individuals but also from entire communities. The introduction of the Don't Let the Bed Bugs Bite Act gave federal officials a chance to reverse the 1938 decision not to subsidize local efforts at bedbug eradication for low-income communities.[41] The newly formed Norwood Tenants' Association echoed cries of past activists in infested communities. They demanded greater power to protect their own homes and health, and they called for government intervention—on their terms—against a neglectful landlord and soaring housing prices. Residents' struggle both honored the private dwelling—its importance as a family haven and a source of dignity—and united residents as a voice for political and environmental change. Together they decided to forego most chemical pesticides for control of bedbugs and mice, choosing methods that relied on low-toxicity technologies and changes to the domestic environment.[42]

In the history of public health campaigns for household pest control, it has been rare for vigilance about domestic nature and the creatures we call pests to cross the threshold of the home. Even when the state has entered residents' private spaces to urge meticulous cleanliness, it seldom balanced its calls for good environmental citizenship with improved services and care for the communities most entangled in unjust ecological webs. Or, as in the case of the Baltimore Plan of the 1940s and 1950s, householders who possessed the richest knowledge of infested domestic spaces did not become empowered to maintain healthy environmental conditions through either engagement with state actors or engagement with domestic ecologies and technologies. The Henry Horner Homes IPM project exhibited a rare combination of features that changed not just the biological ecology of the project but also the broader social ecology with which biological ecology is inextricably interwoven. Residents gained and exercised the power to demand state support for urban environmental change through their struggle for racial and environmental justice. They also gained and exercised the environmental and technical knowledge necessary to maintain their home environments in a way that was both healthy for human bodies and informed by the intricacies of insect bodies.

Given the rarity of situations like that at Horner, it is perhaps unsurprising that creatures like Norway rats, German cockroaches, and now bedbugs have persisted as unwanted companions in American homes. Rachel Carson wrote in *Silent Spring* that "minute causes produce mighty effects"—referring to tiny molecules of pesticides that work their way through ecosystems and bodies to disrupt their ecologies.[43] Likewise, the mightiest of causes—racism, classism, urban disinvestment—have brought the most minute and mundane effects into the homes of low-income people. The creatures we call pests have stayed with us through a century in which housing and health officials and ecologists and pesticide proponents alike have promised modern and healthy living environments. Pests have violated such notions of modernity so long as we have underestimated their unruliness, their relationship to urban politics, and the niche created for them by social inequality.

NOTES

INTRODUCTION: HISTORY, ECOLOGY, AND THE POLITICS OF PESTS

Epigraph: "Clean Up," by Arthur Corwin, M.D., c. 1916, originally appeared in *Clean Living* (May 1916): 2. The archive is the Chicago Municipal Reference Collection.

1 Domestic advice writers, exterminators, and entomologists disputed the value of many products that claimed to kill bedbugs. See, for example, Laura Thorne Hunter, *Domestic Pests: What They Are and How to Remove Them* (London: John Bale and Sons, 1938), 40; and Michael Potter, "The History of Bedbug Management—with Lessons from the Past," *American Entomologist* 57 (2011): 14–25.

2 Some very poor households in the United States experienced continuing bedbug infestation despite claims about "eradication" during the mid-twentieth century. See Robert Usinger, *Monograph on Cimicidae (Hemiptera-Heteroptera)* (College Park, Md.: Entomological Society of America, 1966), 169; and Young Lords Party and Michael Abramson, *Palante: Young Lords Party* (New York: McGraw Hill, 1971), 140–41.

3 David J. Moore and Dini Miller, "Field Evaluations of Insecticide Treatment Regimens for Control of the Common Bedbug, *Cimex lectularius*," *Pest Management Science* 65 (2009): 332–38.

4 Norwood Tenants Association, "Norwood Tenants Say, 'We're Not Leaving,'" Press Release, July 11, 2007, online at http://www.norwoodtenants.org/2007/07/norwood-tenants-say-were-not-leaving.html, accessed on December 28, 2010.

5 For discussion of thermal bedbug treatments, see William Quarles, "Thermal Pest Eradication in Structures," *IPM Practitioner* 28, no. 5–6 (2006): 1–8.

6 Patricia Simms, "Bedbug History Can Haunt Renters," *Capitol Times* (Wisconsin), August 21, 2006.

7 Maril Hazlett, "The Story of *Silent Spring* and the Ecological Turn," PhD diss., University of Kansas, 2003; and Maril Hazlett, "'Woman vs. Man vs. Bugs': Gender and Popular Ecology in Early Reactions to *Silent Spring*," *Environmental History* 9 (2004): 701–29.

8 Among the pesticide histories most important for this study are James

Whorton, *Before* Silent Spring: *Pesticides and Public Health in pre-DDT America* (Princeton, N.J.: Princeton University Press, 1975); Thomas Dunlap, *DDT: Scientists, Citizens, and Public Policy* (Princeton, N.J.: Princeton University Press, 1981); Edmund Russell, *War and Nature: Fighting Humans and Insects with Chemicals from World War I to* Silent spring (Cambridge: Cambridge University Press, 2001); Pete Daniel, *Toxic Drift: Pesticides and Health in the Post–World War II South* (Baton Rouge: Louisiana State University Press, 2005); Linda Nash, *Inescapable Ecologies: A History of Environment, Disease, and Knowledge* (Berkeley: University of California Press, 2006); Hazlett, "Story of *Silent Spring* and the Ecological Turn"; Hazlett, "Woman vs. Man vs. Bugs"; James McWilliams, *American Pests: The Losing War on Insects from Colonial Times to DDT* (New York: Columbia University Press, 2008); and Frederick Davis, "Unraveling the Complexities of Joint Toxicity of Multiple Chemicals at the Tox Lab and the FDA," *Environmental History* 13 (2008): 674–83. For histories focused on mosquitoes or mosquito-borne disease, see Gordon Patterson, *The Mosquito Crusades: A History of the American Anti-Mosquito Movement from the Reed Commission to the First Earth Day* (New Brunswick, N.J.: Rutgers University Press, 2009); and Eric Carter, *Enemy in the Blood: Malaria, Environment, and Development in Argentina* (Tuscaloosa: University of Alabama Press, 2012).

9   Several geographers and historians have documented complexities such as these in the history of pest control. See, for example, Eric Carter, "Development Narratives and the Uses of Ecology: Malaria Control in Northwest Argentina, 1890–1940," *Journal of Historical Geography* 33 (2007): 619–50; Edmund Russell, "Speaking of Annihilation: Mobilizing for War against Human and Insect Enemies, 1914–1945," *Journal of American History* 82 (1996): 1505–29; and Ian Shaw, Paul Robbins, and J. P. Jones. "A Bug's Life and the Spatial Ontologies of Mosquito Management," *Annals of the Association of American Geographers* 100 (2010): 373–92.

10   McWilliams, *American Pests,* 4.

11   For discussion of some of the emotional strains and toxic dangers of household work, see Harriet G. Rosenberg, "The Home Is the Workplace: Hazards, Stress, and Pollutants in the Household," in Wendy Chavkin, ed., *Double Exposure: Women's Health Hazards on the Job and at Home,* 219–45 (New York: Monthly Review Press, 1984).

12   Barbara Boyd, "Natural History in Housekeeping," *Washington Post,* January 21, 1911.

13   For discussions of the home's place in public and private life, especially as it relates to environment and health, see Alyson Blunt and Robyn Dowling, *Home* (London: Routledge, 2006); Liz Bondi, "Gender, Class, and Urban Space: Public and Private Space in Contemporary Urban Landscapes," *Urban Geography* 19 (1998): 160–85; Louise Crabtree, "Sustainability Begins at Home? An Ecological Exploration of Sub/Urban Australian Community-Focused

Housing Initiatives," *Geoforum* 36 (2005): 519–35; Mona Domosh, "Geography and Gender: Home, Again?" *Progress in Human Geography* 22 (1998): 276–82; bell hooks, "Homeplace: A Site of Resistance," in *Yearning: Race, Gender, and Cultural Politics* (Cambridge, Mass.: South End Press, 1999), 41–50; Suellen Hoy, *Chasing Dirt: The American Pursuit of Cleanliness* (New York: Oxford, 1995); Maria Kaika, *City of Flows: Modernity, Nature, and the City* (New York: Routledge, 2005); Sallie Marston, "The Social Construction of Scale," *Progress in Human Geography* 24 (2000): 219–42; Adam Rome, "Political Hermaphrodites: Gender and Environmental Reform in Progressive America," *Environmental History* (2006): 440–63; Virginia Scharff, ed., *Seeing Nature through Gender* (Lawrence: University of Kansas Press, 2003); Susan Smith, "Living Room?" *Urban Geography* 25 (2004): 89–91; Susan Strasser, *Never Done: A History of American Housework* (New York: Pantheon, 1982); Susan Strasser, *Waste and Want: A Social History of Trash* (New York: Henry Holt, 1999); Nancy Tomes, *The Gospel of Germs: Men, Women, and the Microbe in American Life* (Cambridge: Harvard University Press, 1998); Lawrence Vale, *From the Puritans to the Projects: Public Housing and Public Neighbors* (Cambridge: Harvard University Press, 2000); Rhonda Y. Williams, *The Politics of Public Housing: Black Women's Struggles against Urban Inequality* (London: Oxford University Press, 2004); and Gwendolyn Wright, *Building the Dream: A Social History of Housing in America* (New York: Pantheon, 1981).

14 Vale, *From the Puritans to the Projects*, 2000; and Williams, *Politics of Public Housing*, 2004. See also David Theo Goldberg, *The Racial State* (Malden, Mass.: Blackwell, 2002).

15 For discussions of race, justice, and environment, see Elizabeth Blum, *Love Canal Revisited: Race, Class, and Gender in Environmental Activism* (Lawrence: University of Kansas Press, 2008); Robert D. Bullard, *Dumping in Dixie: Race, Class, and Environmental Quality* (Boulder, Colo.: Westview Press, 2000); Giovanna DiChiro, "Nature As Community," in William Cronon, ed., *Uncommon Ground: Rethinking the Human Place in Nature* (New York: Norton, 1996), 298–320; Dianne Glave, *Rooted in the Earth: Reclaiming the African-American Environmental Heritage* (Chicago: Lawrence Hill Books, 2010); Dianne Glave and Mark Stoll, eds., *To Love the Wind and the Rain: African-Americans and Environmental History* (Pittsburgh: University of Pittsburgh Press, 2005); Robert Gottlieb, *Forcing the Spring: The Transformation of the American Environmental Movement* (Washington, D.C.: Island Press, 1993); Andrew Hurley, *Environmental Inequalities: Class, Race, and Industrial Pollution in Gary, Indiana, 1945–1980* (Chapel Hill: University of North Carolina Press, 1995); Gregg Mitman, *Breathing Space: How Allergies Shape Our Lives and Landscapes* (New Haven, Conn.: Yale University Press, 2007); Laura Pulido, "Community, Place, and Identity," in J. P. Jones, H. J. Nast, and S. M. Roberts, eds., *Thresholds in Feminist Geography* (Lanham, Md.: Rowman and Littlefield, 1997); Samuel Kelton Roberts Jr., *Infectious Fears: Politics, Disease, and the Health Effects of Segregation* (Chapel Hill:

University of North Carolina Press, 2009); Kimberly Smith, *African-American Environmental Thought* (Lawrence: University of Kansas Press, 2007); Alan Taylor, "Unnatural Inequalities: Social and Environmental Histories," *Environmental History* 1 (1996): 6–19; and Sylvia Hood Washington, *Packing Them In: An Archaeology of Environmental Racism in Chicago, 1865–1954* (Lanham, Mass.: Lexington, 2005).

16   For literature on public housing, see John Atlas and Peter Dreier, "From Projects to Communities: How to Redeem Public Housing," *The American Prospect* 10 (1992): 74–85; Blunt and Dowling, *Home*, 2006; Jason Hackworth, "Public Housing and the Rescaling of Regulation in the U.S.A.," *Environment and Planning A* 35 (2003): 531–49; Jeffrey Klee, "Public Housing and the Power of Architecture," MA thesis, University of Delaware, 2001; Susan Popkin et al., "The Gautreaux Legacy: What Might Mixed-Income and Dispersal Strategies Mean for the Poorest Public Housing Tenants," *Housing Policy Debate* 11 (2000): 911–42; Gail Radford, *Modern Housing for America: Policy Struggles in the New Deal Era* (Chicago: University of Chicago Press, 1996); Vale, *From the Puritans to the Projects*, 2000; and Williams, *Politics of Public Housing*, 2004. For other urban planning and sanitary schemes, see W. Theodore Durr, "The Conscience of a City: A History of the Citizens' Planning and Housing Association and Efforts to Improve Housing for the Poor in Baltimore, Maryland, 1937–1954," PhD diss., Johns Hopkins University, 1972; Elizabeth Fee, Linda Shopes, and Linda Zeidman, *The Baltimore Book: New Views of Local History, Critical Perspectives on the Past* (Philadelphia: Temple University Press, 1991); Howard Gillette, *Between Justice and Beauty: Race, Planning, and the Failure of Urban Policy in Washington, D.C.* (Philadelphia: University of Pennsylvania Press, 2006); Peter Geoffrey Hall, *Cities of Tomorrow: An Intellectual History of Urban Planning and Design in the Twentieth Century*, 3d ed. (Oxford: Blackwell, 2002); David Harvey, *Spaces of Hope* (Berkeley: University of California Press, 2000); David Harvey, *Justice, Nature, and the Geography of Difference* (Cambridge, Mass.: Blackwell Publishers, 1996); Jennifer Light, *The Nature of Cities: Ecological Visions and the American Urban Professions, 1920–1960* (Baltimore, Md.: Johns Hopkins University Press, 2009); and Rachel Weber, "Extracting Value from the City: Neoliberalism and Urban Redevelopment," *Antipode* 34 (2002): 519–40. The critique of notions of modernity here also draws on Bruno Latour's suggestions for an anthropology of the modern, which argues that practices that seek to purify nature from culture (pests from homes and the city) obscure the very impossibility of this project. Bruno Latour, *We Have Never Been Modern*, trans. C. Porter (Cambridge: Harvard University Press, 1993). For broad critiques of modernism, see James Holston, *The Modernist City: An Anthropological Critique of Brasília* (Chicago: University of Chicago Press, 1989); and James C. Scott, *Seeing Like a State: How Certain Schemes to Improve the Human Condition Have Failed* (New Haven, Conn.: Yale University Press, 1998).

17 For an updated study of Baltimore, the subject of chapter 4, see Judith Easterbrook, Timothy Shields, Sabra Klein, and Gregory Glass, "Norway Rat
Population in Baltimore, Maryland in 2004," *Vector-Borne and Zoonotic Diseases* 5 (2005): 296–99.

PART I. THE PROMISES OF MODERN PEST CONTROL

1   "The Cause of Typhoid Fever in Washington and How It Can Be Prevented,"
     Washington Post, August 2, 1908, SM2; Sherman Aldrich, "Leasing: The
     Chicago Leasing Experience," paper presented at the Seminar on Manag-
     ing Low-Rent Housing: A Record of Current Experiences and Practice in
     Public Housing, Washington, D.C., June 13–24, 1938, 95; "A New War—On
     Vermin," *New York Times*, October 9, 1921, 2; and Rockefeller Foundation
     Trustees' Confidential Report, "Draft Report: The Fitness of the Environ-
     ment," 1950, folder 478, box 58, series 200, RG 1.2: Series 200, Rockefeller
     Foundation Archives, Rockefeller Archive Center, Sleepy Hollow, New
     York.
2   John Muir, *My First Summer in the Sierra* (Boston: Houghton-Mifflin, 1911), 211.
3   These sketches are inspired in part by Jakob von Uexkull, *Foray into the
     Worlds of Animals and Humans*, trans. Joseph O'Neil (Minneapolis: Univer-
     sity of Minnesota Press, 2010). A growing number of environmental schol-
     ars have called for research on cities to examine the place of nonhumans
     and the integration of human and nonhuman worlds in urban areas. These
     sketches are an attempt to understand how political ecologies were also
     natural ecologies. See Bruce Braun, "Writing a More-Than-Human Urban
     Geography," *Progress in Human Geography* 29 (2005): 635–50; Noel Castree,
     "False Antithesis? Marxism, Nature, and Actor-Networks," *Antipode* 34
     (2002): 111–46; Matthew Gandy, *Concrete and Clay: Reworking Nature in New
     York City* (Cambridge, Mass.: MIT Press, 2002); Linda Nash, "The Agency
     of Nature or the Nature of Agency?" *Environmental History* 10 (2005): 67–69;
     Chris Philo, "Animals, Geography, and the City: Notes on Inclusions and
     Exclusions," *Environment and Planning D* 13 (1995): 655–81; Sarah Whatmore,
     Hybrid Geographies: Natures, Cultures, Spaces (Thousand Oaks, Calif.: Sage,
     2002); Jennifer Wolch, "Anima Urbis," *Progress in Human Geography* 26 (2002):
     721–42; and Jennifer Wolch, Alec Brownlow, and Unna Lassiter, "Construct-
     ing the Animal Worlds of Inner-City Los Angeles," in ed. Chris Philo and
     Chris Wilbert, *Animal Spaces, Beastly Places: New Geographies of Human-Ani-
     mal Relations* (London: Routledge, 2000), 71–97.

1. FLIES: AGENTS OF INTERCONNECTION IN PROGRESSIVE ERA CITIES

1   Most of this description comes from L. O. Howard, *The House Fly: Disease
     Carrier* (New York: Frederick Stokes, 1911), 16–25; and Luther S. West, *The*

Housefly: Its Natural History, Medical Importance, and Control (Ithaca, N.Y.: Comstock, 1951), 101.

2   Howard, *House Fly*, 28, 44; and von Uexkull, *Foray into the Worlds*, 98. For a review of olfaction in houseflies, see West, *Housefly*, 73–79.

3   L. O. Howard, *Fighting the Insects* (New York: Century, 1931), 142.

4   C. H. Richardson, "The Response of the House-fly (*Musca domestica* L) to Ammonia and Other Substances," *New Jersey Agricultural Experiment Station Bulletin* 292 (1916): 3–19. See also Hugh Raffles, *Insectopedia* (New York: Pantheon, 2010), 315. For a later review of oviposition in houseflies, see West, *Housefly*, 92–94.

5   L. O. Howard, "A Contribution to the Study of the Insect Fauna of Human Excrement," *Proceedings of the Washington Academy of Sciences* 2 (1900): 541, 554; and L. O. Howard, "Economic Loss to the People of the United States through Insects That Carry Disease," *USDA Bureau of Entomology Bulletin* 78 (1909): 25. For discussion of Howard's career and the emergence of medical entomology, see H. Geong, "Exerting Control: Biology and Bureaucracy in the Development of American Entomology, 1870–1930," PhD diss., University of Wisconsin–Madison, 1999; and H. Geong, "Carving a Niche for Medical Entomology," *American Entomologist* 47 (2001): 236–43.

6   C. F. Hodge and Jean Dawson, *Civic Biology* (Boston: Ginn and Company, 1918), 234.

7   "Inspiration for Shoo-fly," *Madison County* [Montana] *Monitor*, January 19, 1906, 4. Fly species that bite humans probably prompted more "shooing" than *M. domestica*, which has a rough tongue-like mouthpart but cannot bite.

8   Catharine Beecher and Harriet Beecher Stowe, *The American Woman's Home* (New Brunswick, N.J.: Rutgers University Press, 2002), 277. For elite discussion of screens and their use, see, for example, Mae Savell Croy, *Putnam's Household Handbook* (New York: Putnam, 1916), 22.

9   Lydia Maria Child's 1833 guide is one example that omits flies while providing advice about other pests. Lydia Maria Child, *The American Frugal Housewife*, reprint of twelfth edition, 1833 (Bedford, Mass.: Chapman-Billies, 1990), 19.

10   The British naturalist James Samuelson exemplifies the wonder of nineteenth-century authors at the role of flies as decomposers in the order of the natural world. See James Samuelson, *Humble Creatures: The Earthworm and the Common Housefly: In Eight Letters* (London: Van Voorst, 1858), 75. L. O. Howard also called flies' assistance to decomposing bacteria their only positive quality. Howard, *House Fly*, 22.

11   Naomi Rogers, "Germs with Legs: Flies, Disease, and the New Public Health," *Bulletin of the History of Medicine* 63 (1989): 599–617; Rennie Doane, *Insects and Disease: A Popular Account of the Way in Which Insects May Spread or Cause Some of Our Common Diseases* (New York: Henry Holt, 1910), 57; Howard, *House Fly* 45; West, *Housefly*, 5; and E. P. Felt, "Methods of Controlling the

House Fly and Thus Preventing the Dissemination of Disease," *New York Medical Journal* (April 2, 1910): 685–87.

12   For examples of pre-1900 English-language publications, see J. Leidy, "Flies As a Means of Communicating Contagious Diseases," *Proceedings of the Academy of Natural Sciences of Philadelphia* (1871), 297; "The Fly in Its Sanitary Aspect," *Lancet* 2 (1871): 270; and G. E. Nicholas, "The Fly in Its Sanitary Aspect," *Lancet* 2 (1873): 724. See also J. F. M. Clark, *Bugs and the Victorians* (New Haven, Conn.: Yale University Press, 2009), 216–36.

13   George Kober, "Report on the Prevalence of Typhoid Fever in the District of Columbia," in *Report of the Health Officer of the District of Columbia* (Washington, D.C.: Department of Health 1895), 252–92, 266, 258.

14   Vincent J. Cirillo, "'Winged Sponges': Houseflies As Carriers of Typhoid Fever in 19th- and Early 20th-Century Military Camps," *Perspectives in Biology and Medicine* 49 (2006): 52–63; and Walter Reed, Edward Shakespeare, and Victor Vaughan, *Abstract of Report on the Origin and Spread of Typhoid Fever in the U.S. Military Camps during the Spanish War of 1898* (Washington, D.C.: Government Print Office, 1900).

15   Alice Hamilton, Maud Gernon, and Gertrude Howe, *An Inquiry into the Causes of the Recent Epidemic of Typhoid Fever in Chicago* (Chicago: City Homes Association, 1903), 9.

16   Blood-sucking vectors are actually intermediate hosts for pathogens; microbes such as the malaria plasmodium use the vector's body to complete part of its life cycle. Mechanical vectors were not thought to serve as intermediate hosts.

17   Howard, "Contribution to the Study of the Insect Fauna of Human Excrement," 1900; and Howard, *House Fly* 39. A wide array of sources discuss possible diseases carried by houseflies as well as related species. See Simon Flexner and Paul Clark, "Contamination of the Fly with Poliomyelitis Virus," *Journal of the American Medical Association* 56 (1911): 1717–18; E. Austen, "The House-Fly, Its Life History, Importance As a Disease Carrier, and Practical Measures for Its Suppression," *British Museum Economics Series* (1913): 1–12; Charles T. Brues, "Insects As Carriers of Infection: An Entomological Study of the 1916 Epidemic," in *A Monograph on the Epidemic of Poliomyelitis (Infantile Paralysis) in New York City in 1916* (New York: M. B. Brown, 1917), 136–78; Daniel Jackson, *Pollution of New York Harbor As a Menace to Health by the Dissemination of Intestinal Diseases through the Agency of the Common House Fly* (New York: Merchant's Association, 1907); S. Moore, "Diseases Probably Caused by Flies," *British Medical Journal* (1893): 1154; and J. C. Torrey, "Numbers and Types of Bacteria Carried by City Flies," *Journal of Infectious Disease* 10 (1912): 166–77. Brues focused more on other species of flies but admitted the possible role of houseflies in polio. See also Naomi Rogers, "Dirt, Flies, and Immigrants: Explaining the Epidemiology of Poliomyelitis, 1900–1916," *Journal of the History of Medicine and Allied Sciences* 44 (1989): 486–505. Flies were

chiefly blamed for intestinal diseases, but some people also blamed them for tuberculosis. See E. Hayward, "The Fly As a Carrier of Tuberculosis Infection," *New York Medical Journal* (1904): 643–44.

18 American Civic Association, "Fight the Flies," *National Geographic Magazine* 21 (1910): 383–85; and George Kober, *Report of the Committee on Social Betterment* (Washington, D.C.: President's Homes Commission, 1908), 87.

19 Howard cites one investigator who counted twelve hundred "specks" on a square foot of window glass. Howard, *House Fly*, 27–32.

20 Ibid., 16–38.

21 Felt, "Methods of Controlling the House Fly," 685; and F. C. Bishopp, W. E. Dove, and D. C. Parman, "Points of Economic Importance in the Biology of the House Fly," *Journal of Economic Entomology* 8 (1915): 65–69.

22 Howard, *House Fly*, 51–56. Experiments used chalk dust or dyes to make released flies recognizable upon recapture. E. P. Felt, New York state entomologist, used three hundred to five hundred feet as the distance from any fly-breeding hazard within which one is likely to find flies. Felt, "Methods of Controlling the House Fly."

23 Some historians have proposed the "narrowing hypothesis," explaining that public health agencies narrowed their focus from the entire environment onto germs following 1900. See John Cassedy, *Charles V. Chapin and the Public Health Movement* (Cambridge: Harvard University Press, 1962), 93–109; John Duffy, *The Sanitarians: A History of American Public Health* (Urbana: University of Illinois Press, 1990); Gottlieb, *Forcing the Spring*, 1993; Gregg Mitman, Michelle Murphy, and Chris Sellers, "Introduction: A Cloud over History," *Osiris* 19 (2004): 1–17; and Paul Starr, *The Social Transformation of American Medicine* (New York: Basic Books, 1982). Judith Leavitt, Naomi Rogers, and Nancy Tomes each offer their own nuanced readings of the introduction of germ theory into public health, showing ways in which the new paradigm shifted the targets and spaces of public health but did not eliminate interest in sanitation. Judith Walzer Leavitt, *Typhoid Mary: Captive to the Public's Health* (Boston: Beacon Press, 1996); Naomi Rogers, *Dirt and Disease: Polio before FDR* (New Brunswick, N.J.: Rutgers University Press, 1992); Rogers, "Germs with Legs"; and Tomes, *Gospel of Germs*. The evidence surrounding medical entomology suggests that health officials' responses to germ theory varied from city to city and among officials; some pursued a greater focus on sanitation in light of medical entomology findings, while others narrowed their sights on destroying confirmed or supposed vectors.

24 Gordon Patterson, *The Mosquito Wars: A History of Mosquito Control in Florida* (Gainesville: University of Florida Press, 2004). For state control over infested landscapes, see also Timothy Mitchell, "Can the Mosquito Speak?" in *Rule of Experts: Egypt, Techno-politics, Modernity* (Berkeley: University of California Press, 2002), 19–53.

25 Hamilton, Gernon, and Howe, *An Inquiry*, 5.

26   For discussion of the workings of sanitary and unsanitary privies, see Richard Messer, "Designs for Privies," *American Journal of Public Health* 7 (1917): 190–96. See also Hamilton, Gernon, and Howe's own description of malfunctioning privies, *An Inquiry*, 5–7.

27   Robert Archey Woods and Albert Joseph Kennedy, *Handbook of Settlements* (1911; reprint, Urbana: University of Illinois Library, 1970, 54.

28   Hamilton, Gernon, and Howe, *An Inquiry*, 5.

29   Ibid., 9.

30   Ibid., 11.

31   Ibid., 15.

32   "Asks Hull House to Bring Proof," *Chicago Daily Tribune*, April 15, 1903, 16; Alice Hamilton, "The Common House Fly As a Carrier of Typhoid," *Journal of the American Medical Association* 42 (1904): 1034; Alice Hamilton, "The Fly As a Carrier of Typhoid," *Journal of the American Medical Association* 40 (1903): 576–83; and Harold Platt, *Shock Cities: The Environmental Transformation and Reform of Manchester and Chicago* (Chicago: University of Chicago Press, 2005), 333–61.

33   The topic of Hull-House's and other Progressives' relationships to diverse immigrant and ethnic communities in Chicago has prompted considerable scholarly controversy. Maureen Flanagan has argued that women's activist groups across ethnicity and class united based on their interest in reordering city agendas and budgets to support family life and health rather than capitalist interests. This is a rather different angle from Rivka Shpak Lissak's, however; Lissak has focused on the conflict between cultural pluralism and assimilation, concluding that Jane Addams and Hull-House began from an assimilationist view of the ethnic communities they aimed to serve. These two conclusions are not mutually exclusive, and together they may accurately capture the dynamic nature of activism and community-building. Hull-House's educational activities served the somewhat discordant goals of assimilation and empowerment. They provided paternalistic education in the context of activism that broadened political participation and demanded direct government support for healthy neighborhood environments. To any extent that ethnicity was a factor of interest to Hamilton, Gernon, and Howe in the typhoid study—they certainly mentioned ethnicity in their description of community—they did not seem to blame ethnic traditions for the environmental conditions in the nineteenth ward. Maureen Flanagan, *Seeing with Their Hearts: Chicago Women and the Vision of a Good City, 1871–1933* (Princeton, N.J.: Princeton University Press, 2002), 86–93; and Rivka Shpak Lissak, *Pluralism and Progressives: Hull House and the New Immigrants, 1890–1919* (Chicago: University of Chicago Press, 1989). See also Noralee Frankel and Nancy Dye, eds., *Gender, Class, Race, and Reform in the Progressive Era* (Lexington: University of Kentucky Press, 1994).

34   Woods and Kennedy, *Handbook of Settlements*, 53.

35   Jane Addams, *Twenty Years at Hull-House: With Autobiographical Notes*, ed. V. B. Brown (Boston: St. Martin's 1999), 98–99, 152–55.

36   Flanagan, *Seeing with Their Hearts*, 86–93.

37   Kober, "Report on the Prevalence of Typhoid Fever in the District of Columbia," 282.

38   Howard, *House Fly*, 9.

39   Howard, "Contribution to the Study of the Insect Fauna of Human Excrement"; and Howard, *House Fly* 39.

40   Howard, "Contribution to the Study of the Insect Fauna of Human Excrement," 554.

41   Julie Husband and Jim O'Loughlin, *Daily Life in the Industrial United States, 1870–1900* (Westport, Conn.: Greenwood, 2004), 32; and Sarah Hinman, "Spatial and Temporal Structure of Typhoid in Washington, D.C.," PhD diss., Louisiana State University, 2007.

42   James Borchert, *Alley Life in Washington: Family, Community, Religion, and Folklife in the City, 1850–1970* (Champaign: University of Illinois Press, 1982), 1–2; and Frederick Weller, *Neglected Neighbors: Stories of Life in the Alleys, Tenements, and Shanties of the National Capital* (Philadelphia: Winston, 1909), 9.

43   Borchert, *Alley Life in Washington*, ix, 57–58.

44   Weller, *Neglected Neighbors*, 32, 22.

45   Frederick Lord, "Flies and Tuberculosis," *Boston Medical and Surgical Journal* 24 (1904): 651–54.

46   George Kober, *The History and Development of the Housing Movement in the District of Columbia* (Washington, D.C.: Washington Sanitary Homes Company, 1907), 55–56; and Weller, *Neglected Neighbors*, 248. According to Howard Gillette, reformers assumed that the "sanitary housing" would relieve pressure on the housing market, so that somewhat better homes would trickle down to poor blacks and other very low-income residents. See Gillette, *Between Justice and Beauty*, 108–20.

47   Sanborn maps from 1903 show that residential or mixed residential-business blocks in the District commonly had at least one stable and sometimes as many as ten. *Sanborn Fire Insurance Maps*, Washington, D.C., vol. 1–2, 1903–1916, Library of Congress.

48   *Annual Reports of the Health Officer of the District of Columbia* (*ARHODC*) (1906), 40; *ARHODC* (1907), 112; *ARHODC* (1908, 87); and Howard, *Loss through Insects That Carry Disease*, 33.

49   *ARHODC* (1906), 28.

50   Ibid., 40; *ARHODC* (1907), 112; *ARHODC* (1908), 87; and Howard, *Loss through Insects That Carry Disease*, 33.

51   Howard, *House Fly* 25.

52   *ARHODC* (1906), 40; *ARHODC* (1907), 112; *ARHODC* (1908), 87; and Howard, *Loss through Insects That Carry Disease*, 33.

53 W. D. Pierce, "Why American Cities Must Fight Insects," *American City*, August 1919, 146–48.

54 W. M. Esten and C. J. Mason, "Sources of Bacteria in Milk," *Storrs Experiment Station Bulletin 51* (1908): 94–98. For further discussion of flies' flights, see N. Cobb, "The House Fly," *National Geographic*, May 21, 1910, 371–80; and N. Cobb, "Notes on the Distances Flies Can Travel," *National Geographic*, May 21, 1910, 380–83.

55 Pierce, "Why American Cities Must Fight Insects," 146–48; W. D. Pierce, ed., *Sanitary Entomology: The Entomology of Disease, Hygiene, and Sanitation* (Boston: R. G. Badger, 1921).

56 Flexner and Clark, "Contamination of the Fly with Poliomyelitis Virus," 1717–18. At least one study argued that flies carrying infection kept them very close to the source of contagion, meaning that people beyond polluted areas need not worry about them. G. L. Cox, F. C. Lewis, and E. F. Glynn, "The Number and Varieties of Bacteria Carried by the Common House Fly in Sanitary and Insanitary City Areas," *Journal of Hygiene* 12 (1912): 290–319.

57 Weller, *Neglected Neighbors*, 73.

58 Ibid., 94.

59 Hamilton, Gernon, and Howe, *An Inquiry*, 20.

60 "Asks Hull House to Bring Proof," *Chicago Daily Tribune*; and Platt, *Shock Cities*, 333–61. Other social movements also appealed to this sense of self-interest; see, for example, Adam Fairclough, *Better Day Coming: Blacks and Equality, 1890–2000* (New York: Viking, 2001), 163.

61 Flanagan, *Seeing with Their Hearts*, chapter 5; Hoy, *Chasing Dirt*, chapter 3; and Suellen Hoy, "Municipal Housekeeping: The Role of Women in Improving Urban Sanitation Practices, 1880–1917," in Martin Melosi, ed., *Pollution and Reform in American Cities* (Austin: University of Texas Press, 1980), 173–98.

62 Mary Waring, *Prophylactic Topics: Common Sense Subjects for the Use of the People, Especially the Home-makers* (Chicago: Fraternal Press, 1916). For further discussion of Waring and flies, see Anne Meis Knupfer, *Toward a Tenderer Humanity and a Nobler Womanhood: African-American Women's Clubs in Turn-of-the-Century Chicago* (New York: NYU Press, 1996), 49; and Elizabeth Blum, "Women, Environmental Rationale, and Activism during the Progressive Era," in Dianne Glave and Mark Stoll, eds., *"To Love the Wind and the Rain": African-Americans and Environmental History* (Pittsburgh: University of Pittsburgh Press, 2006), 77–92.

63 Marion Talbot, *House Sanitation: A Manual for Housekeepers* (Boston: Whitcomb and Barrows, 1913), 99–100. Other African-American health reformers urged fly control and personal cleanliness in domestic space as a way to build respect and protect well-being in black communities. A. Wilberforce Williams, "Preventive Measures, First Aid Remedies, Hygienics, and Sanitation," *Chicago Defender*, March 30, 1918, 16.

64   L. O. Howard and F. C. Bishopp, "The House Fly and How to Suppress It," *USDA Farmers' Bulletin* 1408 (1926): 17–18.

65   Howard, *House Fly*, xvi.

66   "The Cause of Typhoid Fever in Washington and How It Can Be Prevented," *Washington Post*, August 2, 1908, SM2.

67   Howard and Bishopp, "House Fly and How to Suppress It," 17–18.

68   Washington's health commissioner, Dr. William Woodward, commented that even Kober's investigation of the 1895 typhoid outbreak relied on emergency funding rather than permanent allocations, a mark of the District's failure to proactively address disease hazards. William Woodward, *Report of the Health Officer of the District of Columbia* (Washington, D.C.: Department of Health, 1895), 252.

69   Howard, *Economic Loss Through Insects That Carry Disease*, 33.

70   Weller, *Neglected Neighbors*, 248.

71   For discussions of relationships between urban waste sources and rural and suburban farms, see Marc Linder and Lawrence Zacharias, *Of Cabbages and Kings County: Agriculture and the Formation of Modern Brooklyn* (Iowa City: University of Iowa Press, 1999), 44–51; and Richard Wines, *Fertilizer in America: From Waste Recycling to Resource Exploitation* (Philadelphia: Temple University Press, 1985). See also Dawn Day Biehler, "Flies, Manure, and Window Screens: Medical Entomology and Environmental Reform in Early-Twentieth-Century U.S. Cities," *Journal of Historical Geography* 36 (2010): 68–78.

72   *ARHODC* (1907), 31.

73   *ARHODC* (1906), 40.

74   *ARHODC* (1908), 69; and *ARHODC* (1916), 29. For discussion of city inspection as a diffuse form of governance, see T. Crook, "Sanitary Inspection and the Public Sphere in Late Victorian and Edwardian Britain: A Case Study in Liberal Governance," *Social History* 32 (2007): 369–93.

75   Weller, *Neglected Neighbors*, 94–96.

76   Susan Craddock, *City of Plagues: Disease, Poverty, and Deviance in San Francisco* (Minneapolis: University of Minnesota Press, 2000); and Joanna Dyl, "The War on Rats versus the Right to Keep Chickens: Plague and the Paving of San Francisco, 1907–1908," in Andrew Isenberg, ed., *The Nature of Cities: Culture, Landscape, and Urban Space* (Rochester, N.Y.: University of Rochester Press, 2006), 38–61. For further discussion of horses in cities, see Clay McShane and Joel Tarr, *The Horse in the City: Living Machines in the Nineteenth Century* (Baltimore, Md.: Johns Hopkins University Press, 2007); and Ann Norton Greene, *Horses at Work: Harnessing Power in Industrial America* (Cambridge: Harvard University Press, 2008).

77   Geong, "Carving a Niche for Medical Entomology," 240; Howard, *House Fly*, 16–18; and F. C. Cook, "Experiments in the Destruction of Fly Larvae in Horse Manure," *Bulletin of the Department of Agriculture* 118 (1914).

78   McWilliams, *American Pests*, chapter 5; see also Howard, *Fighting the Insects*.

At the same time, another chronicler of Howard's career credits him with founding biological control in the United States. Louise Russell, "Leland Ossian Howard: A Historical Review," *Annual Review of Entomology* 23 (1978): 1–17, 7.

79 "Plans Death to Flies," *Washington Post*, August 7, 1910, M2.

80 C. F. Hodge, "How You Can Make Your Home, Town, or City, Flyless," *Nature and Culture* 3 (1911): 9–23, 16. See also G. S. Graham-Smith, *Flies in Relation to Disease: Non-bloodsucking Flies* (Cambridge: Cambridge University Press, 1913).

81 See, for example, American Civic Association, "Fight the Flies," 383–85.

82 C. F. Hodge, "House Flies: Outline for Practical Lessons and Plans for Flyless Homes," pamphlet, University of Oregon Archives, 1913.

83 C. F. Hodge, "A Practical Point in the Study of Typhoid or Filth Fly," *Nature Study Review* 6 (1910): 195–99; C. F. Hodge, "A Plan to Exterminate the Typhoid or Filth-disease Fly," *La Follette's Weekly* 3 (1911): 7–8; Hodge, "How You Can Make Your Home, Town, or City, Flyless"; C. F. Hodge, "Exterminating the Fly," *California Outlook*, 1911; and Hodge and Dawson, *Civic Biology*, 117–18.

84 Sally Gregory Kohlstedt, *Teaching Children Science: Hands-on Nature Study in North America, 1890–1930* (Chicago: University of Chicago Press, 2010), 72–76; 125–26.

85 Thanks to Adam Shapiro for helping me think about the relationship between the nature-study movement and biological citizenship as expressed through nature-study textbooks. Adam Shapiro, *Trying Biology: The Scopes Trial, Textbooks, and the Anti-evolution Movement in American Schools* (Chicago: University of Chicago Press, 2013).

86 C. F. Hodge, *Nature Study and Life* (Boston: Ginn and Company, 1902), 12.

87 Hodge, "House Flies."

88 Hodge, *Nature Study and Life*, 78.

89 Hodge and Dawson, *Civic Biology*, 110.

90 Ibid., 121; Chicago Board of Health, "The First Swat," *Clean Living*, May 1916, 16; and Eleanor Gates, *Swat the Fly* (New York: Arrow, 1915).

91 Chicago Board of Health, *Clean Living*, February 1917, 11.

92 Hodge and Dawson, *Civic Biology*, 117.

93 North Carolina State Board of Health, "Flies Are a Disgrace," *Board of Health Special Bulletin* 21 (May 1914).

94 Margaret Humphreys, *Yellow Fever and the South* (Baltimore, Md.: Johns Hopkins University Press, 1999), 152–53; 161–62; and Margaret Humphreys, *Malaria: Poverty, Race, and Public Health in the United States* (Baltimore, Md.: Johns Hopkins University Press, 2001), 47–57, 74–87.

95 Tomes, *Gospel of Germs*. See also Roger Miller, "Selling Mrs. Consumer: Advertising and the Creation of Suburban Socio-spatial Relations, 1910–1930," *Antipode* 23 (1991): 263–301. Miller found that early advertising for refrigerators and other household appliances reinforced the notion that women

were responsible for health and other concerns at the scale of the individual household.

96   Howard, *House Fly*, 534. See also Howard, "Economic Loss to the People of the United States through Insects That Carry Disease." This figure represents the contemporary value of the dollar. Margaret Humphreys has pointed out that Howard did promote screening for mosquitoes in areas where malaria was endemic. Humphreys, *Malaria*, 47. See also W. Herms, "The House Fly in Its Relation to Public Health," *Bulletin of the College of Agriculture* [California], 1911, 215.

97   *ARHODC* (1912).

98   Chicago Board of Health, "Our Greatest Enemy Is Not Foreign, but Domestic," *Clean Living* (July 1916). For a contradictory message, see Chicago Board of Health, "Implements of Safety," *Clean Living* (May 1916).

99   Waring, *Prophylactic Topics*, 41; see also Jacqueline Wolf, *Don't Kill Your Baby: Public Health and the Decline of Breastfeeding in the Nineteenth and Twentieth Centuries* (Columbus: Ohio State University Press, 2001), Appendix A2.

100 Research by Rima Apple and Jacqueline Wolf has identified different relationships among health experts and mothers in the Progressive Era that influenced shifting infant feeding practices. Both Apple and Wolf note the dramatic drop in breastfeeding by 1910, including early weaning. Apple ascribes the drop to Progressives' promotion of "scientific motherhood," including specially formulated infant foods and feeding practices. Wolf, however, argues that large numbers of women adopted early weaning in the nineteenth century and that many of the "scientific" alternatives to breastfeeding promoted by Progressives were actually attempts to make so-called artificial feeding safer. Wolf found significant evidence of efforts by health experts to promote breastfeeding as protection against diarrheal disease, but the "scientific" alternatives had the unintended consequence of hastening the trend away from the breast. Wolf, *Don't Kill Your Baby*; and Rima Apple, *Mothers and Medicine: A Social History of Infant Feeding, 1890–1950* (Madison: University of Wisconsin Press, 1987).

101 Marston, "Social Construction of Scale."

102 Wolf, *Don't Kill Your Baby*, 18.

103 Weller, *Neglected Neighbors*, 31.

104 *Annual Reports of the Department of Health of the City of New York* (*ARDHCNY*) (1912) 37; and *ARDHCNY* (1915), 37. Chicago mandated screening of homes as well as stables. City Council of the City of Chicago, "An Ordinance Requiring Dwellings, Tenement Houses, etc., to Be Screened against Flies," *Journal of the Proceedings of the City Council of Chicago*, 1917, 319; and City Council of the City of Chicago, "An Ordinance Requiring Stables to Be Screened against Flies," *Journal of the Proceedings of the City Council of Chicago*, 1917, 320.

105 Roy Lubove, *The Progressives and the Slums: Tenement House Reform in New York City, 1890–1917* (Westport, Conn.: Greenwood Press, 1974), 4–10, 118.

D. Becker, "The Visitor to the New York City Poor, 1843–1920," PhD diss., Columbia University, 1960; and R. Padernacht, "The Contributions of the New York Association for Improving the Condition of the Poor to Child Welfare, 1843–1939," PhD diss., St. John's University, 1976.

106 Many authors have pointed out the role of household technologies as tools of public health governance. Michel Foucault, "American Neo-liberalism (I)," in *The Birth of Biopolitics: Lectures at the College de France, 1978–1979* (New York: Macmillan, 2008), 215–38; Maria Kaika, "Interrogating the Geographies of the Familiar: Domesticating Nature and Constructing the Autonomy of the Modern Home," *International Journal of Urban and Regional Research* 28 (2004): 265–86; Thomas Osborne, "Security and Vitality: Drains, Liberalism, and Power in the Nineteenth Century," in Andrew Barry, Nikolas Rose, and Thomas Osborne, eds., *Foucault and Political Reason: Liberalism, Neo-Liberalism, and Rationalities of Government* (Chicago: University of Chicago Press, 1996), 99–122; and Chris Otter, "Cleansing and Clarifying: Technology and Perception in Nineteenth-Century London," *Journal of British Studies* 43 (2004): 40–65.

107 Association for Improving the Condition of the Poor (AICP), *Flies and Diarrheal Disease* (New York: Department of Health, 1914), 7.

108 D. Armstrong, "The House-fly and Diarrheal Disease among Children," *Journal of the American Medical Association* 62 (1914): 200–1; and AICP, *Flies and Diarrheal Disease* (1914).

109 AICP, *Flies and Diarrheal Disease* (1914), 11.

110 Ibid., 5–6.

111 Ibid., 29.

112 Ibid., 10.

113 Ibid. The AICP also concluded that children old enough to walk spent so much of their time playing outdoors that any protection rendered by screens was meaningless.

114 Russell Lynes, *The Domesticated Americans* (New York: Harper and Row, 1963), 129–32. Lynes offers anecdotes that contradict the remembrances of Rennie Doane and Luther West that householders tolerated the presence of flies.

115 Barbara Sicherman, *Alice Hamilton: A Life in Letters* (Cambridge: Harvard University Press, 1984), 145–46. Health experts continued to wonder about flies and disease transmission for many years afterward. See, for example, B. Greenberg, "Flies and Disease," *Scientific American* 213, no. 1 (1965): 92–99.

116 Esten and Mason, "Sources of Bacteria in Milk."

117 *ARHODC* (1917), 28–29.

118 Howard, *House Fly*, 2; Howard, *Fighting the Insects*, 140; and Edith Abbott, *The Tenements of Chicago, 1908–1935* (Chicago: University of Chicago Press, 1936), 477–78. The decline of flies recalls what Theodore Steinberg has called the "death of the organic city" as sanitary regulations and technologies

eliminated ecological connections among humans and other urban animals, wastes, and food. Theodore Steinberg, *Down to Earth: Nature's Role in American History* (New York: Oxford University Press, 2002), chapter 10.

2. BEDBUGS: CREATURES OF COMMUNITY IN MODERNIZING CITIES

1   Bedbug host-seeking has remained a mysterious process, even as entomologists applied novel techniques in a flurry of new bedbug research since the insects' resurgence in the United States. For an English-language review of older research, much of which was published in German, see Usinger, *Monograph of Cimicidae*, 17–21. See also Hugo Hartnack, *202 Common Household Pests of North America* (Chicago: Hartnack Publishing, 1939), 244. What remains fairly clear is that even bedbugs on the way to a meal tend to stop and meander. James Suchy and Vernard Lewis, "Host-Seeking Behavior in the Bedbug, *Cimex lectularius,*" *Insects* 2 (2011): 22–35.

2   Hartnack, *202 Common Household Pests of North America*, 238–44; Willard Wright, "The Bedbug—Its Habits and Life History and Methods of Control," *Public Health Reports* supplements, no. 175 (1944), 2–3. See also Usinger, *Monograph of Cimicidae*, 37–38, on the content of saliva and prevalence of allergy to it among humans.

3   These folk remedies are based on Archie William Friedberg, interview by Sue Chin, October 1992, Lower East Side Tenement Museum; and Reece Sailer, "The Bedbug: An Old Bedfellow That's Still with Us," *Pest Control* (October 1952): 22–24, 70–72, 23.

4   Usinger, *Monograph of Cimicidae*, 27, 171–72; and Wright, "The Bedbug," 4.

5   There is some disagreement whether females actually flee traumatic insemination. Alastair Stutt and Michael Siva-Jothy have disputed the notion that females flee based on even sex ratios in chicken coops, but other investigators found sex ratios skewed toward males and found that females are the life stage most likely to disperse, although that does not necessarily indicate that they do so to avoid traumatic insemination. Margie Pfiester, Philip G. Koehler, and Roberto M. Pereira found that females were most likely to be found alone. Cornell's Integrated Pest Management Program insists that traumatic insemination may be a factor in bedbug dispersal within a home. Margie Pfiester, Philip G. Koehler, and Roberto M. Pereira, "Effect of Population Structure and Size on Aggregation Behavior of *Cimex lectularius* (Hemiptera: Cimicidae)," *Journal of Medical Entomology* 46 (2009): 1015–20; Alastair Stutt and Michael Siva-Jothy, "Traumatic Insemination and Sexual Conflict in the Bed Bug *Cimex lectularius,*" *Proceedings of the National Academy of Sciences* 98 (2001): 5683–87; and the New York State IPM Program, "Bedbug FAQs," online at http://www.nysipm.cornell.edu/whats_bugging_ you/bed_bugs/bedbugs_faqs.asp#avoid, accessed on August 15, 2012.

6   Wright, "The Bedbug," 4–5; Sailer, "The Bedbug," 22–23; and C. L. Marlatt,

"The Bedbug," USDA *Farmers' Bulletin* 754 (1916): 2, 5, 8–9.

7   Hartnack, *202 Common Household Pests of North America*, 252–53; and James H. Collins, "Fighting the Bedbug," *Scientific American*, June 1924, 392, 439.

8   Collins, "Fighting the Bedbug."

9   The Swedish naturalist Peter Kalm found bedbugs among the English colonists in 1748 but not among aboriginal Americans. Glenn Herrick, *Insects Injurious to the Household and Annoying to Man* (New York: Macmillan, 1914), 108. The entomologist Robert Usinger also conducted linguistic investigations that attest to the lack of bedbugs in North America before European colonization. Usinger, *Monograph on Cimicidae*, 3.

10   Sailer, "The Bedbug," 22–23.

11   Usinger, *Monograph on Cimicidae*, 3.

12   Attilio Caccini, "Some Reasons for Exterminating the 'Brown Peril,'" *New York Times*, June 28, 1908, SM11. Despite Caccini's insistence that American infestations were worse than those in Europe, bedbug histories from England seem to show widespread, almost universal infestation in large cities like London. On the other hand, several European societies had public bedbug-control programs far more comprehensive than those in the United States; see Hartnack, *202 Common Household Pests of North America*, 289–300. For an excellent review of bedbug history, including European history, see Potter, "History of Bedbug Management."

13   Hartnack, *202 Common Household Pests of North America*, 257–58.

14   Clarence Weed, *Insects and Insecticides: A Practical Manual* (New York: Orange Judd Company, 1904), 325.

15   "The Midnight Toilers," *New York Times*, August 26, 1885, 2.

16   Caccini, "Some Reasons for Exterminating the 'Brown Peril.'"

17   Potter, "History of Bedbug Management," 15; and John Southall, *A Treatise of Buggs* (London: John Roberts, 1730).

18   Sailer, "The Bedbug."

19   Friedberg, interview, October 1992.

20   Beecher and Stowe, *American Woman's Home*, 277.

21   Potter, "History of Bedbug Management," 18.

22   Caccini, "Some Reasons for Exterminating the 'Brown Peril.'"

23   Child, *American Frugal Housewife*, 10.

24   "Midnight Toilers," *New York Times*, 2.

25   Mabel Hyde Kittredge, *Housekeeping Notes: How to Furnish and Keep House in a Tenement Flat* (Boston: Whitcomb and Barrows, 1911), 43, 16.

26   Talbot, *House Sanitation*, 85.

27   Potter, "History of Bedbug Management," 19; and Hunter, *Domestic Pests*, 40.

28   See, for example, Herrick, *Insects Injurious to the Household*, 119.

29   Herrick, *Insects Injurious to the Household*, 118; and George Hockenyos, "Bedbug Spraying," *Pests* (May 1940): 12.

30   Sailer, "The Bedbug," 22–23.

31 Ibid.

32 Marlatt, "The Bedbug," 5; Herrick, *Insects Injurious to the Household,* 118; and Sailer, "The Bedbug," 23–24. For a discussion of rising expectations of cleanliness from household technologies such as these, see Elizabeth Shove, *Comfort, Cleanliness, and Convenience: The Social Organization of Normality* (Oxford: Berg, 2004). For a history of beds, including many mentions of the bugs that shared them with people, see Lawrence Wright, *Warm and Snug: The History of the Bed* (London: Routledge, 1962). Wright dates the origins of metal bed frames back to no later than the 1500s, but wooden and adorned ones seem to have persisted even after metal ones became available. Afford-able metal bed frames seem to become more widespread by the mid-nine-teenth century; see Wright, *Warm and Snug,* 165–67.

33 For discussion of the advantage that affluent families enjoyed in bedbug con-trol, see Potter, "History of Bedbug Management."

34 Caccini, "Some Reasons for Exterminating the 'Brown Peril.'"

35 "A New War—On Vermin," *New York Times,* 1921; and Collins, "Fighting the Bedbug."

36 Sailer, "The Bedbug," 23.

37 Ibid.

38 Hartnack, *202 Common Household Pests of North America,* 252–53; Herrick, *Insects Injurious to the Household,* 111; and Marlatt, "The Bedbug," 1.

39 Hartnack, *202 Common Household Pests of North America,* 252–53.

40 J. Johnstone Jervis, "Disinfestation of Bug-Infested Furniture by Hydrocy-anic Acid," *Public Health* 48 (1935): 203–7.

41 Marion Harland, "Helping Hand," *Chicago Daily Tribune,* September 5, 1916, 13. See also S. Maria Elliott, *Household Hygiene* (Chicago: American School of Home Economics, 1905), 159; Hunter, *Domestic Pests,* 40; and Kittredge, *Housekeeping Notes,* 43.

42 Sailer, "The Bedbug," 23.

43 Herrick, *Insects Injurious to the Household,* 111.

44 See, for example, Weller, *Neglected Neighbors,* chapter 11.

45 Hartnack, *202 Common Household Pests of North America,* 285.

46 Jervis, "Disinfestation of Bug-Infested Furniture by Hydrocyanic Acid."

47 Abbott, *Tenements of Chicago,* 480.

48 Kittredge, *Housekeeping Notes,* 43.

49 Abbott, *Tenements of Chicago,* 243.

50 The study counted each double bed as two bedding units.

51 Abbott, *Tenements of Chicago,* 261, 267–68.

52 James Borchert also writes of reformers' worries about families that took in boarders. Borchert, *Alley Life in Washington,* 57.

53 Maurice Hall, "The Bedbug," *Public Health Reports Supplements* 129 (1937), 2.

54 W. Harvey and H. Hill, *Insect Pests* (Brooklyn: Chemical Publishing Company, 1941), 20–31; Usinger, *Monograph on Cimicidae,* 37–38; and P. Venkatachalam

and B. Belavadi, "Loss of Haemoglobin Iron Due to Excessive Biting by Bed-bugs," *Transactions of the Royal Society for Tropical Medicine and Hygiene* 56 (1962): 218–21.

55 Hartnack, *202 Common Household Pests of North America*, 242; and Sailer, "The Bedbug."

56 Pierce, *Sanitary Entomology*, 20–21.

57 Marlatt, "The Bedbug," 9–10; and Hall, "The Bedbug."

58 Hall, "The Bedbug," 2.

59 Robert Snetsinger, *The Ratcatcher's Child: The History of the Pest Control Industry* (Cleveland: Franzak and Foster, 1983); and "N. N. Sameth, Headed Extermination Firm," *New York Times*, February 22, 1955, 21.

60 "A New War—On Vermin," *New York Times*, 1921; and Collins, "Fighting the Bedbug."

61 Collins, "Fighting the Bedbug."

62 Rodman M. Brown, "The Relationship between a Building Official and Pest Control Operators," *Pests* (March 1939): 12–13.

63 Joel Connolly, "Public Health Aspects of Insect and Rodent Control," *Exterminators Log*, December 1935, 10–13. For a more critical view of the industry, see Edward D. Bocker, "Public Health Value of the Exterminating and Fumigating Industry," *Exterminators Log*, April 1934, 16.

64 George Sanders, "The Exterminator in the Field of Preventative Medicine," *Exterminators Log*, January 1934, 8.

65 For the adoption of "science" and "humanitarianism" in exterminators' national trade association motto, see the September 1933 issue of *Exterminators Log*. See also William Buettner, "Greeting," *Exterminators Log*, October 1933, 2; and Hugo Hartnack, *202 Common Household Pests of North America*, 1939.

66 Hockenyos, "Bedbug Spraying."

67 For discussion of unruliness of bodies, chemicals, and environments as a problem in occupational health, see Linda Nash, "The Fruits of Ill-Health: Pesticides and Workers' Bodies in Post–World War II California," *Osiris* 19 (2004): 203–19.

68 L. O. Howard, *Progress in Economic Entomology* (Washington, D.C.: Department of Agriculture, 1899), 150–51.

69 R. H. Creel, F. M. Faget, and W. D. Wrightson, "Hydrocyanic Acid Gas: Its Practical Use As a Routine Fumigant," *Public Health Reports* 30 (1915): 3537–50; and R. H. Creel and F. M. Faget, "Cyanide Gas for the Destruction of Insects with Special Reference to Mosquitoes, Fleas, Body Lice, and Bedbugs," *Public Health Reports* Reprint 343 (1916): 1464–75.

70 Howard, *Progress in Economic Entomology*, 151–52.

71 Aime Cousineau and F. G. Legg, "Hydrocyanic Acid Gas and Other Toxic Gases in Commercial Fumigation," *American Journal of Public Health* 25 (1935): 277–87.

72 Zyklon B, the formulation of HCN used by the Nazis, consisted of the chemical mixed with a solid medium, from which the HCN would evaporate to produce deadly fumes. Edmund Russell's book on insecticides and war briefly mentions HCN. Russell, *War and Nature*, 42.

73 Creel, Faget, and Wrightson, "Hydrocyanic Acid Gas." Masks may have been insufficient to protect HCN workers because the gas could be absorbed through the skin. P. Drinker, "Hydrocyanic Acid Gas Poisoning by Absorption through the Skin," *Journal of Industrial Hygiene* 14 (1932): 1–2.

74 Marlatt, "The Bedbug," 11; see also E. A. Back and R. T. Cotton, *Hydrocyanic Acid Gas As a Fumigant for Destroying Household Insects* (Washington, D.C.: Government Printing Office, 1932).

75 W. R. Beattie, "The Use of Hydrocyanic Acid Gas for Exterminating Household Insects," *Science* 14, no. 247 (1901): 285–89. HCN was first used for household fumigation in 1898, but it did not become popular for household use immediately. L. O. Howard and C. Popenoe, "Hydrocyanic Acid-Gas against Household Insects," *USDA Farmers' Bulletin* 163 (1912).

76 See examples cited in R. Hartigan, "Exterminator's Tort Liability for Personal Injury or Death," *American Law Reports* 4 (1983): 987.

77 Cousineau and Legg, "Hydrocyanic Acid Gas and Other Toxic Gases in Commercial Fumigation." In one notable instance, however, naval discipline failed to prevent sailors' deaths, prompting New York City to further investigate and regulate HCN fumigations. "Two Die in Vain Effort to Rescue Another in Gas-Filled Ship," *New York Times*, July 24, 1921, 1.

78 C. L. Williams, "Fumigants," *Public Health Reports* 46 (1931): 1013–31.

79 C. L. Williams, "Hydrocyanic Acid Gas Absorbed in Bedding," *Pests* (November 1938): 15–17.

80 Beattie, "Use of Hydrocyanic Acid Gas for Exterminating Household Insects."

81 Cousineau and Legg, "Hydrocyanic Acid Gas and Other Toxic Gases in Commercial Fumigation."

82 See, for example, W. G. Campbell, Acting Chief, to Eastern District Chief, September 19, 1917; Special Files Relating to the Enforcement of the Food and Drug Act, 1907–1920, Box 11, File 52-Hydrocyanic Acid; Records of the Bureau of Chemistry, RG 88, National Archives and Records Administration, College Park, Md. For further discussion of the history of pesticide regulation, see Whorton, *Before Silent Spring*; Dunlap, *DDT*; and Daniel, *Toxic Drift*. Pesticide regulation in general remained lax; HCN was not the only substance to receive little attention.

83 Health Department of the City of New York, "The Recent Fatalities from Hydrocyanic Acid Gas Fumigation," *Weekly Bulletin of the Department of Health of the City of New York* 7 (1923): 1–2; and "Two Die in Vain Effort to Rescue Another in Gas-Filled Ship," *New York Times* (1921), 1.

84 The Cook County Coroner's chemist published a paper on the accident that

sanitarians and toxicologists in other countries would later cite in their own studies on hydrocyanic acid gas poisoning. William D. McNally, "Six Deaths Following Fumigation with Hydrogen Cyanide," *Medical Journal and Record* 119 (1924): 143–44.

85 McNally, "Six Deaths Following Fumigation with Hydrogen Cyanide."

86 William Buettner, "Insurance and the Fumigation Business," *Exterminators Log*, January 1934, 11; and Committee on Legislation, "Legislation," *Exterminators Log*, October 1935, 8.

87 "A New War—On Vermin," *New York Times* (1921); Collins, "Fighting the Bedbug"; Hockenyos, "Bedbug Spraying"; and Hartnack, 202 *Common Household Pests of North America*, 87, 257.

88 Collins, "Fighting the Bedbug."

89 Industry leaders used similar arguments when the state of California excluded them from lists of professionals allowed to buy the toxic pesticide thallium. James Munch, "Thallium." *Exterminators Log*, July 1937, 8; and Al Cossetta, "Editor's Note," *Exterminators Log*, February 1938, 10.

90 "Legislation," *Exterminators Log*, November 1933, 6.

91 Cousineau and Legg, "Hydrocyanic Acid Gas and Other Toxic Gases in Commercial Fumigation"; and F. S. Pratt, "Discussion [Response to Cousineau and Legg]," *American Journal of Public Health* 25 (1935): 290–93.

92 C. L. Williams, "Discussion [Response to Cousineau and Legg]," *American Journal of Public Health* 25 (1935): 287–89. Williams also compared deaths from HCN and other fumigants to deaths from automobile exhaust and other gases to make the point that risks were small and regulators should spend time crafting reasonable legislation rather than adopting ill-considered laws on an emergency basis. C. L. Williams, "Fumigation Deaths As Compared with Deaths from Other Poisonous Gases," *Public Health Reports* 49 (1934): 697–99.

93 "Free Fumigator Whose Mixture Killed 6 in Flat," *Chicago Tribune*, March 14, 1923, 4.

94 "Pertinent Questions Asked of an Exterminator," *Exterminators Log*, February 1933, 3.

95 Hugo Hartnack, "Some Experiences with the Chicago Fumigating Ordinance," *Exterminators Log*, July 1934, 7.

96 Hartnack, 202 *Common Household Pests of North America*, 290–92.

97 "Medicine and the Law: Deaths after HCN Fumigation," *Lancet* (1935): 1065–66; and "Parliamentary Intelligence: Aldershot Fumigation Deaths," *Lancet* (1935): 1067.

98 C. L. Williams, "Fumigants."

99 W. A. Evans, "How to Keep Well: To Make Fumigation Safe," *Chicago Daily Tribune*, June 22, 1931, 12.

100 Cousineau and Legg, "Hydrocyanic Acid Gas and Other Toxic Gases in Commercial Fumigation."

101   Arnold Mallis, *Handbook of Pest Control* (Los Angeles: McNair-Dorland, 1960), 1074–76.

102   Some of the material in this section has been previously published in Dawn Biehler, "Permeable Homes: A Historical Political Ecology of Insects and Pesticides in U.S. Public Housing," *Geoforum* 40 (2009): 1014–23.

103   Hall, *Cities of Tomorrow*, 248–54; Radford, *Modern Housing for America*, chapter 3; and Catherine Wurster, *Modern Housing* (Houghton Mifflin: Boston, 1934).

104   Martin Meyerson and Edward Banfield, *Politics, Planning, and the Public Interest* (New York: Free Press, 1955), 18.

105   Abraham Goldfeld, *Toward Fuller Living through Public Housing and Leisure Time Activities* (New York: National Public Housing Conference, 1934), 3.

106   National Association of Housing Officials (NAHO), *Disinfestation of Dwellings and Furnishings: Problems and Practices in Low-Rent Housing* (Chicago: National Association of Housing Officials, 1939), 4.

107   Aldrich, "Leasing," 89.

108   NAHO, *Disinfestation of Dwellings and Furnishings*, 8.

109   Potter, "History of Bedbug Management."

110   Hartnack, *202 Common Household Pests of North America*, 259–61.

111   Hunter, *Domestic Pests*, 40. See also Michael Potter's review of bedbug history for discussion of extensive public engagement with bedbug control in Europe. Potter, "History of Bedbug Management."

112   NAHO, *Disinfestation of Dwellings and Furnishings*, 27.

113   However, see above reference to a fumigating accident in Britain; *The Lancet* still pronounced that HCN must not be banned because of its value in bedbug eradication.

114   NAHO, *Disinfestation of Dwellings and Furnishings*, 25.

115   Aldrich, "Leasing," 90.

116   Marston, "Social Construction of Scale"; Vale, *From the Puritans to the Projects*, 3–5; and Williams, *Politics of Public Housing*, 3–8.

117   Williams, *Politics of Public Housing*, 3.

118   Ibid., chapter 1.

119   "The Residents in Low-Rent Housing Like Their Homes," *Journal of Housing* (April 1947): 10–11.

120   For discussion of the negative reputation of American public housing, see Paul Grogan and Tony Proscio, "The Fall (and Rise) of Public Housing," Harvard University Joint Center for Housing Studies September 1, 2000, online at http://www.jchs.harvard.edu/research/publications/fall-and-rise-public-housing, accessed on March 21, 2013.

121   Blunt and Dowling, *Home*, chapter 3; Hackworth, "Public Housing and the Rescaling of Regulation in the USA"; and Vale, *From the Puritans to the Projects*, 8, 183–84.

122   "Find U.S. Pays Rent Money to Its Own Tenants," *Chicago Daily Tribune*, November 24, 1938, 5.

123 "Find U.S. Pays Rent Money to Its Own Tenants," *Chicago Daily Tribune* (1938); and Abraham Goldfeld, *The Diary of a Housing Manager* (Chicago: NAHO, 1938).

124 NAHO, *Disinfestation of Dwellings and Furnishings*, 8.

125 Unfortunately, any descriptions or images of this device seem to have been lost to history.

126 Abraham Goldfeld, quoted in Aldrich, "Leasing," 92.

127 NAHO, *Disinfestation of Dwellings and Furnishings*, 8. For further discussion of this case, see Biehler, "Permeable Homes."

128 This description is based on Hartnack, *202 Common Household Pests of North America*, 152–53; and George Hockenyos, "The Era of Pest Prevention," *Pests and Their Control* (August 1946): 8, 10.

129 New York City Housing Authority, *East River Houses: Public Housing in East Harlem* (New York: New York City Housing Authority, 1941), 11.

130 Russell, "Speaking of Annihilation," 1510.

3. GERMAN COCKROACHES: PERMEABLE HOMES IN THE POSTWAR ERA

1 Mallis, *Handbook of Pest Control* (1960), 171; and G. E. Gould, "Recent Developments in Roach Control," *Pests* (December 1943): 12–13, 22–23.

2 Bureau of Entomology and Plant Quarantine, *Cockroaches and Their Control* (Washington, D.C.: Government Printing Office, 1950), 4.

3 Vernon Kellogg, *American Insects* (New York: Holt and Company, 1908), 128; and Weed, *Insects and Insecticides*, 322.

4 James A. G. Rehn, "Man's Uninvited Fellow Traveler—The Cockroach," *Scientific Monthly* 61 (1945): 265–76.

5 Arnold Mallis, *Handbook of Pest Control* (Los Angeles: McNair-Dorland, 1954), 148.

6 Herrick, *Insects Injurious to the Household*, 127. For further historical discussion of cockroaches, see David George Gordon, *The Compleat Cockroach* (Berkeley: Ten Speed Press, 1996).

7 Herrick, *Insects Injurious to the Household*, 129.

8 M. Allen Pond, "What Can the Sanitary Engineer Contribute to Housing?" *Journal of Housing* 4 (1947): 237–39. New York's renowned exterminator Nathan Sameth suggested that roaches spread via dumbwaiters. "A New War—On Vermin," *New York Times* (1921).

9 Hartnack, *202 Common Household Pests of North America*, 86.

10 Louis Roth and Edwin Willis, *The Medical and Veterinary Importance of Cockroaches* (Washington, D.C.: Smithsonian Institution, 1957), 19.

11 Ibid., 19–20; and W. A. Janssen and S. E. Wedberg, "The Common House Roach, *Blattella germanica* Linn., As a Potential Vector of *Salmonella typhimurium* and *Salmonella typhosa*," *American Journal of Tropical Medicine and Hygiene* 1 (1952): 337–43.

12   H. Frings, "An Ounce of Prevention," *Pests and Their Control* (February 1948): 24–26; for a review, see Roth and Willis, *Medical and Veterinary Importance of Cockroaches*, 28.

13   Roth and Willis, *Medical and Veterinary Importance of Cockroaches*, 29.

14   These researchers examined the American cockroach, not the German cockroach, but the same sentiment applies. R. S. Bitter and O. B. Williams, "Enteric Organisms from the American Cockroach," *Journal of Infectious Disease* 85 (1949): 87–90.

15   Herrick, *Insects Injurious to the Household*, 138.

16   Beecher and Stowe, *American Woman's Home*, 277.

17   Kittredge, *Housekeeping Notes*, 30–31.

18   Child, *American Frugal Housewife*, 19.

19   F. L. Washburn, "Cockroaches," *Eleventh Annual Report of the State Entomologist of Minnesota* (1906).

20   Weed, *Insects and Insecticides*, 323.

21   Herrick, *Insects Injurious to the Household*, 139.

22   Mallis, *Handbook of Pest Control* (1960), 168.

23   For assertions about the harmlessness of pyrethrum to humans, see, for example, Bureau of Entomology and Plant Quarantine, *Cockroaches and Their Control*, 6; and Herrick, *Insects Injurious to the Household*, 139.

24   Herrick, *Insects Injurious to the Household*, 139–41.

25   Hartnack, *202 Common Household Pests of North America*, 87.

26   Herrick called HCN one of the most efficient solutions for roach infestation. Herrick, *Insects Injurious to the Household*, 138.

27   NAHO, *Disinfestation of Dwellings and Furnishings*, 8.

28   U.S. Public Health Service, *DDT for Control of Household Insects Affecting Health* (Atlanta: Federal Security Agency, 1946); and Bureau of Entomology and Plant Quarantine, *DDT . . . for Control of Household Pests* (Washington, D.C.: Government Printing Office, 1947).

29   Hockenyos, "Era of Pest Prevention."

30   Ibid.

31   Arthur Bartlett, "Chemical Marvels Take the 'Bugs' out of Living," *Popular Science* (May 1945): 150–54.

32   See, for example, Public Health Service, *DDT for Control of Household Insects Affecting Health.*

33   Medical and toxicological researchers considered the possibility of chronic poisoning during the late 1940s, but these notions seldom made it into public discussion. Minutes of the Interdepartmental Committee on Pest Control, May 18, 1951, and June 4, 1952; President's Committee on the Environment, Subcommittee on Pesticides; Records of the Food and Drug Administration RG 88, National Archives and Records Administration, College Park, Md.; and President's Science Advisory Committee, *The Use of Pesticides* (Washington, D.C.: President's Science Advisory Committee, 1963).

34   Hockenyos, "Era of Pest Prevention."

35   Division of Insects Affecting Man and Animals, *Cockroaches and Their Control* (Washington, D.C.: Government Printing Office, 1950), 5.

36   Ibid.

37   Mallis, *Handbook of Pest Control* (1954), 1000–1. Mallis indicates that even after the introduction of DDT, some exterminators might turn to HCN for jobs that demanded quick control, such as in a restaurant whose reputation would suffer if it was known to be infested.

38   Strasser, *Never Done*, 9.

39   See, for example, Public Health Service, *DDT for Control of Household Insects Affecting Health.*

40   Mitchell Zavon, "Insecticides and Other Pesticides of Home and Garden," *Modern Medicine* (August 20, 1962): 90–101.

41   Hockenyos, "Bedbug Spraying," 12.

42   Hockenyos, "Era of Pest Prevention."

43   Sailer, "The Bedbug," 22.

44   Ibid., 72.

45   "Hints to the Housing Manager: DDT-Impregnated Paint," *Journal of Housing* (November 1945): 199.

46   Division of Insects Affecting Man and Animals, *Cockroaches and Their Control*, 9.

47   Dwight Metzler, "DDT for Controlling Household Pests," *Journal of Housing* (July 1946): 151.

48   Metzler, "DDT for Controlling Household Pests."

49   Examples of these gaps in treatment are revealed in James Oleniak, "Tenant Sales and Services," *Journal of Housing* (August–September 1955): 296; and F. E. Wood, W. H. Robinson, Sandra K. Kraft, and Patricia Zungoli, "Survey of Attitudes and Knowledge of Public Housing Residents toward Cockroaches," *Bulletin of the Entomological Society of America* 27 (1981): 9–13.

50   Chipman Chemical Company, "New and Different … P-C-H Roach Powder," *Pests and Their Control* (November 1946): 31.

51   "Hints to the Housing Manager: Effective Insecticide," *Journal of Housing* (October 1946): 230. The *Journal of Housing* misprinted the name of the powder as PGH; the actual name is PCH.

52   Oleniak, "Tenant Sales and Services," 296. For more coercive tenant relations policies relating to infestation, see, for example, E. W. Blum, "Garbage Disposal Habits Improve under Penalty Plan," *Journal of Housing* 5, no. 4 (1948): 111–12.

53   Frances Morton Froelicher, interview by Betty Key, Baltimore, Md., October 18, 1977, Citizens' Planning and Housing Collection, Series 1: Organizational Records, Box 2: Highlights and Histories, University of Baltimore Archives.

54   Williams, *Politics of Public Housing*, 8; and Sarah Ruffin, interview by the author, Chicago, June 2006.

55   Williams, *Politics of Public Housing*, 78–79.

56   Louella Webster, "*La Cucaracha* and the Housing Shortage," *American Home* (May 1948): 156–60.

57   Webster, "*La Cucaracha* and the Housing Shortage."

58   Committee on the Hygiene of Housing, *An Appraisal Method for Measuring the Quality of Housing: A Yardstick for Health Officers, Housing Officials, and Planners* (New York: American Public Health Association, 1946).

59   Pond, "What Can the Sanitary Engineer Contribute to Housing?" 238.

60   Division of Insects Affecting Man and Animals, *Cockroaches and Their Control*, 4.

61   Mallis, *Handbook of Pest Control* (1954), 169.

62   National Commission on Urban Problems, *Building the American City* (Washington, D.C.: Government Printing Office, 1969), 10; and Kenneth Jackson, *Crabgrass Frontier: The Suburbanization of the United States* (New York: Oxford University Press, 1987), chapters 11–12.

63   New York City Housing Authority, "25-Year Public Housing Jubilee," *New York City Housing Authority Management Newsletter* (January–February 1961): 1; and J. S. Fuerst and Rosalyn Kaplan, "Chicago's Public Housing Program Saves Babies' Lives," *The Child* (June–July 1951), 178–81.

64   Radford, *Modern Housing for America*, 191–92.

65   NAHO, "Screen Doors Causing Trouble," in *Managing Low-Rent Housing Conference: A Record of Current Experiences and Practice in Public Housing* (Washington, D.C.: NAHO, 1938).

66   NAHO Maintenance Committee, *Maintenance Men Look at Housing Design* (Chicago: NAHO, 1948).

67   Pond, "What Can the Sanitary Engineer Contribute to Housing?" For further observations of housing quality, see Dwight F. Metzler, "A Study of Housing Regulation and Enforcement in the City of Chicago and Cook County, Illinois," MS thesis, University of Kansas, 1947.

68   Metzler, "DDT for Controlling Household Pests."

69   New York City Housing Authority, *Pre-examination Training Course Material for Resident Buildings Superintendent and Assistant Resident Buildings Superintendent* (New York: New York City Housing Authority, 1952), 85.

70   Hackworth, "Public Housing and the Rescaling of Regulation in the USA"; Radford, *Modern Housing for America*, 188–94; and Williams, *Politics of Public Housing*, 54–55. See also J. S. Fuerst, *When Public Housing Was Paradise: Building Community in Chicago* (Champaign-Urbana: University of Illinois Press, 2005).

71   Vale, *From the Puritans to the Projects*, 237–38.

72   Radford, *Modern Housing for America*, 188–94.

73   Atlas and Dreier, "From Projects to Communities."

74   Radford, *Modern Housing for America*, 188–94.

75   Vale, *From the Puritans to the Projects*, 236–41; and Atlas and Dreier, "From Projects to Communities."

76 Nicholas Bloom, *Public Housing That Worked: New York in the Twentieth Century* (Philadelphia: University of Pennsylvania Press, 2008). Bloom uses NYCHA's success to suggest that other housing authorities' management practices caused projects to "fail," but other histories have shown that federal public housing policy, negative popular discourse about public housing in the United States, and urban disinvestment in general bear considerable culpability. James Hanlon, "Review of *Public Housing That Worked: New York in the Twentieth Century* by Nicholas Dagen Bloom." *H-Urban, H-Net Reviews* (September 2008), online at http://www.h-net.org/reviews/showrev.pho?id=15772, accessed on August 15, 2012; R. Allen Hays, *The Federal Government and Urban Housing: Ideology and Change in Public Policy* (Albany: State University of New York Press, 1995); and Alexander von Hoffman, "A Study in Contradictions: The Origins and Legacy of the Housing Act of 1949," *Housing Policy Debate* 11 (2000): 299–326.

77 C. Peter Rydell, *Factors Affecting Maintenance and Operating Costs in Federal Public Housing Projects* (New York: Rand, 1970).

78 Radford, *Modern Housing for America*, 188–94; and Vale, *From the Puritans to the Projects*, 237–41.

79 "Vermin Control Drive Started; Newest Materials, Methods Used," *Journal of Housing* 4 (1947): 213.

80 C. L. Walker, "How to Get Rid of Household Pests," *Readers Digest* (April 1952): 109–12.

81 "'Three-in-One' Insecticide Kills Roaches, Ants, Lice, Other Pests," *Journal of Housing* (December 1947): 365; and Mallis, *Handbook of Pest Control* (1954), 955.

82 Quoted in "'Three-in-One' Insecticide Kills Roaches, Ants, Lice, Other Pests."

83 New York City Housing Authority, *Pre-examination Training Course Material for Resident Buildings Superintendent and Assistant Resident Buildings Superintendent*, 80.

84 Arnold Lehman, "The Major Toxic Actions of Insecticides," *Bulletin of the New York Academy of Medicine* 25, no. 6 (June 1949): 382–87; U.S. Congress, House, Select Committee to Investigate the Use of Chemicals in Food Products, *Chemicals in Food Products: Hearing before the Select Committee to Investigate the Use of Chemicals in Food Products*, 81st Cong., 2d sess., September 14–December 15, 1950, 388–90; and Arnold Lehman, "Chemicals in Foods: A Report to the Association of Food and Drug Officials on Current Developments," *Bulletin of the Association of Food and Drug Officials of the US* 15 (1951): 82–89. See also Rachel Carson, *Silent Spring* (Boston: Houghton Mifflin, 1962), 21–24; and Davis, "Unraveling the Complexities of Joint Toxicity of Multiple Chemicals at the Tox Lab and the FDA."

85 Minutes of the Interdepartmental Committee on Pest Control, June 4, 1952; President's Committee on the Environment, Subcommittee on Pesticides;

Records of the Food and Drug Administration RG 88, National Archives and Records Administration, College Park, Md.

86 Mallis, *Handbook of Pest Control* (1954), 955.

87 Justus Ward, "A Dynamic Statute for Pesticides," *USDA Yearbook of Agriculture* (1966): 271–79.

88 Justus Ward, "Toxicity Criteria Used in Judging the Labeling of Pesticides," *American Journal of Public Health* 45 (1955): 723–28.

89 Saint Prillerman, interview by the author, Fulton, Md., March 2012.

90 New York City Housing Authority, *Pre-examination Training Course Material for Resident Buildings Superintendent and Assistant Resident Buildings Superintendent.*

91 Such practices are largely lost to history for the 1950s, but by the 1970s it was certainly commonplace for residents of multifamily public housing to supplement the housing authority's pesticide applications, and the practice remains common today. See F. E. Wood, "Cockroach Control in Public Housing: Is It an Overwhelming Problem?" *Pest Control* (June 1980): 14–16; Michael Surgan et al., *Pest Control in Public Housing, Schools, and Parks: Urban Children at Risk* (Albany, N.Y.: Office of the Attorney General, 2002); Jill Viehweg, interview by the author, Denver, Colo., June 2006; and Ruffin interview.

92 David Shangle, interview by the author, Chicago, June 2006; Wood, "Cockroach Control in Public Housing"; and F. E. Wood, interview by the author, College Park, Md., February 2009.

93 Walter Ebeling, *Urban Entomology* (Berkeley: University of California Division of Agricultural Sciences 1975), 57–59.

94 Ibid.

95 Donald Cochran, "Insecticide Resistance," in Michael Rust, John Owens, and Donald Reierson, eds., *Understanding and Controlling the German Cockroach* (New York: Oxford University Press, 1995), 171–92.

96 Ebeling, *Urban Entomology*, 57–58.

97 Ibid.

98 Mallis, *Handbook of Pest Control* (1954), 164.

99 For a review of resistant flies, see Carson, *Silent Spring*, 267–68, 273–74. See also Ebeling, *Urban Entomology*, 57–59.

100 Walter Ebeling, "Past, Present, and Future Directions in the Management of Structure-Infesting Insects," in Gordon W. Frankie and Carl S. Koehler, eds., *Perspectives in Urban Entomology* (New York: Academic Press, 1978), 221–47. 229.

101 Ebeling, *Urban Entomology*, 226.

102 Mallis, *Handbook of Pest Control* (1954), 152, 164.

103 Mallis, *Handbook of Pest Control* (1960), 169.

104 Ebeling, *Urban Entomology*, 226.

105 Carson, *Silent Spring*, 27.

106 Ebeling, *Urban Entomology*, 242.

107   H. Shuyler, "Are German and Oriental Roaches Changing Their Habits?" *Pest Control* (September 1956): 9–10.

108   Ebeling, *Urban Entomology*, 226.

109   M. S. Johnson and A. J. Hill, "Partial Resistance of a Strain of Bedbugs to DDT Residual," *Medical News Letter* 12 (1948): 26–28.

110   C. S. Lofgren, J. C. Keller, and G. S. Burden, "Resistance Tests with the Bedbug and Evaluation of Insecticides for Its Control," *Journal of Economic Entomology* 51 (1958): 241–44; Usinger, *Monograph of Cimicidae*, 46–49; Mallis, *Handbook of Pest Control* (1960), 404; and Robert Snetsinger, personal communication, March 13, 2012.

111   J. R. Busvine, "Insecticide Resistance in Bed-bugs," *Bulletin of the World Health Organization* 19 (1959): 1041–52; Arnold Mallis and A. C. Miller, "Prolonged Resistance in the House Fly and Bed Bug," *Journal of Economic Entomology* 57 (1964): 608–9; and Usinger, *Monograph on Cimicidae*, 46–49.

112   Usinger, *Monograph of Cimicidae*, vi.

113   Mallis, *Handbook of Pest Control* (1954), 378.

114   Ebeling, *Urban Entomology*, 463–67.

115   Woody Klein, *Who Has Seen the Slums?* (New York: Citizens' Housing and Planning Council, 1959), 10.

116   Young Lords Party and Abramson, *Palante*, 140–41.

117   Prillerman interview. Maryland Extension entomologist Eugene Wood never saw bedbugs in the urban communities to which he dedicated much of his career in the mid- to late twentieth century, but he sometimes heard of hikers in the Adirondack mountains picking them up in backcountry lean-tos. Wood interview.

118   Mitman, *Breathing Space*, 161.

4. NORWAY RATS: BACK-ALLEY ECOLOGY IN THE CHEMICAL AGE

1   The visual description of this neighborhood is based on two films: U.S. Public Health Service, *No Good on Earth: A Study of the Rat*, 31 minutes (Baltimore, Md.: Stark Films, 1932); and Baltimore Redevelopment Commission, *The Baltimore Plan*, 20 minutes (Evanston, Ill.: Encyclopedia Britannica Films, 1953).

2   The topic of neophobia, the fear of new things, comes up often in discussions of rat control. For a discussion of this behavior's implications for rat control, see Robert Timm, "Norway Rats," in Scott Hyngstrom, Robert Timm, and Gary Larson, eds., *Prevention and Control of Wildlife Damage*, B105-B120 (Lincoln: University of Nebraska Cooperative Extension, 1994).

3   For discussions of rat reproduction and population dynamics in Baltimore, see David Davis, "A Comparison of Reproductive Potential of Two Rat Populations," *Ecology* 32 (1951): 469–75; and John Calhoun, "A Method for Self-Control of Population Growth among Mammals Living in the Wild," *Science* 109, no. 2831 (1949): 333–35. Another researcher in Baltimore in the 1940s and

1950s found that domestic pets made little contribution to rat control. See William Jackson, "Food Habits of Baltimore, Maryland, Cats in Relation to Rat Populations," *Journal of Mammalogy* 32 (1951): 458–61.

4   Rockefeller Foundation Trustees' Confidential Report, "Draft Report: The Fitness of the Environment," 1950, folder 478, box 58, series 200, RG 1.2: Series 200, Rockefeller Foundation Archives, Rockefeller Archive Center, Sleepy Hollow, New York (hereafter RAC). For the tendency of indoor rats to harbor more ectoparasites, see B. E. Holsendorf, "Rat Harborage and Rat Proofing," *Public Health Reports Supplements* 131 (1937): 75–81.

5   William McNeill mentions practices and taboos surrounding marmots among nineteenth-century Mongolians that may have been inherited across many generations. William McNeill, *Plagues and Peoples* (1976; New York: Doubleday, 1998), 167–72. Daniel Defoe's 1722 novel *A Journal of the Plague Year*, based on accounts of a 1664–65 outbreak of bubonic plague in London, mentions that officials and physicians called for the killing of rats along with cats, dogs, and mice. This evidence suggests that health advisers at the time suspected urban animal populations broadly as plague carriers. Daniel Defoe, *A Journal of the Plague Year* (1722; New York: Random House, 2001), 116.

6   The folklorist D. L. Ashliman has collected stories from Syria, China, and throughout Europe. See D. L. Ashliman, "The Pied Piper of Hameln and Related Legends from Other Towns," 1999–2011, online at http://www.pitt.edu/~dash/hameln.html, accessed on May 31, 2012.

7   Holsendorf, "Rat Harborage and Ratproofing."

8   For example, "Fatal Bite from a Rat," *New York Times*, May 1, 1876; and Beecher and Stowe, *American Woman's Home*, 277.

9   Snetsinger, *Ratcatcher's Child*.

10   "Dick, the Rat," *New York Times*, January 30, 1876, 10.

11   Guenter B. Risse, "'A Long Pull, a Strong Pull, and All Together': San Francisco and Bubonic Plague, 1907–1908," *Bulletin of the History of Medicine* 66 (1992): 260–86.

12   Craddock, *City of Plagues*; Dyl, "War on Rats versus the Right to Keep Chickens"; and Risse, "'Long Pull, a Strong Pull, and All Together.'" For further discussion of health regulations and state discipline imposed on immigrant and socially marginalized communities, see Kay Anderson, *Vancouver's Chinatown: Racial Discourse in Canada, 1875–1980* (Montreal: McGill-Queen's University Press, 1991); Alan M. Kraut, *Silent Travelers: Germs, Genes, and the "Immigrant Menace"* (Baltimore, Md.: Johns Hopkins University Press, 1995); Leavitt, *Typhoid Mary*; Mary Poovey, *Making a Social Body: British Cultural Formation, 1830–1864* (Chicago: University of Chicago Press, 1995); Roberts, *Infectious Fears*; Nyan Shah, *Contagious Divides: Epidemics and Race in San Francisco's Chinatown* (Berkeley: University of California Press, 1999); and Washington, *Packing Them In*.

13 U.S. Public Health Service, *No Good on Earth: A Study of the Rat.*

14 See, for example, "Fatal Bite from a Rat," *New York Times*, May 1, 1876; "Perhaps Killed by the Bite of a Rat," *New York Times*, July 5, 1879, 2; W. A. Evans, "How to Keep Well," *Chicago Tribune*, October 28, 1924, 8; "Second Case of 'Rat Fever' Is Found in City," *Chicago Tribune*, August 31, 1924, 3; and "Victim of Rat Bite Fever Reported Recuperating," *Chicago Tribune*, September 1, 1925, 5.

15 See, for example, "Ferocity of Montreal Rats," *New York Times*, July 15, 1883. A central plot point in the 1955 animated film *Lady and the Tramp*, based on stories written in the 1930s and 1940s and set in 1909, concerns a rat that stalks a human baby in its crib. *Lady and the Tramp*, 76 minutes (Burbank, Calif.: Walt Disney Productions, 1955).

16 "Dick, the Rat," *New York Times.*

17 Holsendorf, "Rat Harborage and Rat Proofing."

18 U.S. Public Health Service, *No Good on Earth: A Study of the Rat.*

19 Martin Millspaugh, Gurney Breckenfeld, and Miles Colean, *The Human Side of Urban Renewal: A Study of the Attitude Changes Produced by Neighborhood Rehabilitation* (Baltimore, Md.: Fight-Blight, 1956), 3. See also Ralph J. Johnson, Huntington Williams, and Roy McCaldin, "The Quality of Housing 'Before' and 'After' Rehabilitation," *American Journal of Public Health and the Nation's Health* 2 (1958): 189–96.

20 Quoted in Ira DeA. Reid, *The Negro Community of Baltimore* (Baltimore, Md.: Baltimore Urban League, 1935), 17.

21 Reid, *Negro Community of Baltimore*, 17. For more discussion of segregation patterns in Baltimore, see Fee, Shopes, and Zeidman, *Baltimore Book*; Cynthia Neverdon-Morton, "Black Housing Patterns in Baltimore City, 1885–1953," *Maryland Historian* (spring–summer 1985): 25–39; Sherry Olson, *Baltimore: The Building of an American City* (Baltimore, Md.: Johns Hopkins University Press, 1997); and Antero Pietila, *Not in My Neighborhood: How Bigotry Shaped a Great American City* (Chicago: Ivan Dee, 2010).

22 Baltimore Redevelopment Agency, *Baltimore Plan.*

23 *Annual Report of the Health Department of the City of Baltimore* (ARHDCB), 1938, 346.

24 Citizens' Planning and Housing Association Collection, Series 1: Organizational Records, Box 5: 1950–51 Annual Report; University of Baltimore Archives.

25 Weber, "Extracting Value from the City"; Committee on the Hygiene of Housing, *Appraisal Method*; and Committee on the Hygiene of Housing, *Basic Principles of Healthful Housing* (New York: American Public Health Association, 1941).

26 Durr, "Conscience of a City," 71–72, 90, 97.

27 Baltimore Redevelopment Agency, *Baltimore Plan.*

28 Ibid.

29 *ARHDCB* 1945, 45.

30 Curt Richter, "The Development and Use of Alpha-Naphthyl Thiourea (ANTU) As a Rat Poison," *Journal of the American Medical Association* 129 (1946): 927–31. For a dramatization of these problems, see Baltimore Redevelopment Agency, *Baltimore Plan.*

31 Williams, *Politics of Public Housing,* 79; Froelicher, interview by Betty Key; and Citizens' Planning and Housing Association Collection, Series 1: Organizational Records, Box 5: 1943–44 Annual Report; University of Baltimore Archives.

32 Citizens' Planning and Housing Association Collection, Series 1: Organizational Records, Box 5: 1943–44 Annual Report; University of Baltimore Archives.

33 Durr, "Conscience of a City," 71–72, 90, 97. For further statistics about crowding in Baltimore's African-American communities, see Reid, *Negro Community of Baltimore,* 15–17.

34 Williams, *Politics of Public Housing,* chapter 2.

35 Ibid.

36 Smith, *African-American Environmental Thought,* 91–92; and Dianne Glave, "Rural African-American Women, Gardening, and Progressive Reform in the South," in Dianne Glave and Mark Stoll, eds., *"To Love the Wind and the Rain": African-Americans and Environmental History* (Pittsburgh: University of Pittsburgh Press, 2006), 37–50.

37 Roscoe Brown, "The National Negro Health Week Movement," *Journal of Negro Education* 6 (1937): 553–64. For reviews of African-American health activism, see also David McBride, *From TB to AIDS: Epidemics among Urban Blacks since 1900* (Albany: State University of New York Press, 1991); Sandra Crouse Quinn and Stephen B. Thomas, "The National Negro Health Week, 1915 to 1951: A Descriptive Account," *Minority Health Today* 2 (2001): 44–49; and Susan L. Smith, *Sick and Tired of Being Sick and Tired: Black Women's Health Activism in America, 1890–1950* (Philadelphia: University of Pennsylvania Press, 1995).

38 Smith, *African-American Environmental Thought,* 80–82.

39 D. Holmes, "Lights and Shadows," *Baltimore Afro-American,* May 6, 1944, 4.

40 C. Miles, "South Side Housing Shortage," *Chicago Tribune,* June 23, 1940, S2.

41 Woman's City Club of Chicago, "Rats and a Clean City," *Bulletin,* March 1934, 59.

42 Abbott, *Tenements of Chicago,* 121, 189–90, 406, 465.

43 Miles, "South Side Housing Shortage"; and Abbott, *Tenements of Chicago,* 480.

44 John Essex, "Rat Infestation and Rodent Control," in *The Chicago-Cook County Health Survey* (New York: Columbia University Press, 1949), 318. "US to Hire 554 Relief Clients in War on Rats," *Chicago Tribune,* October 25, 1935, 13.

45 Essex, "Rat Infestation and Rodent Control," 318–19.

46   Snetsinger, *Ratcatcher's Child*, chapter 4.

47   William O. Buettner, Letter Regarding Public-Private Competition to Transient Relief Board, January 1934, reprinted in *Exterminators Log*, January 1934, 7. Exterminators often used the phrase "second line of defense" to describe their relationship to the medical or health world. See also, for example, Al Cossetta, "The Importance of Our Profession," *Exterminators Log*, April 1935, 4.

48   Buettner, Letter Regarding Public-Private Competition to the Transient Relief Board.

49   Essex, "Rat Infestation and Rodent Control," 319.

50   Ibid.

51   Ibid.

52   "Rats Have a Picnic," *Chicago Defender*, June 22, 1940, 14.

53   Essex, "Rat Infestation and Rodent Control," 318–19.

54   *Pests and Their Control*, "Editorial," November 1940, 4.

55   Essex, "Rat Infestation and Rodent Control," 319; and "Citizens Urged to Help in War on Rat Menace," *Chicago Tribune*, June 4, 1946, 4.

56   Essex, "Rat Infestation and Rodent Control," 320–21.

57   Ibid., 322.

58   C. Kirkpatrick, "Stealthy Foe Eats Millions in Food Yearly," *Chicago Tribune*, June 17, 1946, 1.

59   Harold Smith, "Rat Ravages Cost Chicago 74 Millions," *Chicago Tribune*, December 21, 1948, A6; and "Mayor's Group Asks Merchants to Join Drive against Rats," *Chicago Tribune*, July 23, 1949, 7.

60   "Open West Area Drive on Rats," *Chicago Tribune*, May 16, 1943, W1; for discussion of African-American women and gardening, see Glave, "Rural African-American Women, Gardening, and Progressive Reform in the South."

61   William Buettner, letter to John J. Davis, August 15, 1938, reprinted in Snetsinger, *Ratcatcher's Child*, 88. See also E. C. Jaeger, "Rodent Control and Rat-proofing of Buildings," *Exterminators Log*, June 1935, 12–13.

62   Hartnack, *202 Common Household Pests of North America*, 35.

63   "The Public Health Comes First," (editorial) *Chicago Tribune*, August 16, 1946, 16.

64   Hartnack, *202 Common Household Pests of North America*, 35.

65   Thomas Murray, "Essentials of a Municipal Rat Control Program," reprinted in *Pests* (July 1947): 8–10.

66   Rockefeller Foundation Trustees' Bulletin, "Draft of Report on Rats in War and Peace," 1948, folder 478, Box 50, series 200, RG 1.2, Rockefeller Foundation Archive, RAC.

67   Christine Keiner, "Wartime Rat Control, Rodent Ecology, and the Rise and Fall of Chemical Rodenticides," *Endeavour* 29 (2005): 119–25; see also Timm, "Norway Rats."

68   E. Stellar, "An Appreciation of Curt Richter," in E. M. Blass, ed., *The Psychobiology of Curt Richter* (Baltimore, Md.: York Press, 1976). A small number of DuPont workers helped discover phenyl thiourea when they detected a bitter taste in the factory air—the result of a gene found in 15 percent of humans—but suffered no apparent ill effects. Dr. Herbert Fox was the DuPont scientist who pursued examinations of workers' families to determine that a simple recessive gene was responsible for the ability to taste phenyl thiourea. Richter thought that if rats also varied in their ability to taste the substance, he might use it to learn about taste and feeding behavior, but instead, it was toxic to his rats. Curt Richter, "Experiences of a Reluctant Rat-Catcher: The Common Norway Rat—Friend or Enemy?" *Proceedings of the American Philosophical Society* 112 (1968): 403–15.

69   Richter said that this enhanced sensory system did not enable rats to choose more nutritious food, only to be more prone to reject foods—hence their bait shyness, which is cursed by pest-control operators. See Rockefeller Foundation Trustees' Bulletin, "Draft of Report on Rats in War and Peace," 6.

70   Richter, "Development and Use of Alpha-Naphthyl Thiourea (ANTU) As a Rat Poison." A 1958 review all but dismissed the danger of ANTU poisoning in humans, though it confessed that nonfatal cases may have gone unreported. Certainly, compared with popular but deadly thallium sulfate, which California had already restricted, ANTU was a lesser threat. Earl Brewer and Robert J. Haggerty, "Toxic Hazards: Rat Poisons III—Thallium, Strychnine, and ANTU," *New England Journal of Medicine* 259 (1958): 1038–40; and Rockefeller Foundation Trustees' Bulletin, "Draft of Report on Rats in War and Peace."

71   Richter, "Experiences of a Reluctant Rat-Catcher." In this case, the city block meant the land enclosed by four streets, including the alley that typically ran down the spine of these units according to Baltimore's prevailing style of housing.

72   "They Made Rat Traps for All Baltimore," *Baltimore Afro-American*, July 31, 1943, 9.

73   Richter, "Development and Use of Alpha-Naphthyl Thiourea (ANTU) As a Rat Poison."

74   "Health Department Film to Feature City Rats," *Baltimore Evening Sun*, March 31, 1943; Keiner, "Wartime Rat Control, Rodent Ecology, and the Rise and Fall of Chemical Rodenticides"; and Richter, "Experiences of a Reluctant Rat-Catcher."

75   Curt Richter, "Incidence of Rat Bites and Rat Bite Fever in Baltimore," *Journal of the American Medical Association* 128 (1945): 324–26.

76   Ibid.

77   ARBCHD lists reported typhus cases in the Communicable Diseases section. See reports for the 1930s and 1940s.

78   Richter, "Incidence of Rat Bites and Rat Bite Fever in Baltimore"; and William

Sallow, "An Analysis of Rat Bites in Baltimore, 1948–52," *Public Health Reports* 68 (1953): 1239–42. For further discussion of Johns Hopkins's studies of and relationship with the Eastern Health District, see Elizabeth Fee, *Disease and Discovery: A History of the Johns Hopkins School of Hygiene and Public Health, 1916–1939* (Baltimore, Md.: Johns Hopkins University Press, 1987).

79   Richter, "Experiences of a Reluctant Rat-Catcher."

80   John Emlen, "Rodent Ecology and Control: Report on Activities under Research Project Supported by the Rockefeller Foundation International Health Division," 1946, folder 481, box 59, series 200, RG 1.2, Rockefeller Foundation Archives, RAC; and Richter, "Development and Use of Alpha-Naphthyl Thiourea (ANTU) As a Rat Poison."

81   Keiner, "Wartime Rat Control, Rodent Ecology, and the Rise and Fall of Chemical Rodenticides"; "Rat-drive Row Investigation," *Baltimore Sun*, May 18, 1943; "Drive on Rats May Get New Lease on Life," *Baltimore Sun*, May 1943; and "Dr. Richter May Abandon Rat Project," *Baltimore Sun*, June 4, 1943.

82   Richter, "Experiences of a Reluctant Rat-Catcher"; Hugh H. Smith, "HHS Diary note, 15 February," 1945, folder 478, box 58, Series 200, RG 1.2, Rockefeller Foundation Archives, RAC; Bureau of the Biological Survey, *Report of the Conference of Field Representatives of Economic Investigations*, Ogden, Utah, April 23–28, 1928; and Holsendorf, "Rat Harborage and Rat Proofing." The application of ecology to issues of disease seemed novel to many American administrators and scholars, but British ecologists such as Julian Huxley and Charles Elton had already begun to integrate the study of health with that of animal populations and communities. For a discussion of these contributions, see Gregg Mitman, "In Search of Health: Landscape and Disease in American Environmental History," *Environmental History* 10 (2005): 184–209. For later development of disease ecology, see Warwick Anderson, "Natural Histories of Infectious Disease: Ecological Vision in Twentieth-Century Biomedical Science," *Osiris* 19 (2004): 39–61; J. D. Mayer, "Geography, Ecology, and Emerging Infectious Diseases," *Social Science and Medicine* 50 (2000): 937–52; and J. D. Mayer, "The Political Ecology of Disease As One New Focus for Medical Geography," *Progress in Human Geography* 20 (1996): 441–56.

83   Rockefeller Foundation Trustees' Confidential Report, "Draft Report: The Fitness of the Environment."

84   The School of Hygiene and Public Health professed its interest in rodent control in terms of "population problems," a phrase that seemed to connote issues of human and animal overpopulation. Johns Hopkins University School of Hygiene and Public Health, "A Proposal for Studies on Rodent Ecology and Control," 1945, folder 478, box 58, series 200, RG 1.2, Rockefeller Foundation Archive, RAC.

85   Quoted in Sumner Matteson, "John T. Emlen Jr.: A Naturalist for All Seasons, Part 2: Of Adventure, Innovation, and Conscience, 1934–1959," *The Passenger Pigeon* 60 (1998): 123–67. For more about Emlen's work with Richter's

program, see John T. Emlen, "Baltimore's Community Rat Control Program," *American Journal of Public Health* 37 (1947): 721–27.

86   For discussion of Davis's attitudes toward disease in ecology, see John J. Christian, "In Memoriam: David E. Davis, 1913–1994," *The Auk* 112 (1995): 491–92.

87   Rockefeller Foundation International Health Division, "Resolution 48009," 1948, folder 478, box 58, series 200, RG 1.2 Rockefeller Foundation Archives, RAC. In some reports of 1946 and 1947, Davis gave a more varied and detailed account of population recovery, but by 1948 seemed to settle on the six- to twelve-month figure.

88   *ARHDCB* 1943, 236–44; and *ARHDCB* 1944, 237–46.

89   Rockefeller Foundation Trustees' Confidential Report, "Draft Report: The Fitness of the Environment"; Rockefeller Foundation International Health Division, "Resolution 49013," 1949, folder 478, box 58, series 200, RG 1.2, Rockefeller Foundation Archives, RAC. For further discussion of rat population recovery, see John T. Emlen, Allen W. Stokes, and Charles P. Winsor, "The Rate of Recovery of Decimated Populations of Brown Rats in Nature," *Ecology* 29 (1948): 133–45.

90   David E. Davis and W. T. Fales, "The Distribution of Rats in Baltimore, Maryland," *American Journal of Hygiene* 49 (1949): 247–54.

91   John B. Calhoun, *The Ecology and Sociology of the Norway Rat* (Bethesda, Md.: U.S. Public Health Service, 1962).

92   Rockefeller Foundation Trustees' Confidential Report, "Draft Report: The Fitness of the Environment."

93   Ibid.

94   Davis and Fales, "Distribution of Rats in Baltimore, Maryland"; and David E. Davis and W. T. Fales, "The Rat Population of Baltimore, 1949," *American Journal of Hygiene* 52 (1950): 143–46.

95   David E. Davis, "Principles of Rat Management," *Pest Control* (November 1948): 9–12; David Davis, "Report on Rodent Ecology Project at Johns Hopkins School of Hygiene and Public Health from January 1 to December 31, 1946," 1947, folder 481, box 59, series 200, RG 1.2, Rockefeller Foundation Archives, RAC. Notice that the meaning of "balance" here is not the ideal state often implied in the phrase "balance of nature" as used by environmentalists. Rather, as Davis explained in a 1948 proposal, this balance is a limit brought about by a combination of environmental factors that keeps populations at a constant level, whether or not that level is ideal according to human values. See Rodent Ecology Project of the Johns Hopkins School of Hygiene and Public Health, "A Proposal for the Study of the Characteristics of Animal Populations," 1948, folder 481, box 59, series 200, RG 1.2, Rockefeller Foundation Archives, RAC.

96   David E. Davis, John T. Emlen, and Allen W. Stokes, "Studies on the Home Range of the Brown Rat," *Journal of Mammalogy* 29 (1948): 207–25; and Emlen,

"Rodent Ecology and Control: Report on Activities under Research Project Supported by the Rockefeller Foundation International Health Division."

97 Rodent Ecology Project of the Johns Hopkins School of Hygiene and Public Health, "A Proposal for the Study of the Characteristics of Animal Populations (continuation)," folder 479, box 58, series 200, RG 1.2, Rockefeller Foundation Archives, RAC.

98 Davis, "Principles of Rat Management."

99 Rockefeller Foundation Trustees' Bulletin, "Draft of Report on Rats in War and Peace."

100 R. F. Griggs, Letter Regarding Rodenticides to A. Warren, 1945, folder 478, box 58, series 200, RG 1.2, Rockefeller Foundation Archives, RAC.

101 Johns Hopkins University School of Hygiene and Public Health, "Proposed Program for the Continuation of the Rodent Ecology Project of the Johns Hopkins School of Hygiene and Public Health," 1947, folder 479, box 58, series 200, RG 1.2, Rockefeller Foundation.

102 H. H. Smith, "HHS Diary note 1, 22–24 March, 1949," folder 479, box 58, series 200, RG 1.2, Rockefeller Foundation Archives, RAC.

103 Curt Richter, "Rat Control—Report to the Mayor of Baltimore," 1944, folder 478, box 58, series 200, RG 1.2, Rockefeller Foundation Archives, RAC; and Richter, "Experiences of a Reluctant Rat-Catcher." This martial approach recalls Edmund Russell's arguments in *War and Nature*.

104 W. W. Cort, Letter Regarding Rodent Ecology Program to H. H. Smith, March 28, 1949, folder 479, box 58, series 200, RG 1.2, Rockefeller Foundation Archives, RAC; and H. H. Smith, "HHS Diary note, 20 May," 1949, folder 479, box 58, series 200, RG 1.2, Rockefeller Foundation Archives, RAC.

105 J. Wilfrid Davis et al., "Endemic Typhus in Baltimore," *Southern Medical Journal* 41 (1948): 21–26.

106 *ARHDCB* 1946, 39; and *ARHDCB* 1947, 61.

107 *ARHDCB* 1947, 240.

108 Millspaugh, Breckenfeld, and Colean, *Human Side of Urban Renewal*, 4.

109 Rockefeller Foundation Trustees' Confidential Report, "Draft Report: The Fitness of the Environment."

110 Ibid.

111 Citizens' Planning and Housing Association Collection, University of Baltimore Langsdale Library Special Collections, CPHA Series 1: Organizational Records, Box 5: 1950–1 Annual Report.

112 Rockefeller Foundation Trustees' Confidential Report, "Draft Report: The Fitness of the Environment."

113 Citizens' Planning and Housing Association Collection, University of Baltimore Langsdale Library Special Collections, CPHA Series 1: Organizational Records, Box 5: 1950–1 Annual Report.

114 Rockefeller Foundation Trustees' Confidential Report, "Draft Report: The Fitness of the Environment."

115 Ibid.

116 Citizens' Planning and Housing Association Collection, University of Baltimore Langsdale Library Special Collections, CPHA Series 1: Organizational Records, Box 5: 1950–1 Annual Report.

117 Ibid.

118 "City Donates $500 to Clean Block Drive," *The Afro-American*, June 28, 1947, 1; and "'Get the New Look' Slogan of '48 Clean Block Drive," *The Afro-American*, June 22, 1948, 1.

119 Different commentators counted the blocks and calculated homeownership rates differently within the pilot area. The Citizens' Housing and Planning Association counted twenty-seven blocks and over 50 percent homeowners, but the authors of a later study counted fourteen blocks and 40 percent homeowners. CPHA's figure appears here for consistency because the one-hundred-block count cited earlier was also from that organization's report. See also Millspaugh, Breckenfeld, and Colean, *Human Side of Urban Renewal*, 5.

120 Ibid., 5, 11.

121 Ibid., 10. For the difference in rates of working outside the home between white and black women in Baltimore, see also Reid, *Negro Community of Baltimore*, 15.

122 Citizens' Planning and Housing Association Collection, Series 1: Organizational Records, Box 5: 1950–1 Annual Report; University of Baltimore Archives. For further discussion of red-lining, the denial of homebuyer and home-improvement loans to African-American communities in Baltimore, see Pietila, *Not in My Neighborhood*.

123 "Rat Infestation Proved Recurrent by Johns Hopkins Scientists," *Baltimore Sun*, February 24, 1954.

124 Davis and Fales, "Rat Population of Baltimore, 1949." Davis never explained exactly how he had gauged the growing proportion of indoor rats.

125 Richter, "Incidence of Rat Bites and Rat Bite Fever in Baltimore"; Holsendorf, "Rat Harborage and Rat-Proofing"; and Davis et al., "Endemic Typhus in Baltimore."

126 Davis did examine the likelihood that a greater population of rats would increase the potential for disease transmission. David E. Davis, "The Relation Between the Level of Population and the Prevalence of Leptospira, Salmonella, and Capillaria in Norway Rats," *Ecology* 32 (1951): 465–68.

127 "No Place for Displaced Rats," *Baltimore Sun*, March 17, 1952.

128 Citizens' Planning and Housing Association Collection, Series 1: Organizational Records, Box 2: Fact Sheet (1954); University of Baltimore Archives.

129 Ralph Matthews Jr., "The *Afro* Goes on a Hunt for a Murderer," *The Afro-American*, June 1952.

130 J. A. Last, "The Missing Link: The Story of Karl Paul Link," *Toxicological Sciences* 66 (2002): 4–6.

131 Brewer and Haggerty, "Toxic Hazards." By the 1950s, some researchers did see ANTU as relatively safe, although it is "highly toxic to pigs, to cats, and especially to dogs." Bait-shyness, the behavior in which rats avoid poisons, was also a problem with ANTU. T. B. Gaines and W. J. Hayes, "Bait Shyness to ANTU in Wild Norway Rats," *Public Health Reports* 67 (1952): 306–11.

132 H. E. Stark, "Trip Report: Conference on Rodent Control," August 28, 1967, folder 122, box 18, series 100, RG 1.2, Rockefeller Foundation Archive, RAC.

133 John Calhoun, "A Method for Self-Control of Population Growth among Mammals Living in the Wild," *Science* 109, no. 2831 (1949): 333–35; and John Calhoun, "Mortality and Movement of Brown Rats," *Journal of Wildlife Management* 12 (1948): 167–72.

134 This "after" description is based on photographs from Millspaugh, Breckenfeld, and Colean, *Human Side of Urban Renewal.*

135 Alan M. Beck, *The Ecology of Stray Dogs: A Study of Free-Ranging Urban Animals* (Baltimore, Md.: York Press, 1973).

136 Millspaugh, Breckenfeld, and Colean, *Human Side of Urban Renewal*, 9, 51, 62, 111.

137 "Rats Are Only a Symptom," *Chicago Daily Tribune*, June 14, 1947, 10.

PART 2. PERSISTENCE AND RESISTANCE IN THE AGE OF ECOLOGY

1 Some authors, such as Christopher Foreman, have assumed that African-Americans have little historical tradition of environmental involvement and use this as part of the basis for criticizing the environmental justice movement. The history of pest control suggests that environmental thought among African-Americans is both historically deeper and more holistic than Foreman and others have charged. Christopher Foreman, *The Promise and Peril of Environmental Justice* (Washington, D.C.: Brookings Institution, 1998), 13–15.

5. THE ECOLOGY OF INJUSTICE: RATS IN THE CIVIL RIGHTS ERA

1 Wright probably was not referring to the common name of *Rattus rattus*, the black rat, here but rather the rat's color, which he used to further reinforce the parallel with Bigger Thomas. *Rattus norvegicus*, Norway rats, were the species found in Chicago homes, and indeed most infested homes in the United States. The range of fur colors found among Norway rats does include black.

2 Richard Wright, *Native Son* (New York: Harper, 1940). For further interpretation of Bigger's relationship to the rat in *Native Son*, see James Smethurst, "Invented by Horror: The Gothic and African American Literary Ideology in Native Son," *African American Review* (spring 2001): 29–40.

3 "Nearly Bit Kids," *New York Amsterdam News*, October 5, 1957, 16.

4 For further discussion of rats as emblems and parts of the ecology of

environmental injustice, see Andrew Hurley, "Floods, Rats, and Toxic Waste: Allocating Environmental Hazards since World War II," in Andrew Hurley, ed., *Common Fields: An Environmental History of St. Louis* (Saint Louis: Missouri Historical Society Press, 1997), 241–62.

5   "Rat Poison," (Editorial) *New York Amsterdam News*, October 19, 1957, 6; and James Hicks, "See for Yourself," *New York Amsterdam News*, October 19, 1957, 7.

6   "Rat Poison," *New York Amsterdam News.*

7   For example, see "Nearly Bit Kids," *New York Amsterdam News*; "Wonder Why Harlem Is Mad? Here's Your Answer," *New York Amsterdam News*, July 25, 1959, 10; and Al Nall, "Three More Kids Bitten by Rats," *New York Amsterdam News*, January 4, 1958, 1.

8   L. Jackson, "Pulse of the Public: Element of Doubt," *New York Amsterdam News*, November 9, 1957, 6; and Mabelle McAdon, "Pulse of the Public: Didn't Like Rats," *New York Amsterdam News*, August 22, 1959, 10.

9   "We Apologize (An Editorial)," *New York Amsterdam News*, July 25, 1959. 1.

10   James Ferribee, "2-Legged Rats," *New York Amsterdam News*, November 14, 1959, 10.

11   "Landlords to Be Made to Exterminate Rats," *New York Amsterdam News*, October 3, 1959, 2; "Commissioner Reports Decrease in Rat Bites," *New York Amsterdam News*, February 20, 1960. 26; "Rat Infestation Drive Lands 800 Landlords," *New York Amsterdam News*, May 28, 1960., 7; "1 Landlady Pays Fine, Other Faces Court," *New York Amsterdam News*, September 3, 1960, 26; and James Clinton, "Rats in Urban America," *Public Health Reports* 84, no. 1 (1969): 1–6, 3. According to Clinton, while the city focused on Harlem, bites in Brooklyn rose.

12   J. Booker, "Baby Crippled for Life by Rat Bites, Dad Sues," *New York Amsterdam News*, October 12, 1957, 1; J. Booker, "Rat Bite Victims May Go Back to Face Rats," *New York Amsterdam News*, October 19, 1957; and "Child Wins $90,000 for Rat Bite," *New York Amsterdam News*, May 27, 1961, 1.

13   National Commission on Urban Problems, *Building the American City*, 10.

14   Garbage can theft continues to be a serious problem in rat control. Gregory Glass, personal communication, July 2009.

15   There is a rich literature about the history of urban disinvestment and its relationship to suburbanization. See Robert Beauregard, "If Only the City Could Speak: The Politics of Representation," in Helen Liggett and David C. Perry, eds., *Spatial Practices: Critical Explorations in Social/Spatial Theory* (Thousand Oaks, Calif.: Sage, 1995), 59–80; Robert Beauregard, *Voices of Decline: The Postwar Fate of U.S. Cities* (New York: Routledge, 2003); Jackson, *Crabgrass Frontier*, chapters 11–12; and Douglas Massey and Nancy Denton, *American Apartheid: Segregation and the Making of the Underclass* (Cambridge: Harvard University Press, 1993).

16 National Commission on Urban Problems, *Building the American City*, 10.

17 G. Todd, "Life in Harlem, USA!" *New York Amsterdam News*, January 11, 1964, 1.

18 See, for example, "Wonder Why Harlem Is Mad? Here's Your Answer," *New York Amsterdam News*, 1959.

19 "City Sewer Rat Control Across the Nation," *Pest Control* (August 1963): 9; and Clinton, "Rats in Urban America," 4.

20 New York had had a "rat court" since no later than 1920, which addressed sanitary violations including rats. See W. B. Cobb, "A Court of Prevention: The Municipal Term Court of the City of New York," *Journal of the American Institute of Criminal Law and Criminology* 11 (1920): 47–59.

21 See, for example, "Jesse Gray Accuses Cops of Conspiracy," *New York Amsterdam News*, February 15, 1964, 42; and Ferribee, "2-Legged Rats."

22 For reviews of the state of housing code law and enforcement in the 1960s, see J. C. Fossum, "Rent Withholding and the Improvement of Substandard Housing," *California Law Review* 53 (1965): 304–36; and Frank Grad, *Legal Remedies for Housing Code Violations* (Washington, D.C.: National Commission on Urban Problems, 1968), 63.

23 Grad, *Legal Remedies for Housing Code Violations*, 5.

24 See, for example, "Lefkowitz Moves on Slum Violator," *New York Amsterdam News*, September 1, 1960, 24; and "1 Landlady Pays Fine, Other Faces Court," *New York Amsterdam News*, 26.

25 H. G. Scott, "Rat Bite: Epidemiology and Control," *Journal of Environmental Health* 27 (1965): 900–2. Rates remained steady at about ten bites per hundred thousand in most cities, but investigators claimed the sheer number of bites grew with rising populations in poor neighborhoods.

26 For example, an eight-month-old infant in Washington, D.C., died from an apparent rat attack, but the coroner did not immediately rule out the possibility that the rat bites occurred after death. "Was Baby Killed by Rat Bites Here? Coroner's Probe Awaited," *Washington Daily News*, July 18, 1967, 5.

27 Scott, "Rat Bite," 901–2.

28 J. S. Cole, R. W. Stoll, and R. J. Bulger, "Rat-Bite Fever: Report of Three Cases," *Annals of Internal Medicine* 71 (1969): 979–81. See also A. Lieberman, "The Case of the Rampaging Ravenous Rodents," *Journal of the Indiana State Medical Association* (December 1964): 1351–54. One physician claimed that his patient had fallen into a coma due to either the *Spirilla* or *Streptobacilli* form, and possibly both; he only thought to test for these because the patient's baby had died the previous day of blood loss from a rat attack. The title of his account of this case and his tone suggest a flippant attitude toward the death and illness that this family suffered.

29 H. G. Scott, *Operation Rat: A Rat Eradication Program for the American People* (U.S. Public Health Service, Office of Equal Opportunity, 1965). Rat-borne diseases continue to receive little attention today, and the few scholars and

physicians who do study them believe they are underdiagnosed and under-appreciated. Gregory Glass, personal communication, July 2009. See also Joseph Vinetz, Gregory Glass, Charles Flexner, et al., "Sporadic Urban Leptospirosis," *Annals of Internal Medicine* 125 (1996): 794–98; James Childs, Brian Schwartz, Tom Ksiazek, et al., "Risk Factors Associated with Antibodies to Leptospires in Inner-City Residents of Baltimore: A Protective Role for Cats," *American Journal of Public Health* 82 (1992): 597–99; and James Childs, Gregory Glass, and James LeDuc, "Rodent Sightings and Contacts in an Inner-City Population of Baltimore, Maryland, U.S.A." *Bulletin of the Society of Vector Ecology* 16 (1991): 245–55.

30   Rarely, cases of rat-bite fever resulted not from exposure to vermin but from the bites of laboratory rats or pet rats. Russell Blattner, "Comments on Current Literature: Rat-Bite Fever," *Journal of Pediatrics* 67 (1965): 884–86.

31   Scott, "Rat Bite," mentions the practice of rat vigil, as does the *New York Amsterdam News*. See for example, "Rat Ranch Product," *New York Amsterdam News*, September 30, 1961, 6.

32   "'Rats, Rats? Rats!' Starts New TV Urban Series," *Baltimore Afro-American*, November 30, 1968, 32. Psychologists asserting this response included Dr. Robert Derbyshire, Dr. Cornelius Kruse, and Dr. Matthew Tayback, who appeared in a Johns Hopkins University program on rat control. This argument echoes psychological explanations for asthma cited in Mitman, *Breathing Space*, chapter 4. See also E. D. Huttman, "Public Housing: The Negative Psychological Effects on Family Living," paper presented at the American Orthopsychiatric Association Annual Meeting, March 21–24, 1971; Daniel Wilner, et al., *The Housing Environment and Family Life: A Longitudinal Study on the Effects of Housing on Morbidity and Mental Health* (Baltimore, Md.: Johns Hopkins University Press, 1962). On a somewhat different note, education-reform advocate Jonathan Kozol wrote about an African-American boy named Stephen so beaten down by his circumstances that he identified the difference between himself and a rat by his own lack of a tail. Jonathan Kozol, *Death at an Early Age: The Destruction of the Hearts and Minds of Negro Children in the Boston Public Schools* (New York: Plume, 1967), 7.

33   "Dead Rats Help Win Harlem Rent Strike," *Chicago Defender*, December 31, 1963, A1, 3. See also Clinton, "Rats in Urban America," 3.

34   For further discussion of Gray and the rent strikes, see Mandi Isaacs Jackson, "Harlem's Rent Strike and Rat War: Representation, Housing Access, and Tenant Resistance in New York, 1958–1964," *American Studies* 47 (2006): 53–79; and Robert Sullivan, *Rats: Observations on the History and Habitat of the City's Most Unwanted Inhabitants* (New York: Bloomsbury, 2004), chapter 7. Sullivan calls Gray an "interpreter of rats" for his ability to represent the political and cultural meanings of rats.

35   Fossum, "Rent Withholding and the Improvement of Substandard Housing"; and Grad, *Legal Remedies for Housing Code Violations*. Both Fossum and Grad

cite Gray as the key figure in redefining the rent strike as a tool for residents to overcome substandard housing conditions. Other New York tenant activists had used rent strike tactics some decades earlier, but Gray revived the strategy with his own theatrical variations. See also Joel Schwartz, "Tenant Power in the Liberal City, 1943–1971," in R. Lawson and M. Naison, eds., *The Tenant Movement in New York City, 1904–1984* (New Brunswick, N.J.: Rutgers University Press, 1986), 134–208.

36 "Strike against Slum Rent May Reach Chicago Area," *Chicago Defender*, December 3, 1963, 27; and George Todd, "In Rent Strike: Tenants Planning Rat Exhibition," *New York Amsterdam News*, December 28, 1963, 1.

37 Fossum, "Rent Withholding and the Improvement of Substandard Housing," 332.

38 "Rats at the Courthouse," *New York Amsterdam News*, January 4, 1964, 3.

39 "Rent Strikes Hit Chicago! Rats, Squalor Spur W. Side Rent Strike," *Chicago Defender*, January 9, 1964, 1.

40 E. S. Williams, "Save E/S-W/S [sic] TV," *New York Amsterdam News*, March 14, 1964, 8; and Arnold Perl, "Who Do You Kill?" directed by Tom Gries, *Eastside/Westside* (November 1963).

41 "Strike against Slum Rent May Reach Chicago Area," *Chicago Defender*; and "Harlem Slum Fighter: Jesse Gray," *New York Times*, December 31, 1963, 32.

42 "'Rat March' on State Capitol," *Chicago Defender*, February 17, 1964, A7.

43 Fossum, "Rent Withholding and the Improvement of Substandard Housing."

44 S. H. Schanberg, "Rent Cuts Sought in Rat War," *New York Times*, March 3, 1964, 1.

45 "Sy Posner Warring on Rats," *New York Amsterdam News*, May 30, 1964, 50.

46 Schanberg, "Rent Cuts Sought in Rat War."

47 Mitman, *Breathing Space*, chapter 4.

48 Schwartz, "Tenant Power in the Liberal City."

49 Whitney M. Young, "The Urban League and Its Strategy," *Annals of the American Academy of Political and Social Science* 357, no. 1 (1965): 102–7. For discussions of Martin Luther King's advocacy for the domestic Marshall Plan idea, see Nick Kotz, *Judgment Days: Lyndon Baines Johnson, Martin Luther King Jr., and the Laws That Changed America* (Boston: Houghton Mifflin, 2005), 381–83. See also E. L. Payne, "Voice of Negro Is Muted on Capitol Hill," *Chicago Defender*, August 14, 1967, 8.

50 P. J. Sloyan, "What Rat Program? LBJ Asked Cabinet," *Fort Lauderdale News and Sun-Sentinel*, August 21, 1966, 4C.

51 Letter, James E. Jones to Lyndon Johnson, "The Pied Piper of HUD," August 1967, Legislative/Agriculture, Box 5–1 Pest Control—General, White House Central Files (hereafter WHCF), Lyndon Baines Johnson Presidential Library (hereafter LBJ Library).

52 For an example of educational materials that gloss over negative relationships between tenants and landlords, see Rileigh Coleman, *The Dirty Rat Coloring*

Book (Cleveland, Ohio: Division of Health, Community Action for Youth, 1964).

53 National Commission on Urban Problems, *Building the American City*, 487–88.

54 I. Sprague, "The Proposed New Rat Control Program Should Be in HUD," June 20, 1967, Lyndon Baines Johnson Library, Office Files of Irvine Sprague, Rat Bill. Although Johnson focused on poverty and urban problems, he also focused on environmental policy. Martin Melosi, "Lyndon Johnson and Environmental Policy," in Robert A. Divine, ed., *The Johnson Years, Volume Two: Vietnam, the Environment, and Science*, 113–49 (Lawrence: University of Kansas Press, 1988).

55 Scott, "Rat Bite," 902.

56 Ibid. See also Clinton, "Rats in Urban America," 4.

57 Lyndon B. Johnson, "Statement by the President on the Rent Supplement Program Upon Signing the Independent Offices Appropriation Bill," September 7, 1966. Available online by Gerhard Peters and John T. Woolley, *The American Presidency Project*, http://www.presidency.ucsb.edu/ws/?pid=27836, accessed on November 30, 2012.

58 Congress, House, "Rat Extermination Act of 1967," H. Res. 749, 90th Cong., 1st sess., *Congressional Record* 113 (July 20, 1967): H19548–19556; and "Republicans Laugh As Slum Dwellers Battle Rats," *The Democrat* 7 (1967): 3.

59 "Rat Extermination Act of 1967."

60 "Shoot Them Down," *Chicago Defender*, September 16, 1967, 10.

61 Joseph Califano, *The Triumph and Tragedy of Lyndon Johnson: The White House Years* (New York: Simon & Schuster, 1991), 212–13.

62 Memo, Loyd Hackler to L. Levinson, "Rat Attack, and Rat Bill," July 21, 1967, WHCF, Legislative/Agriculture. Box 5–1 Pest Control—Executive, LBJ Library; see also "Was Baby Killed by Rat Bites Here? Coroner's Probe Awaited," *Washington Daily News* (1967).

63 Memo, J. Hedge to J. Gaither, Rat photographs, August 28, 1967, WHCF, Legislative/Agriculture, Box 5–1 Pest Control—Executive, LBJ Library.

64 Jones, "Pied Piper of HUD." See Lyndon Johnson Presidential Library folder 5–1 Legislative/Agriculture—General for more examples of constituent letters.

65 Richard Wetzel, urban rodent-control contact following Detroit's civil unrest, note to C. E. Faulkner, August 7, 1967, Entry 230, Box 126, RG 22, NARA—College Park, Md.

66 "Congress Rapped for Snub of Rat Control Measure," *Chicago Defender*, August 16, 1967, 15.

67 B. Washington, "Slum Building Tour Reveals Common Plight," *Chicago Defender*, August 7, 1967, 6.

68 E. L. Payne, "Congress to Blame for Riots: Young," *Chicago Defender*, October 30, 1967, 7.

69   "Demonstration on Rat Bill Incites Capitol Hill Melee," *Washington Post*, August 8, 1967.

70   San Francisco Bay Area Television Archive, "Rev. Dr. Martin Luther King, Jr. on Urban Riots," online at https://diva.sfsu.edu/collections/sfbatv/bundles/190101, accessed on May 18, 2012. Thanks to Lisa Uddin for suggesting this reference to me.

71   For a review of existing urban rat-control programs as of the 1960s, see Municipal Reference Library, "Rodent Infestation Programs in Other Major Cities," Legislative Reference Bureau, Milwaukee, 1967.

72   "Fine Is $50 in Rat Case," *Milwaukee Journal*, June 17, 1960.

73   Wally Lanford Meyer, "Rat Menace Exists in Outlying Areas As Well As Inner-City," *Milwaukee Metro*, January 11, 1967.

74   "Bounty Proposed on Inner Core Rats," *Milwaukee Sentinel*, December 8, 1967.

75   E. Boynton, "Thinking It Over: Rats Are Not a Laughing Matter," *Chicago Defender*, September 9, 1967, 11.

76   City of Milwaukee Health Department, *Pest Control* (Milwaukee: Health Department Housing and Sanitation Division, 1967).

77   City of Milwaukee Health Department, "Intensive Rodent Control Program Grant Application," City of Milwaukee Reference Bureau, 1968, p. 23. The idea that rural people of color were unready for urban life echoes theories from the early 1900s, as discussed in chapter 1 of this book. Borchert, *Alley Life in Washington*, ix, 57–58. Assumptions about African-American culture read off from visual cues also recall criticisms of uncritical landscape interpretation. See Gillian Rose, *Feminism and Geography: The Limits of Geographical Knowledge* (Cambridge: Polity, 1993).

78   Clinton, "Rats in Urban America."

79   City of Milwaukee Health Department, "Intensive Rodent Control Program Grant Application," 23.

80   City of Milwaukee Health Department, "Renewal Grant Application—Intensive Rodent Control Program," City of Milwaukee Reference Bureau, 1970.

81   Spencer Coggs, interview with the author, Madison, Wisc., April 2006; and Ruth Hopgood, interview with the author, Milwaukee, Wisc., April 2006.

82   Hopgood, interview with the author.

83   City of Milwaukee Health Department, "Intensive Rodent Control Project Continuation Grant Application," 13–14.

84   Municipal Reference Library, "Rodent Infestation Programs in Other Major Cities," City of Milwaukee, 1967; City of Milwaukee Health Department, "Intensive Rodent Control Project Renewal Grant Application," City of Milwaukee, 1971, 11–13. The history of garbage disposal systems helps shape the ecology of pests in cities. See Martin V. Melosi, *Garbage in the Cities: Refuse, Reform, and the Environment, 1880–1980* (College Station: Texas A&M University Press, 1981).

85   City of Milwaukee Health Department, "Intensive Rodent Control Program Grant Application," 1968, 22. The assignment of responsibility for rats to individuals amid systematic ecological and political injustice recalls other case studies examined by political ecologists. See, for example, Agarwal, *Environmentality*; Julie Guthman and E. Melanie DuPuis, "Embodying Neoliberalism: Economy, Culture, and the Politics of Fat," *Environment and Planning D* 24 (2006): 427–48; Becky Mansfield, "Health As a Nature-Society Question," *Environment and Planning A* 40 (2008): 1015–19; Mayer, "Political Ecology of Disease As One New Focus for Medical Geography"; and Paul Robbins, *Lawn People: How Grasses, Weeds, and Chemicals Make Us Who We Are* (Philadelphia: Temple University Press, 2007).

86   City of Milwaukee Health Department, "Intensive Rodent Control Project Continuation Grant Application," Attachment 1.

87   See City of Milwaukee Health Department Rodent Control Annual Reports, 1968–1973.

88   The scholar Arun Agarwal developed the concept of environmental citizenship as an elaboration of Michel Foucault's biological citizenship. Both ideas refer to the heightened sense of self-awareness that citizens develop through exposure to disciplinary messages and routine practices imposed by government. Agarwal, *Environmentality*.

89   Coggs, interview with the author; Hopgood, interview with the author.

90   General Accounting Office, *The Urban Rat Control Program Is in Trouble* (Washington, D.C.: General Accounting Office, 1975), 17–20; and Nancy Coombe and John S. Marr, "Rat Bites Support Need for In-Home Control," *Journal of Environmental Health* 42 (1980): 321–26.

91   Houston Branch of the Black Panther Party, "Houston Branch Implements People's Free Pest Control Program," *The Black Panther*, September 25, 1972, 8; Lindsay Glavac, "A Message to Urban Youths—Down for the Cause," *Wayne State South End*, February 9, 2006; Students and Neighbors Action Program, "Rat Control: People's Science in Philadelphia," *Science for the People* 4, no. 6 (1972): 20–21; and David Hilliard, ed., *The Black Panther Party: Service to the People Programs* (Albuquerque: University of New Mexico Press, 2008), 71–73. For further discussion of Service to the People programs, see Nikolas C. Heynen, "Bending the Bars of Empire from Every Ghetto to Feed the Kids: The Black Panther Party's Radical Anti-Hunger Politics of Social Reproduction and Scale," *Annals of the Association of American Geographers* 99 (2009): 406–22; and Alondra Nelson, *Body and Soul: The Black Panther Party and the Fight against Medical Discrimination* (Minneapolis: University of Minnesota Press, 2011). I am grateful to Melanie McCalmont for bringing SNAP to my attention.

92   "Architects of Pride's Success: From 'Dudes' to 'Black Capitalists'," *Washington Post*, March 23, 1969, 53.

93   James Kidney, "D.C. Teenagers Beam with Pride at 'Their' Pride, Inc.," *Chicago Defender*, September 7, 1967, 16.

94 Smithsonian Institution Archives, Record Unit 390, Box 11: Education Department, Anacostia Museum, 1967–1989, Folder: Rat Exhibit.

95 "Mayfield Asks $1 Million to Rid Ghetto of Rats," *Chicago Defender*, March 9, 1968, 14. Mayfield's big dreams illustrate that some black activists saw pest control as one means to self-determination, environmental improvement, and perhaps even financial gain. Mayfield himself was a controversial figure. A very young man when he first gained attention among civil rights leaders, Mayfield fell in and out of favor with activists a half-generation older—for example, Marion Barry and Father James Groppi. He advocated revolution, praised rioters in D.C. who damaged downtown businesses, and stoked anti-Semitism in comments about the loss of money from black ghettos.

96 John Kinard and Esther Nighbert, "The Anacostia Neighborhood Museum, Smithsonian Institution, Washington, D.C.," *Museum International* 24 (1972): 103–9; Zora Felton-Martin and Gail Lewis, *Different Drummer: John Kinard and the Anacostia Museum* (Washington, D.C.: Anacostia Museum, 1989); Jeffrey Stewart and Fath Davis Ruffins, "A Faithful Witness: Afro-American Public History in Historical Perspective," in Susan Benson, Stephen Brier, and Roy Rosenzweig, eds., *Presenting the Past: Essays on History and the Public* (Philadelphia: Temple University Press, 1986), 307–38; and Smithsonian Institution Archives, Record Unit 390, Box 11: Education Department, Anacostia Museum, 1967–1989, Folder: Rat Exhibit.

97 Students and Neighbors Action Program, "Rat Control—People's Science in Philadelphia."

98 Glavac, "Message to Urban Youths"; and Houston Branch of the Black Panther Party, "Houston Branch Implements People's Free Pest Control Program," *The Black Panther*, September 25, 1972, 8.

99 Sam Durant, ed., *Black Panther: The Revolutionary Art of Emory Douglas* (New York: Rizzoli, 2007); and Colette Gaiter, "The Revolution Will Be Visualized: Emory Douglas in the Black Panther," *Bad Subjects* 65 (2004), online at http://bad.eserver.org/issues/2004/65/gaiter.html, accessed on November 30, 2012.

100 Gil Scott-Heron, "Whitey On the Moon," *Small Talk at 125th and Lenox*, Flying Dutchman Records, 1970. Thanks to Paul Robbins for suggesting that I investigate Scott-Heron's poem, and to Amy Smith Muise for helping me articulate its nonfinancial meanings.

101 John E. Davies, Walter F. Edmundson, and Americo Raffonelli, "The Role of House Dust in Human DDT Pollution," *American Journal of Public Health* 65 (1975): 53–57; J. F. Finklea et al., "Pesticides and Pesticide Hazards in Urban Households," *Journal of the South Carolina Medical Association* 65 (1969): 31–33; William S. Hoffman, William I. Fishbein, and Morten B. Andelman, "The Pesticide Content of Human Fat Tissue," *Archives of Environmental Health* 9 (1964): 387–94; Julian E. Keil, et al., "DDT and DDE Residues in Blood

from Children, South Carolina—1970," *Pesticide Monitoring Journal* 6 (1972): 1–3; Secretary's Commission on Pesticides and Their Relationship to Environmental Health, *Report: Pesticides and Their Relationship to Environmental Health* (Washington, D.C.: U.S. Department of Health, Education, and Welfare, 1969); and Task Force on Environmental Problems of the Inner City, *Our Urban Environment and Our Most Endangered People* (Washington, D.C.: Environmental Protection Agency, 1971), 1–9, 26–28, 35.

102 Examples of optimism about warfarin abound in municipal rat-control operations and at the federal level. See, for example, the Records of the Fish and Wildlife Service, which include correspondence with congressional representatives and ephemera about warfarin. Fish and Wildlife Service Region 5, *Municipal Rat Control* 1 (1951), Box 79, Entry 230, Records of the Fish and Wildlife Service RG 22, NARA—College Park, Md.; A. Suomela, letter to E. P. Radwan, March 5, 1956, Box 129, Entry 230, Records of the Fish and Wildlife Service RG 22, NARA—College Park, Md.; J. Jacobsen, letter to A. C. Powell, 1964 (undated), Box 82, Entry 230, Records of the Fish and Wildlife Service RG 22, NARA—College Park, Md.; and L. A. Parker, letter to A. C. Powell, November 5, 1964, Box 82, Entry 230, Records of the Fish and Wildlife Service RG 22, NARA—College Park, Md.

103 David C. Drummond, "Rats Resistant to Warfarin," *New Scientist* (June 23, 1966): 771–72.

104 William B. Jackson, "Anticoagulant Resistance in Europe: Part I," *Pest Control* (March 1969): 51–55; and William B. Jackson, "Anticoagulant Resistance in Europe: Part II," *Pest Control* (April 1969): 40–43.

105 William B. Jackson and Dale E. Kaukeinen, "The Problem of Anticoagulant Resistance in the United States," paper presented at the Fifth Vertebrate Pest Conference, Fresno, Calif., March 7–9, 1972, pp. 142–48; and William B. Jackson, P. T. Spear, and C. Wright, "Resistance of Norway Rats to Anticoagulant Rodenticides Confirmed in the United States," *Pest Control* (1971): 13–14.

106 Jackson, "Anticoagulant Resistance in Europe: Part I"; and Jackson, "Anticoagulant Resistance in Europe: Part II."

107 William Jackson, interview with the author, Bowling Green, Ohio, June 2006.

108 Ibid.; Stephen Frantz and Constance Padula, "Recent Developments in Anticoagulant Rodenticide Resistance Studies: Surveillance and Application in the United States," *Proceedings of the Ninth Vertebrate Pest Conference* (1980): 80–88; and Stephen Frantz, interview with the author, Troy, N.Y., July 16, 2006.

109 A. Daniel Ashton and William B. Jackson, "Field Testing of Rodenticides in a Resistant-Rat Area of Chicago," *Pest Control* (August 1979): 14–16; and Jackson, interview with the author.

110 Rockefeller Foundation Officer Harold Stark paraphrased this quote from

Davis's statements. H. E. Stark, "Trip Report: Conference on Rodent Control," August 28, 1967.

111   Joe E. Brooks and Alan M. Bowerman, "Analysis of the Susceptibilities of Several Populations of *Rattus Norvegicus* to Warfarin," *Journal of Hygiene 73* (1974): 401–8; Joe E. Brooks and Alan M. Bowerman, "Anticoagulant Resistance in Wild Norway Rats in New York," *Journal of Hygiene 71* (1973): 217–22; William B. Jackson et al., "Anticoagulant Resistance in Norway Rats as Found in U.S. Cities: Part I," *Pest Control* (April 1975): 12–16; and William B. Jackson et al., "Anticoagulant Resistance in Norway Rats as Found in U.S. Cities: Part II," *Pest Control* (May 1975): 14–24.

112   Ashton and Jackson, "Field Testing of Rodenticides in a Resistant-Rat Area of Chicago."

113   "America's Strange New Breed of Super Rats That Chemicals Can't Kill," *San Francisco Examiner and Chronicle*, November 10, 1974.

114   "Austin, City Meeting Ends Following Profanity," *Chicago Tribune*, September 30, 1977.

115   D. Schneidman, "Blizzard of '79 Sets Chicago Back in Its War on Rats," *Chicago Tribune*, September 27, 1979.

116   Louis Fitzgerald, "Critique," *Chicago Defender*, March 20, 1979.

117   R. Toth, "Rats! They Can Become a Super World Menace," *Chicago Sun-Times*, October 21, 1979.

118   For coverage of clean-up efforts in 1979, see "2nd Ward Wages All-Out War on Rodents," *Chicago Defender*, September 8, 1979.

119   Jackson, interview with the author.

120   Brooks and Bowerman, "Analysis of the Susceptibilities of Several Populations of *Rattus norvegicus* to Warfarin"; Brooks and Bowerman, "Anticoagulant Resistance in Wild Norway Rats in New York"; Jackson et al., "Anticoagulant Resistance in Norway Rats as Found in U.S. Cities: Part I"; and Jackson et al., "Anticoagulant Resistance in Norway Rats as Found in U.S. Cities: Part II."

121   Ashton and Jackson, "Field Testing of Rodenticides in a Resistant-Rat Area of Chicago"; and Jackson, interview with the author.

122   Although urban predators do not contribute significantly to rat control, rodenticides were feared to make a significant contribution to wildlife mortality when birds of prey or cats ate rats.

123   It has been surmised that a single gene controls anticoagulant resistance in rats, a gene closely linked with coat color, and that this gene can also predispose rats to cross-resistance to other anticoagulants. A. MacNicoll, "Resistance to 4-hydroxycoumarin Anticoagulants in Rodents," in E. Glass, ed., *Pesticide Resistance: Strategies and Tactics for Management* (Washington, D.C.: National Academies Press, 1986), 87–99. See also Frantz and Padula, "Recent Developments in Anticoagulant Rodenticide Resistance Studies"; and Frantz interview. For more contemporary studies of urban rats and genetics, see L.

C. Gardner-Santana et al., "Commensal Ecology, Urban Landscapes, and Their Influence on the Genetic Characteristics of City-Dwelling Norway Rats (*Rattus norvegicus*)," *Molecular Ecology* 18 (2009): 2766–78.

124　Massey and Denton, *American Apartheid*, 76.

125　City of Milwaukee Health Department, *Intensive Rodent Control Progress Report 69–73* (Milwaukee: City of Milwaukee Health Department, 1973).

6. INTEGRATING URBAN HOMES: COCKROACHES AND SURVIVAL

1　Audre Lorde, "Eye to Eye: Black Women, Anger, and Hatred," in Lorde's *Sister Outsider: Essays and Speeches* (Berkeley, Calif.: The Crossing Press, 1984), 145–75.

2　Camille Dungy, *Black Nature: Four Centuries of African American Nature Poetry* (Athens: University of Georgia Press, 2009); Margaret Kissam Morris, "Audre Lorde: Textual Authority and the Embodied Self," *Frontiers* 23 (2002): 168–88; and Alexis Pauline Gumbs, "We Can Learn to Mother Ourselves: The Queer Survival of Black Feminism," PhD diss., Duke University, 2010.

3　Sarah Ruffin, interview with the author; Jill Viehweg, interview with the author; and David Shangle, interview with the author.

4　Hazlett, "Woman vs. Man vs. Bugs."

5　Hugh Raffles has also discussed comparisons of people and pests. For example, the description of Rwandan Tutsis as "cockroaches" helped to both rally and justify their extermination by the Hutu. Raffles, *Insectopedia*, 146.

6　Meyerson and Banfield, *Politics, Planning, and the Public Interest*.

7　Ibid.

8　This narrative of the CHA's battle for integration is based largely on Meyerson and Banfield, *Politics, Planning, and the Public Interest*. See also Devereaux Bowly Jr., *The Poorhouse: Subsidized Housing in Chicago, 1895–1976* (Carbondale: Southern Illinois University Press, 1978), 113–14; Massey and Denton, *American Apartheid*, 227–29; and "Move-ins Begin at Henry Horner Remake," *Chicago Tribune*, May 16, 2004.

9　Bowly, *Poorhouse*; Fuerst, *When Public Housing Was Paradise*; Alexander Kotlowitz, *There Are No Children Here* (New York: Doubleday, 1991), 19–24; and Ruffin interview.

10　*Hills v. Gautreaux*, 425 U.S. 284 (U.S. Supreme Court 1976).

11　Ronald Shaw, "Final Push for National Legislation: The Chicago Freedom Movement," *Journal of the Illinois State Historical Society* 94 (2001): 304–32.

12　Chicago Freedom Movement, "Project Open City," 1966, CFM40 Archive, Middlebury College, online at http://cfm40.middlebury.edu/files/project%20open%20city.pdf, accessed on March 29, 2013. See also James Ralph Jr., "Home Truths: Dr. King and the Chicago Freedom Movement," *American Visions* 9 (1994): 30–34. The Freedom Movement was controversial in part because some African-American leaders in Chicago felt that housing integration was largely a concern for middle-class blacks and should be a low priority for the civil rights movement, but it seems that King and Raby sought integration in part for the improvement in housing conditions that it was likely to provide.

13   Much scholarship and popular discourse about public housing condemns high-rise architecture, but research on pests does not seem to consider this aspect of building style an important factor in infestation.

14   Atlas and Dreier, "From Projects to Communities."

15   John Perkins, *Insects, Experts, and the Insecticide Crisis: The Quest for New Pest Management Strategies* (New York: Plenum Press, 1982).

16   For an introduction to these principles, see Mary Louise Flint and Robert van den Bosch, *Introduction to Integrated Pest Management* (New York: Plenum Press, 1981). This volume was a posthumous publication for van den Bosch; he died in 1978.

17   For discussions of IPM, see Richard Baker, "Integrated Pest Management: Accentuate the 'I,'" *Pest Management* (August 1982): 19–21; Flint and van den Bosch, *Introduction to Integrated Pest Management*; Marcos Kogan, "Integrated Pest Management: Historical Perspectives and Contemporary Developments," *Annual Reviews in Entomology* 43 (1998): 243–70; and Perkins, *Insects, Experts, and the Insecticide Crisis*. For further background on ecosystem ecology, see Stephen Bocking, *Ecologists and Environmental Politics: A History of Contemporary Ecology* (New Haven, Conn.: Yale University Press, 1997); and Frank B. Golley, *A History of the Ecosystem Concept in Ecology* (New Haven, Conn.: Yale University Press, 1993).

18   Robert van den Bosch, *The Pesticide Conspiracy* (Garden City, N.J.: Doubleday, 1978).

19   For a review of these studies, see Eldon P. Savage, Thomas J. Keefe, and H. William Wheeler, *National Household Pesticide Usage Study, 1976–1977* (Fort Collins, Colo.: Epidemiologic Pesticide Studies Center, 1979), 5–7.

20   Helga Olkowski, *Common Sense Pest Control* (Berkeley: Consumers' Cooperative of Berkeley, 1971).

21   Ibid., 37.

22   Ibid.

23   William Olkowski, "A Model Ecosystem Management Program," paper presented at Tall Timbers Conference on Ecological Animal Control by Habitat Management, in *Tall Timbers Conference on Ecological Animal Control by Habitat Management* 5 (1973): 103–17.

24   Helga Olkowski and William Olkowski, "Entomophobia in the Urban Ecosystem: Some Observations and Suggestions," *Bulletin of the Entomological Society of America* 22 (1976): 313–17, 315.

25   Olkowski, *Common Sense Pest Control*, 36.

26   William Olkowski, "The Birth of the I-House," ms., personal archives of Helga and William Olkowski, January 21, 1977.

27 Helga Olkowski, William Olkowski, and Tom Javits, *The Integral Urban House: Self-reliant Living in the City* (San Francisco: Sierra Club Books, 1979).

28 Gordon W. Frankie and Hanna Levenson, "Insect Problems and Insecticide Use: Public Opinion, Information, and Behavior," in Gordon W. Frankie and Carl S. Koehler, eds., *Perspectives in Urban Entomology* (New York: Academic Press, 1978), 359–99, 364; and Hanna Levenson and Gordon W. Frankie, "A Study of Homeowner Attitudes and Practices toward Arthropod Pests and Pesticides in Three U.S. Metropolitan Areas," in Gordon W. Frankie and Carl S. Koehler, eds., *Urban Entomology: Interdisciplinary Perspectives* (New York: Praeger, 1983), 67–106. Other surveys from the late 1960s through the 1970s found that between 72 and 93 percent of all households used pesticides either indoors or outdoors. For a review of these studies, see Savage, Keefe, and Wheeler, *National Household Pesticide Usage Study*, 5–7. See also Carl S. Koehler, "Domestic Pesticide Consumption, Commodities Treated, and the More Important Pests against Which These Treatments Are Directed," 1970, folder 194, box 36, series 900, RG 3.2, Rockefeller Foundation Archive, RAC.

29 Mallis, *Handbook of Pest Control* (1954), 183. Despite the spread of pesticide resistance among cockroaches during the 1950s, Mallis's 1960 guide did not show any greater interest in boric acid than the previous edition. Interest in boric acid sometimes arose among housing managers—in part based on Ebeling's research—but some commercial pest controllers worried that it would be an ineffective and dangerous tool in the hands of untrained householders and staff. Irving Bengelsdorf, "Boric Acid Held Best Roach Killer: Cheap, Safe Powder Tests Better Than Potent Insecticides," *The Apartment Journal* (1966): 20–21; and National Pest Control Association, "Pest Control Group Warns: Boric Acid for Household Roaches? Not Unless You Really Know How to Do It," press release, May 1975, Rutgers University Special Collections and University Archives, Consumers' Research Collection, Files on Pests and Pesticides, Box 696, File 26.

30 Walter Ebeling, R. E. Wagner, and Donald A. Reierson, "Influence of Repellency on the Efficacy of Blatticides I. Learned Modification of Behavior of the German Cockroach," *Journal of Economic Entomology* 59 (1966): 1374–88. See also Walter Ebeling, Donald A. Reierson, and R. E. Wagner, "Influence of Repellency on the Efficacy of Blatticides II. Laboratory Experiments with German Cockroaches," *Journal of Economic Entomology* 60 (1967): 1375–90.

31 Frederick Plapp, "Insecticides in the Urban Environment," in Gordon Frankie and Carl Koehler, eds., *Perspectives in Urban Entomology* (New York: Academic Press, 1978), 401–8.

32 Assumptions of cultural universalism have long been characteristic of American environmentalism. See, for example, Jennifer Price, *Flight Maps: Adventures with Nature in Modern America* (New York: Basic Books, 1999); and Julie Guthman, "If They Only Knew: Color-Blindness and Universalism in California Alternative Food Institutions," *Professional Geographer* 60 (2008): 387–97.

33   Frank Graham, *Since Silent Spring* (Boston: Houghton Mifflin, 1970), 139, 214.

34   Several IPM educators admitted to this author in casual conversation that they do not practice the rigorous pest prevention techniques that they promote in community outreach, and that they do not suffer any additional trouble from roaches.

35   Ruffin interview.

36   Kotlowitz, *There Are No Children Here*, 28.

37   Ruffin interview.

38   Ray Lopez, interview with the author, New York, July 2009; Ruffin interview; and Viehweg interview.

39   Harry Bernton and Halla Brown, "Insect Allergy: Preliminary Studies of the Cockroach," *Journal of Allergy* 35 (1964): 506–13; Harry Bernton and Halla Brown, "Cockroach Allergy II: The Relation of Infestation to Sensitization," *Southern Medical Journal* 60 (1967): 852–55. See also Mitman, *Breathing Space*, chapter 4.

40   "Can Cockroaches Cause Asthma?" *British Medical Journal* 6063 (1977): 734; Bann Kang et al., "Analysis of Indoor Environment and Atopic Allergy in Urban Populations with Bronchial Asthma," *Annals of Allergy* 62 (1989): 30–34; Bann Kang, Charles Wu, and Jessie Johnson, "Characteristics and Diagnoses of Cockroach-Sensitive Bronchial Asthma," *Annals of Allergy* 68 (1992): 237–44; Bann Kang, Jessie Johnson, and Chris Veres-Thorner, "Atopic Profile of Inner-City Asthma with a Comparative Analysis on the Cockroach-Sensitive and Ragweed-Sensitive Subgroups," *Journal of Allergy and Clinical Immunology* 92 (1993): 802–11; Daniel Garcia et al., "Cockroach Allergy in Kentucky: A Comparison of Inner-City, Suburban, and Rural Small Town Populations," *Annals of Allergy* 72 (1994): 203–8; John Roberts, "Cockroaches Linked with Asthma," *British Medical Journal* 7047 (1996): 1630; and David L. Rosenstreich et al., "The Role of Cockroach Allergy and Exposure to Cockroach Allergen in Causing Morbidity among Inner-City Children with Asthma," *New England Journal of Medicine* 336 (1997): 1356–63. In addition to asthma and cockroach exposure, residents of poor-quality housing, and especially renters, faced an array of other indoor health problems such as lead or mold. Christian Warren, *Brush with Death: A Social History of Lead Poisoning* (Baltimore, Md.: Johns Hopkins University Press, 2000); and Susan Smith, Robin Knill-Jones, and Ann McGuckin, eds., *Housing for Health* (Essex, UK: Longman Group, 1991).

41   Herrick, *Insects Injurious to the Household*, 133.

42   Kang et al., "Analysis of Indoor Environment and Atopic Allergy in Urban Populations with Bronchial Asthma."

43   Ruffin interview.

44   Shangle interview.

45   Safer Pest Control Project, "Safer Solutions: Integrated Pest Management in Public Housing," brochure, 2002; Ruffin interview; and Viehweg interview.

46 "The Residents in Low-Rent Housing Like Their Homes," *Journal of Housing*.

47 For discussion of sense of smell and embodied perceptions of ill health, see Joy Parr, "Smells Like? Sources of Uncertainty in the History of the Great Lakes Environment," *Environmental History* 11 (2006): 269–99.

48 Ruffin interview; Shangle interview; and Viehweg interview.

49 Safer Pest Control Project, "Safer Solutions: Integrated Pest Management in Public Housing"; Ruffin interview; and Viehweg interview.

50 William Olkowski, Helga Olkowski, and Linda Laub, *Urban Integrated Pest Management in California: An Assessment and Action Plan* (Berkeley, Calif.: Center for the Integration of Applied Sciences, 1980), 13. See also Katherine A. Streimer et al., *Report on the Environmental Assessment of Pesticide Regulatory Programs* (Sacramento: California Department of Food and Agriculture Division of Pest Management, 1978), 37.

51 Olkowski, Olkowski, and Laub, *Urban Integrated Pest Management in California*, 9.

52 National Research Council Committee on Urban Pest Management, *Urban Pest Management: A Report* (Washington, D.C.: National Academy Press, 1980), 141.

53 Philip Landrigan et al., "Pesticides and Inner-City Children: Exposures, Risks, and Prevention," *Environmental Health Perspectives* 107, supplement 3 (1999): 431–37.

54 National Research Council Committee on Urban Pest Management, *Urban Pest Management*, 10.

55 See, for example, Devra Davis and A. K. Ahmed, "Exposures from Indoor Spraying of Chlorpyrifos Pose Greater Health Risks to Children Than Currently Estimated," *Environmental Health Perspectives* 106 (1998): 299–301.

56 Hoffman, Fishbein, and Andelman, "Pesticide Content of Human Fat Tissue."

57 Industry leaders before the civilian release of DDT observed that low-income people purchased more pesticides than people of other income levels. See "Aerosol Insecticides," *Soap and Sanitary Chemicals* (October 1945): 124–26. The most important compilation of research on social differences and pesticides in its day is found in Secretary's Commission on Pesticides and Their Relationship to Environmental Health, "Report: Pesticides and Their Relationship to Environmental Health." For other reviews, reports, and empirical pieces published between 1960 and 1980 that address social difference in pesticide body loads, see, for example, Davies, Edmundson, and Raffonelli, "Role of House Dust in Human DDT Pollution"; Finklea et al., "Pesticides and Pesticide Hazards in Urban Households"; Keil et al., "DDT and DDE Residues in Blood from Children, South Carolina—1970"; National Research Council Committee on Urban Pest Management, *Urban Pest Management*; and Olkowski, Olkowski, and Laub, *Urban Integrated Pest Management in California*. These reports generally conclude that low income predicts higher pesticide exposure, as does being a person of color.

58 National Research Council, *Pest Control: An Assessment of Present and Alternative Technologies, Volume I: Contemporary Pest Control Practices and Prospects* (Washington, D.C.: National Academies Press, 1975), 155, 170. This focus on agricultural chemicals reflects a pattern of emphasis on production over social reproduction—that is, a focus on activities that produce commodities versus those involved in producing bodies and subjects. For discussion of the privileging of production, see, for example, Isabella Bakker and Rachel Silvey, *Beyond States and Markets: The Challenges of Social Reproduction* (London: Routledge, 2008); and Marston, "Social Construction of Scale."

59 National Research Council Committee on Urban Pest Management, *Urban Pest Management 7*. See also Flint and Van Den Bosch, *Introduction to Integrated Pest Management*, 203.

60 See, for example, Olkowski, *Common Sense Pest Control*; and Olkowski, Olkowski, and Javits, *Integral Urban House*.

61 Ebeling et al., "Influence of Repellency on the Effectiveness of Blatticides I"; and Shangle interview. See also Wood, "Cockroach Control in Public Housing."

62 Most of these insights about pest control in public housing come from David Shangle and Eugene Wood; Shangle interview; and Wood interview.

63 Charles Wright, "A Survey of Cockroach Species Found in Some North Carolina Apartment Projects," *Pest Control* (June 1965): 14–15.

64 William Olkowski and Helga Olkowski, *Delivering Integrated Pest Management: Pest Control Services for Cockroaches, Mice, Rats, and Flies in Public and Private Buildings* (Berkeley, Calif.: Bio-Integral Resource Center, 1984); and William Olkowski and Helga Olkowski, *Contracting for Pest Control Services: Cockroaches, Mice, Rats, and Flies in Public and Private Buildings: A Consumers' Guide* (Berkeley, Calif.: Bio-integral Resource Center, 1984).

65 Some pest controllers insist that roaches only enter apartments that have sanitation problems, but those "problems" may be minor lapses rather than blatant violations of hygiene. Frantz interview; Shangle interview; and Wood interview.

66 Wood, "Cockroach Control in Public Housing."

67 Williams, *Politics of Public Housing*, 78–79.

68 Wood interview; Wood, "Cockroach Control in Public Housing"; F. E. Wood et al., "Survey of Attitudes and Knowledge of Public Housing Residents toward Cockroaches," *Bulletin of the Entomological Society of America* 27 (1981): 9–13; and Gary L. Piper and Gordon W. Frankie, *Integrated Management of Urban Cockroach Populations: Final Report* (Washington, D.C.: Environmental Protection Agency, 1978).

69 For a review of resistance research up to 1960, see Mallis, *Handbook of Pest Control* (1960), 169.

70 Wood, "Cockroach Control in Public Housing."

71 Ibid.

72　Ibid.

73　National Research Council Committee on Urban Pest Management, *Urban Pest Management*, 175.

74　The literature discussing the decline of American public housing is rich. See, for example, Grogan and Proscio, "Fall (and Rise) of Public Housing." While Grogan and Proscio tend to focus on the dangers of concentrating poverty in the projects and therefore praise economic integration efforts since the 1990s, Rhonda Williams places her emphasis upon the agency of very low-income residents who struggled against neglectful management and a broader public that was often hostile toward the projects. Therefore, while still critical of racial segregation in public housing and of the state for failing to fulfill its promises to residents, Williams arrives at a much more positive view of the projects as a human community and as a public good. Lawrence Vale similarly allows a positive view of the projects as a public good and is critical of American social biases against public housing, blaming these in part for policies that left projects to decline physically and socially. Vale, *From the Puritans to the Projects*; Williams, *Politics of Public Housing*.

75　Williams, *Politics of Public Housing*, especially 54–56, 71–72, 143–52. Some scholars of the history of public housing might also say that the difference between the first and subsequent cohorts of public housing residents resulted when managers stopped being selective about tenants they admitted to the projects; this would presume that open admission let in residents who did not maintain proper sanitation in their units. See Atlas and Dreier, "From Projects to Communities."

76　Andrea Gill, "Moving to Integration? The Origins of Chicago's Gautreaux Program and the Limits of Voucher-Based Housing Mobility," *Journal of Urban History* 38 (2012): 662–86.

77　On the cheapness of public housing, see Atlas and Dreier, "Public Housing."

78　Grogan and Proscio, "Fall (and Rise) of Public Housing," 3.

79　Kotlowitz, *There Are No Children Here*, 27.

80　Adam Walinsky, "What It's Like to Be in Hell," *New York Times*, December 4, 1987.

81　Atlas and Dreier, "From Projects to Communities."

82　For discussion of the theory of IPM, see William Olkowski et al., "Ecosystem Management: A Framework for Urban Pest Control," *Bioscience* 26 (1976): 384–89; and Flint and van den Bosch, *Introduction to Integrated Pest Management*.

83　For other examples of this sort of activism, see Blum, *Love Canal Revisited*; M. David Naguib Pellow, *The Garbage Wars: The Struggle for Environmental Justice in Chicago* (Cambridge, Mass.: MIT Press, 2002); and Hurley, *Environmental Inequalities*.

84　Chicago Freedom Movement, "Project Open City."

85　General Accounting Office, *HOPE VI Resident Issues and Changes in*

Neighborhoods Surrounding Grant Sites (Washington, D.C.: General Accounting Office, 2003); and James Hanlon, "Success by Design: HOPE VI, New Urbanism, and the Neoliberal Transformation of Public Housing in the United States," *Environment and Planning A* 42 (2010): 80–98.

86 Gill, "Moving to Integration."

87 Ruffin interview.

88 For a more complete discussion of the politics of public housing in Chicago after *Gautreaux*, including a case study of Henry Horner Homes, see Popkin et al., "The Gautreaux Legacy"; Gill, "Moving to Integration"; and Carlos Morales, "Hearing Set for Horner Redevelopment," *Chicago Tribune*, August 6, 1995.

89 Ruffin interview.

90 Ibid.; and Viehweg interview.

91 See Blum, "Women, Environmental Rationale, and Activism during the Progressive Era." See also Celene Krauss, "Challenging Power: Toxic Waste Protests and the Politicization of White, Working-Class Women," in N. A. Naples, ed., *Community Activism and Feminist Politics: Organizing across Race, Class, and Gender* (New York: Routledge, 1998), 129–50; Vernice Miller, Moya Hallstein, and Susan Quass, "Feminist Politics and Environmental Justice: Women's Community Activism in West Harlem, New York," in Dianne Rocheleau, Barbara Thomas-Slayter, and Esther Wangari, eds., *Feminist Political Ecology: Global Issues and Local Experiences* (London: Routledge, 1996), 62–85; Laura Pulido, "Ecofeminist Natures: Race, Gender, Feminist Theory, and Political Action," *Environment and Planning D* 18 (2000): 122–24; and Sandra Harding, *The Science Question in Feminism* (Ithaca, N.Y.: Cornell University Press, 1986). These renderings of "standpoint epistemology" argue that knowledge constructed "from below" is better positioned to get at the truth; by contrast, Donna Haraway has argued that no standpoint is innocent or even unitary. Donna Haraway, "Situated Knowledges: The Science Question in Feminism and the Privilege of Partial Perspective," in *Simians, Cyborgs, and Women: The Reinvention of Nature.* (New York: Routledge, 1991), 183–201.

92 Williams, *Politics of Public Housing*; and hooks, "Homeplace."

93 This victory was incomplete for reasons that cannot be fully discussed here; in short, because of changing federal and local funding priorities, the number of units available to low-income tenants would decrease. The CHA (and other housing authorities that reduce units) assume that after renovations some residents who were temporarily relocated will decide not to return. For further discussion of recent changes in public housing that have decreased the number of units available for very low-income people, see Hackworth, "Public Housing and the Rescaling of Regulation in the U.S.A."

94 Olkowski and Olkowski, *Contracting for Pest Control Services.*

95 Ruffin interview; Shangle interview; and Viehweg interview.

96   Ibid.

97   Ruffin interview.

98   Barbara Brenner, personal communication with the author, New York City, July 2006; and Viehweg interview. See also H. P. Hynes et al., "'Where Does the Damp Come From?' Investigations into the Indoor Environment and Respiratory Health in Boston Public Housing," *Journal of Public Health Policy* 24 (2003): 401–26; and H. P. Hynes et al., "Public Health and the Physical Environment in Boston Public Housing: A Community-Based Survey and Action Agenda," *Planning Practice and Research* 15 (2000): 31–49.

99   "Polikoff Combats 'Residential Apartheid,' with Gautreaux, Sacrifices Inner City Shelter Needs for Open Housing Goal," *Chicago Reporter*, March 1978; and Rita McLennon and William Wilen, "CHA Reform at Horner Homes a Housing Model," *Chicago Tribune*, March 22, 2004.

100 John Handley, "Move-ins Begin at Henry Horner Remake," *Chicago Tribune*, May 16, 2004.

101 Carlos Morales, "Hearing Set for Horner Redevelopment," *Chicago Tribune*, August 6, 1995.

102 General Accounting Office, *HOPE VI Resident Issues and Changes in Neighborhoods Surrounding Grant Sites*.

103 T. A. Rehner et al., "Depression among Victims of South Mississippi's Methyl Parathion Disaster," *Health and Social Work* 35 (2000): 33–40.

104 Kenneth G. McCann et al., "Chicago Area Methyl Parathion Response," *Environmental Health Perspectives* 110, supplement 6 (2002): 1075–78; and Daniel Johnson, "Illegal Use of Methyl Parathion Endangers Detroit Area Residents," *Michigan Toxics Watch* (summer 1995).

105 Kathy Seikel, personal communication with the author, Crystal City, Va., June 2006; and Vanessa Villareal, "Districts Tackle Pesticide Clean-up," *Army Corps of Engineers Newsletter*, 1997.

106 O. Ibitayo, "Relocated Citizens' Perceptions and Attitudes Regarding Indoor Application of Toxic Agricultural Pesticides," *Journal of Contingencies and Crisis Management* 8 (2000): 141–50.

107 Ebeling, Wagner, and Reierson, "Influence of Repellency on the Efficacy of Blatticides I."

108 Both Donna Haraway and Bruno Latour have developed the notion that we learn from or *translate* the performances of nonhumans within ecological webs. See, for example, Donna Haraway, *When Species Meet* (Minneapolis: University of Minnesota Press, 2007); and Latour, *We Have Never Been Modern*.

EPILOGUE

1   William Quarles, "Bed Bugs Bounce Back," *IPM Practitioner* 29, no. 3–4 (2007): 1–8; and Tim Myles et al., "Bed Bugs in Toronto," *Centre for Urban and Community Studies Research Bulletin* 19 (2003): 1–4.

2   Hockenyos, "Bedbug Spraying"; and Robert Snetsinger, personal communication.

3   Sailer, "The Bedbug."

4   Usinger, *Monograph on Cimicidae*, vi.

5   The breakdown of class lines is far from the only theme, although it is common. Another common narrative portrays the way families have learned about bedbug biology and ecology in their home environments. Another related theme concerns the struggle to cleanse the home environment; many videos and blog posts chronicle meticulous and lengthy efforts to bring nature in the home under control.

6   Sarah Makuta, "Bloomingdales Bedbug," *New York Post*, September 25, 2010; Matt Skoller Band, *Bone to Pick with You* (Chicago: Groove-tongue Records, 1996); and Matt Hubbard, "Audition Day," *30 Rock*, directed by Beth McCarthy Miller, November 5, 2009.

7   Skolander, "Bedbugs in New York," August 29, 2010, online at http://www.youtube.com/watch?v=lKoLffiCDb8, accessed on August 15, 2012.

8   Task forces made up of municipal administrators, city council members, pest management professionals, and residents have convened in New York, Chicago, and several other major cities. Agencies such as the EPA are also commissioning studies to understand bedbug control best practices under the often-difficult conditions found in apartment buildings. National Center for Healthy Housing, *What's Working for Bed Bug Control in Multifamily Housing: Reconciling Best Practices with Research and the Realities of Implementation* (Washington, D.C.: Environmental Protection Agency, 2010).

9   Michael Potter, Panel 1, Congressional Bed Bug Forum, November 18, 2010; and Brian Hendy, Panel 2, Congressional Bed Bug Forum, November 18, 2010.

10 Congress, House, "Don't Let the Bed Bugs Bite Act of 2009," 111th Cong., 1st sess., HR 2248, May 5, 2009.

11 Potter, Congressional Bed Bug Forum.

12 Ibid.

13 Associated Press, "'SNL' Star Sues over Bedbugs in Her Loft." *USA Today*, November 11, 2006.

14 Potter, Congressional Bed Bug Forum.

15 Ibid.; and Potter, "History of Bedbug Management."

16 Daniel E. Kass et al., "Developing a Comprehensive Pesticide Health Effects Tracking System for an Urban Setting: New York City's Approach," *Environmental Health Perspectives* 112 (2004): 1419–23; and Rosenstreich et al., "The Role of Cockroach Allergy and Exposure to Cockroach Allergen in Causing Morbidity among Inner-City Children with Asthma."

17 M. David Pellow, *Garbage Wars: The Struggle for Environmental Justice in Chicago* (Cambridge, Mass.: MIT Press, 2002), 133.

18 Glass, interview with the author, July 2009; City of Baltimore, Council Resolution Concerning Bureau of Vector Control, Legislative File Number

07–0272R, March 15, 2007. Thanks to Yvette Williams for bringing this resolution to my attention.

19   G. K. Butterfield, Congressional Bed Bug Forum, November 18, 2010.

20   Dini Miller and Michael Potter, Panel 1, Congressional Bed Bug Forum, November 18, 2010.

21   NAHO, "Disinfestation of Dwellings and Furnishings."

22   Dini Miller and Michael Potter, Panel 1, Congressional Bed Bug Forum, November 18, 2010.

23   Potter, Congressional Bed Bug Forum.

24   Miller and Potter, Panel 1, Congressional Bed Bug Forum.

25   John Del Signore, "Bedbugs Tormenting Howard Stern, DDT-Hating Hippies Blamed," The Gothamist, September 28, 2010.

26   Silvia Salazar, testimony at Stop Bedbugs-DC Summit, March 27, 2009; and Silvia Salazar, Panel 4, Congressional Bed Bug Forum, November 18, 2010.

27   Potter, Congressional Bed Bug Forum.

28   Landrigan et al., "Pesticides and Inner-City Children."

29   E. Carlton, H. L. Moats, M. Feinberg, P. Shepard, P. Garfinkel, R. Whyatt, and D. Evans, "Pesticide Sales in Low-Income, Minority Neighborhoods," Journal of Community Health 29 (2002): 231–44; and Mannes interview.

30   Deroy Murdock, "Pesticide Patrol Fallout," Washington Times, February 13, 2002.

31   Most notably, see Landrigan et al., "Pesticides and Inner-City Children."

32   Barbara Brenner et al., "Integrated Pest Management in an Urban Community: A Successful Partnership for Prevention," Environmental Health Perspectives 111 (2003): 1649–1653; Stuart Greenberg, Cockroach Allergen Reduction Using Precision-Targeted IPM and the Lead Dust Cleaning Protocol (Cleveland, Ohio: Environmental Health Watch, 2003); Anthhu Hoang, interview with the author, New York, July 2009; Safer Pest Control Project, "Safer Solutions"; and State of New York, "Complaint for Declaratory and Injunctive Relief: State of New York against Department of Housing and Urban Development," Albany, N.Y.: U. S. District Court for the Eastern District of New York, 2004.

33   Dini Miller and Frank Meek, "Cost and Efficacy Comparison of Integrated Pest Management Strategies with Monthly Spray Insecticide Applications for German Cockroaches in Public Housing," Journal of Economic Entomology 97 (2004): 559–69; and Changlu Wang and Gary W. Bennett, "Comparative Study of Integrated Pest Management and Baiting for German Cockroach Management in Public Housing," Journal of Economic Entomology 99 (2006): 879–85.

34   Stuart Greenberg, personal communication with the author, Cleveland, Ohio, August 2009; Hoang interview; and Lopez interview.

35   Rosenberg. "Home Is the Workplace."

36   Michael Potter, Panel 1, Congressional Bed Bug Forum.

37 "New War—On Vermin"; and Collins, "The Bedbug."

38 Harland, "Helping Hand."

39 Michael Potter, Panel 1, Congressional Bed Bug Forum. This comment also recalls Bruno Latour's criticism of the "proliferation of hybrids" accompanied by "purification practices" that deny those hybrids; both bedbugs and personal electronic devices are hybrids of a sort, but Americans are often deluded and seduced by the presumed modernity of the latter, ignoring the immediacy of the former. Latour, *We Have Never Been Modern.*

40 Potter's argument also resonates with the work of geographers who seek to end the valorization of public space over private space and those who recognize that unruly nature shares in even the most seemingly tame spaces. For works elevating the importance of home, see Blunt and Dowling, *Home*; Harriet Bulkeley and Nicky Gregson, "Crossing the Threshold: Municipal Waste Policy and Household Waste Generation," *Environment and Planning A* 41 (2009): 929–45; Crabtree, "Sustainability Begins at Home?"; Domosh, "Geography and Gender: Home, Again?"; Scharff, *Seeing Nature through Gender*; and Strasser, *Waste and Want.* For works concerned with domesticated nature, see Donna Haraway, *The Companion Species Manifesto: Dogs, People, and Significant Otherness* (Chicago: Prickly Paradigm, 2003); Maria Kaika, "Interrogating the Geographies of the Familiar: Domesticating Nature and Constructing the Autonomy of the Modern Home," *International Journal of Urban and Regional Research* 28 (2004): 265–86; Maria Kaika and Erik Swyngedouw, "Fetishizing the Modern City: The Phantasmagoria of Urban Technological Networks," *International Journal of Urban and Regional Research* 24 (2000): 120–38; Sharon Moran, "Under the Lawn: Engaging the Water Cycle," *Ethics, Place, and Environment* 11 (2008): 129–45; Emma Power, "Furry Families: Making a Human-Dog Family through Home," *Social and Cultural Geography* 9 (2008): 535–55; and J. A. Smith, "Beyond Dominance and Affection: Living with Rabbits in Post-humanist Households," *Animals and Society* 11 (2003): 181–97.

41 NAHO, "Disinfestation of Dwellings and Furnishings."

42 Silvia Salazar, testimony at Congressional Bedbug Forum.

43 Carson, *Silent Spring*, 189.

SELECTED BIBLIOGRAPHY

ARCHIVAL COLLECTIONS

Chicago Municipal Reference Collection
    Chicago Board of Health Reports
    Clean Living (newsletter)
City of Milwaukee Legislative Reference Bureau
City of New York Municipal Reference Bureau
    Annual Reports of the Department of Health of the City of New York
    (ARDHCNY)
Consumers' Research, Inc. Collection, Rutgers University Special Collections
    and University Archives
    Files on Pests and Pesticides, Insecticides and Chemicals
Enoch Pratt Free Library Local History Collection (Baltimore)
    Files on Rats-Baltimore-Extermination
Langsdale Library Special Collections, University of Baltimore
    Citizens' Planning and Housing Association Collection
Library of Congress
    Sanborn Fire Insurance Maps
Lower East Side Tenement Museum
    Oral histories
Lyndon B. Johnson Presidential Library
Maryland Historical Society
    Annual Reports of the Health Department of the City of Baltimore
    (ARHDCB)
National Archives and Records Administration
    Record Group 22—Records of the Fish and Wildlife Service
    Record Group 88—Records of the Food and Drug Administration
Olkowski, Helga and William—Personal Archive
Rockefeller Foundation Archives, Rockefeller Archive Center (RAC)
    Record Group 1.2, Series 200—Records of the Rodent Ecology Project
Smithsonian Institution Archives
Washington, D.C., Historical Society
    Annual Reports of the Health Officer of the District of Columbia (ARHODC)

BOOKS, ARTICLES, REPORTS, AND DISSERTATIONS

Abbott, Edith. *The Tenements of Chicago, 1908–1935*. Chicago: University of Chicago Press, 1936.

Addams, Jane. *Twenty Years at Hull-House: With Autobiographical Notes*, edited by V. B. Brown. Boston: St. Martin's, 1999.

Agrawal, Arun. *Environmentality: Technologies of Government and the Making of Subjects*. Durham, N.C.: Duke University Press, 2005.

Aldrich, Sherman. "Leasing: The Chicago Leasing Experience." Paper presented at the Seminar on Managing Low-Rent Housing: A Record of Current Experiences and Practice in Public Housing, Washington, D.C., June 13–24, 1938.

American Civic Association. "Fight the Flies." *National Geographic Magazine* 21 (1910): 383–85.

Anderson, Kay. *Vancouver's Chinatown: Racial Discourse in Canada, 1875–1980*. Montreal: McGill-Queen's University Press, 1991.

Anderson, Warwick. "Natural Histories of Infectious Disease: Ecological Vision in Twentieth-Century Biomedical Science." *Osiris* 19 (2004): 39–61.

Apple, Rima. *Mothers and Medicine: A Social History of Infant Feeding, 1890–1950*. Madison: University of Wisconsin Press, 1987.

Armstrong, D. "The House-Fly and Diarrheal Disease among Children." *Journal of the American Medical Association* 62 (1914): 200–1.

Ashliman, D. L. "The Pied Piper of Hameln and Related Legends from Other Towns." 1999–2011. Online at http://www.pitt.edu/~dash/hameln.html. Accessed on May 31, 2012.

Ashton, A. Daniel, and William B. Jackson. "Field Testing of Rodenticides in a Resistant-Rat Area of Chicago." *Pest Control* (August 1979): 14–16.

Association for Improving the Condition of the Poor. *Flies and Diarrheal Disease*. New York: Department of Health, 1915.

———. *Flies and Diarrheal Disease*. New York: Department of Health, 1914.

Atlas, John, and Peter Dreier. "From Projects to Communities: How to Redeem Public Housing." *The American Prospect* 10 (1992): 74–85.

Austen, E. "The House-Fly, Its Life History, Importance As a Disease Carrier, and Practical Measures for Its Suppression." *British Museum Economics Series* (1913): 1–12.

Back, E. A., and R. T. Cotton. *Hydrocyanic Acid Gas As a Fumigant for Destroying Household Insects*. Washington, D.C.: Government Printing Office, 1932.

Baker, Richard L. "Integrated Pest Management: Accentuate the 'I'." *Pest Management* (August 1982): 19–21.

Bakker, Isabella, and Rachel Silvey. *Beyond States and Markets: The Challenges of Social Reproduction*. London: Routledge, 2008.

Baltimore Redevelopment Commission. *The Baltimore Plan*. 20 minutes. Evanston, Ill.: Encyclopedia Britannica Films, 1953.

Bartlett, Arthur. "Chemical Marvels Take the 'Bugs' out of Living." *Popular Science* (May 1945): 150–54.

Beattie, W. R. "The Use of Hydrocyanic Acid Gas for Exterminating Household Insects." *Science* 14, no. 247 (1901): 285–89.

Beauregard, Robert A. "If Only the City Could Speak: The Politics of Representation." In *Spatial Practices: Critical Explorations in Social/Spatial Theory*, edited by Helen Liggett and David C. Perry, 59–80. Thousand Oaks, Calif.: Sage, 1995.

———. *Voices of Decline: The Postwar Fate of U.S. Cities.* New York: Routledge, 2003.

Beck, Alan M. *The Ecology of Stray Dogs: A Study of Free-Ranging Urban Animals.* Baltimore, Md.: York Press, 1973.

Becker, D. "The Visitor to the New York City Poor, 1843–1920." PhD dissertation, Columbia University, 1960.

Beecher, Catharine, and Harriet Beecher Stowe. *The American Woman's Home.* New Brunswick, N.J.: Rutgers University Press, 2002.

Bengelsdorf, Irving. "Boric Acid Held Best Roach Killer: Cheap, Safe Powder Tests Better Than Potent Insecticides." *The Apartment Journal* (1966): 20–21.

Bernton, Harry S., and Halla Brown. "Cockroach Allergy II: The Relation of Infestation to Sensitization." *Southern Medical Journal* 60 (1967): 852–55.

———. "Insect Allergy: Preliminary Studies of the Cockroach." *Journal of Allergy* 35 (1964): 506–13.

Biehler, Dawn Day. "Flies, Manure, and Window Screens: Medical Entomology and Environmental Reform in Early-Twentieth-Century U.S. Cities." *Journal of Historical Geography* 36 (2010): 68–78.

———. "Permeable Homes: A Historical Political Ecology of Insects and Pesticides in U.S. Public Housing." *Geoforum* 40 (2009): 1014–23.

Bishopp, F. C., W. E. Dove, and D. C. Parman. "Points of Economic Importance in the Biology of the House Fly." *Journal of Economic Entomology* 8 (1915): 65–69.

Bitter, Ruth S., and O. B. Williams. "Enteric Organisms from the American Cockroach." *Journal of Infectious Disease* 85 (1949): 87–90.

Blattner, Russell J. "Comments on Current Literature: Rat-Bite Fever." *Journal of Pediatrics* 67 (1965): 884–86.

Bloom, Nicholas. *Public Housing That Worked: New York in the Twentieth Century.* Philadelphia: University of Pennsylvania Press, 2008.

Blum, Elizabeth. *Love Canal Revisited: Race, Class, and Gender in Environmental Activism.* Lawrence: University of Kansas Press, 2008.

———. "Women, Environmental Rationale, and Activism during the Progressive Era." In *"To Love the Wind and the Rain": African-Americans and Environmental History*, edited by Dianne Glave and Mark Stoll, 77–92. Pittsburgh: University of Pittsburgh Press, 2006.

Blum, E. W. "Garbage Disposal Habits Improve under Penalty Plan." *Journal of Housing* 5, no. 4 (1948): 111–12.

Blunt, Alyson, and Robyn Dowling. *Home.* London: Routledge, 2006.

Bocker, Edward D. "Public Health Value of the Exterminating and Fumigating Industry." *Exterminators Log,* April 1934, 16.

Bocking, Stephen. *Ecologists and Environmental Politics: A History of Contemporary Ecology.* New Haven, Conn.: Yale University Press, 1997.

Bondi, Liz. "Gender, Class, and Urban Space: Public and Private Space in Contemporary Urban Landscapes." *Urban Geography* 19 (1998): 160–85.

Borchert, James. *Alley Life in Washington: Family, Community, Religion, and Folklife in the City, 1850–1970.* Champaign: University of Illinois Press, 1982.

Bowly, Devereaux, Jr. *The Poorhouse: Subsidized Housing in Chicago, 1895–1976.* Carbondale: Southern Illinois University Press, 1978.

Braun, Bruce. "Writing a More-Than-Human Urban Geography." *Progress in Human Geography* 29 (2005): 635–50.

Brenner, Barbara, Steven Markowitz, Maribel Rivera, Harry Romero, Matthew Weeks, Elizabeth Sanchez, Elena Deych, Anjali Garg, James Godbold, Mary S. Wolff, Philip J. Landrigan, and Gertrud Berkowitz. "Integrated Pest Management in an Urban Community: A Successful Partnership for Prevention." *Environmental Health Perspectives* 111 (2003): 1649–53.

Brewer, Earl, and Robert J. Haggerty. "Toxic Hazards: Rat Poisons III—Thallium, Strychnine, and ANTU." *New England Journal of Medicine* 259 (1958): 1038–40.

Brooks, Joe E., and Alan M. Bowerman. "Analysis of the Susceptibilities of Several Populations of *Rattus Norvegicus* to Warfarin." *Journal of Hygiene* 73 (1974): 401–8.

———. "Anticoagulant Resistance in Wild Norway Rats in New York." *Journal of Hygiene* 71 (1973): 217–22.

Brown, Rodman M. "The Relationship between a Building Official and Pest Control Operators." *Pests* (March 1939): 12–13.

Brown, Roscoe C. "The National Negro Health Week Movement." *Journal of Negro Education* 6 (1937): 553–64.

Brues, Charles T. "Insects As Carriers of Infection: An Entomological Study of the 1916 Epidemic." In *A Monograph on the Epidemic of Poliomyelitis (Infantile Paralysis) in New York City in 1916.* New York: M. B. Brown, 1917.

Buettner, William O. "Greeting." *Exterminators Log,* October 1933, 2.

———. "Insurance and the Fumigation Business." *Exterminators Log,* January 1934, 11.

Bulkeley, Harriet, and Nicky Gregson. "Crossing the Threshold: Municipal Waste Policy and Household Waste Generation." *Environment and Planning A* 41 (2009): 929–45.

Bullard, Robert D. *Dumping in Dixie: Race, Class, and Environmental Quality.* Boulder, Colo.: Westview Press, 2000.

Bureau of the Biological Survey. *Report of the Conference of Field Representatives of Economic Investigations.* Conference held in Ogden, Utah, April 23–28, 1928.

Bureau of Entomology and Plant Quarantine. *Cockroaches and Their Control.* Washington, D.C.: Government Printing Office, 1950.

———. *DDT . . . for Control of Household Pests.* Washington, D.C.: Government Printing Office, 1947.

Busvine, James R. "Insecticide Resistance in Bed-bugs." *Bulletin of the World Health Organization* 19 (1959): 1041–52.

Calhoun, John B. *The Ecology and Sociology of the Norway Rat.* Bethesda, Md.: U.S. Public Health Service, 1962.

———. "A Method for Self-Control of Population Growth among Mammals Living in the Wild." *Science* 109, no. 2831 (1949): 333–35.

———. "Mortality and Movement of Brown Rats." *Journal of Wildlife Management* 12 (1948): 167–72.

Califano, Joseph. *The Triumph and Tragedy of Lyndon Johnson: The White House Years.* New York: Simon & Schuster, 1991.

Carlton, E., H. L. Moats, M. Feinberg, P. Shepard, P. Garfinkel, R. Whyatt, and D. Evans. "Pesticide Sales in Low-Income, Minority Neighborhoods." *Journal of Community Health* 29 (2002): 231–44.

Carson, Rachel. *Silent Spring.* Boston: Houghton Mifflin, 1962.

Carter, Eric. "Development Narratives and the Uses of Ecology: Malaria Control in Northwest Argentina, 1890–1940." *Journal of Historical Geography* 33 (2007): 619–50.

———. *Enemy in the Blood: Malaria, Environment, and Development in Argentina.* Tuscaloosa: University of Alabama Press, 2012.

Cassedy, John. *Charles V. Chapin and the Public Health Movement.* Cambridge: Harvard University Press, 1962.

Castree, Noel. "False Antithesis? Marxism, Nature, and Actor-Networks." *Antipode* 34 (2002): 111–46.

Chicago Freedom Movement. "Project Open City." 1966, CFM40 Archive, Middlebury College. Online at http://cfm40.middlebury.edu/files/project%20open%20city.pdf. Accessed on March 29, 2013.

Child, Lydia Maria. *The American Frugal Housewife.* Reprint of twelfth edition, 1833. Bedford, Mass.: Chapman-Billies, 1990.

Childs, James, Brian Schwartz, Tom Ksiazek, R. Ross Graham, James LeDuc, and Gregory Glass. "Risk Factors Associated with Antibodies to Leptospires in Inner-City Residents of Baltimore: A Protective Role for Cats." *American Journal of Public Health* 82 (1992): 597–99.

Childs, James, Gregory Glass, and James LeDuc. "Rodent Sightings and Contacts in an Inner-City Population of Baltimore, Maryland, U.S.A." *Bulletin of the Society of Vector Ecology* 16 (1991): 245–55.

Chipman Chemical Company. "New and Different . . . P-C-H Roach Powder." *Pests and Their Control* (November 1946): 31.

Christian, John J. "In Memoriam: David E. Davis, 1913–1994." *The Auk* 112 (1995): 491–92.

Cirillo, Vincent J. "'Winged Sponges': Houseflies As Carriers of Typhoid Fever in Nineteenth- and Early Twentieth-Century Military Camps." *Perspectives in Biology and Medicine* 49 (2006): 52–63.

City Council of the City of Chicago. "An Ordinance Requiring Dwellings, Tenement Houses, etc., To Be Screened against Flies." *Journal of the Proceedings of the City Council of Chicago* (1917): 319.

———. "An Ordinance Requiring Stables To Be Screened against Flies." *Journal of the Proceedings of the City Council of Chicago* (1917): 320.

City of Milwaukee Health Department. *Pest Control.* Milwaukee: Health Department Housing and Sanitation Division, 1967.

Clark, J. F. M. *Bugs and the Victorians.* New Haven, Conn.: Yale University Press, 2009.

Clinton, James M. "Rats in Urban America." *Public Health Reports* 84, no. 1 (1969): 1–6.

Cobb, N. "The House Fly." *National Geographic* (May 21, 1910): 371–80.

———. "Notes on the Distances Flies Can Travel." *National Geographic* (May 21, 1910): 380–83.

Cobb, W. Bruce. "A Court of Prevention: The Municipal Term Court of the City of New York." *Journal of the American Institute of Criminal Law and Criminology* 11 (1920): 47–59.

Cochran, Donald. "Insecticide Resistance." In *Understanding and Controlling the German Cockroach,* edited by Michael Rust, John Owens, and Donald Reierson, 171–92. New York: Oxford University Press, 1995.

Cole, J. S., R. W. Stoll, and R. J. Bulger. "Rat-Bite Fever: Report of Three Cases." *Annals of Internal Medicine* 71 (1969): 979–81.

Coleman, Rileigh. *The Dirty Rat Coloring Book.* Cleveland, Ohio: Division of Health, Community Action for Youth, 1964.

Collins, James H. "Fighting the Bedbug." *Scientific American* (June 1924): 392, 439.

Committee on the Hygiene of Housing. *An Appraisal Method for Measuring the Quality of Housing: A Yardstick for Health Officers, Housing Officials, and Planners.* New York: American Public Health Association, 1946.

———. *Basic Principles of Healthful Housing.* New York: American Public Health Association, 1941.

Congress, House, "Don't Let the Bed Bugs Bite Act of 2009." 111th Congress, 1st Session, HR 2248, May 5, 2009.

———. "Rat Extermination Act of 1967." H. Res. 749, 90th Cong., 1st session, *Congressional Record* 113 (July 20, 1967): H19548–19556.

Connolly, Joel. "Public Health Aspects of Insect and Rodent Control." *Exterminators Log,* December 1935, 10–13.

Cook, F. C. "Experiments in the Destruction of Fly Larvae in Horse Manure." *Bulletin of the Department of Agriculture* 118 (1914): 1–26.

Coombe, Nancy, and John S. Marr. "Rat Bites Support Need for In-Home Control." *Journal of Environmental Health* 42 (1980): 321–26.

Cossetta, Al. "Editor's Note." *Exterminators Log*, February 1938, 10.

———. "The Importance of Our Profession." *Exterminators Log*, April 1935, 4.

Cousineau, Aime, and F. G. Legg. "Hydrocyanic Acid Gas and Other Toxic Gases in Commercial Fumigation." *American Journal of Public Health* 25 (1935): 277–87.

Cox, G. L., F. C. Lewis, and E. F. Glynn. "The Number and Varieties of Bacteria Carried by the Common House Fly in Sanitary and Insanitary City Areas." *Journal of Hygiene* 12 (1912): 290–319.

Crabtree, Louise. "Sustainability Begins at Home? An Ecological Exploration of Sub/Urban Australian Community-Focused Housing Initiatives." *Geoforum* 36 (2005): 519–35.

Craddock, Susan. *City of Plagues: Disease, Poverty, and Deviance in San Francisco.* Minneapolis: University of Minnesota Press, 2000.

Creel, R. H., and F. M. Faget. "Cyanide Gas for the Destruction of Insects with Special Reference to Mosquitoes, Fleas, Body Lice, and Bedbugs." *Public Health Reports* Reprint 343 (1916): 1464–75.

Creel, R. H., F. M. Faget, and W. D. Wrightson. "Hydrocyanic Acid Gas: Its Practical Use As a Routine Fumigant." *Public Health Reports* 30 (1915): 3537–50.

Crook, T. "Sanitary Inspection and the Public Sphere in Late Victorian and Edwardian Britain: A Case Study in Liberal Governance." *Social History* 32 (2007): 369–93.

Croy, Mae Savell. *Putnam's Household Handbook.* New York: Putnam, 1916.

Daniel, Pete. *Toxic Drift: Pesticides and Health in the Post–World War II South.* Baton Rouge: Louisiana State University Press, 2005.

Davies, John E., Walter F. Edmundson, and Americo Raffonelli. "The Role of House Dust in Human DDT Pollution." *American Journal of Public Health* 65 (1975): 53–57.

Davis, David E. "A Comparison of Reproductive Potential of Two Rat Populations." *Ecology* 32 (1951): 469–75.

———. "Principles of Rat Management." *Pest Control* (November 1948): 9–12.

———. "The Relation between the Level of Population and the Prevalence of Leptospira, Salmonella, and Capillaria in Norway Rats." *Ecology* 32 (1951): 465–68.

Davis, David E., and W. T. Fales. "The Distribution of Rats in Baltimore, Maryland." *American Journal of Hygiene* 49 (1949): 247–54.

———. "The Rat Population of Baltimore, 1949." *American Journal of Hygiene* 52 (1950): 143–46.

Davis, David E., John T. Emlen, and Allen W. Stokes. "Studies on the Home Range of the Brown Rat." *Journal of Mammalogy* 29 (1948): 207–25.

Davis, Devra L., and A. K. Ahmed. "Exposures from Indoor Spraying of Chlorpyrifos Pose Greater Health Risks to Children Than Currently Estimated." *Environmental Health Perspectives* 106 (1998): 299–301.

Davis, Frederick. "Unraveling the Complexities of Joint Toxicity of Multiple Chemicals at the Tox Lab and the FDA." *Environmental History* 13 (2008): 674–83.

Davis, J. Wilfrid, Wilmer Schulze, C. LeRoy Ewing, and George W. Schucker. "Endemic Typhus in Baltimore." *Southern Medical Journal* 41 (1948): 21–26.

Defoe, Daniel. *A Journal of the Plague Year.* 1722; reprint, New York: Random House, 2001.

DiChiro, Giovanna. "Nature As Community." In *Uncommon Ground: Rethinking the Human Place in Nature*, edited by William Cronon, 298–320. New York: Norton, 1996.

Division of Insects Affecting Man and Animals. *Cockroaches and Their Control.* Washington, D.C.: Government Printing Office, 1950.

Doane, Rennie. *Insects and Disease: A Popular Account of the Way in Which Insects May Spread or Cause Some of Our Common Diseases.* New York: Henry Holt, 1910.

Domosh, Mona. "Geography and Gender: Home, Again?" *Progress in Human Geography* 22 (1998): 276–82.

Drinker, P. "Hydrocyanic Acid Gas Poisoning by Absorption through the Skin." *Journal of Industrial Hygiene* 14 (1932): 1–2.

Drummond, David C. "Rats Resistant to Warfarin." *New Scientist* (June 23, 1966): 771–72.

Duffy, John. *The Sanitarians: A History of American Public Health.* Urbana: University of Illinois Press, 1990.

Dungy, Camille. *Black Nature: Four Centuries of African American Nature Poetry.* Athens: University of Georgia Press, 2009.

Dunlap, Thomas. *DDT: Scientists, Citizens, and Public Policy.* Princeton, N.J.: Princeton University Press, 1981.

Durant, Sam, ed. *Black Panther: The Revolutionary Art of Emory Douglas.* New York: Rizzoli, 2007.

Durr, W. Theodore. "The Conscience of a City: A History of the Citizens' Planning and Housing Association and Efforts to Improve Housing for the Poor in Baltimore, Maryland, 1937–1954." PhD dissertation, Johns Hopkins University, 1972.

Dyl, Joanna. "The War on Rats versus the Right to Keep Chickens: Plague and the Paving of San Francisco, 1907–1908." In *The Nature of Cities: Culture, Landscape, and Urban Space*, edited by Andrew Isenberg, 38–61. Rochester, N.Y.: University of Rochester Press, 2006.

Easterbrook, Judith, Timothy Shields, Sabra Klein, and Gregory Glass. "Norway Rat Population in Baltimore, Maryland in 2004." *Vector-Borne and Zoonotic Diseases* 5 (2005): 296–99.

Ebeling, Walter. "Past, Present, and Future Directions in the Management of Structure-Infesting Insects." In *Perspectives in Urban Entomology*, edited by Gordon W. Frankie and Carl S. Koehler, 221–47. New York: Academic Press, 1978.

————. *Urban Entomology.* Berkeley: University of California Division of Agricultural Sciences, 1975.

Ebeling, Walter, Donald A. Reierson, and R. E. Wagner. "Influence of Repellency on the Efficacy of Blatticides II. Laboratory Experiments with German Cockroaches." *Journal of Economic Entomology* 60 (1967): 1375–90.

Ebeling, Walter, R. E. Wagner, and Donald A. Reierson. "Influence of Repellency on the Efficacy of Blatticides I. Learned Modification of Behavior of the German Cockroach." *Journal of Economic Entomology* 59 (1966): 1374–88.

Elliott, S. Maria. *Household Hygiene.* Chicago: American School of Home Economics, 1905.

Emlen, John T. "Baltimore's Community Rat Control Program." *American Journal of Public Health* 37 (1947): 721–27.

Emlen, John T., Allen W. Stokes, and Charles P. Winsor. "The Rate of Recovery of Decimated Populations of Brown Rats in Nature." *Ecology* 29 (1948): 133–45.

Essex, John J. "Rat Infestation and Rodent Control." In *The Chicago-Cook County Health Survey,* 316–36. New York: Columbia University Press, 1949.

Esten, W., and C. Mason. "Sources of Bacteria in Milk." *Storrs Agricultural Experiment Station Bulletin* 51 (1908): 94–98.

Fairclough, Adam. *Better Day Coming: Blacks and Equality, 1890–2000.* New York: Viking, 2001.

Fee, Elizabeth. *Disease and Discovery: A History of the Johns Hopkins School of Hygiene and Public Health, 1916–1939.* Baltimore, Md.: Johns Hopkins University Press, 1987.

Fee, Elizabeth, Linda Shopes, and Linda Zeidman. *The Baltimore Book: New Views of Local History, Critical Perspectives on the Past.* Philadelphia: Temple University Press, 1991.

Felt, E. P. "Methods of Controlling the House Fly and Thus Preventing the Dissemination of Disease." *New York Medical Journal* (April 2, 1910): 685–87.

Felton-Martin, Zora, and Gail Lewis. *Different Drummer: John Kinard and the Anacostia Museum.* Washington, D.C.: Anacostia Museum, 1989.

Finklea, J. F., J. E. Keil, S. H. Sandifer, and R. H. Gadsden. "Pesticides and Pesticide Hazards in Urban Households." *Journal of the South Carolina Medical Association* 65 (1969): 31–33.

Flanagan, Maureen. *Seeing with Their Hearts: Chicago Women and the Vision of a Good City, 1871–1933.* Princeton, N.J.: Princeton University Press, 2002.

Flexner, Simon, and Paul Clark. "Contamination of the Fly with Poliomyelitis Virus." *Journal of the American Medical Association* 56 (1911): 1717–18.

Flint, Mary Louise, and Robert van den Bosch. *Introduction to Integrated Pest Management.* New York: Plenum Press, 1981.

Foreman, Christopher. *The Promise and Peril of Environmental Justice.* Washington, D.C.: Brookings Institution, 1998.

Fossum, John C. "Rent Withholding and the Improvement of Substandard Housing." *California Law Review* 53 (1965): 304–36.

Foucault, Michel. "American Neo-liberalism (I)." In *The Birth of Biopolitics: Lectures at the College de France, 1978–1979*. New York: Macmillan, 2008.

Frankel, Noralee, and Nancy Dye, eds. *Gender, Class, Race, and Reform in the Progressive Era*. Lexington: University of Kentucky Press, 1994.

Frankie, Gordon W., and Hanna Levenson. "Insect Problems and Insecticide Use: Public Opinion, Information, and Behavior." In *Perspectives in Urban Entomology*, edited by Gordon W. Frankie and Carl S. Koehler, 359–99. New York: Academic Press, 1978.

Frantz, Stephen, and Constance Padula. "Recent Developments in Anticoagulant Rodenticide Resistance Studies: Surveillance and Application in the United States." *Proceedings of the Ninth Vertebrate Pest Conference* (1980): 80–88.

Frings, H. "An Ounce of Prevention." *Pests and Their Control* (February 1948): 24–26.

Fuerst, J. S. *When Public Housing Was Paradise: Building Community in Chicago*. Champaign-Urbana: University of Illinois Press, 2005.

Fuerst, J. S., and Rosalyn Kaplan. "Chicago's Public Housing Program Saves Babies' Lives." *The Child* (June–July 1951): 178–81.

Gaines T. B., and W. J. Hayes, "Bait Shyness to ANTU in Wild Norway Rats." *Public Health Reports* 67 (1952): 306–11.

Gaiter, Colette. "The Revolution Will Be Visualized: Emory Douglas in the Black Panther." *Bad Subjects* 65 (2004). Online at http://bad.eserver.org/issues/2004/65/gaiter.html. Accessed on November 30, 2012.

Gandy, Matthew. *Concrete and Clay: Reworking Nature in New York City*. Cambridge, Mass.: MIT Press, 2002.

Garcia, Daniel, Mark Corbett, James Sublett, Stephen Pollard, Joseph Meiners, John Karibo, Hobert Pence, and Joseph Petrosko. "Cockroach Allergy in Kentucky: A Comparison of Inner-City, Suburban, and Rural Small Town Populations." *Annals of Allergy* 72 (1994): 203–8.

Gardner-Santana, L. C., D. E. Norris, C. M. Fornadel, E. R. Hinson, S. L. Klein, and G. E. Glass. "Commensal Ecology, Urban Landscapes, and Their Influence on the Genetic Characteristics of City-Dwelling Norway Rats (*Rattus norvegicus*)." *Molecular Ecology* 18 (2009): 2766–78.

Gates, Eleanor. *Swat the Fly*. New York: Arrow, 1915.

General Accounting Office. *HOPE VI Resident Issues and Changes in Neighborhoods Surrounding Grant Sites*. Washington, D.C.: General Accounting Office, 2003.

———. *The Urban Rat Control Program Is in Trouble*. Washington, D.C.: General Accounting Office, 1975.

Geong, H. "Carving a Niche for Medical Entomology." *American Entomologist* 47 (2001): 236–43.

———. "Exerting Control: Biology and Bureaucracy in the Development of American Entomology, 1870–1930." PhD dissertation, University of Wisconsin–Madison, 1999.

Gill, Andrea. "Moving to Integration? The Origins of Chicago's Gautreaux Program and the Limits of Voucher-Based Housing Mobility." *Journal of Urban History* 38 (2012): 662–86.

Gillette, Howard. *Between Justice and Beauty: Race, Planning, and the Failure of Urban Policy in Washington, D.C.* Philadelphia: University of Pennsylvania Press, 2006.

Glave, Dianne. *Rooted in the Earth: Reclaiming the African-American Environmental Heritage.* Chicago: Lawrence Hill Books, 2010.

———. "Rural African-American Women, Gardening, and Progressive Reform in the South." In *"To Love the Wind and the Rain": African-Americans and Environmental History*, edited by Dianne Glave and Mark Stoll, 37–50. Pittsburgh: University of Pittsburgh Press, 2006.

Glave, Dianne, and Mark Stoll, eds., *"To Love the Wind and the Rain": African-Americans and Environmental History.* Pittsburgh: University of Pittsburgh Press, 2005.

Goldberg, David Theo. *The Racial State.* Malden, Mass.: Blackwell, 2002.

Goldfeld, Abraham. *The Diary of a Housing Manager.* Chicago: National Association of Housing Officials, 1938.

———. *Toward Fuller Living through Public Housing and Leisure Time Activities.* New York: National Public Housing Conference, 1934.

Golley, Frank B. *A History of the Ecosystem Concept in Ecology.* New Haven, Conn.: Yale University Press, 1993.

Gordon, David George. *The Compleat Cockroach.* Berkeley: Ten Speed Press, 1996.

Gottlieb, Robert. *Forcing the Spring: The Transformation of the American Environmental Movement.* Washington, D.C.: Island Press, 1993.

Gould, G. E. "Recent Developments in Roach Control." *Pests* (December 1943): 12–13, 22–23.

Grad, Frank P. *Legal Remedies for Housing Code Violations.* Washington, D.C.: National Commission on Urban Problems, 1968.

Graham, Frank. *Since Silent Spring.* Boston: Houghton Mifflin, 1970.

Graham-Smith, G. S. *Flies in Relation to Disease: Non-bloodsucking Flies.* Cambridge: Cambridge University Press, 1913.

Greenberg, B. "Flies and Disease." *Scientific American* 213, no. 1 (1965): 92–99.

Greenberg, Stuart. *Cockroach Allergen Reduction Using Precision-Targeted IPM and the Lead Dust Cleaning Protocol.* Cleveland, Ohio: Environmental Health Watch, 2003.

Greene, Ann Norton. *Horses at Work: Harnessing Power in Industrial America.* Cambridge: Harvard University Press, 2008.

Grogan, Paul, and Tony Proscio. "The Fall (and Rise) of Public Housing."

Harvard University Joint Center for Housing Studies, September 1, 2000. Online at http://www.jchs.harvard.edu/research/publications/fall-and-rise-public-housing. Accessed on March 21, 2013.

Gumbs, Alexis Pauline. "We Can Learn To Mother Ourselves: The Queer Survival of Black Feminism." PhD dissertation, Duke University, 2010.

Guthman, Julie. "If They Only Knew: Color-blindness and Universalism in California Alternative Food Institutions." *Professional Geographer* 60 (2008): 387–97.

Guthman, Julie, and E. Melanie DuPuis. "Embodying Neoliberalism: Economy, Culture, and the Politics of Fat." *Environment and Planning D* 24 (2006): 427–48.

Hackworth, Jason. "Public Housing and the Rescaling of Regulation in the U.S.A." *Environment and Planning A* 35 (2003): 531–49.

Haggerty, Robert J. "Toxic Hazards: Rat Poisons III—Thallium, Strychnine, and ANTU." *New England Journal of Medicine* 259 (1958): 1038–40.

Hall, Maurice. "The Bedbug." *Public Health Reports Supplements* 129 (1937): 1–7.

Hall, Peter Geoffrey. *Cities of Tomorrow: An Intellectual History of Urban Planning and Design in the Twentieth Century.* Third edition. Oxford: Blackwell, 2002.

Hamilton, Alice. "The Common House Fly As a Carrier of Typhoid." *Journal of the American Medical Association* 42 (1904): 1034.

———. "The Fly As a Carrier of Typhoid." *Journal of the American Medical Association* 40 (1903): 576–83.

Hamilton, Alice, Maud Gernon, and Gertrude Howe. *An Inquiry into the Causes of the Recent Epidemic of Typhoid Fever in Chicago.* Chicago: City Homes Association, 1903.

Hanlon, James. "Review of *Public Housing That Worked: New York in the Twentieth Century* by Nicholas Dagen Bloom." *H-Urban, H-Net Reviews* (September 2008). Online at http://www.h-net.org/reviews/showrev.pho?id=15772. Accessed on August 15, 2012.

———. "Success by Design: HOPE VI, New Urbanism, and the Neoliberal Transformation of Public Housing in the United States." *Environment and Planning A* 42 (2010): 80–98.

Haraway, Donna. *The Companion Species Manifesto: Dogs, People, and Significant Otherness.* Chicago: Prickly Paradigm, 2003.

———. "Situated Knowledges: The Science Question in Feminism and the Privilege of Partial Perspective." In *Simians, Cyborgs, and Women: The Reinvention of Nature,* 183–201. New York: Routledge, 1991.

———. *When Species Meet.* Minneapolis: University of Minnesota Press, 2007.

Harding, Sandra. *The Science Question in Feminism.* Ithaca, N.Y.: Cornell University Press, 1986.

Hartigan, R. "Exterminator's Tort Liability for Personal Injury or Death." *American Law Reports* 4 (1983): 987.

Hartnack, Hugo. "Some Experiences with the Chicago Fumigating Ordinance." *Exterminators Log,* July 1934, 7.

——. *202 Common Household Pests of North America*. Chicago: Hartnack Publishing, 1939.

Harvey, David. *Justice, Nature, and the Geography of Difference*. Cambridge, Mass.: Blackwell Publishers, 1996.

——. *Spaces of Hope*. Berkeley: University of California Press, 2000.

Harvey, William C., and Harry Hill. *Insect Pests*. Brooklyn, N.Y.: Chemical Publishing Company, 1941.

Hays, R. Allen. *The Federal Government and Urban Housing: Ideology and Change in Public Policy*. Albany: State University of New York Press, 1995.

Hayward, E. "The Fly As a Carrier of Tuberculosis Infection." *New York Medical Journal* (1904): 643–44.

Hazlett, Maril. "The Story of *Silent Spring* and the Ecological Turn." PhD dissertation, University of Kansas, 2003.

——. "'Woman vs. Man vs. Bugs': Gender and Popular Ecology in Early Reactions to *Silent Spring*." *Environmental History* 9 (2004): 701–29.

Herms, W. "The House Fly in Its Relation to Public Health." *Bulletin of the College of Agriculture* [California], 1911.

Herrick, Glenn. *Insects Injurious to the Household and Annoying to Man*. New York: Macmillan, 1914.

Heynen, Nikolas C. "Bending the Bars of Empire from Every Ghetto to Feed the Kids: The Black Panther Party's Radical Anti-Hunger Politics of Social Reproduction and Scale." *Annals of the Association of American Geographers* 99 (2009): 406–22.

Hilliard, David, ed. *The Black Panther Party: Service to the People Programs*. Albuquerque: University of New Mexico Press, 2008.

Hinman, Sarah. "Spatial and Temporal Structure of Typhoid in Washington, D.C." PhD dissertation, Louisiana State University, 2007.

Hockenyos, George L. "Bedbug Spraying." *Pests* (May 1940): 12.

——. "The Era of Pest Prevention." *Pests and Their Control* (August 1946): 8, 10.

Hodge, C. F. "Exterminating the Fly." *California Outlook* (1911).

——. "House Flies: Outline for Practical Lessons and Plans for Flyless Homes." Pamphlet, University of Oregon Archives, 1913.

——. "How You Can Make Your Home, Town, or City, Flyless." *Nature and Culture* 3 (1911): 9–23.

——. *Nature Study and Life*. Boston: Ginn and Company, 1902.

——. "A Plan to Exterminate the Typhoid or Filth-disease Fly." *La Follette's Weekly* 3 (1911): 7–8.

——. "A Practical Point in the Study of Typhoid or Filth Fly." *Nature Study Review* 6 (1910): 195–99.

Hodge, C. F., and Jean Dawson. *Civic Biology*. Boston: Ginn and Company, 1918.

Hoffman, Alexander von. "A Study in Contradictions: The Origins and Legacy of the Housing Act of 1949." *Housing Policy Debate* 11 (2000): 299–326.

Hoffman, William S., William I. Fishbein, and Morten B. Andelman. "The

Pesticide Content of Human Fat Tissue." *Archives of Environmental Health* 9 (1964): 387–94.

Holsendorf, B. E. "Rat Harborage and Rat Proofing." *Public Health Reports Supplements* 131 (1937): 75–81.

Holston, James. *The Modernist City: An Anthropological Critique of Brasília*. Chicago: University of Chicago Press, 1989.

hooks, bell. "Homeplace: A Site of Resistance." In *Yearning: Race, Gender, and Cultural Politics*, 41–50. Cambridge, Mass.: South End Press, 1999.

Houston Branch of the Black Panther Party. "Houston Branch Implements People's Free Pest Control Program." *The Black Panther*, September 25, 1972, 8.

Howard, L. O. "A Contribution to the Study of the Insect Fauna of Human Excrement." *Proceedings of the Washington Academy of Sciences* 2 (1900): 541–604.

———. "Economic Loss to the People of the United States through Insects That Carry Disease." *USDA Bureau of Entomology Bulletin* 78 (1909).

———. *Fighting the Insects*. New York: Century, 1931.

———. *The House Fly: Disease Carrier*. New York: Frederick Stokes, 1911.

———. *Progress in Economic Entomology*. Washington, D.C.: Department of Agriculture, 1899.

Howard, L. O., and C. Popenoe. "Hydrocyanic Acid-Gas against Household Insects." *USDA Farmers' Bulletin* 163 (1912).

Howard, L. O., and F. C. Bishopp. "The House Fly and How to Suppress It." *USDA Farmers' Bulletin* 1408 (1925).

Hoy, Suellen M. *Chasing Dirt: The American Pursuit of Cleanliness*. New York: Oxford University Press, 1995.

———. "Municipal Housekeeping: The Role of Women in Improving Urban Sanitation Practices, 1880–1917." In *Pollution and Reform in American Cities*, edited by Martin V. Melosi, 173–98. Austin: University of Texas Press, 1980.

Hubbard, Matt. "Audition Day." *30 Rock*, directed by Beth McCarthy Miller. November 5, 2009.

Humphreys, Margaret. *Malaria: Poverty, Race, and Public Health in the United States*. Baltimore, Md.: Johns Hopkins University Press, 2001.

———. *Yellow Fever and the South*. Baltimore, Md.: Johns Hopkins University Press, 1999.

Hunter, Laura Thorne. *Domestic Pests: What They Are and How to Remove Them*. London: John Bale and Sons, 1938.

Hurley, Andrew. *Environmental Inequalities: Class, Race, and Industrial Pollution in Gary, Indiana, 1945–1980*. Chapel Hill: University of North Carolina Press, 1995.

———. "Floods, Rats, and Toxic Waste: Allocating Environmental Hazards since World War II." In *Common Fields: An Environmental History of St. Louis* edited by Andrew Hurley, 241–62. Saint Louis: Missouri Historical Society Press, 1997.

Husband, Julie, and Jim O'Loughlin. *Daily Life in the Industrial United States, 1870–1900*. Westport, Conn.: Greenwood, 2004.

Huttman, E. D. "Public Housing: The Negative Psychological Effects on Family Living." Paper presented at the American Orthopsychiatric Association Annual Meeting, Washington, D.C., March 21–24, 1971.

Hynes, H. Patricia, Doug Brugge, Julie Watts, and Jody Lally. "Public Health and the Physical Environment in Boston Public Housing: A Community-Based Survey and Action Agenda." *Planning Practice and Research* 15 (2000): 31–49.

Hynes, H. Patricia, Doug Brugge, Neal-Dra Osgood, John Snell, Jose Vallarino, and John Spengler. "'Where Does the Damp Come From?' Investigations into the Indoor Environment and Respiratory Health in Boston Public Housing." *Journal of Public Health Policy* 24 (2003): 401–26.

Ibitayo, O. "Relocated Citizens' Perceptions and Attitudes Regarding Indoor Application of Toxic Agricultural Pesticides." *Journal of Contingencies and Crisis Management* 8 (2000): 141–50.

Jackson, Daniel. *Pollution of New York Harbor As a Menace to Health by the Dissemination of Intestinal Diseases through the Agency of the Common House Fly*. New York: Merchant's Association, 1907.

Jackson, Kenneth. *Crabgrass Frontier: The Suburbanization of the United States*. New York: Oxford University Press, 1987.

Jackson, Mandi Isaacs. "Harlem's Rent Strike and Rat War: Representation, Housing Access, and Tenant Resistance in New York, 1958–1964." *American Studies* 47 (2006): 53–79.

Jackson, William B. "Anticoagulant Resistance in Europe: Part I." *Pest Control* (March 1969): 51–55.

———. "Anticoagulant Resistance in Europe: Part II." *Pest Control* (April 1969): 40–43.

———. "Food Habits of Baltimore, Maryland, Cats in Relation to Rat Populations." *Journal of Mammalogy* 32 (1951): 458–61.

Jackson, William B., and Dale E. Kaukeinen. "The Problem of Anticoagulant Resistance in the United States." Paper presented at the Fifth Vertebrate Pest Conference, Fresno, California, March 7–9, 1972.

Jackson, William B., J. E. Brooks, A. M. Bowerman, and Dale E. Kaukeinen. "Anticoagulant Resistance in Norway Rats As Found in U.S. Cities: Part I." *Pest Control* (April 1975): 12–16.

———. "Anticoagulant Resistance in Norway Rats As Found in U.S. Cities: Part II." *Pest Control* (May 1975): 14–24.

Jackson, William B., P. T. Spear, and C. Wright. "Resistance of Norway Rats to Anticoagulant Rodenticides Confirmed in the United States." *Pest Control* (1971): 13–14.

Jaeger, E. C. "Rodent Control and Rat-proofing of Buildings." *Exterminators Log*, June 1935, 12–13.

Janssen, W. A., and S. E. Wedberg. "The Common House Roach, *Blattella germanica* Linn., As a Potential Vector of *Salmonella typhimurium* and *Salmonella typhosa.*" *American Journal of Tropical Medicine and Hygiene* 1 (1952): 337–43.

Jervis, J. Johnstone. "Disinfestation of Bug-Infested Furniture by Hydrocyanic Acid." *Public Health* 48 (1935): 203–7.

Johnson, Daniel. "Illegal Use of Methyl Parathion Endangers Detroit Area Residents." *Michigan Toxics Watch* (summer 1995).

Johnson, Lyndon B. *Statement by the President on the Rent Supplement Program upon Signing the Independent Offices Appropriation Bill.* University of California, 1966. Online at http://www.presidency.ucsb.edu/ws/print.php?pid=27836. Accessed on November 30, 2012.

Johnson, M. S., and A. J. Hill. "Partial Resistance of a Strain of Bedbugs to DDT Residual." *Medical News Letter* 12 (1948): 26–28.

Johnson, Ralph J., Huntington Williams, and Roy McCaldin. "The Quality of Housing 'before' and 'after' Rehabilitation." *American Journal of Public Health and the Nation's Health* 2 (1958): 189–96.

Kaika, Maria. *City of Flows: Modernity, Nature, and the City.* New York: Routledge, 2005.

———. "Interrogating the Geographies of the Familiar: Domesticating Nature and Constructing the Autonomy of the Modern Home." *International Journal of Urban and Regional Research* 28 (2004): 265–86.

Kaika, Maria, and Erik Swyngedouw. "Fetishizing the Modern City: The Phantasmagoria of Urban Technological Networks." *International Journal of Urban and Regional Research* 24, no. 1 (2000): 120–38.

Kang, Bann, Charles Wu, and Jessie Johnson. "Characteristics and Diagnoses of Cockroach-Sensitive Bronchial Asthma." *Annals of Allergy* 68 (1992): 237–44.

Kang, Bann, Jessie Johnson, and Chris Veres-Thorner. "Atopic Profile of Inner-City Asthma with a Comparative Analysis on the Cockroach-Sensitive and Ragweed-Sensitive Subgroups." *Journal of Allergy and Clinical Immunology* 92 (1993): 802–11.

Kang, Bann, J. Jones, J. Johnson, and I. J. Kang. "Analysis of Indoor Environment and Atopic Allergy in Urban Populations with Bronchial Asthma." *Annals of Allergy* 62 (1989): 30–34.

Kass, Daniel, Audrey Thier, Jessica Leighton, James Cone, and Nancy Jeffrey. "Developing a Comprehensive Pesticide Health Effects Tracking System for an Urban Setting: New York City's Approach." *Environmental Health Perspectives* 112 (2004): 1419–23.

Keil, J. E., W. Weston, C. B. Loadholt, S. H. Sandifer, and J. J. Colcolough. "DDT and DDE Residues in Blood from Children, South Carolina—1970." *Pesticide Monitoring Journal* 6 (1972): 1–3.

Keiner, Christine. "Wartime Rat Control, Rodent Ecology, and the Rise and Fall of Chemical Rodenticides." *Endeavour* 29 (2005): 119–25.

Kellogg, Vernon. *American Insects.* New York: Holt and Company, 1908.

Kinard, John, and Esther Nighbert. "The Anacostia Neighborhood Museum, Smithsonian Institution, Washington, D.C." *Museum International* 24 (1972): 103–9.

Kittredge, Mabel Hyde. *Housekeeping Notes: How to Furnish and Keep House in a Tenement Flat*. Boston: Whitcomb and Barrows, 1911.

Klee, Jeffrey. "Public Housing and the Power of Architecture." MA thesis, University of Delaware, 2001.

Klein, Woody. *Who Has Seen the Slums?* New York: Citizens' Housing and Planning Council, 1959.

Knupfer, Anne Meis. *Toward a Tenderer Humanity and a Nobler Womanhood: African-American Women's Clubs in Turn-of-the-Century Chicago*. New York: NYU Press, 1996.

Kober, George. *The History and Development of the Housing Movement in the District of Columbia*. Washington, D.C.: Washington Sanitary Homes Company, 1907.

———. *Report of the Committee on Social Betterment*. Washington, D.C.: President's Homes Commission, 1908.

———. "Report on the Prevalence of Typhoid Fever in the District of Columbia." In *Report of the Health Officer of the District of Columbia*, 252–92. Washington, D.C.: Department of Health, 1895.

Kogan, Marcos. "Integrated Pest Management: Historical Perspectives and Contemporary Developments." *Annual Reviews in Entomology* 43 (1998): 243–70.

Kohlstedt, Sally Gregory. *Teaching Children Science: Hands-On Nature Study in North America, 1890–1930*. Chicago: University of Chicago Press, 2010.

Kotlowitz, Alexander. *There Are No Children Here*. New York: Doubleday, 1991.

Kotz, Nick. *Judgment Days: Lyndon Baines Johnson, Martin Luther King Jr., and the Laws That Changed America*. Boston: Houghton Mifflin, 2005.

Kozol, Jonathan. *Death at an Early Age: The Destruction of the Hearts and Minds of Negro Children in the Boston Public Schools*. New York: Plume, 1967.

Krauss, Celene. "Challenging Power: Toxic Waste Protests and the Politicization of White, Working-Class Women." In *Community Activism and Feminist Politics: Organizing across Race, Class, and Gender*, edited by N. A. Naples, 129–50. New York: Routledge, 1998.

Kraut, Alan M. *Silent Travelers: Germs, Genes, and the "Immigrant Menace."* Baltimore, Md.: Johns Hopkins University Press, 1995.

Landrigan, Philip J., Luz Claudio, Steven Markowitz, Gertrud Berkowitz, Barbara Brenner, Harry Romero, James G. Wetmur, Thomas D. Matte, Andrea C. Gore, James Godbold, and Mary S. Wolff. "Pesticides and Inner-City Children: Exposures, Risks, and Prevention." *Environmental Health Perspectives* 107, supplement 3 (1999): 431–37.

Last, J. A. "The Missing Link: The Story of Karl Paul Link." *Toxicological Sciences* 66 (2002): 4–6.

Latour, Bruno. *We Have Never Been Modern*, translated by C. Porter. Cambridge: Harvard University Press, 1993.

Leavitt, Judith Walzer. *Typhoid Mary: Captive to the Public's Health.* Boston: Beacon Press, 1996.

Lehman, Arnold. "Chemicals in Foods: A Report to the Association of Food and Drug Officials on Current Developments." *Bulletin of the Association of Food and Drug Officials of the U.S.* 15 (1951): 82–89.

———. "The Major Toxic Actions of Insecticides." *Bulletin of the New York Academy of Medicine* 25 (June 1949): 382–87.

Leidy, J. "Flies As a Means of Communicating Contagious Diseases." *Proceedings of the Academy of Natural Sciences of Philadelphia* (1871): 297.

Levenson, Hanna, and Gordon W. Frankie. "A Study of Homeowner Attitudes and Practices toward Arthropod Pests and Pesticides in Three U.S. Metropolitan Areas." In *Urban Entomology: Interdisciplinary Perspectives,* edited by Gordon W. Frankie and Carl S. Koehler, 67–106. New York: Praeger, 1983.

Lieberman, A. "The Case of the Rampaging Ravenous Rodents." *Journal of the Indiana State Medical Association* (December 1964): 1351–54.

Light, Jennifer. *The Nature of Cities: Ecological Visions and the American Urban Professions, 1920–1960.* Baltimore, Md.: Johns Hopkins University Press, 2009.

Linder, Marc, and Lawrence Zacharias. *Of Cabbages and Kings County: Agriculture and the Formation of Modern Brooklyn.* Iowa City: University of Iowa Press, 1999.

Lissak, Rivka Shpak. *Pluralism and Progressives: Hull House and the New Immigrants, 1890–1919.* Chicago: University of Chicago Press, 1989.

Lofgren, C. S., J. C. Keller, and G. S. Burden. "Resistance Tests with the Bedbug and Evaluation of Insecticides for Its Control." *Journal of Economic Entomology* 51 (1958): 241–44.

Lord, Frederick. "Flies and Tuberculosis." *Boston Medical and Surgical Journal* 24 (1904): 651–54.

Lorde, Audre. "Eye to Eye: Black Women, Anger, and Hatred." In *Sister Outsider: Essays and Speeches,* 145–75. Berkeley, Calif.: Crossing Press, 1984.

Lubove, Roy. *The Progressives and the Slums: Tenement House Reform in New York City, 1890–1917.* Westport, Conn.: Greenwood Press, 1974.

Lynes, Russell. *The Domesticated Americans.* New York: Harper and Row, 1963.

MacNicoll, A. "Resistance to 4-hydroxycoumarin Anticoagulants in Rodents." In *Pesticide Resistance: Strategies and Tactics for Management,* edited by E. Glass, 87–99. Washington, D.C.: National Academies Press, 1986.

Mallis, Arnold. *Handbook of Pest Control.* Los Angeles: McNair-Dorland Company, 1954.

———. *Handbook of Pest Control.* Los Angeles: McNair-Dorland, 1960.

Mallis, Arnold, and A. C. Miller. "Prolonged Resistance in the House Fly and Bed Bug." *Journal of Economic Entomology* 57 (1964): 608–9.

Mansfield, Becky. "Health As a Nature-Society Question." *Environment and Planning A* 40 (2008): 1015–19.

Marlatt, C. L. "The Bedbug." *USDA Farmers' Bulletin 754* (1916): 1–12.

Marston, Sallie. "The Social Construction of Scale." *Progress in Human Geography* 24 (2000): 219–42.

Massey, Douglas, and Nancy Denton. *American Apartheid: Segregation and the Making of the Underclass.* Cambridge: Harvard University Press, 1993.

Matteson, Sumner. "John T. Emlen Jr.: A Naturalist for All Seasons, Part 2: Of Adventure, Innovation, and Conscience, 1934–1959." *The Passenger Pigeon* 60 (1998): 123–67.

Matt Skoller Band. "Bad Bed Bugs." *Bone to Pick with You.* Groove-tongue Records, 1996.

Mayer, J. D. "Geography, Ecology, and Emerging Infectious Diseases." *Social Science and Medicine* 50 (2000): 937–52.

———. "The Political Ecology of Disease As One New Focus for Medical Geography." *Progress in Human Geography* 20 (1996): 441–56.

McBride, David. *From TB to AIDS: Epidemics among Urban Blacks since 1900.* Albany: State University of New York Press, 1991.

McCann, Kenneth G., C. Michael Moomey, Kenny D. Runkle, Daniel O. Hryhorczuk, J. Milton Clark, and Dana B. Barr. "Chicago Area Methyl Parathion Response." *Environmental Health Perspectives* 110, supplement 6 (2002): 1075–78.

McNally, William D. "Six Deaths Following Fumigation with Hydrogen Cyanide." *Medical Journal and Record* 119 (1924): 143–44.

McNeill, William. *Plagues and Peoples.* New York: Doubleday, 1998.

McShane, Clay, and Joel Tarr. *The Horse in the City: Living Machines in the Nineteenth Century.* Baltimore, Md.: Johns Hopkins University Press, 2007.

McWilliams, James. *American Pests: The Losing War on Insects from Colonial Times to DDT.* New York: Columbia University Press, 2008.

Melosi, Martin V. *Garbage in the Cities: Refuse, Reform, and the Environment, 1880–1980.* College Station: Texas A&M University Press, 1981.

———. "Lyndon Johnson and Environmental Policy." In *The Johnson Years, Volume Two: Vietnam, the Environment, and Science,* edited by Robert A. Divine, 113–49. Lawrence: University of Kansas Press, 1988.

Messer, Richard. "Designs for Privies." *American Journal of Public Health* 7 (1917): 190–96.

Metzler, Dwight F. "DDT for Controlling Household Pests." *Journal of Housing* (July 1946): 151.

———. "A Study of Housing Regulation and Enforcement in the City of Chicago and Cook County, Illinois." MS thesis, University of Kansas, 1947.

Meyerson, Martin, and Edward Banfield. *Politics, Planning, and the Public Interest.* New York: Free Press, 1955.

Miller, Dini, and Frank Meek. "Cost and Efficacy Comparison of Integrated Pest Management Strategies with Monthly Spray Insecticide Applications for German Cockroaches in Public Housing." *Journal of Economic Entomology* 97 (2004): 559–69.

Miller, Roger. "*Selling Mrs. Consumer*: Advertising and the Creation of Suburban Socio-spatial Relations, 1910–1930." *Antipode* 23 (1991): 263–301.

Miller, Vernice, Moya Hallstein, and Susan Quass. "Feminist Politics and Environmental Justice: Women's Community Activism in West Harlem, New York." In *Feminist Political Ecology: Global Issues and Local Experiences*, edited by Dianne Rocheleau, Barbara Thomas-Slayter, and Esther Wangari, 62–85. London: Routledge, 1996.

Millspaugh, Martin, Gurney Breckenfeld, and Miles Colean. *The Human Side of Urban Renewal: A Study of the Attitude Changes Produced by Neighborhood Rehabilitation*. Baltimore, Md.: Fight-Blight, Inc., 1956.

Mitchell, Timothy. *Rule of Experts: Egypt, Techno-politics, Modernity*. Berkeley: University of California Press, 2002.

Mitman, Gregg. *Breathing Space: How Allergies Shape Our Lives and Landscapes*. New Haven, Conn.: Yale University Press, 2007.

———. "In Search of Health: Landscape and Disease in American Environmental History." *Environmental History* 10 (2005): 184–209.

Mitman, Gregg, Michelle Murphy, and Christopher Sellers. "Introduction: A Cloud over History." *Osiris* 19 (2004): 1–17.

Moore, David J., and Dini Miller. "Field Evaluations of Insecticide Treatment Regimens for Control of the Common Bedbug, *Cimex lectularius*." *Pest Management Science* 65 (2009): 332–38.

Moore, S. "Diseases Probably Caused by Flies." *British Medical Journal* (1893): 1154.

Moran, Sharon. "Under the Lawn: Engaging the Water Cycle." *Ethics, Place, and Environment* 11 (2008): 129–45.

Morris, Margaret Kissam. "Audre Lorde: Textual Authority and the Embodied Self." *Frontiers* 23 (2002): 168–88.

Muir, John. *My First Summer in the Sierra*. Boston: Houghton-Mifflin, 1911.

Munch, James. "Thallium." *Exterminators Log*, July 1937, 8.

Municipal Reference Library. "Rodent Infestation Programs in Other Major Cities." Milwaukee, Wisc.: Municipal Reference Library, 1967.

Murdock, Deroy. "Pesticide Patrol Fallout." *Washington Times*, February 13, 2002.

Murray, Thomas. "Essentials of a Municipal Rat Control Program." *Pests* (July 1947): 8–10.

Myles, Tim, Beth Brown, Bobbi Bedard, Rajan Bhooi, Kailynn Bruyere, Ai-Linn Chua, Michelle Mascal, Rashmi Menezes, Alka Salwan, and Mitsuko Takahashi. "Bed Bugs in Toronto." *Centre for Urban and Community Studies Research Bulletin* 19 (2003): 1–4.

Nash, Linda. "The Agency of Nature or the Nature of Agency?" *Environmental History* 10 (2005): 67–69.

———. "The Fruits of Ill-Health: Pesticides and Workers' Bodies in Post–World War II California." *Osiris* 19 (2004): 203–19.

———. *Inescapable Ecologies: A History of Environment, Disease, and Knowledge*. Berkeley: University of California Press, 2006.

National Association of Housing Officials (NAHO). *Disinfestation of Dwellings and Furnishings: Problems and Practices in Low-Rent Housing*. Chicago: NAHO, 1939.

———. "Screen Doors Causing Trouble." In *Managing Low-Rent Housing Conference: A Record of Current Experiences and Practice in Public Housing*. Washington, D.C.: NAHO, 1938.

National Association of Housing Officials Maintenance Committee. *Maintenance Men Look at Housing Design*. Chicago: NAHO, 1948.

National Center for Healthy Housing. *What's Working for Bed Bug Control in Multifamily Housing: Reconciling Best Practices with Research and the Realities of Implementation*. Washington, D.C.: Environmental Protection Agency, 2010.

National Commission on Urban Problems. *Building the American City*. Washington, D.C.: Government Printing Office, 1969.

National Research Council. *Pest Control: An Assessment of Present and Alternative Technologies, Volume 1: Contemporary Pest Control Practices and Prospects*, Washington, D.C.: National Academies Press, 1975.

National Research Council Committee on Urban Pest Management. *Urban Pest Management: A Report*. Washington, D.C.: National Academy Press, 1980.

Nelson, Alondra. *Body and Soul: The Black Panther Party and the Fight against Medical Discrimination*. Minneapolis: University of Minnesota Press, 2011.

Neverdon-Morton, Cynthia. "Black Housing Patterns in Baltimore City, 1885–1953." *Maryland Historian* (spring–summer 1985): 25–39.

New York City Housing Authority. *East River Houses: Public Housing in East Harlem*. New York: New York City Housing Authority, 1941.

———. "25-Year Public Housing Jubilee." *New York City Housing Authority Management Newsletter* (January–February 1961): 1.

———. *Pre-examination Training Course Material for Resident Buildings Superintendent and Assistant Resident Buildings Superintendent*. New York: New York City Housing Authority, 1952.

New York State IPM Program. "Bedbug FAQs." Online at http://www.nysipm .cornell.edu/whats_bugging_you/bed_bugs/bedbugs_faqs.asp#avoid. Accessed on August 15, 2012.

Nicholas, G. E. "The Fly in Its Sanitary Aspect." *Lancet* 2 (1873): 724.

North Carolina State Board of Health. "Flies Are a Disgrace." *Board of Health Special Bulletin* 21 (May 1914).

Norwood Tenants Association. "Norwood Tenants Say, 'We're Not Leaving.'" Press release, July 11, 2007. Online at http://www.norwoodtenants. org/2007/07/norwood-tenants-say-were-not-leaving.html. Accessed on December 28, 2010.

Oleniak, James. "Tenant Sales and Services." *Journal of Housing* (August–September 1955): 296.

Olkowski, Helga. *Common Sense Pest Control*. Berkeley, Calif.: Consumers Cooperative of Berkeley, 1971.

Olkowski, Helga, and William Olkowski. "Entomophobia in the Urban Eco-system: Some Observations and Suggestions." *Bulletin of the Entomological Society of America* 22 (1976): 313–17.

Olkowski, Helga, William Olkowski, and Tom Javits. *The Integral Urban House: Self-reliant Living in the City.* San Francisco: Sierra Club Books, 1979.

Olkowski, William. "A Model Ecosystem Management Program." Paper presented at the Tall Timbers Conference on Ecological Animal Control by Habitat Management, Tallahassee, Fla., March 1–2, 1973.

Olkowski, William, and Helga Olkowski. *Contracting for Pest Control Services: Cockroaches, Mice, Rats, and Flies in Public and Private Buildings: A Consumers' Guide.* Berkeley, Calif.: Bio-integral Resource Center, 1984.

———. *Delivering Integrated Pest Management: Pest Control Services for Cockroaches, Mice, Rats, and Flies in Public and Private Buildings.* Berkeley, Calif.: Bio-integral Resource Center, 1984.

Olkowski, William, Helga Olkowski, and Linda Laub. *Urban Integrated Pest Management in California: An Assessment and Action Plan.* Berkeley, Calif.: Center for the Integration of Applied Sciences, 1980.

Olkowski, William, Helga Olkowski, Robert van den Bosch, and R. Hom. "Ecosystem Management: A Framework for Urban Pest Control." *Bioscience* 26 (1976): 384–89.

Olson, Sherry. *Baltimore: The Building of an American City.* Baltimore, Md.: Johns Hopkins University Press, 1997.

Osborne, Thomas. "Security and Vitality: Drains, Liberalism, and Power in the Nineteenth Century." In *Foucault and Political Reason: Liberalism, Neo-Liberalism, and Rationalities of Government,* edited by Andrew Barry, Nikolas Rose, and Thomas Osborne, 99–122. Chicago: University of Chicago Press, 1996.

Otter, Chris. "Cleansing and Clarifying: Technology and Perception in Nineteenth-Century London." *Journal of British Studies* 43 (2004): 40–65.

Padernacht, R. "The Contributions of the New York Association for Improving the Condition of the Poor to Child Welfare, 1843–1939." PhD dissertation, St. John's University, 1976.

Parr, Joy. "Smells Like? Sources of Uncertainty in the History of the Great Lakes Environment." *Environmental History* 11 (2006): 269–99.

Patterson, Gordon. *The Mosquito Crusades: A History of the American Anti-Mosquito Movement from the Reed Commission to the First Earth Day.* New Brunswick, N.J.: Rutgers University Press, 2009.

———. *The Mosquito Wars: A History of Mosquito Control in Florida.* Gainesville: University Press of Florida, 2004.

Pellow, M. David Naguib. *The Garbage Wars: The Struggle for Environmental Justice in Chicago.* Cambridge, Mass.: MIT Press, 2002.

Perkins, John H. *Insects, Experts, and the Insecticide Crisis: The Quest for New Pest Management Strategies.* New York: Plenum Press, 1982.

Perl, Arnold. "Who Do You Kill?" Directed by Tom Gries. *Eastside/Westside.* November 1963.

Pfiester, Margie, Philip G. Koehler, and Roberto M. Pereira. "Effect of Population Structure and Size on Aggregation Behavior of *Cimex lectularius* (Hemiptera: Cimicidae)." *Journal of Medical Entomology* 46 (2009): 1015–20.

Philo, Chris. "Animals, Geography, and the City: Notes on Inclusions and Exclusions." *Environment and Planning D* 13 (1995): 655–81.

Pierce, W. D., ed. *Sanitary Entomology: The Entomology of Disease, Hygiene, and Sanitation.* Boston: R. G. Badger, 1921.

———. "Why American Cities Must Fight Insects." *American City* (August 1919): 146–48.

Pietila, Antero. *Not in My Neighborhood: How Bigotry Shaped a Great American City.* Chicago: Ivan Dee, 2010.

Piper, Gary L., and Gordon W. Frankie. *Integrated Management of Urban Cockroach Populations: Final Report.* Washington, D.C.: Environmental Protection Agency, 1978.

Plapp, Frederick. "Insecticides in the Urban Environment." In *Perspectives in Urban Entomology,* edited by Gordon Frankie and Carl Koehler, 401–8. New York: Academic Press, 1978.

Platt, Harold. *Shock Cities: The Environmental Transformation and Reform of Manchester and Chicago.* Chicago: University of Chicago Press, 2005.

Pond, M. Allen. "What Can the Sanitary Engineer Contribute to Housing?" *Journal of Housing* 4 (1947): 237–39.

Poovey, Mary. *Making a Social Body: British Cultural Formation, 1830–1864.* Chicago: University of Chicago Press, 1995.

Popkin, Susan J., Larry F. Buron, Diane K. Levy, and Mary K. Cunningham. "The Gautreaux Legacy: What Might Mixed-Income and Dispersal Strategies Mean for the Poorest Public Housing Tenants." *Housing Policy Debate* 11 (2000): 911–42.

Potter, Michael. "The History of Bedbug Management—with Lessons from the Past." *American Entomologist* (2011): 14–25.

Power, Emma. "Furry Families: Making a Human-Dog Family through Home." *Social and Cultural Geography* 9 (2008): 535–55.

Pratt, F. S. "Discussion [Response to Cousineau and Legg]." *American Journal of Public Health* 25 (1935): 290–93.

President's Science Advisory Committee. *The Use of Pesticides.* Washington, D.C.: President's Science Advisory Committee, 1963.

Price, Jennifer. *Flight Maps: Adventures with Nature in Modern America.* New York: Basic Books, 1999.

Pulido, Laura. "Community, Place, Identity." In *Thresholds in Feminist Geography,* edited by J. P. Jones, H. J. Nast, and S. M. Roberts, 11–28. Lanham, Md.: Rowan and Littlefield, 1997.

———. "Ecofeminist Natures: Race, Gender, Feminist Theory, and Political Action." *Environment and Planning D* 18 (2000): 122–24.

Quarles, William. "Bed Bugs Bounce Back." *IPM Practitioner* 29, no. 3–4 (2007): 1–8.

———. "Thermal Pest Eradication in Structures." *IPM Practitioner* 28, no. 5–6 (2006): 1–8.

Quinn, Sandra Crouse, and Stephen B. Thomas. "The National Negro Health Week, 1915 to 1951: A Descriptive Account." *Minority Health Today* 2 (2001): 44–49.

Radford, Gail. *Modern Housing for America: Policy Struggles in the New Deal Era.* Chicago: University of Chicago Press, 1996.

Raffles, Hugh. *Insectopedia.* New York: Pantheon, 2010.

Ralph, James, Jr. "Home Truths: Dr. King and the Chicago Freedom Movement." *American Visions* 9 (1994): 30–34.

Reed, Walter, Edward Shakespeare, and Victor Vaughan. *Abstract of Report on the Origin and Spread of Typhoid Fever in the U.S. Military Camps during the Spanish War of 1898.* Washington, D.C.: Government Print Office, 1900.

Rehn, James A. G. "Man's Uninvited Fellow Traveler—The Cockroach." *Scientific Monthly* 61 (1945): 265–76.

Rehner, T. A., J. R. Kolbo, R. Trump, C. Smith, and D. Reid. "Depression among Victims of South Mississippi's Methyl Parathion Disaster." *Health and Social Work* 35 (2000): 33–40.

Reid, Ira DeA. *The Negro Community of Baltimore.* Baltimore, Md.: Baltimore Urban League, 1935.

Richardson, C. H. "The Response of the House-fly (*Musca domestica* L.) to Ammonia and Other Substances." *New Jersey Agricultural Experiment Station Bulletin* 292 (1916): 3–19.

Richter, Curt. "The Development and Use of Alpha-Naphthyl Thiourea (ANTU) As a Rat Poison." *Journal of the American Medical Association* 129 (1946): 927–31.

———. "Experiences of a Reluctant Rat-Catcher: The Common Norway Rat—Friend or Enemy?" *Proceedings of the American Philosophical Society* 112 (1968): 403–15.

———. "Incidence of Rat Bites and Rat Bite Fever in Baltimore." *Journal of the American Medical Association* 128 (1945): 324–26.

Risse, Guenter B. "'A Long Pull, a Strong Pull, and All Together': San Francisco and Bubonic Plague, 1907–1908." *Bulletin of the History of Medicine* 66 (1992): 260–86.

Robbins, Paul. *Lawn People: How Grasses, Weeds, and Chemicals Make Us Who We Are.* Philadelphia: Temple University Press, 2007.

Roberts, John. "Cockroaches Linked with Asthma." *British Medical Journal* 312 (1996): 1630.

Roberts, Samuel Kelton, Jr. *Infectious Fears: Politics, Disease, and the Health Effects of Segregation.* Chapel Hill: University of North Carolina Press, 2009.

Rogers, Naomi. *Dirt and Disease: Polio before FDR.* New Brunswick, N.J.: Rutgers University Press, 1992.

———. "Dirt, Flies, and Immigrants: Explaining the Epidemiology of Poliomyelitis, 1900–1916." *Journal of the History of Medicine and Allied Sciences* 44 (1989): 486–505.

———. "Germs with Legs: Flies, Disease, and the New Public Health." *Bulletin of the History of Medicine* 63 (1989): 599–617.

Rome, Adam. "Political Hermaphrodites: Gender and Environmental Reform in Progressive America." *Environmental History* (2006): 440–63.

Rose, Gillian. *Feminism and Geography: The Limits of Geographical Knowledge.* Cambridge, Mass.: Polity, 1993.

Rosenberg, Harriet G. "The Home Is the Workplace: Hazards, Stress, and Pollutants in the Household." In *Double Exposure: Women's Health Hazards on the Job and at Home*, edited by Wendy Chavkin, 219–45. New York: Monthly Review Press, 1984.

Rosenstreich, David L., Peyton Eggleston, Meyer Kattan, Dean Baker, Raymond Slavin, Peter Gergen, Herman Mitchell, Kathleen McNiff-Mortimer, Henry Lynn, Dennis Ownby, Floyd Malveaux, and National Cooperative Inner-City Asthma Study. "The Role of Cockroach Allergy and Exposure to Cockroach Allergen in Causing Morbidity among Inner-City Children with Asthma." *New England Journal of Medicine* 336 (1997): 1356–63.

Roth, Louis M., and Edwin R. Willis. *The Medical and Veterinary Importance of Cockroaches.* Washington, D.C.: Smithsonian Institution, 1957.

Russell, Edmund. "Speaking of Annihilation: Mobilizing for War against Human and Insect Enemies, 1914–1945." *Journal of American History* 82 (1996): 1505–29.

———. *War and Nature: Fighting Humans and Insects with Chemicals from World War I to Silent Spring.* Cambridge: Cambridge University Press, 2001.

Russell, Louise. "Leland Ossian Howard: A Historical Review." *Annual Review of Entomology* 23 (1978): 1–17.

Rydell, C. Peter. *Factors Affecting Maintenance and Operating Costs in Federal Public Housing Projects.* New York: Rand, 1970.

Safer Pest Control Project. "Safer Solutions: Integrated Pest Management in Public Housing." Brochure, 2002.

Sailer, Reece I. "The Bedbug: An Old Bedfellow That's Still with Us." *Pest Control* (October 1952): 22–24, 70–72.

Sallow, William. "An Analysis of Rat Bites in Baltimore, 1948–52." *Public Health Reports* 68 (1953): 1239–42.

Samuelson, James. *Humble Creatures: The Earthworm and the Common Housefly: In Eight Letters.* London: Van Voorst, 1858.

Sanders, George. "The Exterminator in the Field of Preventative Medicine." *Exterminators Log*, January 1934, 8.

Savage, Eldon P., Thomas J. Keefe, and H. William Wheeler. *National Household Pesticide Usage Study, 1976–1977.* Fort Collins, Colo.: Epidemiologic Pesticide Studies Center, 1979.

Scharff, Virginia. *Seeing Nature through Gender*. Lawrence: University Press of Kansas, 2003.

Schwartz, Joel. "Tenant Power in the Liberal City, 1943–1971." In *The Tenant Movement in New York City, 1904–1984*, edited by Ronald Lawson and Mark Naison, 134–208. New Brunswick, N.J.: Rutgers University Press, 1986.

Scott, Harold George. *Operation Rat: A Rat Eradication Program for the American People*. U.S. Public Health Service, Office of Equal Opportunity, 1965.

———. "Rat Bite: Epidemiology and Control." *Journal of Environmental Health* 27 (1965): 900–2.

Scott, James C. *Seeing Like a State: How Certain Schemes to Improve the Human Condition Have Failed*. New Haven, Conn.: Yale University Press, 1998.

Scott-Heron, Gil. "Whitey on the Moon." *Small Talk at 125th and Lenox*. Flying Dutchman Records, 1970.

Secretary's Commission on Pesticides and Their Relationship to Environmental Health. "Report: Pesticides and Their Relationship to Environmental Health." Washington, D.C.: U.S. Department of Health, Education, and Welfare, 1969.

Shah, Nyan. *Contagious Divides: Epidemics and Race in San Francisco's Chinatown*. Berkeley: University of California Press, 1999.

Shapiro, Adam. *Trying Biology: The Scopes Trial, Textbooks, and the Anti-evolution Movement in American Schools*. Chicago: University of Chicago Press, 2013.

Shaw, Ian, Paul Robbins, and J. P. Jones. "A Bug's Life and the Spatial Ontologies of Mosquito Management." *Annals of the Association of American Geographers* 100 (2010): 373–92.

Shaw, Ronald. "Final Push for National Legislation: The Chicago Freedom Movement." *Journal of the Illinois State Historical Society* 94 (2001): 304–32.

Shove, Elizabeth. *Comfort, Cleanliness, and Convenience: The Social Organization of Normality*. Oxford: Berg, 2004.

Shuyler, H. "Are German and Oriental Roaches Changing Their Habits?" *Pest Control* (September 1956): 9–10.

Sicherman, Barbara. *Alice Hamilton: A Life in Letters*. Cambridge: Harvard University Press, 1984.

Skolander. "Bedbugs in New York." August 29, 2010. Online at http://www.youtube.com/watch?v=lKoLffiCDb8. Accessed on August 15, 2012.

Smethurst, James. "Invented by Horror: The Gothic and African American Literary Ideology in Native Son." *African American Review* (spring 2001): 29–40.

Smith, J. A. "Beyond Dominance and Affection: Living with Rabbits in Posthumanist Households." *Animals and Society* 11 (2003): 181–97.

Smith, Kimberly. *African-American Environmental Thought*. Lawrence: University of Kansas Press, 2007.

Smith, Susan. "Living Room?" *Urban Geography* 25 (2004): 89–91.

Smith, Susan, Robin Knill-Jones, and Ann McGuckin, eds. *Housing for Health*. Essex, UK: Longman Group, 1991.

Smith, Susan L. *Sick and Tired of Being Sick and Tired: Black Women's Health Activism in America, 1890–1950*. Philadelphia: University of Pennsylvania Press, 1995.

Snetsinger, Robert. *The Ratcatcher's Child: The History of the Pest Control Industry*. Cleveland, Ohio: Franzak and Foster, 1983.

Southall, John. *A Treatise of Buggs*. London: John Roberts, 1730.

Starr, Paul. *The Social Transformation of American Medicine*. New York: Basic Books, 1982.

State of New York. "Complaint for Declaratory and Injunctive Relief: State of New York against Department of Housing and Urban Development." Albany: U.S. District Court for the Eastern District of New York, 2004.

Steinberg, Theodore. *Down to Earth: Nature's Role in American History*. New York: Oxford University Press, 2002.

Stellar, E. "An Appreciation of Curt Richter." In *The Psychobiology of Curt Richter*, edited by E. M. Blass. Baltimore, Md.: York Press, 1976.

Stewart, Jeffrey, and Fath Davis Ruffins. "A Faithful Witness: Afro-American Public History in Historical Perspective." In *Presenting the Past: Essays on History and the Public*, edited by Susan Benson, Stephen Brier, and Roy Rosenzweig, 307–38. Philadelphia: Temple University Press, 1986.

Strasser, Susan. *Never Done: A History of American Housework*. New York: Pantheon, 1982.

———. *Waste and Want: A Social History of Trash*. New York: Henry Holt, 1999.

Streimer, Katherine A., Mary Louise Flint, Robert B. McCray, and Mary Jean Haley. *Report on the Environmental Assessment of Pesticide Regulatory Programs*. Sacramento: California Department of Food and Agriculture, 1978.

Students and Neighbors Action Program. "Rat Control—People's Science in Philadelphia." *Science for the People* 4, no. 6 (1972): 20–21.

Stutt, Alastair, and Michael Siva-Jothy. "Traumatic Insemination and Sexual Conflict in the Bed Bug *Cimex lectularius*." *Proceedings of the National Academy of Sciences* 98 (2001): 5683–87.

Suchy, James, and Vernard Lewis. "Host-Seeking Behavior in the Bedbug, *Cimex lectularius*." *Insects* 2 (2011): 22–35.

Sullivan, Robert. *Rats: Observations on the History and Habitat of the City's Most Unwanted Inhabitants*. New York: Bloomsbury, 2004.

Surgan, Michael, Thomas Congdon, Christine Primi, Stephanie Lamster, and Jennifer Louis-Jacques. *Pest Control in Public Housing, Schools, and Parks: Urban Children at Risk*. Albany, N.Y.: Office of the Attorney General, 2002.

Talbot, Marion. *House Sanitation: A Manual for Housekeepers*. Boston: Whitcomb and Barrows, 1913.

Task Force on Environmental Problems of the Inner City. *Our Urban Environment and Our Most Endangered People*. Washington, D.C.: Environmental Protection Agency, 1971.

Taylor, Alan. "Unnatural Inequalities: Social and Environmental Histories." *Environmental History* 1 (1996): 6–19.

Timm, Robert. "Norway Rats." In *Prevention and Control of Wildlife Damage*, edited by Scott Hyngstrom, Robert Timm, and Gary Larson, B105–B120. Lincoln: University of Nebraska Cooperative Extension, 1994.

Tomes, Nancy. *The Gospel of Germs: Men, Women, and the Microbe in American Life*. Cambridge: Harvard University Press, 1998.

Torrey, J. C. "Numbers and Types of Bacteria Carried by City Flies." *Journal of Infectious Disease* 10 (1912) 166–77.

Uexkull, Jakob von. *Foray into the Worlds of Animals and Humans*, translated by Joseph O'Neil. Minneapolis: University of Minnesota Press, 2010.

United States Supreme Court. *Hills v. Gautreaux*. 425 U.S. 284 (1976).

U.S. Congress, House. Select Committee to Investigate the Use of Chemicals in Food Products. *Chemicals in Food Products: Hearing before the Select Committee to Investigate the Use of Chemicals in Food Products*. 81st Congress, 2nd session, September 14–December 15, 1950.

Usinger, Robert L. *Monograph on Cimicidae (Hemiptera-Heteroptera)*. College Park, Md.: Entomological Society of America, 1966.

U.S. Public Health Service. *DDT for Control of Household Insects Affecting Health*. Atlanta, Ga.: Federal Security Agency, 1946.

———. *No Good on Earth: A Study of the Rat*. 31 minutes. Baltimore, Md.: Stark Films, 1932.

Vale, Lawrence. *From the Puritans to the Projects: Public Housing and Public Neighbors*. Cambridge: Harvard University Press, 2000.

van den Bosch, Robert. *The Pesticide Conspiracy*. Garden City, N.J.: Doubleday, 1978.

Venkatachalam, P. S., and B. Belavadi. "Loss of Haemoglobin Iron Due to Excessive Biting by Bedbugs." *Transactions of the Royal Society for Tropical Medicine and Hygiene* 56 (1962): 218–21.

Villarreal, Vanessa. *Districts Tackle Pesticide Clean-Up*. Army Corps of Engineers Newsletter, 1997.

Vinetz, Joseph, Gregory Glass, Charles Flexner, Paul Mueller, and David Kaslow. "Sporadic Urban Leptospirosis," *Annals of Internal Medicine* 125 (1996): 794–98.

Walker, C. L. "How to Get Rid of Household Pests." *Readers Digest* (April 1952): 109–12.

Wang, Changlu, and Gary W. Bennett. "Comparative Study of Integrated Pest Management and Baiting for German Cockroach Management in Public Housing." *Journal of Economic Entomology* 99 (2006): 879–85.

Ward, Justus. "A Dynamic Statute for Pesticides." *USDA Yearbook of Agriculture* (1966): 271–79.

———. "Toxicity Criteria Used in Judging the Labeling of Pesticides." *American Journal of Public Health* 45 (1955): 723–28.

Waring, Mary. *Prophylactic Topics: Common Sense Subjects for the Use of the People, Especially the Home-makers*. Chicago: Fraternal Press, 1916.

Warren, Christian. *Brush with Death: A Social History of Lead Poisoning*. Baltimore, Md.: Johns Hopkins University Press, 2000.

Washburn, F. L. "Cockroaches." *Eleventh Annual Report of the State Entomologist of Minnesota*, 1906.

Washington, Sylvia Hood. *Packing Them In: An Archaeology of Environmental Racism in Chicago, 1865–1954*. Lanham, Mass.: Lexington, 2005.

Weber, Rachel. "Extracting Value from the City: Neoliberalism and Urban Redevelopment." *Antipode* 34 (2002): 519–40.

Webster, Louella. "*La Cucaracha* and the Housing Shortage." *American Home* (May 1948): 156–60.

Weed, Clarence. *Insects and Insecticides: A Practical Manual*. New York: Orange Judd Company, 1904.

Weller, Frederick. *Neglected Neighbors: Stories of Life in the Alleys, Tenements, and Shanties of the National Capital*. Philadelphia: Winston, 1909.

West, Luther S. *The Housefly: Its Natural History, Medical Importance, and Control*. Ithaca, N.Y.: Comstock, 1951.

Whatmore, Sarah. *Hybrid Geographies: Natures, Cultures, Spaces*. Thousand Oaks, Calif.: Sage, 2002.

Whorton, James C. *Before Silent Spring: Pesticides and Public Health in Pre-DDT America*. Princeton, N.J.: Princeton University Press, 1975.

Williams, A. Wilberforce. "Preventive Measures, First Aid Remedies, Hygienics, and Sanitation." *Chicago Defender* (March 30, 1918): 16.

Williams, C. L. "Discussion [Response to Cousineau and Legg]." *American Journal of Public Health* 25 (1935): 287–89.

———. "Fumigants." *Public Health Reports* 46 (1931): 1013–31.

———. "Fumigation Deaths As Compared with Deaths from Other Poisonous Gases." *Public Health Reports* 49 (1934): 697–99.

———. "Hydrocyanic Acid Gas Absorbed in Bedding." *Pests* (November 1938): 15–17.

Williams, Rhonda Y. *The Politics of Public Housing: Black Women's Struggles against Urban Inequality*. London: Oxford University Press, 2004.

Wilner, Daniel M., Rosabelle Price Walkey, Thomas C. Pinkerton, and Matthew Tayback. *The Housing Environment and Family Life: A Longitudinal Study on the Effects of Housing on Morbidity and Mental Health*. Baltimore, Md.: Johns Hopkins Press, 1962.

Wines, Richard A. *Fertilizer in America: From Waste Recycling to Resource Exploitation*. Philadelphia: Temple University Press, 1985.

Wolch, Jennifer. "Anima Urbis." *Progress in Human Geography* 26 (2002): 721–42.

Wolch, Jennifer, Alec Brownlow, and Unna Lassiter. "Constructing the Animal Worlds of Inner-City Los Angeles." In *Animal Spaces, Beastly Places: New Geographies of Human-Animal Relations*, edited by Chris Philo and Chris Wilbert, 71–97. London: Routledge, 2000.

Wolf, Jacqueline. *Don't Kill Your Baby: Public Health and the Decline of Breastfeeding in the Nineteenth and Twentieth Centuries*. Columbus: Ohio State University Press, 2001.

Woman's City Club of Chicago. "Rats and a Clean City." *Woman's City Club of Chicago Bulletin*, March 1934, 59.

Wood, F. E. "Cockroach Control in Public Housing: Is It an Overwhelming Problem?" *Pest Control* (June 1980): 14–16.

Wood, F. E., W. H. Robinson, Sandra K. Kraft, and Patricia Zungoli. "Survey of Attitudes and Knowledge of Public Housing Residents toward Cockroaches." *Bulletin of the Entomological Society of America* 27 (1981): 9–13.

Woods, Robert Archey, and Albert Joseph Kennedy. *Handbook of Settlements*. 1911; reprint, Urbana: University of Illinois Library, 1970.

Woodward, William. *Report of the Health Officer of the District of Columbia*. Washington, D.C.: Department of Health, 1895.

Wright, Charles. "A Survey of Cockroach Species Found in Some North Carolina Apartment Projects." *Pest Control* (June 1965): 14–15.

Wright, Gwendolyn. *Building the Dream: A Social History of Housing in America*. New York: Pantheon Books, 1981.

Wright, Lawrence. *Warm and Snug: The History of the Bed*. London: Routledge, 1962.

Wright, Richard. *Native Son*. New York: Harper, 1940.

Wright, Willard H. "The Bedbug—Its Habits and Life History and Methods of Control." *Public Health Reports*, supplements, no. 175 (1944): 1–9.

Wurster, Catherine. *Modern Housing*. Boston: Houghton Mifflin, 1934.

Young, Whitney M. "The Urban League and Its Strategy." *Annals of the American Academy of Political and Social Science* 357 (1965): 102–7.

Young Lords Party and Michael Abramson. *Palante: Young Lords Party*. New York: McGraw Hill, 1971.

Zavon, Mitchell R. "Insecticides and Other Pesticides of Home and Garden." *Modern Medicine* (1962): 90–101.

INDEX

Orleans, 94–95; in New York City, 13, 83, 85, 87, 100–102; nonvolatile baits for, 200–201; as nymphs, 83; odor of, 83; ootheca (egg case), 83, 23*fig.*; and organophosphates, 102, 105–6, 191; Oriental cockroaches, 83; and PCH mixed with DDT, 94; persistence of, 85, 192–96, 204, 211; poetry about, 177; population reservoirs of, 96; and positive thigmotaxis, 84, 23*fig.*; on posters, 168, 147*fig.*; preventive control of, 88, 103, 200–201; in public housing, 88, 94–95, 97–106, 108–10, 168, 178–81, 187–89, 192–93, 195–97, 200–201; range of, 106; reintroduction of, 94–96, 110; reproductive cycle of, 83, 86–88, 99, 102, 104–5, 108; and resistance, 102–6, 108–10, 170, 187, 190–91, 193–95, 268n29; saliva of, 189; shame concerning, 4, 84, 94, 177–78; sketches of, 83–84, 108; sticky feet of, 83; stigma of, 181, 187, 200; stress caused by, 84, 86; as symbols, 179, 194, 196; tenacious populations of, 94; traps for, 87–88
code enforcement systems, 9; in Baltimore, 116–18, 127, 130–31, 133–34, 154; and bedbugs, 63, 65; block-by-block, 117–18; in Chicago, 53, 63, 120, 122, 173; and flies, 53–54; in New York City, 151–52, 154–55; and rats, 116–18, 120, 122–23, 127, 130–31, 133–34, 151–52, 154–55, 159, 173; in Washington, D.C., 53. *See also* inspectors, health/housing
Collins, Henry and Willa Mae, 151–53
Collins, Keith, 151–53
Commission on Urban Problems, U.S., 158
Committee on Pest Control Activities (Chicago), 121
Common Sense Pest Control (Olkowski), 183–86
communism, 98
communities of color. *See* blacks;

ethnicity; race
community involvement: and cockroaches, 199–202; and communal pest control, 75–82, 91–95, 106, 108–9, 190, 194–96, 214; decline of, 194–95; and Horner Mothers' Guild, 199–202, 204; and rat control, 113, 118–20, 122–23, 125–27, 130, 132–34, 137–38, 165, 167–68, 173–74; and volunteers, 125–27, 130, 165, 167–68, 173–74, 200–202
composting bins/toilets, 185
Congress, U.S.: and agricultural/aesthetic pests, 158–59; and alley homes, 36–37, 39; and bedbugs, 206–7, 209, 213; and chlordane, 101; and cockroaches, 208; and DDT, 91; disciplining black communities, 160–62; and funding for suburbs, 109; mocking in, 159–61, 163, 209; and public housing, 74, 99; and rat control, 158–63, 175. *See also names of federal acts and laws*
Congress of Racial Equality (CORE), 156
Connecticut, 58, 158
conservationists, 181
consumer products/services, 47; and appliances, 59–60, 90, 229n95, 234n32; and chlordane, 100–101; and DDT, 90–91; and exterminators, 65–66, 71–72, 74, 121; and HCN fumigation, 71–72; and Integrated Pest Management (IPM), 186; and over-the-counter remedies, 211
Consumer Reports, 100
contamination of food and drink, 11; caused by flies, 30–31, 38–39, 48–49, 19*fig.*; contaminated milk, 48–49; and typhoid fever, 30
Cornell University, 86
coroners, 69, 121, 236n84, 257n26
corrosive sublimate (mercuric chloride), 58–59
Corwin, Arthur, 3–5, 45, 17*fig.*
coumarin, 170

budgetary priorities of, 29, 40–42, 53–54, 99, 120–22, 135, 150, 153–54, 165, 181, 198, 228n68, 273n93; and chlordane, 100–102, 104; and cockroaches, 95, 100–102, 104, 187; and DDT, 84, 93, 95; exterminators' licenses required by, 67–68, 71; and flies, 29, 32, 35–36, 38–44, 47, 50–54, 228n68; and HCN fumigation, 66–74, 77–78, 81; and Hull-House, 53, 225n33; and Integrated Pest Management (IPM), 211–12; laws/regulations of, 49, 65–76, 81–82, 100–102, 131–32, 152, 237n92; "municipal housekeeping" movement, 40; neglect of buildings, 176, 178, 181, 187, 195–96, 272n74; power over private spaces, 29, 32, 50–53, 69, 77–78, 231n106; and rats, 112, 114, 116, 120–23, 125, 127, 135, 150–52, 157, 162, 165, 208–9; revolving funds of, 150, 154; waste management, 28–29, 53, 119, 122. *See also* housing authorities; public health; *names of cities*

governments, state, 99, 156–57, 163; funding from, 163. *See also names of states*

Gray, Jesse, 155–57, 161, 166, 174–75, 258nn34–35

Great Depression, 112, 117, 119–20, 130

Great Society, 158, 175

Great War. *See* World War I

Greeks, 33

grocers, 40, 49; and cockroaches, 83–84, 86, 187

guns, 101

H

Hamilton, Alice, 33–34, 44, 53, 225n33

Haraway, Donna, 273n91, 274n108

Harland, Marion, 61

Harlem (New York City), 107, 150–53, 155–57, 167, 258nn34–35, 144*fig.*; Community Council on Housing, 155–56,

166; Harlem Hospital, 151; West Harlem Environmental Action, 211–12

Hartnack, Hugo: and bedbugs, 57, 62, 70, 72–73, 75–76; and cockroaches, 86, 88; and rats, 123

Hawai'i, 106

Hazlett, Maril, 6–7, 178

HCN (hydrocyanic acid gas), 91; absorbed through skin, 236n73; agricultural use of, 66–68, 73; and "airing-out" periods, 67–69, 71–72, 76–77, 80; and bedbugs, 56–57, 66–82, 88, 91, 108, 236n73, 236n75, 21*fig.*, 22*fig.*; in Boston, 71; in Britain, 73, 76; as chemical weapon, 67, 82; in Chicago, 69–70, 72–73, 75–78, 82; and cockroaches, 88; commerce/shipping use of, 67–69; and coroner's inquests, 69, 236n84; cost of fumigation, 70–71, 73, 77, 79, 81, 88; court cases involving, 72; in cracks/crevices, 66–69, 91; DDT compared to, 89–94; deaths caused by, 67, 69–73, 236n84, 237n92; in Detroit, 71; difficult to contain, 57, 66–70, 73, 76, 81, 91–92; and evacuations, 68, 70–71, 76–77, 88–89, 91; gas chambers/vaults for, 71, 77, 80; generators for, 80, 21*fig.*; guidelines for, 73; and indicator chemicals, 67; masks as insufficient for, 236n73; and murders/suicides, 67; in New York City, 69; prussic acid pills, 67; in public housing, 75–82, 88, 91; risks of, 66–71, 76, 81, 84, 88–90, 237n92; safety measures for, 66–73, 76–77, 81–82, 236n73; and sentinels, 67, 69, 71; as "ultimate weapon," 56–57, 71; used in citrus orchards, 66; used rarely after DDT introduction, 91, 93, 241n37; warning gases mixed with, 67, 71; and warning placards, 71; and Zyklon B, 67, 236n72

health departments/officials. *See* public health

healthy housing, 9, 140, 215; and bedbug control, 69, 73; and cockroach control, 95, 110, 194, 196, 198–200; and fly control, 40; and HCN fumigation, 69, 73; healthy homes movement, 211–12; and "municipal housekeeping" movement, 40; and Parnell, Alverta, 95, 194; and rat control, 116–19, 122, 133–34, 157–58, 167; as right of citizenship, 199–200

hellebore, 44

hemlock, 113

Henry Horner Homes (Chicago), 178–81, 187–92, 197–202, 204, 214–15, 273n93; Mothers' Guild, 198–202, 204

hepatitis, 207

Herrick, Glenn, 86–88

high-rise architecture, 76, 181, 197, 267n13

hikers, 245n117

Hockenyos, George, 70, 89–90, 92, 205

Hodge, Clifton, 44–47, 54, 16fig.

holistic environmental change, 7–9, 14; and fly control, 42, 53; and Integrated Pest Management (IPM), 198, 202; and rat control, 137, 152, 159, 171, 174, 209, 255n1

Holmes, Dwight, 119

home economics/economists: and bedbugs, 59, 61–63; and cockroaches, 87–88; and flies, 32, 41

homelessness, 117

homeowners. See property owners

Home Sanitation (Talbot), 41

hooks, bell, 203

hopelessness, 155, 258n32

HOPE VI, 198–99, 202

horse corpses, 50–51

horse manure. See manure

horse stables: in Chicago, 40; closing of, 54; and flies, 27, 31–32, 35, 37–38, 40–42, 50, 52, 54, 20fig.; in New York City, 50, 20fig.; in Washington, D.C., 27, 31, 35, 37, 41–43, 52, 226n47

hotels, 71, 106–7, 115, 205–7

houseflies. See flies

household technologies, 50, 231n106, 234n32. See also appliances

housewifery guides, 29–30, 222n9

housewives. See women

Housing Act (1937), 74, 93, 99, 117

Housing Act (1949), 135, 159, 179

housing authorities: in Baltimore, 95, 116–18, 193–94; and bedbugs, 13, 75–77, 79–80, 206; in Chicago, 13, 75–80, 99, 178–81, 189, 196–202, 214; and cockroaches, 93–95, 98–102, 104, 109, 178–81, 193–94, 197, 199–202, 268n29; corruption in, 95, 116–18; federal, 93–94, 97, 100, 118, 243n76; and HOPE VI, 198; in New York City, 81, 99–102, 191, 243n76; and rats, 116–18. See also public housing

housing/housing reform, 7, 9–11, 13–14, 139–40; and alley homes, 36–37, 39–40, 42–43, 49, 53–54; in Baltimore, 112, 115–19, 129–35, 154, 162, 250n71, 254n122, 26fig.; and bedbugs, 6, 13, 57, 60–65, 70, 73–75, 77–82; in Chicago, 13, 36, 62–63, 75, 77–78, 82, 120, 122, 172, 178–81, 198–99, 266n12; and cockroaches, 84–86, 88–89, 94–95, 97–98, 106; and "domestic Marshall Plan," 157, 159, 161; in Europe, 57; and flies, 29, 33, 35–40, 42–43, 49, 53–54; in Houston, 168; in Milwaukee, 11, 162–65; in New York City, 49–50, 58, 79, 81, 83, 100–102, 150–53, 155–57, 243n76, 20fig.; and overcrowding, 63, 179; in Philadelphia, 167; and rats, 4, 13, 112, 115–20, 122–24, 129–35, 151–54, 156–59, 162–68, 172, 250n71; and suburban housing, 85, 90, 97, 99, 103, 109, 133, 150, 153, 157, 175, 256n15; and urban renewal, 116–17, 135, 150, 159; and vouchers, 198–99; in Washington, D.C., 36–37, 39–40, 42–43, 49, 53–54, 62, 166. See also affordable housing; apartments; public housing; rental homes; tenements housing market, private, 74, 77–78, 82, 97, 110, 125, 152, 176, 180, 198–99, 201, 214

housing shortages, 60, 70, 95, 98

Houston (Tex.), 168

Howard, Leland O.: and flies, 28–29, 31–32, 35–38, 41–44, 53–54, 222n10, 224n19; as founder of biological control, 228n78; and HCN fumigation, 67; and screens, 47–48, 230n96

Howe, Gertrude, 33–34, 225n33

Hull, O. W., 69, 72

Hull-House (Chicago): and bedbugs, 62–63; and flies, 32–36, 38, 40, 53–54, 225n33, 227n60; and rats, 120, 122

human bodies, 6–7, 140; and bedbugs, 4, 11, 56, 92; and burdens of pesticides, 169, 191–92; and chlordane, 102; and cockroaches, 102, 178, 189–90, 201, 215; and DDT, 85, 89, 92; and rats, 116

human rights, 168

Humphreys, Margaret, 230n96

Hunter, Laura, Thorne, 76

Huxley, Julian, 251n82

hyacinths, 158

hydrocyanic acid gas. See HCN (hydrocyanic acid gas)

I

Ida B. Wells Homes (Chicago), 76, 179

illegal practices: and bedbugs, 210–11; dumping of waste, 28, 30, 38, 50, 53; and flies, 28, 30, 38, 50, 53; and methyl parathion disaster, 202–3, 210–11; in New York City, 50

immigrants, 9; and bedbugs, 63, 65, 72; in Chicago, 35, 40, 63, 225n33; chicken-raising practices of, 43, 114; economic unity with, 35; and flies, 35–36, 40, 50–51, 53; as "foreign colonies," 36; Hartnack as, 72; in New York City,

50–51; and rats, 43; in San Francisco, 43, 114, 126

inequalities, 8–9, 14, 140, 204, 215; and bedbugs, 206; and flies, 41, 53–54; and pesticides, 169; racial, 41, 53, 151, 159, 169, 173, 198; and rats, 151, 159, 169, 173; structural, 54, 151

infants: "artificial feeding" of, 51; baby bottles, 7, 28, 31, 40, 49; and body burdens of pesticides, 211; breastfeeding of, 48–49, 51, 230n100; in Chicago, 48, 120; and cockroaches, 86; early weaning of, 48–49, 230n100; and flies, 28, 30–31, 40, 47–51, 19fig.; infant mortality, 28, 47–49; nets for cribs/prams, 51; in New York City, 50–51, 156; rat attacks on, 114, 120, 151–52, 154–56, 247n15, 257n26, 257n28, 144fig.; in Washington, D.C., 40

infectious diseases, 11, 31, 81, 115–16, 207–8; and resistance, 174. See also names of infectious diseases, e.g., typhoid fever

infestations, 4–11, 13–14, 140, 211; of bedbugs, 6, 46, 56–57, 59–63, 65, 70, 74–75, 77, 79–80, 82, 92–93, 107, 118, 205–10, 212–14, 233n12; of cockroaches, 70, 83, 86, 93–97, 99–100, 104–6, 109–10, 178–79, 187, 189–91, 198, 203; of flies, 35, 41–44, 46–47, 49, 53; and Integrated Pest Management (IPM), 182, 184, 186; of rats, 13, 97, 99, 113–14, 116, 118–21, 125–26, 129, 135, 138, 150–55, 157, 159–60, 163, 165, 167–69, 173, 175–76; in Washington, D.C., 35, 43

influenza epidemic, 71

infrastructure, urban, 7, 13–14, 30; and cockroaches, 195; modernization of, 10, 44; and rats, 153, 157, 162, 165

insecticides, 45, 67, 82, 87, 96, 185, 210, 236n72. See also names and types of insecticides

insects, 7, 32, 185, 187, 194. See also common names of insects inspectors, health/housing, 14; in Baltimore, 117, 131, 134; and bedbugs, 65; in Chicago, 34, 120; and flies, 34, 42–43, 54; in Milwaukee, 165; and preventive pest control, 89–90; and rats, 117, 120, 131, 134, 165; in Washington, D.C., 42

Integral Urban Home (Berkeley), 185–86

Integrated Pest Management (IPM), 140, 178–79, 181–87, 192–93, 197–204, 211–12, 214; and aesthetic injury level, 184, 187; agricultural, 182–85; in city parks, 184–85; costs of, 212; and cultural attitudes toward pests, 184–86, 268n32; in domestic environments, 182–86, 192–93, 197–204, 211–12, 214; and economic injury level, 182, 184; and "ecosystem managers," 182–86, 193–94, 200; and education, 183–86, 269n34; and entomophobia, 184–85; and feedback loops, 182–83; and Henry Horner Homes (Chicago), 197–204, 214–15; and Integral Urban Home (Berkeley), 185–86; and Safer Pest Control Project (SPCP), 200, 204; and tolerance levels for infestations, 184, 186–87

integration, concept of, 180–82, 185–86, 197–99, 266n12; economic integration, 199, 272n74. See also Integrated Pest Management (IPM)

Intensive Rodent Control Program (Milwaukee), 145fig.

Internet remedies, 210–11

Irish-Americans, 33

iron sulfate, 44

Italians, 33, 43, 50, 114

J

Jackson, Howard, 127

Jackson, Jesse, 161

Jackson, William, 164, 170–74

Jane Addams Houses (Chicago), 76

The Jeffersons (television sitcom), 206

Johns Hopkins University, 164; Medical School, 124, 126–28; School of Hygiene and Public Health, 128–30, 251n84

Johnson, Lyndon, 157–62, 168–69, 174–75, 260n54

Jones, James, 161

Jones, James Earl, 156

A Journal of the Plague Year (Defoe), 246n5

judicial system. See court cases

Julia Lathrop Homes (Chicago), 179

K

kala-azar, 64

Kalm, Peter, 233n9

Kennelly, Edward, 180

kerosene, 55, 59, 213, 232n3

King, Martin Luther Jr., 157, 161, 180

kitchens, 6; and bedbugs, 63; and cockroaches, 13, 83–84, 86–87, 94, 102–4, 108, 187–89, 201; and flies, 7, 28, 35, 40, 52, 54; and Integrated Pest Management (IPM), 184–85, 201; and rats, 111, 129, 131, 136, 164

Kittredge, Mable Hyde, 59, 62–63, 87

Klein, Woody, 107

Kober, George, 30, 35–36, 38, 228n68

Kotlowitz, Alex, 197

Kozol, Jonathan, 258n32

Kratzenberg family, 69–70, 72

Kruse, Cornelius, 258n32

L

Lady and the Tramp (1955 film), 247n15

Lake Park (Chicago), 199

The Lancet (medical journal), 73

landlords, 8–9; absentee, 152, 163, 172; agents of, 151; in Baltimore, 116, 118, 127, 129, 131–33, 138, 154; and bedbugs, 5–6, 60, 65, 75, 206, 210, 214; in Chicago,

M

real estate industry, 95, 97–98, 117; and
red-lining, 133, 254n122
recipes for pest control, 29–30
reconstructive surgery, 154
recycling of household waste, 183
red squill, 124, 135–36
reduction of ecological complexity, 6–7,
113, 125–26, 136–37, 178, 197
Reese, Mamie, 161
reform/reformers, urban, 6–11, 13–14,
140; in Baltimore, 116, 118, 195; and
bedbugs, 57, 62–65, 74, 78, 81, 107;
"breakdown hypothesis" of, 36, 163,
261n77; in Chicago, 32–36, 38, 40, 53,
62–63, 78, 225n33, 227n60; and DDT,
93; and flies, 28–29, 32, 35–44, 47–54;
and HCN fumigation, 74, 78, 81; and
Hull-House, 32–36, 38, 40, 53, 225n33,
227n60; and medical entomology, 10,
13, 28–29, 32, 34–37, 40, 51, 53; in New
York City, 49–52, 150; and rats, 112, 116,
118, 150–51, 163; stigmatizing alley home
residents, 36–37; in Washington, D.C.,
35–40, 42–43, 48–49, 53, 163, 226n46.
See also housing/housing reform
refrigerators, 94, 96, 229n95; top of, 193–94
rehabilitation of housing, 9, 13; in Baltimore, 112, 117, 129–33, 135, 254n122; in
Chicago, 181, 198–202; and rat control,
4, 158–59, 162, 165–66
Rehn, James, 85
Reid, Ira deA., 116
rental homes, 102, 132–33, 138, 151, 153,
155–57, 180, 188
renters. See tenants
resistance, 102–7, 139–40; and agricultural pests, 182; and bedbugs, 5, 106–7,
209–10; behavioral resistance, 102,
104–6, 195, 204; and cockroaches,
102–6, 108–10, 170, 187, 190–91, 193–95,
268n29; cross-resistance, 5, 102–3, 107,
210, 265n123; and DDT, 181; and flies,
104, 170, 181; knockdown resistance

("kdr"), 102; and mosquitoes, 104,
170, 181; physiological resistance, 102,
104, 195; and "super rats," 151, 169–74,
265n123; and warfarin, 151, 169–74
resistance of city residents, 140, 165, 168;
to pest control practices, 195; resistance to screens, 50–52
responsibility, personal/private, 7–8; and
bedbugs, 76, 78; and cockroaches, 99,
101–2, 109, 200, 202; and flies, 8, 44–48,
54, 229n95, 17fig., 18fig., 19fig.; and pesticides, 101–2, 109; and rats, 4, 119, 121,
137, 158, 161–62, 164, 175, 262n85; women
as responsible, 8, 29, 40, 54, 200
restaurants, 49, 69, 171, 241n37
rheumatism, 118
Ribicoff, Abraham, 158
Richter, Curt, 124–30, 132, 135–37, 170,
250nn68–69
roaches. See cockroaches
roach salt. See sodium fluoride
Robbins, Paul, 263n100
Rockefeller Foundation, 39, 124, 128–29,
131, 172, 264n110
Rodent Ecology Research Project (Baltimore), 112–13, 128, 132, 134, 138, 164,
170, 141fig.
rodenticides, 112–14, 124, 128–29, 131,
135–36, 151, 169, 194, 265n122. See also
warfarin
rodents. See rats
Rodriguez, Lucille, 78
Roosevelt, Theodore, 37
row houses, 6, 76, 91, 118, 129, 141fig.
Rudolph, Maya, 208
Ruffin, Sarah, 178, 188–90, 198–202, 204,
212
rural areas, 43, 90, 107; along Mexican
border, 158; rural South, 43, 171, 188;
rural-to-urban migration, 36, 43,
163–64, 261n77; in Scotland, 170; and
warfarin, 170–72. See also agricultural
pests; farms; ranches

WEYERHAEUSER ENVIRONMENTAL BOOKS

Loving Nature, Fearing the State: American Environmentalism and Antigovernment Politics before Reagan by Brian Allen Drake

Whales and Nations: Environmental Diplomacy on the High Seas by Kurt Dorsey

Tangled Roots: The Appalachian Trail and American Environmental Politics by Sarah L. Mittlefehldt

Pests in the City: Flies, Bedbugs, Cockroaches, and Rats by Dawn Day Biehler

WEYERHAEUSER ENVIRONMENTAL CLASSICS

The Great Columbia Plain: A Historical Geography, 1805–1910 by D. W. Meinig

Mountain Gloom and Mountain Glory: The Development of the Aesthetics of the Infinite by Marjorie Hope Nicolson

Tutira: The Story of a New Zealand Sheep Station by Herbert Guthrie-Smith

A Symbol of Wilderness: Echo Park and the American Conservation Movement by Mark Harvey

Man and Nature: Or, Physical Geography as Modified by Human Action by George Perkins Marsh; edited and annotated by David Lowenthal

Conservation in the Progressive Era: Classic Texts edited by David Stradling

DDT, Silent Spring, and the Rise of Environmentalism: Classic Texts edited by Thomas R. Dunlap

The Environmental Moment, 1968–1972 edited by David Stradling

CYCLE OF FIRE BY STEPHEN J. PYNE

Fire: A Brief History

World Fire: The Culture of Fire on Earth

Vestal Fire: An Environmental History, Told through Fire, of Europe and Europe's Encounter with the World

Fire in America: A Cultural History of Wildland and Rural Fire

Burning Bush: A Fire History of Australia

The Ice: A Journey to Antarctica